M000187615

Jurists: Profiles in Legal History

William Twining, General Editor

Ebu's-su'ud

The Islamic Legal Tradition

Colin Imber

Stanford University Press
Stanford, California

Paperback edition first published in the USA by
Stanford University Press
Stanford, California
2009

© Colin Imber, 1997
Originating publisher
Edinburgh University Press
22 George Square, Edinburgh

Transferred to digital print on demand, 2007
Typeset in Monotype Plantin Light
by Koinonia Ltd, Bury

This book is exclusively distributed in the USA, its dependencies,
Canada, Mexico, and the Philippines by Stanford University Press.

Library of Congress Cataloging-in-Publication Data
Imber, Colin.
  Ebu's-su'ud : the Islamic legal tradition / Colin Imber.
    p. cm.
  Includes bibliographical references and index.
  ISBN 978-0-8047-6099-7 (pbk. : alk. paper)
  ISBN 978-0-8047-2927-7 (cl. : alk. paper)
    1. Abu al-Sa'ud Muhammad ibn Muhammad,
1492 or 3–1574 or 5.   2. Hanafites.   3. Islamic law—Turkey—
History.   4. Turkey—History—Ottoman Empire, 1288–1918.   I. Title.
KBP300.A268I43   2009
340.5′9—dc22   2008047278

The Law is the embodiment
Of everything that's excellent.
It has no kind of fault or flaw,
And I, my Lords, embody the Law.

W. S. Gilbert, *Iolanthe*

The object and use of lawyer's language is twofold: partly to prevent information being conveyed to certain descriptions of persons, partly to cause such information to be conveyed to them as shall be false or, at any rate, fallacious: to secure habitual ignorance, or produce occasional misconception.

Jeremy Bentham, *Rationale of Judicial Evidence*

Contents

Abbreviations

Ch   John Rylands Library, Manchester, Chetham's Oriental MS 7979. An anthology of the fatwas of Ebu's-su'ud and others, compiled by Veli b. Yusuf, known as Veli Yegan. Copied 1584.

D   M. E. Düzdağ, *Şeyhülislâm Ebussuûd Efendi Fetvaları Işığında 16. Asır Türk Hayatı*, Istanbul: Enderun Kitabevi (1972).

H   Paul Horster, *Zur Anwendung des Islamischen Rechts im 16. Jahrhundert*, Bonner orientalische Studien, vol. 10, Stuttgart: W. Kohlhammer (1935).

K   Mahmud b. Süleyman el-Kefevi, *Kata'ib a'lam al-akhyar min fuqaha' madhhab al-Nu'man al-mukhtar*, Süleymaniye Library, Istanbul, MS Esad Efendi 548.

MTM   Printed version of the 'New *Qanun*', in *Millî Tetebbü'ler Mecmuası*, vol. 1, Istanbul (1913).

Acknowledgements

My first acknowledgement must be to the series editors, William Twining and Neil MacCormick, for their imaginative step in extending the scope of *Jurists: Profiles in Legal Theory* to the non-Western world, and for inviting me to contribute a volume on an Islamic jurist. This provided me with both the stimulus and the opportunity to fulfil a long-standing ambition to write a study of Ebu's-su'ud. It was also an act of faith, since I must be the only contributor to the series with no legal background or training. I can only hope that the book has merited their confidence. Second, I must acknowledge the generous support of the British Academy. It was the award of a British Academy/Leverhulme Senior Research Fellowship that gave me the time necessary for research and writing. Without this support, the book could not have been written. I am also indebted to a number of academic colleagues, in particular to Norman Calder for many hours of discussion over numerous points of detail. His knowledge of Islamic law is considerably greater than mine, and any good ideas which readers may find in this book are quite probably his. I am grateful also to Colin Heywood, Ian Edge, Rudolf Peters and Cornell Fleischer, whose critical comments on my original proposal for Edinburgh University Press were extremely helpful at the outset of my research. I owe a particular debt of gratitude to Victor Ménage and Christine Woodhead, who both very kindly read the completed manuscript and made numerous suggestions which improved both the content and the style, and to Leslie Peirce, the reader for Stanford University Press, for her perceptive and helpful comments. Finally I must, as always, thank my family for tolerating my obsession with the unsavoury antics of Zeyd and Hind.

Introduction

The only Sultan of the Ottoman Empire whose name is familiar in Western Europe and the United States is Süleyman I (1520–66), known as 'the Magnificent'. For Westerners, the epithet 'magnificent' suggests above all the overwhelming power of the Sultan's armies, his material wealth and the vast extent of his realms. The Ottomans too came to regard Süleyman as the greatest of their Sultans. Within a decade or so of his death, they began to look back nostalgically on his reign as a lost golden age, and to regard the re-establishment of Süleymanic norms as a cure for all ills in the body politic. The Ottomans, however, remembered Süleyman not as 'the Magnificent' but as 'the Law-giver', emphasising that it was above all the legal order of his reign that they sought to recreate. One personality in particular stands out as the representative of this order, and this is the jurist Ebu's-su'ud (c. 1490–1574).

The Ottoman concept of the ideal law was, in essence, very simple. The empire was Islamic, and Islamic law, the *shar'* – or, to give it the name in common use nowadays, the *shari'a* – was the embodiment of legal perfection. The problem was that the *shari'a* is, in many respects, impractical, and has always, in reality, coexisted with secular systems of law. This was as true of the Ottoman Empire as it was (and is) of all Islamic polities. However, an Ottoman tradition which began, it seems, in the early seventeenth century and which modern historians frequently reiterate, asserts that during the reign of Süleyman I, Ebu's-su'ud succeeded in harmonising the secular law with the *shari'a*, creating, in effect, the ideal Islamic legal system.

This book examines the validity of this assertion. I have begun by choosing five areas of the law: the Sultan and legal sovereignty, land tenure and taxation, trusts in mortmain, marriage and the family, and crimes and torts. In each of these areas, I have laid out what seem to be the most important rules and concepts in the Islamic and specifically in the *Hanafi* juristic tradition, and afterwards given the texts of a selection of Ebu's-su'ud's fatwas and other writings on the topic in question, together with a brief analysis. From these materials, the reader may draw his or her own conclusions as to whether Ebu's-su'ud did indeed reconcile Ottoman secular legal practice with the sacred law.

This way of presenting the material, which leaves much of the work to the reader, requires an explanation. There are two reasons. The first is the very obvious one that the texts from which I have worked are inaccessible to most people, either linguistically or because they exist only in manuscript. My first priority has therefore been to provide a representative body of texts in translation. This puts readers in a position to be able to agree or disagree with any conclusions I may have reached. The second reason is the current state of the academic study of Islamic law in general and of Ottoman law in particular.

Before the nineteenth century, traditional jurisprudence was central to the intellectual life of the Islamic world. In the nineteenth century, it became marginalised, and in the twentieth it disappeared in all but name. There has in the twentieth century been a revival of interest in Islamic jurisprudence as a subject of academic research and, after the work of such scholars as Joseph Schacht, Chafik Chéhata and N. J. Coulson, it is certainly possible to say that it has passed the pioneering phase. Nonetheless, it is still at an early stage. Interested scholars are thinly spread out over a vast field, and the extensive secondary literature necessary to support succinct summary and analysis, and debate at a high level, such as students of Western law and jurisprudence can expect, simply does not exist.

If the study of Islamic law in general is at an early stage, then the study of Ottoman law in particular is embryonic. The greatest pioneer in the field was Uriel Heyd, whose work on Ottoman criminal law and the Ottoman fatwa, incomplete at the time of his death, is available thanks to meticulous editing by V. L. Ménage.[1] For Ebu's-su'ud, two works are especially important. The first is Baber Johansen's study of the argument during the sixteenth century over the legal status of lands in Ottoman Egypt.[2] This does not concern Ebu's-su'ud directly, but the juristic formulation of the debate closely parallels Ebu's-su'ud's own statements on the Ottoman laws of land tenure in Hungary, the Balkan peninsula and Anatolia. The second is Jon Mandaville's study of the controversy, in which Ebu's-su'ud was the protagonist, over charitable trusts based on cash endowments.[3] The particular merit of Mandaville's approach is that he presents an admirably clear account both of the strictly legal issues and of their social and historical context. It is an approach which I have tried to imitate.

Since the materials for the study of Islamic and Ottoman law are so meagre, research in these areas, and research on Ebu's-su'ud in particular, must inevitably rely almost entirely on primary sources, and must concentrate largely on details and technicalities. Only when these have been mastered will it be possible to move the debate to a higher level. This, then, accounts for the shape of this book. My aim has been to make a selection of Ebu's-su'ud's fatwas and other writings available in

English and to place them in a legal and historical context so that they make sense to the reader.

Notes

1. Uriel Heyd, *Studies in Old Ottoman Criminal Law*, Oxford: Clarendon Press (1973); idem, 'Some aspects of the Ottoman *fetva*', *Bulletin of the School of Oriental and African* Studies, 32 (1969), 35–56.
2. Baber Johansen, *The Islamic Law of Tax and Rent*, London: Croom Helm (1988).
3. Jon E. Mandaville, 'Usurious piety: the cash waqf controversy in the Ottoman Empire', *International Journal of Middle Eastern Studies*, 10 (1979), 289–308.

PART I

The Historical and Legal Background

1

The Ottoman Empire, the Law and Ebu's-su'ud

The Ottoman Empire and its Legal System

By the mid-sixteenth century, the Ottoman Empire had emerged from obscure origins to the status of a world power. In Europe its territories included almost the entire Balkan peninsula south of the rivers Danube and Sava. To the north of this line, the old Kingdom of Hungary was a directly-ruled Ottoman province, while to the east of Hungary the principalities of Wallachia and Moldavia and the Khanate of the Crimea were tributary to the Ottoman Sultan. In Asia, the territories of the Empire extended over Anatolia, Iraq and Syria, Palestine and the western coastlands of the Arabian peninsula. In north Africa, Egypt was an Ottoman province and Tripoli and Algiers were Ottoman protectorates.

The nucleus of the Empire had come into being 250 years earlier, in about 1300, in north-western Anatolia to the east of Constantinople, as an insignificant principality whose ruler, Osman I, was to give his name to the Ottoman dynasty. By 1400, the fourth Ottoman Sultan, Bayezid I (1389–1402), ruled over much of the Balkan peninsula and western and central Anatolia, either directly or by exercising suzerainty over native dynasties. The Empire which the early Sultans had established was sufficiently cohesive to recover from a catastrophe. In 1402, the Central Asian conqueror Timur – or Tamerlane – defeated Bayezid I at Ankara, dismembering his territories and initiating an eleven-year civil war between his sons. However, after the reunification of the Ottoman dynastic lands under Mehmed I (1413–21), the Empire not only recovered but, in the second half of the fifteenth century, expanded rapidly. In 1453, Mehmed II (1451–81) captured the imperial Byzantine city of Constantinople, establishing it as the Ottoman capital and giving the Ottoman Sultan a claim to have inherited the title of Caesar. In every year from 1453 until his death, Mehmed undertook further campaigns. By the end of his reign, he had eliminated the remaining independent dynasties in the Balkan peninsula, extending the westward boundaries of the Empire to the Adriatic. Similarly, in Anatolia, he had removed all rival dynasties and extended his realm into the mountainous zone to the east of the central plateau. By fortifying the Dardanelles and the

Bosphorus, and by establishing his suzerainty over Wallachia, Moldavia and the Crimea, he had assured Ottoman control of the Black Sea. In the Aegean, he had severely reduced the power of the trading republics of Venice and Genoa, occupying several of their former colonies and confronting their fleets at sea. The territory that he established in Europe and Asia became, in some senses, the nucleus of the Ottoman Empire in the following four centuries.

Ottoman conquest began again on a huge scale after the thirty-year reign of Mehmed II's pacific son, Bayezid II (1481–1512). In only eight years, Bayezid's son, Selim I (1512–20), doubled the size of the Empire by defeating first the Safavid Shah of Iran and annexing territory in south-eastern Anatolia, and then, in 1516–17, defeating the last of the Mamluk Sultans of Cairo, annexing all the territories of the Mamluks in Syria, Palestine, Egypt and the Hijaz. These conquests not only made Selim *de facto* the most powerful Islamic ruler but also, through his acquisition of the Holy Cities of Mecca, Medina and Jerusalem, gave him a claim to spiritual pre-eminence. The conquests did not cease with the Sultan's death. His successor Süleyman I (1520–66) opened his reign with the capture first of Belgrade, which Ottoman sources frequently refer to as 'the gate to Hungary', and then of Rhodes, an island strategically placed for the control of the eastern Mediterranean and the Aegean.

Süleyman's great conquests all fell within the first twenty years of his reign. In 1526, he defeated and killed the king of Hungary, replacing him first with his own nominee and then, in 1541, converting the kingdom to an Ottoman province. In the 1530s, war with the Safavid dynasty led to the annexation of more territory in eastern Anatolia and Iraq. In the same decade, the Ottoman fleet evicted the Venetians from most of their remaining insular and mainland possessions in the Aegean. By the mid-century, the Ottoman Empire had reached almost the limits of its expansion. Conquests after 1550 were on a smaller scale and often ephemeral. The capture of Tripoli in 1551 added to Süleyman's north African domains, Algiers having already accepted Ottoman overlordship in 1519. The reign of Süleyman's son, Selim II (1566–74), saw the conquests of Cyprus and Tunis, but there were no acquisitions on the scale of those of the first half of Süleyman's reign. On land, the distances to be covered and the difficulty of the terrain, particularly on the eastern frontier, rendered further conquest strategically difficult and financially ruinous, while at sea the dependence on the Mediterranean galley as a warship limited the range of the fleet.

Equally important, however, was the nature of the enemy. The conquest of Hungary and expansion into north Africa and the Mediterranean had brought the Ottomans into conflict with the forces of the Habsburg monarchs: the King of Spain and Holy Roman Emperor, Charles V, and his brother, Ferdinand of Austria. In the east, they encountered the

Safavid Shahs of Iran. The Safavid armies were not, at this period, equal to those of the Ottomans, but the barely penetrable mountains on the western borders of Iran made them an invincible enemy. Furthermore, as Shi'i Muslims who were also the leaders of an Islamic spiritual order with many followers among the Sultan's subjects in Iraq and Anatolia, the Shahs presented a mortal danger to the integrity of the Ottoman Empire. It was above all the wars against the Habsburgs and the Safavids that shaped Ottoman imperial consciousness in the sixteenth century. As Holy Roman Emperor, Charles adopted the title of Caesar, to which Süleyman laid a competitive claim. In portraying the Safavids as heretics and enemies of true Sunni Islam, Ottoman propaganda created a counter-image of the Ottoman Sultan as the defender of the orthodox Islamic faith. It was Ebu's-su'ud who provided the most concise and elegant formulation of these claims to imperial and spiritual dominion.

By the mid-sixteenth century, therefore, the Ottoman Empire covered an enormous land area, encompassing extreme variations in climate and terrain. It is hardly surprising then that its most striking feature as a social entity was its diversity. Settled peasants formed the majority of the population, but there were, in addition, numerous groups of tribal, often nomadic or semi-nomadic peoples. Among these were the Vlachs of the Balkan peninsula, the Turcomans in Anatolia and the Balkans, the Kurds in south-eastern Anatolia and northern Iraq, and the Bedouin in Syria, Egypt and Arabia. Although the population was overwhelmingly rural, Istanbul, the Ottoman capital, was probably the largest city in sixteenth-century Europe, and other cities, notably perhaps Thessaloniki, Bursa, Damascus and Cairo, continued to expand as centres of manufacturing and of local and long-distance trade. Linguistically, the Empire was heterogeneous. Turkish was the language of government and of perhaps the majority of the population of Anatolia and the eastern Balkans. It was the language of a minority of the population elsewhere in the Empire where, for example, Greek, Slavonic, Kurdish or Arabic might predominate. Arabic, in its literary form, was the language of Muslim learning and of the law, as it was everywhere in the Islamic world, enjoying much the same status as Latin in Catholic Europe.

To a Western European used to monarchies which attempted to impose uniformity of faith, what must have been most striking was the diversity of religions among the Sultan's subjects. The Ottoman Empire was a Muslim polity, but in its European territories, Muslims, except locally, formed a minority. In its Asian territories where the population was predominantly Muslim, Christians could form a local majority. Equally, there was a large Jewish population, particularly in Istanbul and Thessaloniki and particularly after the settlement of the Jews who had been expelled from Spain in 1492. A typical feature of Ottoman cities was their division into districts according to confessional groups, each centred on a place of worship. There was division too within the main religious groups. A salient feature of popular Islam was the proliferation of dervish orders, whose heterodox practices the Ottoman government tolerated, so long as their adherents also practised the orthodox forms of Muslim worship. The majority of the Christian subjects of the Sultan belonged to the Greek Orthodox or Armenian churches, but there were numerous other Christian groups, including Catholics and Protestants in Hungary.

An inevitable corollary of the Empire's size and of its diversity of peoples and faiths was a legal pluralism. There can be no doubt that villagers and tribesmen in remote rural areas managed their affairs and settled their disputes according to the customs of the village or tribe, without recourse to courts or government officials. Christians and Jews also enjoyed some autonomy in settling intra-communal affairs under the auspices of the ecclesiastical or rabbinic authorities, while Muslims had recourse to the Muslim courts. There were regional differences too in the feudal practices of land tenure and taxation. The Empire in its period of expansion had absorbed a large number of principalities and kingdoms, whose feudal usages often remained embedded in later Ottoman law. What gave Ottoman legal practice its unity was the authority of the Sultan. Anyone who exercised legal power, whether Muslim judges, Christian ecclesiastics, rabbis or secular governors, did so by virtue of appointment by the Sultan, from whom all authority in the Empire flowed. A second unifying factor was the network of Muslim courts. Every town in the Empire had an Islamic judge (qadi) administering Islamic law, whose court was open to anyone of any confession.

The function of the Muslim judges and their deputies was both judicial and administrative. They gave judgement in court cases and also acted as public notaries, issuing certificates validating, for example, marriage, manumission, sale or lease. Among their numerous administrative duties, they were responsible, for example, for levying from the area of their jurisdiction oarsmen for service in the imperial fleet, for victualling the army if it passed through their district, or for fixing and enforcing the daily prices in the market. The judge, in fact, was probably the most important royal official in his locality. The seat of most judgeships was in small towns, and it was in small towns that most judges made their career. There was, however, a hierarchy within the profession. The judges with the highest pay, prestige and opportunity for advancement were, in the mid-sixteenth century, the judges of Istanbul, Edirne, Bursa and Cairo and, at a slightly lower rank, of Damascus, Aleppo and Baghdad.[1] The two senior judges in the Empire were the Military Judge (qadi'asker) of Rumelia and the Military Judge of Anatolia, both of whom were members of the Imperial Council, which met in the Sultan's palace, under the presidency of the Grand Vizier. The Military Judges were responsible, in the name of the Sultan, for most of the judicial appointments in respectively the European and Asian territories of the Empire.

The judges were at the centre of the Ottoman, or indeed of any Islamic legal system, in that they were responsible for the day-to-day application of the law. Nevertheless, they played no part in its development since, although a judge's decree is binding and irrevocable in a particular case, it cannot serve as a precedent in the future. Ottoman judges, it is true, kept detailed records of court proceedings, but for administrative rather than juristic purposes. Alongside the judge stood the mufti, a qualified jurisconsult[2] whose responsa, or fatwas, served as authoritative although non-binding statements of the law. A mufti in himself has no executive powers and a fatwa is not an executive decree. To become legally effective, it must be enacted by a judge or, in the Ottoman Empire, by anyone who exercises power in the Sultan's name. In seeking a solution to a difficult case, a judge might consult a mufti, and then give his judgement on the basis of the fatwa. The judgement would then be effective in the particular case. The fatwa on which it was based would, however, remain valid as an authoritative source of law in future cases. There does not, in the Ottoman Empire, appear to have been an organisation of muftis to parallel the hierarchy of judges. Undoubtedly, every city had learned men willing to exercise this function, particularly among the professors (*mudarris*) at the religious colleges (*madrasa*), but they do not, in the provinces, appear to have had official status.

This was not however true of the Mufti of Istanbul, the Ottoman capital. This muftiship had emerged from obscurity in the fifteenth century to become, by the mid-sixteenth, the supreme office in the Ottoman judicial hierarchy, a development which owed much to the prestige and personalities of two of its holders, Kemalpashazade (1525–34) and Ebu's-su'ud (1545–74).[3] The chief function of the Mufti of Istanbul or, to give him the title by which he became known in later centuries, the *sheikhu'l-islam*, was to issue fatwas in response to questions from the Sultan, his ministers, governors or judges, or from members of the public seeking out-of-court settlements or simply answers to queries. He became, at least from the time of Ebu's-su'ud, the chief source of juristic authority in the Empire. The Mufti of Istanbul, however, was a jurisconsult and not a judge and, as such, he did not sit on the Imperial Council. His opinions did not have executive authority, and, if he wished in any way to change or modify the law, he would need to petition the Sultan to enact his recommendation as a decree. Equally, before any undertaking which might prove controversial, a Sultan would seek a fatwa from the Mufti to legitimise his action.

In the Ottoman Empire, as elsewhere in the Islamic world, it was the colleges attached to the great mosques that provided the training for members of the legal profession, from classes in Arabic and logic at the lowest grade, to the study of jurisprudence, Quranic exegesis and theology at the highest. Although each college was, in its origin, an independent foundation, deriving its income from the endowments of individual benefactors, each one occupied a particular position in a more or less formally established hierarchy of grades, based on location and the salary of its professors. To some extent, too, the grade of the college determined the curriculum taught.[4] In a society where wealth was more or less coterminous with rank, it is not surprising to find that the most prestigious and wealthy colleges were those founded by Sultans, with those endowed by members of the ruling class in the entourage of the Sultan occupying a second tier. In the late fifteenth century and for much of the sixteenth, the Eight Colleges attached to the mosque of Mehmed II in Istanbul occupied the pinnacle of religious and legal education in the Ottoman Empire. In the decades after the completion of the complex in 1557, the colleges attached to the Süleymaniye mosque in Istanbul came to occupy the most prestigious position.

A career as a professor in the colleges offered the trained jurist an alternative to a career as a judge. A professor's first appointment might be to a poorly-endowed provincial college with a small salary, but it offered the possibility of promotion to a higher-grade college and ultimately to a post in one of the royal foundations in Istanbul or another great city.[5] With the right connections, a professor might avoid the lower rungs of the profession altogether. The colleges were also the path to the higher echelons of the judiciary. The Sultan appointed the judges of Istanbul, Bursa, Edirne or other great cities not from among the small-town judges, but from among the teachers in the important colleges, in particular from the Eight. These positions tended, however, to be the preserve of a few influential learned families. The holder of a judgeship in one of the great cities could rise to the position of Military Judge, with a seat on the Imperial Council, and it was normally one of the two Military Judges whom the Sultan selected for the post of *sheikhu'l-islam*. This was to be the pattern of Ebu's-su'ud's career.

The Life of Ebu's-su'ud

Ebu's-su'ud is a Turkish pronunciation of the Arabic name Abu's-su'ud, meaning literally 'father of auspiciousness'. It is with this name alone that Ebu's-su'ud signed legal decrees and fatwas, and by which he is remembered. Biographical sources and a graduation certificate which he himself wrote for a certain Sheikhzade 'Abdu'r-rahman[6] give his full name as Ebu's-su'ud son of Mehmed son of Mustafa al-'Imad. The meaning of the family name al-'Imad none of the sources can explain.

A career like Ebu's-su'ud's in the Ottoman learned profession depended above all on birth and patronage. A future scholar or jurist usually received his early education from his father and so the first step in the profession was to be born into a learned household. It was the household too, through family or professional links, that provided access to a patron whose intervention would be essential to advance a scholarly or legal career. Since learning was, to some extent, hereditary and advancement was through patronage, the most prestigious legal and academic posts in the Ottoman Empire had become, by the late fifteenth century, the preserve of a few, often competing, scholarly dynasties.

It was the household that was the starting point of Ebu's-su'ud's career. His father, Mühiyyü'd-din Mehmed, was a native of Iskilip in northern Anatolia, and it was through him that Ebu's-su'ud acquired both an apprenticeship in learning and his first links with the Ottoman dynasty. Mühiyyü'd-din Mehmed himself had been a pupil of 'Ali Qushji,[7] a scholar famous primarily as a mathematician and astronomer, who had migrated from Samarkand and settled in Istanbul sometime before 1472. Mühiyyü'd-din Mehmed had also married into Ali Qushji's family. Ebu's-su'ud himself refers to 'Ali Qushji as 'my mother's uncle'.[8] Besides 'Ali Qushji, Mühiyyü'd-din Mehmed received instruction from Müeyyedzade 'Abdu'r-rahman, a connection that was to prove crucial in the future career of his son. Müeyyedzade himself was a native of Amasya in northern Anatolia, the capital city of a district whose government was allocated to one of the sons of the reigning Sultan. Its governor in the 1470s was the future Sultan Bayezid II (1481–1512). Müeyyedzade was a protégé of this prince, and it was probably he who brought Ebu's-su'ud's father into Bayezid's circle.[9] Both men came to Istanbul some time after Bayezid's accession to the throne in 1481, and remained, it seems, close friends.

Both of them prospered during Bayezid's reign, with Müeyyedzade rising to become Military Judge of Anatolia in 1501 and of Rumelia in 1505.[10] Mühiyyü'd-din Mehmed's career was very different. Like Müeyyedzade, he was a man of orthodox learning and skilled in the law, but he combined this expertise in the *shari'a* with another role. After his studies with 'Ali Qushji 'he followed the mystic path' and, as a dervish sheikh, he acquired a reputation for miracle-working sanctity.[11] It was probably his reputation as a holy man that had attracted the famously pious Bayezid. Bayezid, the mid-sixteenth-century biographer Tashköprüzade relates, 'loved him greatly and he became known among the people as the Sultan's sheikh. Sultan Bayezid built a lodge for him in Istanbul. Great men used to go to his door and viziers and Military Judges came to him in reverence. Sometimes the Sultan summoned him to his palace and kept him company ... Pious men were in awe of him because of his greatness in science.'[12] Muhiyyü'd-din Mehmed's son, Ebu's-su'ud, was born into this milieu which combined learning and piety with links to the Sultan and the great men of the realm. His father was both a source of learning and a source of patronage.

The date of Ebu's-su'ud's birth is uncertain. The early seventeenth-century writer 'Ata'i's biographical notice gives 30 December 1490.[13] The place of his birth, according to the same source, was a village called Müderris near Istanbul, belonging probably to his father's lodge. His early education, Ebu's-su'ud himself recalled, was with his father: 'With my father Mühiyyü'd-din I studied the gloss on the *Tajrid* by al-Sharif al-Jurjani. I twice studied with him the same scholar's commentary on *al-Miftah*, as well as his commentary on *al-Mawaqif* in its entirety.'[14] By his own account, he continued his education with Seyyid Mehmed el-Qojevi.[15] Seyyid Mehmed must have been a son or other relative of one of Mühiyyü'd-din Mehmed's mystic guides, Muslihü'd-din el-Qojevi;[16] and since he had studied for a while in Amasya, he must have been in the entourage of Prince Bayezid before 1481. During Bayezid's reign, he rose to the position of professor in one of the Eight Colleges.[17] In the reign of Bayezid's successor, Selim I (1512–20), he became first judge of Istanbul and then Military Judge of Rumelia before returning to the Eight Colleges. Seyyid Mehmed's career suggests that his pupil, Ebu's-su'ud, had studied at one of the Eight. Ebu's-su'ud himself mentions only his father and Seyyid Mehmed as his teachers. 'Ata'i however adds that he also studied under Müeyyedzade[18] and, given the latter's friendship with his father, this seems very possible.

As the son of his most revered spiritual master, Ebu's-su'ud received particular favours from Bayezid II. 'Ata'i notes that when news of his extraordinary capabilities reached the Sultan 'the crescent moon of his aspirations became effulgent with the sun of patronage', and the Sultan granted him a daily stipend of thirty aqches, and the honour of 'independently kissing the Sultan's hand'.[19]

In 1512, Bayezid's son Selim I (1512-20) came to the throne, having compelled his father to abdicate. In 1514, Ebu's-su'ud's father Muhiyyü'd-din Mehmed died, followed in 1516 by his father's influential teacher and ally, Müeyyedzade 'Abdu'r-rahman.[20] The loss of these three patrons was not, however, a setback in Ebu's-su'ud's career. He clearly continued to receive his stipend from Selim I since, in 1516, when the Military Judge of Anatolia, Kemalpashazade, offered him a professorship in a provincial college, he turned it down.[21] The post carried a stipend of twenty-five aqches a day, and to have accepted it would have meant a loss of both income and prestige. His first teaching appointment, to the College of Ishaq Pasha in Inegöl, came shortly afterwards. The stipend was thirty aqches daily, equal in value to what he was receiving from the Sultan.

For the next ten years, he followed a career that was typical of a successful member of the learned class. After leaving his post at Inegöl, he seems to have returned to the capital and, ten months later,[22] he received an appointment there as professor in the college of Daud Pasha at forty aqches a day. A few months afterwards, he moved to the College of Mahmud Pasha,[23] also in Istanbul. His return from Inegöl to the capital, evidently in 1520, must have coincided with the accession to the throne of Selim I's son, Süleyman I (1520–66), whose patronage was to secure for him the highest judicial offices. Süleyman also, it seems, became his close personal friend.

It is clear that Ebu's-su'ud would have used his time in the capital to restore his links with the royal dynasty and its entourage. Of his early patrons, Seyyid Mehmed el-Qojevi was still alive but apparently out of office,[24] and he needed new patrons to advance his career. He seems to have found one in the Second Vizier, Mustafa Pasha, since his next appointment in 1524[25] was to the new college which Mustafa Pasha had established at Gebze, a small town a day and a half's journey to the east of Istanbul. He stayed there for a year, moving in 1525/6 to the Sultaniyya College, a foundation of Sultan Mehmed I (1413–21) in Bursa. Unlike Inegöl and Gebze, Bursa was a large commercial city, which had prestige as a former seat of the Sultanate and burying-place, until 1453, of the Ottoman royal family. The Sultaniyya too was a royal foundation, and thus a suitable staging-post between Gebze and Ebu's-su'ud's next appointment. In 1527/8, he became professor at the Müfti College, one of the Eight Colleges of Mehmed II in Istanbul.

This appointment brought Ebu's-su'ud to the top of the teaching hierarchy and made him a candidate for high judicial office. Residence in the capital also gave him immediate access to the sources of power and patronage, and he clearly exploited the opportunities. 'In him', writes the late sixteenth-century biographer, Manq 'Ali, 'there was an inordinate inclination towards men of rulership and government', and his manner was clearly one that impressed. 'He was possessed', Manq 'Ali continues, 'with immense dignity and carefully measured pace. In his assemblies for the great, he rarely hastened to address or speak.' A consequence of his standing among the great is that he never once fell from office or lost the favour of the Sultan.

The late sixteenth-century legal scholar Mahmud of Caffa preserves a short memoir of Ebu's-su'ud's time at the Eight Colleges:

I heard from his student and our master Molla Mehmed, known as 'Abdü'l-Kerimzade: 'I came to the service of Molla Ebu'su'ud on the day he became professor in one of the Eight Colleges. I studied the *Hidaya* with him and then the *Talwih*. I heard from him the *Kashshaf* on Quranic exegesis, and Bukhari on prophetic traditions.[26] I studied profoundly with him, acquiring from him the branches and roots of law, prophetic tradition and Quranic exegesis. I learned from him many sciences: lexicology and style, rhetorical embellishment, essences and adornments, poetics, oratory and rhetorical prose. I did not cease attending on him and his instruction for a single day, until the day he became judge in Bursa. The said Molla's period of teaching in one of the Eight Colleges was five years, no more and no less. On the day he became judge in Bursa, I came to the service of the learned Molla Kemalpashazade Ahmed.[27]

The statement by his pupil that Ebu's-su'ud spent five unbroken years at the Eight Colleges presents a problem. A register of charitable trusts in Istanbul, compiled in 1546, contains copies of three documents dating from 1531 and bearing the signature 'Ebu's-su'ud', whom two of them record as 'judge of the royal estates of Constantinople'.[28] This may indicate that Mahmud of Caffa's informant was wrong, and that Ebu's-su'ud spent a period as judge during his tenure at the Eight Colleges. The signature could, however, belong to another man of the same name, possibly the contemporary jurist Bedrü'd-dinzade Ebu's-su'ud.[29] What is, however, certain is that in 1533 he left the Eight Colleges to become judge of Bursa.

This was a move from the highest academic post in the Empire to one of the senior judicial positions, since the judge of Bursa ranked with those of Istanbul and Edirne at the top of the legal hierarchy. Six months later, in October or November 1533, he became judge in Istanbul, a post which he held for four years.[30] His next promotion came in 1537. An anecdote in the margin of 'Ata'i's biographical dictionary relates how, in this year, when the Sultan was returning from the unsuccessful siege of Corfu and conversing with the two Military Judges, they asked him the reason for the execution of the Grand Vizier Ibrahim Pasha in the previous year. This 'insolent question' so angered the Sultan that he dismissed them on the spot and, in their place, appointed the judge of Cairo, Chivizade Mehmed, as Military Judge of Anatolia, and the judge of Istanbul, Ebu's-su'ud, as Military Judge of Rumelia. On receiving the news, Ebu's-su'ud 'came quickly to the Sultan's encampment' and accepted the appointment.[31] Whether the story is true or not, it illustrates how arbitrary patronage could be, leading as easily to sudden dismissal and sometimes execution as to elevation. That Ebu's-su'ud's career suffered no setbacks during the reigns of four Sultans suggests that he was a man of extraordinary political skill.

He was Military Judge of Rumelia for eight years. A story which has found its way into the biographical tradition suggests that, in the memory of the learned profession at least, it was his administrative reforms that most clearly marked his period in office. 'It is related', 'Ata'i writes, 'that up until his tenure as Military Judge, no care was taken in the registration of candidacies for the posts of judge and professor, and it was therefore possible for everyone to obtain a post through a different route.' When the Military Judge of Anatolia, Chivizade, prevented all but his own protégés from obtaining candidacies, those excluded petitioned the Sultan who, after awarding them positions, put in place a day-book for entering candidacies. Furthermore, 'Ata'i continues, on Ebu's-su'ud's petition, the Sultan decreed that the investiture of candidates should take place once in seven years, with each rank in the legal hierarchy entitled to present a fixed number of candidates for office.[32] The changes which 'Ata'i records did not affect the principle of patronage. Candidacy for office remained in the personal gift of the higher ranks of the learned profession. They did, however, establish an orderly procedure for entry into the profession of judge or professor at a College.

Ebu's-su'ud showed a similar interest in imposing order on the substance of the law itself. Some of the Sultanic decrees to which he refers in his fatwas date from his period as Military Judge, suggesting that their promulgation was on his initiative. It was also during these years that he began his reformulation of the Ottoman laws of land tenure. However, it was his twenty-eight years as *sheikhu'l-islam* that saw his major efforts to systematise the law.

He came to this office in October 1545, at the age of about 55. Since it was usual by this date to appoint a Military Judge to the post, the office of Mufti of Istanbul or *sheikhu'l-islam* was already, it appears, the most prestigious, although probably not the most powerful in the legal hierarchy. By 1545, however, its reputation had clearly sunk since the nine-year tenure of its most illustrious holder, Kemalpashazade (1525–34). Before Ebu's-su'ud's appointment, writes Manq 'Ali, 'the office of Mufti was troubled and passing from hand to hand. The roof of its house was unsupported, until its destiny was delivered to [Ebu's-su'ud] and its keys handed over [to him].'[33] In the eleven years since the death of Kemalpashazade, there had been four Muftis. Only Kemalpashazade's immediate successor Sa'di Chelebi had held office for as much as five years, and it is from his death that Manq 'Ali dates the troubles of the institution. Of Sa'di Chelebi's successors, Chivizade (1539–42) was dismissed, and his successor Qadiri Chelebi resigned after only a year. Qadiri's successor, Fenarizade Mühiyyü'd-din, resigned after only two.[34] After Ebu's-su'ud's time, such rapid changes in office became normal, but this time without diminishing the power and prestige of the institution. It was Ebu's-su'ud's reorganisation that made this possible.

The most important of the Mufti's day-to-day functions was to issue fatwas, responsa composed in answer to legal questions. Before Ebu's-su'ud's period in office, it seems that the procedure for issuing fatwas was largely informal, and dependent for its efficacy and continuity on the personality and competence of the individual office-holder, and on his remaining in post and gaining experience over a number of years. An informal system would also limit the number of fatwas that a Mufti could issue daily. During his tenure of office, Ebu's-su'ud systematised the process of issuing fatwas, so that the task of receiving and drawing up the questions fell to his clerks, whom he also instructed in their proper formulation. The greater the skill of the clerks, the easier was the task of the Mufti, and with this division of labour the volume of fatwas increased. 'Many times,' Manq 'Ali comments, '[Ebu's-su'ud] wrote answers on a thousand slips of paper in a single day, with perfect decisiveness of sense. His answers concerning all the sciences travelled to all horizons like the courses of the stars.'[35] An anecdote which 'Ata'i transmits from one of Ebu's-su'ud's clerks, 'Ashiq Chelebi, confirms what Manq 'Ali says. 'Twice over,' 'Ashiq Chelebi relates, 'the affairs of mankind crowded in on one another, and the questions asked were formidable. He began writing answers after the performance of the dawn prayer and was granted completion by the time of the afternoon call to prayer. He counted them and, on the first occasion, one thousand four hundred and twelve and, on the second occasion, one thousand four hundred and thirteen fatwas were answered and signed.' 'Ashiq Chelebi and, after him, 'Ata'i recounted this story as evidence of divine power working through Ebu's-su'ud,[36] presenting him, like his father, as a miracle-worker.

In reality, the story exemplifies the efficacy of the new procedures which Ebu's-su'ud introduced to the Mufti's office. These relied on a permanent staff, trained in the law and the art of legal formulation. In time, the system which Ebu's-su'ud had instituted became so sophisticated that the framing of the question in a fatwa usually presupposed the answer, and required the Mufti to add no more than a simple 'yes' or 'no' answer and his signature. When, after Ebu's-su'ud's time, rapid changes of *sheikhu'l-islam* became normal, it was the highly-trained permanent staff who effectively did all the work, ensuring continuity and maintaining legal standards in fatwas.[37]

It is, however, clear that Ebu's-su'ud usually did ponder the questions and answer them himself. What in fact seems to have impressed the literary biographers was his ability in his fatwas to write answers which matched the literary style of the questions. His clerk 'Ashiq Chelebi and, following him, Manq 'Ali and 'Ata'i all quote his fatwa on the dissolution of an oath, written in Persian verse in imitation of the question,[38] and the same fatwa turns up from time to time in private literary compilations. Manq 'Ali also quotes a fatwa on the correct recitation of the Quran, which Ebu's-su'ud composed, in the style of the question, in rhymed Arabic prose.[39] These literary pyrotechnics appealed to the highly educated, but what in the end is significant is the fact that most of his fatwas are in Turkish, the language not only of the élite but also of most of the Muslim inhabitants of the capital and of Anatolia and the Balkans. Furthermore, the Turkish style in which he instructed his clerks is clear and simple.[40] His aim, it seems, was to issue fatwas in a style that was easily accessible to the public at large. The fatwa thus became a means of educating the Sultan's subjects in the law.

With his accession to the highest legal offices, as Military Judge of Rumelia in 1537 and as *sheikhu'l-islam* in 1545, Ebu's-su'ud no longer needed any patron but the Sultan. He remained, it seems, an intimate of Süleyman I, keeping him company both in the capital and on military campaigns. Literary sources give hints of the friendship between the two men. It was, Ebu's-su'ud writes in his commentary on the Quran, when returning with the Sultan from one of his Holy Wars, that he passed through Macedonia, 'the seat of the Kingdom of Alexander' the Great.[41] It was as Military Judge of Rumelia that he accompanied the Sultan on the Hungarian campaign of 1541, producing during the campaign a gloss on Zamakhshari's commentary on the Victory chapter in the Koran.[42] Years later, feeling that his advancing years made it an urgent matter, he petitioned the Sultan to allow him to go on the Pilgrimage to Mecca. The Sultan refused 'as there was no one in Istanbul to take his place'.[43] It was Ebu's-su'ud too whom Süleyman chose to lay the foundation stone of the great Süleymaniye mosque in 1550,[44] and to compose the inscription over the portal[45] on its completion seven years later.

At the time at least of his succession in 1566, Süleyman's son, Selim II, seems to have shared his father's reverence for Ebu's-su'ud. The contemporary chronicler, Selaniki Mustafa, describes the scene after Selim's accession, where the dignitaries of state received the Sultan as he entered Istanbul on horseback. 'Ebu's-su'ud', he wrote, 'was the first to approach the Imperial Stirrup. [The Sultan] held tight to [Ebu's-su'ud's] turban with his blessed hands. The people acclaimed with the words: "This degree of honouring and veneration was never seen from a previous Sultan".'[46] In a courtly milieu, which placed extreme importance on ceremonial,[47] this apparently insignificant gesture carried great meaning.

As a man of immense moral and political prestige, it is clear that Ebu's-su'ud would exert his powers of patronage to the advantage of his family and protégés. His eldest son, Mehmed, was born in about 1525,[48] and, if the biographical tradition is to be believed, he became a candidate for office under the patronage of Mühiyyü'd-din Chelebi when the latter was Military Judge of Rumelia. Since the Sultan dismissed Mühiyyü'd-din from this post in 1537, the boy cannot have been more than 12. His first post, in 1548 according to Manq 'Ali,[49] was to the Qasim Pasha College with the unusually high starting salary of fifty aqches per day. He became professor at the Eight Colleges in 1551[50] at the age of about 26. By 1560, he was judge of Damascus, one of the senior judicial posts in the Empire. Damascus, however, was far from the capital and his father's immediate sphere of protection. He was dismissed, Manq 'Ali says, 'for no reason'. He died in 1563, when judge of Aleppo.[51]

His brother Shemsü'd-din Ahmed also died during their father's lifetime. He was born in about 1540, and studied with the biographer Tashköprüzade, before becoming his father's teaching assistant. It was undoubtedly through his father that he came to the attention of the vizier and royal son-in-law, Rüstem Pasha, who 'admired the beauty of his speech, bestowed on him the finest books and adopted him as a son'. Rüstem appointed him, at the age of 17, to the college which he had himself founded, with a daily stipend of fifty aqches.[52] Shemsü'd-din Ahmed was, however, a source of grief to his father since, in defiance of his father's stern prohibition of any form of intoxicant, he became addicted to drugs and died in 1569 when he was not yet 30. 'The cause of his death', Manq 'Ali guardedly writes, 'was that he mixed with certain despicable men, and they gave him a liking for eating a certain concoction.'[53] His pupil, the more forthright Mustafa 'Ali of Gallipoli, states bluntly that he died of diarrhoea, brought on by drug addiction.[54]

In a Turkish elegy composed probably for his son Mehmed, the elderly Ebu's-su'ud expressed his grief at the loss and a desire to follow him in death: 'When I entrusted you to eternity, I wished that I too should find oblivion/ ... Oh Heart! You have put an end to supplication and prayer/ The beloved son did not return. Come then, let us go to him.'[55] Mehmed's death brought him not only grief, but also left him with the burden of educating his two sons. The elder of these, 'Abdü'l-kerim, became his protégé and, through his patronage, received the professorship at the College of Mahmud Pasha, 'in honour of his grandfather,' writes Manq 'Ali, 'and contrary to custom.'[56] By the time of his death in 1573/4, when he was not yet 30, he was already professor at one the colleges attached to the Süleymaniye Mosque.[57] He did not outlive his grandfather. Mehmed's second son, 'Abdü'l-vasi', also became a protégé of Ebu's-su'ud and, as his first appointment, succeeded his brother at the College of Mahmud Pasha. At the time of Ebu's-su'ud's death, and still only in his mid-thirties, he was a professor at the Süleymaniye. Lacking his grandfather's protection, in 'Ata'i's words, 'the swift steed on the path of his prosperity stumbled on the stone of misfortune', and his career did not advance further until 1580, when he received the College of the new Mosque of Sultan Selim II in Edirne, where he died two years later.[58]

Only one of Ebu's-su'ud's sons outlived his father. This was Mustafa, born in 1558 when Ebu's-su'ud was about 70. He became his father's protégé in seeking office and, in 1574, was a professor at the Eight Colleges at the age of 26. This appointment, 'Ata'i says, 'was in honour of his noble father'. When he died in 1599, he had served at the College of Selim II, where he replaced his nephew, twice as judge of Istanbul, and briefly as Military Judge of Anatolia and then of Rumelia. After the death of his father, however, his career was no longer a smooth succession of promotions.[59]

The biographical sources refer to Ebu's-su'ud's sons, but only obliquely to his daughter, in the context of her marriage to his student, Ma'lulzade Mehmed. Ma'lulzade himself was from a prominent learned family, his father having served as Military Judge of Anatolia in 1547,[60] but what is perhaps more important is that the family were seyyids, claiming descent from the Prophet himself. As seyyids, they enjoyed both material privileges and the respect of the pious. By marrying the daughter of the *sheikhu'l-islam*, Ma'lulzade undoubtedly enhanced his own career prospects, himself becoming *sheikhu'l-islam* in 1580.[61] At the same time, Ebu's-su'ud and his offspring must, through this marriage, have acquired some of the moral prestige belonging to the holy family of the Prophet.

It was not only Ebu's-su'ud's immediate descendants that benefited from his patronage. His cousin Ja'fer, the son of his father's brother 'Abdü'n-nebi, was a native of Iskilip who had begun his career in the entourage of Bayezid II's son, Prince Ahmed, in Amasya. When Ebu's-su'ud became Military Judge of Rumelia, he used his powers of patronage to bring Ja'fer to Istanbul, where he embarked on a career which culminated in his six-year period as Military Judge of Anatolia. He died in 1570.[62] His brother, Lutfu'llah, also under Ebu's-su'ud's patronage, was to become, by 1562, a professor at the Eight Colleges, dying in Istanbul in 1568.[63]

Ebu's-su'ud's use of patronage to secure positions for his own relatives was unremarkable, since it was only through patronage that a man could acquire office of any sort. The same was also true of the more humble position of clerk in the suite of an office-holder. The biographical sources record only two of the clerks who worked for Ebu's-su'ud, but in both cases the ties of patronage are obvious. The first of these was 'Ashiq Chelebi, who records, without specifying a date, that he served as Ebu's-su'ud's 'fatwa clerk'.[64] He had previously been Ebu's-su'ud's student and, as a seyyid, must also have known his son-in-law, Ma'lulzade. The other clerk was Veli Yegan (d. 1590). Like Ebu's-su'ud's father and uncle, he was a native of Iskilip, and related in some way to Ebu's-su'ud's family.[65] He became, 'Ata'i says, Ebu's-su'ud's protégé and 'served Ebu's-su'ud for a long time in teaching and issuing fatwas'. Because, 'Ata'i continues, 'he was the late Molla [Ebu'su'ud]'s fatwa clerk, and had fine calligraphy and excellent spelling, he compiled noble anthologies [of fatwas] … He selected and compiled in a single book, the noble fatwas of the scholars of the Ottoman realms: 'Ali Jemali, Kemalpashazade Ahmed, Sa'di, Chivizade and Ebu's-su'ud.'[66] A second scholar who made a systematic compilation of Ebu's-su'ud's fatwas was Buzenzade Mehmed (d. 1575).[67] Like Veli Yegan, he too was from Iskilip and became Ebu's-su'ud's protégé but did not, it appears, serve directly as his fatwa clerk.[68]

When Selim II, the great-grandson of his first royal patron, came to the throne in 1566, Ebu's-su'ud was aged 75 or more. He enjoyed the patronage and respect of the new Sultan, and controlled the senior judicial appointments in the Empire. He had secured offices for relatives and students, who in turn must have supported his position of authority. His mental powers had not declined, and he was still in sufficiently good health to oversee the new cadastral survey of Skopje and Thessaloniki in 1568/9. But this was a public image. In a poem remarkably free of religious feeling, Ebu's-su'ud reflected on the private griefs of old age: 'The season of youth has departed, like the moment of meeting with the beloved. The days of old age have come, like the night time of separation / The turning heavens have rolled up the scroll of my life ... / Limping with weakness, I have passed the boundary of life, and entered a strange clime, like a foreign world/ My stay in the kingdom of health is over. What I see is like a journey to the clime of non-existence.'[69] 'Ata'i tells the story of how, shortly before his own death, he attended the funeral of his grandson 'Abdü'l-kerim and prayed: 'Let no one in our household pass over before me into the valley [of death]'. His request, 'Ata'i concludes, was granted. He died on 23 August 1574. He was buried, after the funeral prayer at the Mosque of Sultan Mehmed, in the courtyard of the school which he had endowed in the Istanbul suburb of Eyüp.[70]

Ebu's-su'ud devoted his entire life from his appointment as judge of Bursa in 1533 until his death in 1574 to the practice of law, and, in this sphere, his influence continued down to the nineteenth century. Nonetheless, his greatest literary work was not, in the estimation of the Ottoman biographical and literary tradition, one of jurisprudence, but his commentary on the Quran, entitled 'The Guide for the sound mind to the virtues of the Noble book'. This the biographers treat together with the commentaries of Zamakhshari (d. 1144) and Baidawi (d. late thirteenth century) as one of the three greatest works of Quranic exegesis.[71] By 1565, Ebu's-su'ud had reached the thirty-eighth chapter of the Quran, when Sultan Süleyman, feeling perhaps that his own death was imminent, demanded a copy of the incomplete work. Ebu's-su'ud made a fair copy, which he sent to the Palace with his son-in-law, Ma'lulzade. On receipt, Süleyman raised Ebu's-su'ud's daily stipend from 200 to 500 aqches and bestowed on him 'coins and goods, garments and honours beyond counting'.[72] In February/March 1566, he sent the completed book to the Sultan, and received for it an additional 100 aqches per day.[73]

The composition of the commentary had occupied Ebu's-su'ud for over thirty years, but, as he makes clear in the exordium, he was subject to constant interruption: 'I was afflicted with managing the affairs of men, in judgeships and once as Military Judge. They interposed themselves between me and what I dreamt of. Important matters piled up and work crowded in ... with the onslaught of vicissitudes and impediments, frequent departures on Holy Wars and campaigns, and moving from house to house.' When he finally settled, with free time to devote to the commentary, the Sultan appointed him Mufti: 'I was ordered to solve the problems of the people, concerning disputes and litigation which broke out between them. I was like someone escaping from rain into the flood ...' What spurred him to finish, despite his constant work, was the knowledge that 'the appointed hour of death was approaching, and that the sun of life was close to setting'.[74] It was in fact not Ebu's-su'ud, but the dedicatee, Sultan Süleyman, who died in 1566, the year of its completion.

'The Guide for the sound mind' was not Ebu's-su`'ud's only exegetical work, although it was by far the most important. The biographers also note his gloss on Zamakhshari's commentary on the Victory chapter of the Quran, mainly, it seems, because of the circumstances of its composition on the Hungarian campaign of 1541. The biographers, and Manq 'Ali in particular, also remark on his skills as a poet, citing in particular an Arabic ode, evidently composed before 1563, which attracted two commentaries.[75] His Arabic elegy on the death of Sultan Süleyman[76] seems also to have circulated widely. The biographers do not accord the same respect to his Turkish verse which, with its lack of artifice and ornamentation, is more appealing to the modern reader. Apart from letters[77] and a prayer book,[78] which he composed in Turkish for the vizier Mehmed Pasha, Ebu's-su'ud's remaining literary works are juristic.

The two commentaries, on the 'Book [i.e. chapter] of sale' in the *Hidaya* of Marghinani and on part of the *Talwih* of Taftazani,[79] he composed probably when he was teaching at the Eight Colleges between 1528 and 1533, since both of these works formed part of the syllabus. His commentary on the *Manar* of Nasafi (d. 1310) dates probably from the same period. These works probably all arose out of Ebu's-su'ud's teaching. His commentary on the 'Book of Holy War' in the *Hidaya*, however, he composed on the order of Sultan Süleyman.[80]

Whatever the motives for their composition, these commentaries belong to the mainstream of juristic literature. They do not appear to have attracted the same esteem as Ebu's-su'ud's Quran commentary or his Arabic verse, and they lacked the relevance to contemporary controversies of his legal treatises. The most important of these he wrote in defence of charitable trusts established with an endowment of cash or moveables, in reply to Chivizade Mehmed who, during his tenure as Military Judge of Rumelia, had declared them illegal. It was on the basis of Ebu's-su'ud's opinion that the Sultan, in 1548, issued a decree reversing Chivizade's ruling.[81] Another treatise, which he composed towards the end of his life for his son Mustafa,[82] was on the subject of another long-running controversy: whether it was permissible to perform the ritual ablution before prayers while wearing boots. The question was clearly important for worshippers who performed ablutions, which included applying water to the feet, out of doors in the depths of winter. Equally practical, although for different reasons, was 'The Judge's Merchandise',[83] an anthology of legal exemplars which Ebu's-su'ud composed in order to assist judges in drawing up documents.

Ebu's-su'ud's output of formal legal treatises is modest and, apart from his work on cash trusts which entered the juristic tradition, not particularly important. He was, as he himself says, caught up 'in managing the affairs of men', leaving little time for formal literary composition. It is not surprising therefore that his most influential writings were those which arose out of his practical day-to-day work, whether this involved solving petty disputes between individuals or major issues of state, such as providing a workable summary of the Ottoman system of land tenure. His writings of this sort survive not because Ebu's-su'ud himself regarded them as having a permanent literary or juristic value, but largely through the efforts of individual biographers, anthologists and keepers of government records.

The fatwas form the most important body of Ebu's-su'ud's legal writings. However, although the existence of his instructions to his fatwa clerks and a treatise on common linguistic errors[84] shows that he had a great concern for their correct format, he never himself collected them or used them as a basis for a legal compendium. It is unlikely that he would have had time to do so since, with his workload as Mufti, he already compared himself to a drowning man, and, until 1566, his greatest literary preoccupation was with his Quran commentary. However, Katib Chelebi in the mid-seventeenth century recorded an anecdote which suggests that he considered his abilities to be inadequate. 'The Mufti Ebu's-su'ud', he writes, 'was asked: "Why didn't you collect the most important problems and compose a book on them?" He replied: "I felt shame before the author of the *Bazzaziyya* and his book. It is a noble book, bringing together the most important questions as required."'[85] He felt simply that he could not emulate or add to the legal compendium of the great Crimean jurist, Ibn Bazzaz (d. 1414).

The collection of his fatwas was a task which remained for others. The first compilers were, it seems, his protégé, Buzenzade Mehmed, and his fatwa clerk, Veli Yegan, who made their collections during Ebu's-su'ud's lifetime. Another collection was made immediately after his death, in the name of the new Sultan, Murad III (1574–95). The compiler seems to have combined the existing collections, possibly those of Buzenzade and Veli Yegan, with the contents of codices of clerks working in the Fatwa Office.[86] This collection possibly formed the main source for subsequent manuscripts. However, the manuscript history of Ebu's-su'ud's fatwas remains to be investigated.

Notes

1. R. C. Repp, *The Müfti of Istanbul*, Oxford: Ithaca Press (1986), p. 45.
2. Kevin Reinhart has pointed out that, as translations of *qadi* and *mufti*, 'judge' and 'jurisconsult' are *faux amis*. Muslims achieve salvation not through Grace but through Right Action, and it is the function of *muftis* and *qadis* to guide Muslims to, and to enforce, Right Action. In this respect, they have a quasi-sacerdotal role in Muslim society. A. Kevin Reinhart, 'Transcendence and social practice: *muftis* and *qadis* as religious interpreters', *Annales Islamologiques*, 27 (1993), 5–25. However, in a mundane legal sense, the terms 'judge' and 'jurisconsult' are accurate enough.
3. Michael M. Pixley, 'The development and role of the Şeyhülislam in early Ottoman history', *Journal of the American Oriental Society*, 96 (1976), 89–96.
4. Ahmed Akgündüz, *Osmanlı Kanunnameleri*, Istanbul: Fey Vakfı yayınları, 4 (1992), p. 663, section 5 (*Kanunname-i ehl-i 'ilm*).
5. Madeline C. Zilfi, 'The *Ilmiye* registers and the Ottoman *medrese* system prior to the *Tanzimat*', *Contributions à l'histoire économique et sociale de l'Empire ottoman*, Collection Turcica III, Louvain: Editions Peeters (1981), pp. 309–27.
6. 'Ata'i, *Hada'iq al-haqa'iq fi takmilat al-Shaqa'iq*, Istanbul: Imperial Press (1851/2), p. 177.
7. Tashköprüzade, *al-Shaqa'iq al-nu'maniyya fi 'ulama' al-dawlat al-'uthmaniyya*, Beirut: Dar al-Kitab al-'Arabi (1975), p. 206.
8. 'Ata'i, *Hada'iq*, p. 83; R. C. Repp, *The Müfti of Istanbul*, p. 273.
9. Tashköprüzade, *al-Shaqa'iq*, p. 177.
10. Ibid.
11. Ibid., p. 206.
12. Ibid.
13. 'Ata'i, *Hada'iq*, p. 183.
14. Manq 'Ali, *al-'Iqd al-manzum fi dhikr afadil al-Rum*, Beirut: Dar al-Kitab al-'Arabi (1975), p. 440. The commentaries by al-Sharif al-Jurjani (1339–1413) are on *al-Tajrid fi 'ilm al-mantiq*, a textbook on logic by Nasir al-Din Tusi (d. 1274); on *Miftah al-'ulum*, a textbook on Arabic grammar and rhetoric by Yusuf b. Abi Bakr al-Sakkaki (d.1229); and on *al-Mawaqif fi 'ilm al-kalam*, a textbook on theology by 'Adud al-Din Iji (d. 1355). These were the foundation texts studied in Ottoman colleges.
15. 'Ata'i, *Hada'iq*, p. 83; Manq 'Ali, *al-'Iqd*, pp. 363–4.
16. Tashköprüzade, *al-Shaqa'iq*, p. 206.
17. Ibid., p. 182.
18. 'Ata'i, *Hada'iq*, p. 184.
19. Ibid.
20. Tashköprüzade, *al-Shaqa'iq*, pp. 206, 177.
21. Manq 'Ali, *al-'Iqd*, p. 440; 'Ata'i, *Hada'iq*, p. 184.
22. 'Ata'i, *Hada'iq*, p. 184. Manq 'Ali, *al-'Iqd*, p. 440, has 'a number of months'.
23. 'Ata'i, *Hada'iq*, p. 184. Manq 'Ali, *al-'Iqd*, p. 440, has the College of 'Ali Pasha. See R. C. Repp, *The Müfti of Istanbul*, p. 276.
24. Tashköprüzade, *al-Shaqa'iq*, p. 182. Seyyid Mehmed died in 1524/5.
25. 'Ata'i, *Hada'iq*, p. 184.
26. The references are to *al-Hidaya*, on jurisprudence by al-Marghinani (d. 1197);

al-Talwih, a commentary by al-Taftazani (d. 1389) on *Tanqih al-usul* on the principles of law by 'Ubayd Allah al-Mahbubi (d. 1346/7); *al-Kashshaf*, a commentary on the Koran by al-Zamakhshari (d. 1144); and to *al-Sahih*, a collection of prophetic traditions by al-Bukhari (d. 870).

27. Mahmud b. Süleyman el-Kefevi, *Kata'ib a'lam al-akhyar min fuqaha' madhhab al-Nu'man al-mukhtar*, Süleymaniye Library, Istanbul, MS Esad Efendi 548 [hereafter: *K*]ff. 65a–b.

28. Ö. L. Barkan and E. H. Ayverdi, *Istanbul vakıflari tahrir defteri: 953 (1546) târîhli*, Istanbul: Baha Matbaası (1970), nos 1,167, 1,178, 1,220. The royal estates were estates around Istanbul, created by Mehmed II after his conquest of the city in 1453, including among other towns and villages the suburb of Eyüp.

29. R. C. Repp, *The Müfti of Istanbul*, p. 277.

30. 'Ata'i, *Hada'iq*, p. 184.

31. Ibid., p. 186.

32. Ibid., p. 184.

33. Manq 'Ali, *al-'Iqd*, p. 441.

34. R. C. Repp, *The Müfti of Istanbul*, pp. 240–72.

35. Manq 'Ali, *al-'Iqd*, p. 441.

36. 'Ata'i, *Hada'iq*, p. 185.

37. Uriel Heyd, 'Some aspects of the Ottoman *fetva*', *Bulletin of the School of Oriental and African Studies*, 32 (1969), 35–56.

38. 'Ashiq Chelebi, ed. G. M. Meredith-Owens, *Meşa'ir üş-şü'ara*, London: E. J. W. Gibb Memorial Series, new series 24 (1971), f. 16a; Manq 'Ali, *al-'Iqd*, p. 442; 'Ata'i, *Hada'iq*, p. 186.

39. Manq 'Ali, *al-'Iqd*, p. 442.

40. The best copy of Ebu's-su'ud's instructions to his clerks is Süleymaniye Library, Istanbul, MS Esad Efendi 1,017. For further references, see Uriel Heyd, 'Some aspects of the Ottoman *fetva*'. Ebu's-su'ud also composed a treatise on the correct use of language: *Fi tashih ba'd al-alfaz al-mutadawala bain al-nas*, Süleymaniye Library, MS Tirnovali 1865; Istanbul University Library, MS TY1496.

41. Ebu's-su'ud, *Irshad al-'aql al-salim ila mazaya al-kitab al-karim*, in margin of Fakhr al-Din Razi, *Mafatih al-Ghaib*, Istanbul: Imperial Press (1872/3), vol. 5, pp. 736–7.

42. 'Ata'i, *Hada'iq*, p. 186.

43. Mahmud b. Süleyman el-Kefevi, *al-Kata'ib*, f. 66a.

44. Jelalzade Mustafa, ed. Petra Kappert, *Tabakat ül-Memalik ve Derecat ül-Mesalik*, Verzeichnis der Orientalischen Handschriften in Deutschland, Supplementband 21, Wiesbaden: Franz Steiner Verlag (1981), f. 152a.

45. See below, Chapter 3, no. (1).

46. Selânikî Mustafa, ed. Mehmet İpşirli, *Tarih-i Selânikî*, İstanbul: Istanbul Üniversitesi Edebiyat Fakültesi yayınları 3,371 (1989), p. 54.

47. On the importance of ceremonial, see Gülru Necipoğlu, *Architecture, Ceremonial and Power: The Topkapı Palace in the Fifteenth and Sixteenth Centuries*, Cambridge, MA: MIT Press (1991).

48. 'Ata'i, *Hadai'iq*, probably deducing from Manq 'Ali's statement that, on his death, 'his age did not exceed forty'. Manq 'Ali, *al-'Iqd*, p. 365.

49. Manq 'Ali, *al-'Iqd*, p. 365.

50. 'Ata'i, *Hada'iq*, p. 43.

51. Manq 'Ali, *al-'Iqd*, p. 365.
52. Ibid., p. 354.
53. Ibid., p. 355.
54. Jan Schmidt, *Pure Water for Thirsty Muslims: A Study of Mustafa 'Ali of Gallipoli's* Kunhü l-ahbar, Leiden: Het Oosters Instituut (1991), p. 266.
55. E. J. W. Gibb, *A History of Ottoman Poetry*, London: Luzac & Co. (repr. 1963), vol. 6, p. 150.
56. Manq 'Ali, *al-'Iqd*, p. 439.
57. Ibid.
58. 'Ata'i, *Hada'iq*, pp. 266–7.
59. Ibid., pp. 428–9.
60. R. C. Repp, *The Müfti of Istanbul*, p. 255.
61. 'Ata'i, *Hada'iq*, p. 281.
62. Manq 'Ali, *al-'Iqd*, p. 399; 'Ata'i, *Hada'iq*, pp. 136–7.
63. 'Ata'i, *Hada'iq*, p. 121.
64. 'Ashiq Chelebi, *Meşa'ir*, f. 16a.
65. 'Ata'i, *Hada'iq*, p. 313.
66. Ibid.
67. Katib Chelebi, ed. Gustav Flügel, *Kashf al-zunun 'an asami al-kutub wa'l-funun*, Leipzig: Oriental Translation Fund of Great Britain and Ireland, 7 vols (1835–58), vol. 4, p. 351.
68. Manq 'Ali, *al-'Iqd*, p. 481.
69. Ziya Pasha, *Kharabat*, Istanbul: Imperial Press (1875/6), vol. 2, p. 156.
70. 'Ata'i, *Hada'iq*, p. 185.
71. Katib Chelebi, *Kashf*, vol. 1, pp. 249–51.
72. 'Ata'i, *Hada'iq*, p. 186.
73. Ibid., p. 186; Manq 'Ali, *al-'Iqd*, p. 444; Mustafa 'Ali of Gallipoli, intro. M. Cavid Baysun, *Mevâ'idü'n-nefâ'is fi kavâ'idi'l-mecâlis*, facsimile, Istanbul: Istanbul Üniversitesi Edebiyat Fakültesi Yayınları 679 (1956), pp. 240–1.
74. Ebu's-su'ud, *Irshad*, vol. 1, pp. 32–8.
75. Katib Chelebi, *Kashf*, vol. 6, pp. 286–7. This gives the date of the death of one of the commentators as 1563/4.
76. Süleymaniye Library, Istanbul, ms Haci Beşir Ağa 676.
77. *Munsha'at-i Ebu's-su'ud*, Süleymaniye Library, Istanbul, ms Esad Efendi 3,291.
78. Ebu's-su'ud, *Du'aname*, Süleymaniye Library, Istanbul, ms Laleli 1,534.
79. Katib Chelebi, *Kashf*, vol. 6, p. 488. For the *Hidaya* and *Talwih*, see above, note 21.
80. Ibid. vol. 6, p. 494.
81. See below, Chapter 6.
82. Katib Chelebi, *Kashf*, vol. 2, p. 56.
83. For excerpts from this work, see below, Chapter 2, nos (35), (36), (37).
84. See above, note 35.
85. Katib Chelebi, *Kashf*, vol. 2, p. 49.
86. Ibid. vol. 4, pp. 352–3.

2

The Law: *shari'a* and *qanun*

The Ottoman Empire was typical of pre-modern Islamic polities in that the *shari'a* coexisted with a secular law which had developed quite independently. This was the *qanun*. Unlike the *shari'a*, which was the law of a religious community, the *qanun* was the law of an Empire, and it is these two distinct bodies of law, one sacred, the other imperial, that Ottoman tradition credits Ebu's-su'ud with bringing into conformity with one another. He did this largely through the medium of fatwas; and so, in order to assess whether or to what extent the tradition is correct, it is necessary first to define three terms: *shari'a*, *qanun* and fatwa.

The *shari'a*

Islamic jurisprudence in its traditional sense had a history of about 1,000 years, from its obscure beginnings in the late eighth and early ninth centuries,[1] until its near-demise in the face of modernism in the late nineteenth. There was no single, unified juristic tradition. Within Islam itself, there was a split between the Shi'a and the Sunnis, and, by the end of the tenth century, the jurisprudence of the Shi'a was distinct from that of the Sunni majority. Within Sunni Islam, there were four separate Schools (*madhhab*), each taking its name from its supposed founder. These were the Hanafi, Shafi'i, Maliki and Hanbali Schools, named respectively after Abu Hanifa, Shafi'i, Malik and Ibn Hanbal.

The differences among the four Schools originated, it seems, in juristic rather than in political division, so that, in the medieval Islamic world, jurists of all four Schools could congregate and debate within a single city or even, as in fourteenth-century Cairo, within a single college.[2] Nonetheless, despite this mixing, there was a tendency for a particular School to dominate a particular geographical area. Thus, by the eleventh century, the Malikis were the dominant School in north Africa and Islamic Spain, and the Hanafis in Iraq and Transoxania. The reasons for the spread of a particular School into a particular area are not always clear. The Maliki School seems to have developed in the Islamic cities of north Africa and Spain, and the Hanafi school in the cities of Iraq, hence their predominance in these regions. The patronage of secular rulers must also have played a part in the geographical distribution of the Schools. It was the Islamic monarchs who, from the eleventh century onwards, established the most prestigious colleges,[3] which maintained the academic traditions of jurisprudence and trained judges in the law, and it was ultimately the monarchs who administered the law through the courts. If a monarch favoured a particular School, then that school would gain ascendancy within the area of his rule.

In the centuries after 1300, the Hanafi School owed its powerful position largely to the patronage of the Ottoman dynasty. From the earliest days of their rule, the Ottoman Sultans appear to have given official status to the Hanafi school, presumably because it was already established in the cities of pre-Ottoman Anatolia which provided the first judges and jurists in the Ottoman realms. By the mid-sixteenth century, the Hanafi School, both in the practice of the courts and in the curriculum of the colleges, had spread with the Ottoman conquest to the Balkan peninsula and Hungary, and had become the predominant School in the Middle East to the west of Iran. Nonetheless, neither the Hanafi, nor any of the other schools represented the law of a kingdom. The Ottoman Sultans were Hanafis, but so too were the Islamic monarchs of northern India and Transoxania. The tradition of jurisprudence was, in itself, independent of political power. Rulers fostered Islamic law and jurisprudence, but they did not create it.

The Hanafi School takes its name from Abu Hanifa, whose death Islamic tradition places in 767. The jurists attribute the foundation of the School to him and to his two disciples, Abu Yusuf (d. 798) and Shaibani (d. 805). These three figures were, for the Hanafis, not simply the founders of the School, but equally the source of the most authoritative juristic opinion. In enunciating a particular rule or opinion, the jurists frequently prefix to it the statement: 'Abu Hanifa said: ...', 'Abu Yusuf said: ...', 'Muhammad [Shaibani] said: ...', or else they attribute the opinion to any combination of these three. In attributing a legal opinion to any one of these founders, they are citing a source of incontrovertible authority.

In reality, these three jurists are far more shadowy figures than the Hanafi tradition would allow. Whether they are, in fact, the authors of the texts and opinions which tradition assigns to them is very far from certain, and they belong in any case to the period before the late tenth and eleventh centuries when Hanafi jurisprudence took its definitive shape. This was the century which saw the full development of legal concepts, the achievement of formal elegance in legal texts, and an increasing precision and flexibility in legal language. In this 'classical age' of the Hanafi tradition, two texts in particular stand out, each of which exemplifies a different genre of legal writing. The first is the 'Epitome' (*mukhtasar*) of Quduri (d. 1037), a jurist working in Baghdad. Quduri's book is a brilliantly concise and elegant summary of the law, giving a definitive shape and logical arrangement to the less well-ordered work of his predecessors. The opening of the chapter on marriage serves as an example of Quduri's style:

> (1) Marriage is contracted by offer and acceptance, by means of two phrases, of which both are expressed in the [imperative or] past tense; or of which one is in the [imperative or] past tense and the other in the future, as when [the suitor] says: 'Marry [your daughter/your ward] to me', and the [father/guardian of the woman] says: 'I have married her to you'.
> The marriage of Muslims in contracted only in the presence of two witnesses who are [male,] free, adult and sane, or [in the presence of] one man and two women. [It is immaterial whether the witnesses] are righteous ('*adil*)[4] or not, or whether they have suffered the penalty for false accusation of fornication (*qadhf*).[5]

The second of these works of the 'classical age' is the 'Summa' (*mabsut*) of the Transoxanian jurist Sarakhsi (d. 1090). In contrast to Quduri's concision, Sarakhsi's work spreads over twenty-four volumes, discussing each point of law in minute detail. The following passage is the opening of the section concerning the rule which forbids a man, in a plural marriage, to take a slave as a wife in addition to a free woman:

> (2) [Sarakhsi] said: It has come down to us from the Apostle of God [Muhammad] (may God bless him and give him peace) that he said: 'A female slave should not be taken in marriage in addition to a free woman'. This is proof that marriage to a female slave in addition to a free woman is not permissible, and that this prohibition is established in law, whether or not the free woman gives her consent. This is the doctrine of our School. Malik (may God have mercy on him) said: 'If the free woman gives her consent, it is permissible, because the prohibition arises from the right of the free woman, and not from the combination [of a free woman and a slave-woman in a plural marriage]. The proof for this is that, if the marriage of the slave precedes, her marriage remains in existence after [the husband's second marriage to] the free woman, bringing the combination into existence ...[6]

Quduri's 'Epitome' and Sarakhsi's 'Summa' exemplify what were to become two of the literary genres of Hanafi jurisprudence. Both were the subject of further exposition and commentary in the following century, when the Syrian jurist Kasani (d. 1189) produced a formal rearrangement of the 'Summa'[7] with some modifications to Sarakhsi's opinions, and the

Transoxanian jurist, Marghinani (d. 1197), used Quduri's 'Epitome' as the basis of one of the most widely-used Hanafi works. This was the *Hidaya*, or 'Guide', a work whose composition and subsequent history typifies the way in which Hanafi literary jurisprudence developed.

Marghinani's starting point was Quduri, whose 'Epitome' he expanded slightly to produce a new text, which he entitled the *Bidaya*, or 'Introduction'. The *Hidaya* is a commentary on this expanded version of Quduri. The chapter on marriage begins like this:

(3) *Marriage is contracted by offer and acceptance, by means of two phrases, both of which are expressed in the past tense*: because, although the grammatical form serves to relate what has happened in the past, in law it is used out of necessity to initiate [a legal act, since the Arabic present tense can also have the sense of the future]. *Or it is contracted by two expressions, of which one is in the past tense and the other in the future, as when [the suitor] says:* 'Marry *[your daughter/ward] to me*', *and [the father/guardian of the woman] says:* 'I have married her to you: because [the first phrase] appoints an agent to [contract] the marriage, and in marriage, one person may act on behalf of both sides, as we shall explain later, God willing.[8]

The success of the *Hidaya* and its widespread circulation in the Hanafi world led to the production of commentaries on the *Hidaya* itself. One of these commentators was Ebu's-su'ud. The following passage is from his commentary on the opening section on the option of defect, in the chapter on sale. The first passage is from the *Hidaya*. The second is Ebu's-su'ud's commentary:

(4) 1. *If the purchaser observes a defect in the object bought, he has a choice. If he wishes, he may take it at its full price, or he may return it*: because flawlessness is an essential quality in an unconditional contract. In the absence of this quality, provided he did not consent [to the defect, the purchaser] has the option, in order that he should suffer no harm from the irrevocability [of the contract]. He may not, however, take [the object] and receive [a discount for] the deficiency in value [caused by the defect], because in the contract itself, the price does not correspond to the [individual] qualities [of the object of sale], and because [the vendor] would not consent to [the object of sale] leaving his ownership for less than the named [price].[9]

2. *If the purchaser observes a defect in the object bought, he has a choice. If he wishes he may take it at the full price, or he may return it.* It is said that this is when the defect cannot be remedied without difficulty, but if it can, then there is no option of defect, as [in the case of] a female slave who

is in a state of ritual purification [for the Pilgrimage, when sexual intercourse with her is forbidden. In this case the purchaser] himself is the cause of her being defective. Or, [as in the case of] dirt on a garment which is not harmed by washing. You should be aware that things such as we have mentioned are not defects to which the garment of option applies. No, they are defects, but they have no effect in law, because of the ease of their removal. His statement: *He may not, however, take [the object] and receive [a discount for] the deficiency in value [caused by the defect], because in the contract itself, the price does not correspond to the [individual] qualities [of the object of sale]*: unless there is something here other than the contract in itself, in which a quality corresponds to a price. An example [of this] is when [the vendor] sells a cloth on condition that it is ten feet for ten pennies, [that is] at a penny a foot. Thus a foot of cloth, despite its being an individual quality, was made to correspond to a price, when [the vendor] declared: 'It is one penny per foot'. It is therefore from this standpoint that, when we find it to be defective, [the purchaser] has the option. He may, if he wishes, take it for its proportional share of the full price; or he may, if he wishes, return it.[10]

The most typical genres of literary jurisprudence, apart from the summa, epitome, commentary and super-commentary, were treatises and fatwas. A treatise (*risala*) was a work dealing with a single topic, often one that was controversial in the jurist's own time. The usual meaning of 'fatwa' is an authoritative legal opinion issued by a qualified jurisconsult, but in practice the term applied to two different types of legal writing.

The Hanafi literary corpus contains many works bearing the title 'Fatwas' (*al-fatawa*), of which the 'Fatwas' of the Transoxanian jurist, Qadikhan (d. 1196) is probably the most famous. The title of such works usually refers to the organisation of the legal materials into sequences of logically-ordered problems, each followed by one or more solutions. The opening of the chapter on loan in the 'Fatwas' of Qadikhan provides an example:

(5) A man borrows something from somebody and the owner is silent.
– The Sun of Imams Sarakhsi (may God Most High have mercy on him) said: Silence does not establish a loan.
A man borrows an animal from someone for carrying [goods].
– The Sheikh Imam 'Ali b. Muhammad al-Bazdawi (may God Most High have mercy on him) said: He may lend it to a [third] person for carrying [goods], because people do not differ greatly in the matter of carrying goods.
A man borrows an animal from someone for riding, or clothes for wearing.

– The same applies when the rider or the wearer are specified.
– But if he himself rides [the animal] or wears [the] clothes after this, the Sheikh Imam 'Ali b. Muhammad al-Bazdawi (may God most High have mercy on him) said: If either [the animal] or [the clothes] are destroyed, he is liable.
– [But] the Sun of Imams Sarakhsi and the Sheikh Imam, known as Khwaharzade (may God Most High have mercy on them) said: He is not liable, and the same applies to all things in the usage of which men do not differ. If he borrows unconditionally, he may lend it to another.[11]

Qadikhan's aim in writing his 'Fatwas' was, he says, to assist working jurists in solving the day-to-day problems of the Muslim community.[12] It would seem, nevertheless, that most if not all of his material came not from legal practice but from the literary tradition of Hanafi law. The contents of his 'Fatwas' and other works of this type do not differ in essence from the contents of other genres of legal writing. It is their organisation rather than specifically their contents which makes them especially useful to legal practitioners. Ebu's-su'ud, according to an Ottoman tradition, was an admirer in particular of the 'Fatwas' of the Crimean jurist Ibn Bazzaz (d. 1414),[13] undoubtedly because the organisation and comprehensive scope of the work made it an invaluable source or reference in solving the legal problems which confronted him every day.

More often, however, the term 'fatwa' applies to an opinion which a jurisconsult issued in response to an ad hoc question, often from a judge seeking a solution to a problem which had arisen in court, or from a member of the public. All Ebu's-su'ud's fatwas belong to this second type. They are the answers to the thousands of questions which he received during his thirty-year period of office as Mufti. Although a handful of originals remain, written on slips of paper in Ebu's-su'ud's own hand, their survival in large numbers is due entirely to later compilers. These made selections from the many thousands of original fatwas, arranged them systematically under legal headings, and copied them into single volumes. Further complete copies of, or selections from, these volumes then passed into general circulation. Without these anthologists, Ebu's-su'ud's fatwas would not have survived. As it is, anthologies of fatwas issued both by Ebu's-su'ud and by his predecessors and, especially, his successors in office became a characteristic genre of Ottoman legal literature.

The epitome, summa, commentary, super-commentary, treatise and the two types of fatwa were the standard forms of Hanafi legal literature. The proliferation in the number and length of texts led from time to time to a need for abridgements, particularly it seems as a result of student demand. The Ottoman jurist Hamidi introduced his 'Compendium of Fatwas' of c. 1475 with the remark that he found students in his day 'shunning long works and inclining towards abridgements'.[14] The creation of new epitomes led, in turn, to the creation of new commentaries. The sixteenth century, for example, saw the compilation of two popular epitomes, the 'Confluence of the Seas' (*Multaqa'l-abhur*) by Ibrahim of Aleppo (d. 1549) and the 'Illumination of Perceptions' (*Tanwir al-absar*) by Tirmirtashi (d. 1595), both of which generated commentaries in the succeeding centuries. The more extensive commentaries, notably perhaps the 'Translucent Sea' (*al-Bahr al-Ra'iq*) by the Egyptian jurist, Ibn Nujaim (d. 1563), a commentary on the 'Treasury of Subtleties' (*Kanz al-daqa'iq*) of Nasafi (d. 1310), belong to the summa type, with the authors' discussions ranging far beyond the limits of the base text. Indeed, Sarakhsi's 'Summa' was itself a commentary on a now lost work by Marwazi.

It is difficult to characterise in modern terms the contents of the texts of the Hanafi, or of any other Islamic school of law. The general word for law is *shar'* or, to give it the form in common use nowadays, *shari'a*. This term has both a metaphysical and a practical usage. In the metaphysical sense, the *shari'a* is the Law of God, which is ultimately unknowable. The science of jurisprudence (*fiqh*) represents the efforts of the jurists to discover God's law, and in this sense legal writings are works of *fiqh* rather than of *shari'a*, works on jurisprudence rather than statements of the law. In practical usage, however, *shari'a* means simply the law as jurists have enunciated it, as distinct from secular law which rulers have promulgated. The *shari'a*, in short, is the law of the Islamic jurists.

However, even this simplified definition is misleading since, in two respects, the *shari'a* does not correspond to a modern understanding of law. In the first place, many of the legal rules which the jurists enunciate are neither enforceable nor intended to be so, and many of the problems which they discuss have no bearing on reality, but relate instead to a self-contained tradition of juristic debate. As a result, the term 'law', in the sense of a system of enforceable rules, does not apply to large areas of the *shari'a*. Second, the *shari'a* is at odds with modern concepts of law, in that many of its provisions concern religious ritual, regulating man's relationship with God rather than man's relationship with man. Questions of ritual purity, prayer, fasting, pilgrimage and alms are as much the concern of jurists as are, for example, marriage, sale, inheritance or homicide. In the sense that it regulates both worldly and religious matters, the *shari'a* is an all-embracing law but, in the sense that many of its provisions have no application in practice, much of it is not, in the modern sense, law at all.

It is possible perhaps to characterise the *shari'a* as an ideal law, in part practical, but whose fulfilment in total remains a pious aspiration rather than an achievable goal. In their presentation of this ideal law, the jurists divide legal obligations into two categories, the 'claims of God' and the 'claims of men'. The claims of God are, for the most part, ritual acts such as prayer and fasting in Ramadan, which every Muslim owes as an obligation to God. To symbolise the supremacy of the Almighty in the life of every Muslim, the jurists invariably place the chapters on ritual at the beginning of their books, beginning always with the chapter on ritual purification. The religious rules in fact made up the area of the law most important in the daily lives of Muslims and, ultimately, in forming the Muslim view of the world. The months of fasting and pilgrimage, together with the other fixed festivals, marked the passing of the year, as the Friday prayer marked the passing of the week, and the five daily prayers the passing of the day. Ritual thus determined the Muslim concept of time. Since most emissions from the body cause a ritual impurity which the believer, as an obligation to God, must remove in the juristically prescribed manner, the simplest physical functions served constantly to remind Muslims of the divine omnipresence. There were also divine intrusions into non-ritual areas of the law. The fixed penalties for five offences, including stoning or the lash for fornication, and flogging for wine-drinking, are also claims of God, as are the obligations which arise from oaths. If a person, intentionally or unintentionally, swears an oath using the formula 'By God! I will do X', he has formed a unilateral contract with God, which obliges him to do X or to perform a penance. The jurists assimilate to oaths the formula for divorce, so that if a husband pronounces a valid formula, the divorce follows automatically. The husband's intention in speaking the words is irrelevant, since it is not his will but the will of God that brings the divorce into effect.[15] The law of manumission operates on exactly the same principle. If a slave-owner merely pronounces a valid formula of manumission, the slave goes free. Again, these are rules which can work only in a deeply religious society, and serve as constant reminders of the omnipotence of God over the lives of Muslims.

However, most of the non-ritual areas of the *shari'a* fall into the category of 'claims of men', and it is by and large this part of the *shari'a* that corresponds to law in its modern, secular sense. In formulating the claims of men, the jurists seem to have envisaged an ideal society, which it is the function of the law to maintain. They achieve this by dividing humankind into contrasting categories, for example, male/female, Muslim/non-Muslim, free/slave, with the possibility of further subdivisions within each category. A non-Muslim, for example, is either a tributary subject of a Muslim sovereign (*dhimmi*), a protected temporary resident in Muslim territory (*musta'min*), or an enemy (*harbi*). Once they have categorised a person in this way, the jurists assign him or her a value and a legal status, with the free, Muslim male occupying the top position in the hierarchy thus created. In this scheme, a woman, for example, has half the value of a man. Her share of an inheritance is worth half that of the equivalent male relative; her compensation for injury is half that owing to a man for an equivalent wound; the testimony of two women is equal to the testimony of one man. However, in the protection of life and property, the law makes no distinction between men and women. Similarly, non-Muslim tributary subjects suffer some legal disabilities. Their testimony, for example, is not admissible against Muslims, and they are subject to discriminatory taxation. But again, in the protection of life and property, they enjoy the same status as Muslims.[16]

Having in this way fixed the legal status and value of each person, the law aims to maintain the status quo thus established by preventing the unjustified enrichment of any individual at the expense of another, and by ensuring that if a person causes a loss to another, he must suffer an equivalent loss himself. It is, it seems, to prevent unjustified enrichment that a contract is invalid if it contains any element of risk or uncertainty. In a contract of sale, for example, the price must be specified and the nature and quantity of the goods known. In a contract of hire, the wages must be specified and the term fixed. By ensuring, as far as possible, that the price is exactly equal to the value of the return, the law is maintaining the status quo between the individuals.[17]

The same principle underlies the law of delicts. Here, the law places an exact price on a human life, and values each limb as a fraction of a whole life, so that, for example, in cases of accidental killing or injury, the sum which the killer or wounder pays in blood-money is precisely equal to the loss which the victim has sustained. If a person damages someone else's property, he must pay a sum precisely equal to the value of the loss. If he takes someone else's property, he must return it or, if it is lost, its equivalent value. If the property is damaged while in his possession, he must return it to its owner, together with a sum equal to the value of the loss through damage. The aim of the law is once more to maintain equivalence between the parties.

It is again perhaps a rule relating to the unlawful removal of property that best exemplifies the importance of this principle in juristic thinking. If a person unlawfully takes and damages property, he must restore to the owner both the property and the value lost. However, a person can also illegally take property and add to its value. The example which the jurists usually give is of a person who misappropriates a piece of white cloth and adds to its value by dyeing it red. In this case, the person who misappropriated the cloth must return it to its owner. The cloth, however, is now worth more than it was when he took it, and so the owner is receiving back something worth more than what was taken. The owner must therefore compensate the man who unlawfully took the cloth for the value of the dye. In this way, neither party gains at the expense of the other.

These rules relating to misappropriation and damage illustrate a cardinal principle underlying many areas of Hanafi law. They also illustrate the tendency of the jurists to allow the strict pursuit of principle to override questions of morality. In cases, for example, of misappropriation or damage, there is clearly a moral difference between the act when it is unintentional and the act when it is malicious. The Hanafi jurists admit this, in that they categorise malicious removal or damage to be a sin (*ithm*), whereas innocent removal or unintended damage is not. A sin, however, has no consequences in law. God may, if He so wishes, punish the sinner, but in law the consequences of misappropriation or damage are the same, whether intentional or not. There are many similar examples of the dichotomy between the moral and legal consequences of an act.[18] In law, strict legal analogy tends to take precedence over morality. However, in cases where strict analogy produces a ruling which appears unjust, it is permissible to give judgement according to equity (*istihsan*), rather than analogy.[19] The equitable ruling must, however, stand alone and cannot provide the basis for analogy. The following case, where a man slaughters a sheep which does not belong to him, provides an example of equity:

(6) A person slaughters a sheep belonging to a butcher. If its leg was tied for slaughter, he is not liable. Otherwise, he is. But if he slaughters a slaughter-animal belonging to another person on one of the [Festival] days [when animals are ritually slaughtered], by equity he is not liable.[20]

It is clear, therefore, that a number of important principles, notably the maintenance of equivalence between individuals, underlie Hanafi law, and that these principles can be sufficiently strong to override considerations of morality. However, to present general principles as the starting point of the law, from which specific rules derive, is to misrepresent the legal method apparent in Hanafi texts. Rather, the starting point of the law is the rules themselves, which the jurists inherited from generation to generation. Hence, the rules which Quduri so brilliantly systematised in the eleventh century remain firmly embedded in the work of, say, Ibrahim of Aleppo in the sixteenth or of Ibn 'Abidin (d. 1836) in the nineteenth. The increasingly minute discussions of the subtleties of each rule led, by analogy, to the creation of new rules. When the jurists do bring forward general principles, it is almost always as an explanation for an individual rule rather than as an introduction to a general legal topic, from which the individual rules derive. Marghinani, for example, discusses some general principles of slavery and marriage when commenting on the rule which forbids a man to manumit a female slave by using the divorce formula; but he is deriving the principle from the rule, rather than the rule from the principle:

> (7) [The master] intended [by the divorce formula] a [construction which] the words cannot bear, because manumission in its lexical sense is the establishment of [legal] capacity, and divorce is the removal of a bond. This is because the slave is assimilated to inanimate objects and is brought to life and given [legal] capacity. A married woman is not like this. She possesses [legal] capacity, but the bond of marriage is a restraint. The restraint is removed by divorce, and her [legal] capacity becomes plain ...[21]

The jurists preferred, in fact, to argue through analogy[22] and example, rather than through a statement of abstract principle, and it was the core of inherited rules that provided the starting point for debate and gave the Hanafi tradition its coherence.

Although it is plain that the *shari'a* owed both its development and its continuing vitality to the use of systematic reasoning, reason alone was not the basis of its legitimacy. The most potent source of legitimisation was the tradition itself. Within the Hanafi School, the attribution of a legal opinion to one or more of the founders of the School – Abu Hanifa, Abu Yusuf or Shaibani – gave it an unquestionable authority. Furthermore, any work of jurisprudence which gained a general acceptance within the School became a source which future jurists could cite as definitive. There was never any sense of a work's going out of date, or of one jurist's opinion superseding another's. Hence the whole field of Hanafi literature was available to a judge or jurist seeking a solution to a particular problem, or for a precedent with which to support his argument.

This need to cite juristic precedent gave rise ultimately to a form of legal literature which consists entirely or almost entirely of quotations, so arranged as to give shape to, and to lend authority to, the author's own arguments. The treatises of most Ottoman jurists, including Ebu's-su'ud, are of this type, as are Ibn Nujaim's monumental commentary, the 'Translucent Sea', and the 'Indian Fatwas' (*al-Fatawa'l-Hindiyya*), a comprehensive survey of Hanafi jurisprudence, compiled on the orders of the Mughal Emperor Awrangzeb (1658–1707). Legal literature of this type is a logical outcome of a reverence for tradition. Ibn Nujaim is able to dismiss an opponent's arguments on the grounds that he is 'someone without [legal] lineage' (*man la salaf lahu*).[23] In other words, an opinion with no precedent in the tradition is invalid.

In short, the Hanafi tradition, like the traditions of the other Islamic legal Schools, was self-contained and, to a degree, self-legitimating. However, the task of the jurist is, in theory, not to create the law, but to discover the Law of God, and so the authority of the jurists alone was not enough to establish the divine credentials of the *shari'a*. To do this, it was necessary to fix its origins in divine revelation.

God had revealed Himself to humankind through the Prophet Muhammad. The first source of revelation was the Quran, the uncreated Word of God, which the Almighty had transmitted to man through the medium of His Prophet. As the literal Word of God, the Quran is, in theory, the primary source of God's Law. The contents of the Holy Book are very varied, but a number of verses are specifically legal and form the basis of statutes in the *shari'a*. The rule, for example, which allows a man to marry up to four wives is Quranic, as is the specification of fasting and the freeing of slaves as forms of penance, or the right of the ruler to take one fifth of war booty as 'God's share'. Some of these Quranic injunctions, most notably perhaps the rules for the division of inheritance,[24] had an important influence on the formation of the law and on actual legal practice. Others, such as the amputation of the hand for theft, gained a revered place in juristic discussion but, because the jurists subjected the rule to so many qualifications, no place in legal practice.[25] The legal ordinances in the Quran are, however, sparse. It was not possible therefore to claim the Quran as the only source of the *shari'a*.

A second source of revelation lay in the recorded words and actions of the Prophet and his Companions. These traditions from the Age of Prophecy became an authoritative source of the law, and one that was considerably more bounteous than the Quran. What seems to have happened is that, during the formative period of the law between the eighth and eleventh centuries, jurists created Traditions in order to give authoritative support to their opinions.[26] Some areas of the law were particularly productive of Traditions. Most notable in this respect are the rules for the conduct of government (*al-siyar*), covering holy war, land tenure, taxation and the status of non-Muslims. Legal discussions of these topics generated a huge number of Traditions, which ultimately came to form the basis of the historiography of the early Islamic conquests.[27] Since many of the Traditions seem to have come into being in a juristic milieu, many of them encapsulate a legal principle, either in the form of a maxim or of an illustrative anecdote about the Prophet or his Companions.

In pious theory, therefore, the foundation of the law is divine revelation in the form of the Quran and the Traditions, and it is therefore common to find Hanafi jurists supporting a particular rule with one or more quotations from these sources. In the case of the Quran, sometimes it really is the source of the rule as, for example, in the following:

(8) *Penance for an oath is ... feeding ten indigent people* ...: The basis for this is the Word of God Most High: 'His penance is feeding ten indigent people' (Quran 5:89).[28]

More often, it is not, but since the Quran possesses the opacity essential to a sacred text, jurists were able to find in it phrases and passages which, creatively interpreted, could support a huge variety of rules and opinions. In the following passage, for example, Marghinani uses the Quran to justify deferred payment in a sale:

(9) *Sale is permissible with an immediate payment or a deferred payment, provided the term is known*: because the Word of God Most High: 'God has made sale lawful' (Quran 2:276) is unrestricted.[29]

The jurists use Traditions in the same way to support rules and opinions.

Although in theory, and sometimes too in practice, they really are the foundation of the law, the sources of revelation rarely override the results of analogical reasoning. The Hanafi jurists sometimes use a Tradition to validate a rule or legal definition when it evades justification by analogy. Here, Marghinani uses Traditions to legitimate the contract of hire, which strict analogy would not permit:

(10) *Hire is a contract on the usufruct for an exchange*: because hire, in its lexical sense, is the sale of the usufruct. Analogy denies its permissibility, because the object of the contract is a beneficial use which [at the time of the contract] is non-existent, and to ascribe the transfer of ownership to what will come into existence in the future is invalid. However [the Hanafis] have permitted it, because men have need of it, and because Traditions testify to its validity. [These traditions] are the Sayings of the Prophet (may God bless him and give him peace): 'Give the hireling his pay before the sweat is dry', and 'Whoever engages a hireling, let him inform him of his wages'.[30]

More often, however, they bring forward a tradition or a Quranic text in addition to an analogical argument. A typical pattern in the *Hidaya* is for the author to quote a rule, to follow it with a supporting Quranic text or Tradition, and to follow this with a justification by analogy. Here Marghinani explains why a Muslim slave belonging to an enemy infidel becomes free when he enters Muslim territory:

(11) *When a slave of an enemy infidel comes to us as a Muslim, he is freed*: because of the words of [the Prophet] (may God bless him and give him peace) concerning the slaves of Ta'if, when they came to him as Muslims: 'They are freedmen of God Most High'; and because, in coming to us, he acquired protection of his person as a Muslim, since one who is already a Muslim cannot be enslaved.[31]

An inevitable corollary of the reverence for precedent and the theory of divine revelation is that the law was extremely conservative. The immediate impression that post-classical Hanafi jurisprudence conveys is that there was no change between the eleventh century and the nineteenth, and since, to be respectable, a legal opinion must always have an ancient lineage, this was probably the impression that the jurists themselves wished to convey. It is not, however, wholly accurate.

It is true that, in the Hanafi school at least, the fundamentals of the law did not alter.[32] Legal concepts as they had developed by the eleventh century remained unchanged in the nineteenth. Jurists continued to discuss the rules and problems that they had inherited from their predecessors, even though these often had no relevance to their own age. Nonetheless, there were developments, although these are evident not as changes in the major outlines of the law, but as modulations in juristic discussion. On the question of land, for example, a number of Hanafi jurists, from Qadikhan onwards, adapted the classical theory of land ownership and taxation to describe the forms of tax and tenure which were prevalent in their own day.[33] Ebu's-su'ud was to draw on this tradition in the sixteenth century for his own formulation of Ottoman land law. In some areas of criminal law, notably theft, where the provisions of the *shari'a* are entirely impractical, a tradition in post-classical jurisprudence effectively transferred responsibility for dealing with offenders to the unfettered discretion of the secular authorities.[34] In its prohibition on lending money at interest, the *shari'a* is equally unrealistic. However, in his defence of charitable trusts which lent cash at interest, Ebu's-su'ud found a way, by manipulating the opinions of Shaibani and Zufar, to justify the activity.[35] Although Ebu's-su'ud's defence of these trusts remained unacceptable to a vociferous group of orthodox pietists, it entered the juristic tradition. At the end of the sixteenth century, Timirtashi restated Ebu's-su'ud's position, and, in his early nineteenth-century commentary on Timirtashi, Ibn 'Abidin quotes Ebu's-su'ud as an authority.[36]

These are examples of the *shari'a* adapting to circumstances. The jurists' recognition of custom (*'urf*) as a source of law gave it further flexibility, although only, as a rule, in accidentals and not in essentials.[37] Custom could, for example, determine which words constitute a valid formula for divorce, but not the legal consequences of pronouncing the formula or the essence of divorce itself.

It would, however, be wrong to overemphasise developments in the law. Even when the post-classical jurists did introduce new themes, such as feudal tenure, they do so within the conceptual framework which they inherited from the founders of the School. What is, in fact, most striking about post-classical jurisprudence is its conservatism and, in many areas, its archaism. Jurists down the ages continued to discuss in minute detail rules such as amputation for theft or stoning for fornication, which had rarely had any application in practice. Equally, they continued to discuss rules and concepts which clearly had their origins in legal reality, but which time had rendered obsolete. The rules for accidental death and injury provide an example. In these cases, the law requires the members of the economic group to which the killer or injurer belonged – the *'aqila* – to pay the blood-money. However, in a response to a question on this subject, Ebu's-su'ud replied bluntly: 'There are no *'aqila* in these lands'.[38] Nonetheless, the non-existence of the *'aqila* did not prevent jurists in Ebu's-su'ud's time and later from continuing to discuss this topic. Furthermore, many, if not most of the cases in the juristic repertory are purely hypothetical, even in areas of the law which had an application in practice.

The jurists in fact never intended large areas of the *shari'a* to function as a practical system of law, and this raises the question of what purpose it served. In part, of course, it did provide the basis of a working system of law and religious ritual, although custom and expedience often modified the exact prescriptions of the jurists. The impracticalities of the *shari'a* served a different purpose.

In the pre-modern Islamic world, jurisprudence occupied the central position in Islamic intellectual life, enjoying much the same prestige as theology in medieval Europe. Theology, Quranic exegesis and the study of Prophetic Traditions existed as independent and prestigious sciences, but each in its different way served to underpin jurisprudence. So too did the natural sciences of astronomy, geography and mathematics. It was celestial events that determined the juristically-fixed times of prayers and festivals. The establishment of the direction of Mecca, towards which Muslims must pray, required a knowledge of longitude and latitude. The correct division of inheritances required the application of complex arithmetic. Furthermore, before a student could even begin to study jurisprudence, he had to master literary Arabic as the language of the law, and logic as a basis of juristic method.[39] To some extent, therefore, jurisprudence was the pre-eminent intellectual pursuit, to which all the sciences were subservient. As such, the discussion of legal minutiae easily became an end in itself, which jurists pursued for sheer intellectual exhilaration. Questions such as the share of an inheritance due to a hermaphrodite might not have much connection with the real world, but they are endlessly fascinating as exercises in legal logic. The ability to solve hypothetical questions conferred intellectual prestige, and also contained a strong element of display. In the festivities, for example, of 1530, which marked the circumcision of the sons of Sultan Süleyman, debate between jurists held in the presence of the Sultan figured as an entertainment beside banqueting, mock-battles and firework displays.[40]

Intellectual prowess in the *shari'a* also served as a marker of piety. Jurisprudence was, after all, an effort to discover God's law, and the analysis of legal problems in minute detail represented an attempt to fathom God's will and to gain a glimpse of the divine infinity. The fact that many problems and their solutions had no bearing on reality is immaterial. God's law is an ideal which the corruption of the age renders for the moment inapplicable, but which it is the jurist's duty to pursue. The law need not be enforceable to be relevant. The same mentality explains the archaism of the law. The ultimate source of law is revelation and, as God's will, it remains valid until the Day of Resurrection. It is the duty of jurists to hand it down from generation to generation. In this way, the maintenance of tradition became an end in itself.

The *shari'a*, therefore, had several functions. In many, although not all areas of the law, it provided the basis of a practical legal system, it supplied the materials for academic learning and intellectual discourse, and it was a means of gaining religious merit. Every Muslim had to know at least the rudiments of the law in order to practise his or her religion, and the greater their knowledge the deeper their piety. The measure of the degree to which a society was Islamic was the degree to which its members adhered to the ordinances of the *shari'a*. It was, in the end, the *shari'a* that was the foundation of Muslim law, religion, learning and piety.

This was the case until the mid-nineteenth century, when most parts of the Muslim world suffered a violent dislocation. It was in this epoch that the economic, military, political and cultural dominance of the West began to influence most aspects of Islamic life, and an effect of the import of the new European sciences, literary as much as technical, was to displace jurisprudence to the margins of intellectual life. In particular, in areas which Europeans colonised directly, the new administrators regarded the *shari'a* not as God's law but as native customs and, from this starting point, developed legal systems on the pattern of metropolitan practice. Hence, for example, the fusion of Islamic law with European civil law traditions produced the *droit musulman algérien*, and the systematisation of *Maliki* law for use in Italian Libya and Eritrea.[41] In India, the British common-law tradition created Anglo-Mohammedan law, on the basis of what was originally Hanafi practice. In thus redefining the *shari'a*, these colonial legal systems introduced notions that were alien to the Islamic tradition. In Hanafi law, for example, the verdict of a court has no status as precedent. It is the opinions of jurists that are definitive. Anglo-Mohammedan law reverses this procedure. European influence was equally strong in the Ottoman Empire, which did not experience direct European colonisation. Here, French practice provided the model for reform, leading, in legal matters, to a process of codification which culminated in the compilation between 1869 and 1876 of the *Mejelle*. This was a codification of certain areas of Hanafi law, made in conscious emulation of the French *Code Civil*. It remained Islamic in content, but was French in its form and concept.[42]

These developments had the effect, therefore, of redefining the *shari'a* strictly as law in its modern sense, and of marginalising it in Islamic intellectual life. The rapid social, economic and political changes in the twentieth century, together with the virtual disappearance of the traditional system of education, completed the process.

The Secular Law

Before the mid-nineteenth century, the *shari'a* had undisputed intellectual and ideological hegemony throughout the Islamic world. However, since it did not provide all the materials necessary for a working legal system, it is inevitable that it should at all times have coexisted with secular laws which drew their authority from custom or from the will of a legitimate sovereign. In the Ottoman Empire, the general term for the secular law was *qanun*, a word which may refer either to a single law or to the secular law as a whole. The term for a code of laws is *qanunname* or 'law-book'. It is specifically the *qanun* that Ebu's-su'ud, according to Ottoman tradition, brought into conformity with the *shari'a*.

In their origin and nature, *qanun* and *shari'a* are quite distinct. What above all determined the nature of *qanun* was the feudal structure of the Ottoman Empire. The Empire's revenues were overwhelmingly agricultural, and went largely towards supporting the Sultan's army. Most of the troops were cavalrymen who drew their income directly from fiefs which they held in return for military service, and who resided on the land which provided their living. The same is true of provincial governors, who normally lived on the revenues of large fiefs within the boundaries of their administrative districts and who, in time of war, served in the field as commanders of the cavalrymen who held fiefs within the area of their civil jurisdiction. Not all sources of revenue were agricultural, and not all fiefs were military. The tax yield from, for example, customs duties or market tolls was substantial and could be allocated to fiefs,[43] and some fiefs were fiscal, with the holder contracting to remit an agreed annual sum to the Sultan's treasury, while retaining the surplus for himself. Other fiefs the Sultan allocated to members of his family, or to members of the governing or the learned class.

The main features of the Ottoman administrative and fiscal system were therefore decentralisation of tax collection and the allocation of revenues to fiefs held in return for a specific, usually military service. In consequence, the most important economic and legal division of the Empire was between taxpayers, who were mostly peasants, and the recipients of taxes, who were mostly fief-holders. By about 1500, the term *ra'iyyet* (pl. *re'aya*), borrowed from the jurists and meaning literally 'flock', had become the standard term for a taxpaying subject, while the term 'askeri, literally 'military', denoted the holder of a fief, or of a salary paid directly from the Sultan's treasury.

The feudal structure of the Empire provided the Sultan with an administration, an army and a flow of revenue to the treasury, but it was, in essence, centrifugal. If the Sultan was weak, fief-holders could begin to act independently of his will, and it was to prevent this happening that the central government kept a close bureaucratic control over the distribution of fiefs. It achieved this by maintaining cadastral registers for each district of the Empire, recording the sources of taxation in each region and its distribution. Through these registers, the Sultan had a record of all the fief-holders in his domains, the taxes due to them, the nominal value of their income, and a record of services due. Failure to perform a service, which usually meant failure to serve on a military campaign when summoned to do so, resulted in the confiscation of the fief. The practice of making cadastral registers of this type dates probably from the time of Bayezid I (1389–1402). It lasted until the late sixteenth century and, during this period, was the primary administrative instrument that enabled the government to keep control of fief-holders in the provinces.

It was not, however, until the late fifteenth century that the Sultan and his government began methodically to codify the laws which governed the relationship between fief-holders and taxpaying subjects. In so doing, they acquired a means of legal control of the Empire's resources which supplemented and strengthened the system of bureaucratic surveillance that was already in place. This reduction to writing of what had previously existed only as feudal custom and administrative practice is the basis of the Ottoman qanun. It is in essence a feudal law.

The process of systematic codification began in the reign of Bayezid II (1481–1512), and created two typical forms of law-book. There was the general law-book containing statutes which were, in part at least, applicable throughout the Empire, and the district law-book. The second type applied only to a particular administrative area, and usually formed the preface to the cadastral survey of the district in question.[44] In character, the law-books are overwhelmingly fiscal, laying down the nature and the rate of the taxes which the fief-holders were entitled to collect. Typically, they also contain criminal statutes, since fief-holders were responsible for law enforcement in their area, and also because they took the income from fines. Law-books also came into existence to regulate other areas of life but, typically, Ottoman qanun means fiscal and criminal law.

The law-book for the district of Bursa, forming the preface to the cadastral survey of 1486, is among the first detailed and systematic expositions of qanun, providing a model for future compilations. The basis of the law, as the codifiers imply in the general heading, was current practice. The law-book, they say, is an 'exposition in detail of the legitimate qanuns which are currently enforced and the recognised customary taxes, which are the bases for the Ottoman registers and the sources of Sultanic decrees'. This formula underlines the notion of custom and practice as the basis of *qanun* and as giving legitimacy to royal legislation. The first clause in the law-book lays down the rates of the annual tax which peasant occupiers must pay on their tenements to the fief-holder. The basic unit of land is the *chift* or 'yoke', nominally the area of land which a peasant can cultivate with a pair of oxen:

(12) *Chift*-tax is thirty-three aqches from a subject noted in the register as holding a whole chift. From half a *chift*, the tax is half of this. From a cottager having the use of less than half a *chift*, [but] who is registered as a cultivator, it is twelve aqches ...[45]

Two other law-books from the reign of Bayezid give some hints as to how the codifiers proceeded. The first is unusual in that it does not deal with taxes, but with market regulations, and consists of the detailed report of a commission which had investigated the prices and quality of foodstuffs and goods, and the practices and malpractices among the traders, in the market of Bursa in 1501. The law-book, if it can be so described, opens with a Sultanic decree, appointing the commission and ordering them to record in detail the prices and quality of goods, and to return the register containing the result:

(13) You should make a detailed record so that the register which you send becomes a law-book, which can be referred to in time of need.[46]

In this case, the remit of the commission was, by codifying current practice, to give it the force of law.

The second law-book is more conventional. It dates from 1499, and lays out the statutes governing the Sultan's estates around Istanbul. Bayezid II's father, Mehmed II (1451–81), had established these estates probably in 1454, and brought them into cultivation by settling on them prisoners-of-war with the legal status of share-cropping slaves. The written core of what was eventually to become the law-book of 1499 in fact dates from the earliest years of the estates. This is the text, which survives only in a sixteenth-century copy, of a warrant which the Sultan issued to an agent on the estates, listing in barest outline the obligations of the share-croppers and the taxes which the agent was to collect. For example:

(14) [The share-croppers] should sow two *müd* of grain, using the *müd* of Edirne, of which one should be wheat, half oats and half barley.
...
They pay the bride-chamber tax, barrel tax and fines at whatever is [the current rate].[47]

The second text relating to the estates, and again surviving in a sixteenth-century copy, dates probably from the 1460s. It is again a set of instructions issued to an agent, in this case because he had petitioned the Sultan. It begins:

> (15) Because the agent so-and-so who holds the [Imperial] estates of Istanbul has sought a law-book from my [i.e. the Sultan's] Exalted Threshold, I have issued this my Imperial Decree ...[48]

What follows is the text of the original warrant, together with a number of additional clauses. What had clearly happened is that an agent on the estates had submitted a series of problems to the Sultan, such as, for example, whether a share-cropper could work on his own account once he had sown the two *müd* of grain which belonged to the Sultan. The additional clauses, which follow no logical order, represent the Sultan's answers to these questions. The text of the original warrant plus the additional clauses forms a rudimentary law-book.

The third document is undated and again survives in a sixteenth-century copy. The preamble makes it clear that it was a reworking of the law-book of the 1460s and came into being for the same reasons:

> (16) The agents who held the [Imperial] estates of Istanbul have requested a law-book from my Sublime Court. A law-book dealing with the [Imperial] estates of Istanbul was previously given to the agents, but because some of its conditions did not conform to the *shari'a* and to custom, I [the Sultan] have newly established this [present] law-book. I have put it into the possession of the said agents and I have commanded that ...[49]

The text of the law-book follows. It is far more systematic than its predecessors and far more detailed, not only adding new regulations, but also, for the first time, closely defining the actual rates of taxation. Whereas, for example, the first two texts state merely:

> (17) [The share-croppers] should pay their *salarliq* according to custom,

the new law-book glosses this clause to read:

> (18) *Salarliq* should be taken at the rate of one bushel for every forty bushels from [the share-croppers'] own share, as they have customarily given it.[50]

The text dates most probably from the reign of Bayezid II, perhaps from the late 1480s. Like the 1486 law-book of Bursa, the preamble shows a concern with its conformity to the *shari'a* and to custom, and the individual clauses establish in detail the modes and rates of taxation. Both these features mark a distinct break from its origins as an agent's warrant. It also formed the foundation of the much longer law-book of 1499. This, like the typical district law-books from the late fifteenth century onwards, forms the preface to a cadastral survey of the Imperial estates, and contains many clauses which arose from attempts to regulate problems which had come to light during the course of the survey.[51]

The source, therefore, of the district law-books is custom, modified through administrative practice and Sultanic decree. The process of their compilation is perhaps more visible in the sixteenth century, since the Ottoman conquests in this period coincided with the full development of the law-book as a form of legal literature. When a Sultan conquered new lands, he would order the compilation of both a new cadastral survey and a new law-book for the area. The new law-book would, as a rule, simply list pre-conquest taxes and note whether these had been confirmed or abolished. In the provinces of eastern and south-eastern Anatolia, for example, which Selim I (1512–20) conquered between 1514 and 1516, the first Ottoman law-books for the area normally state in their preambles that they are compiled 'in accordance with the *qanun* of Hasan Padishah', a reference to the laws in force in the days of the Akkoyunlu Sultan, Uzun Hasan, who had died in 1478. The following three clauses from the 1518 law-book of Siverek are examples of how the Ottomans adapted the '*qanun* of Hasan Padishah':

> (19) From subjects resident in villages, whether Muslim or infidel, who had a *chift* of land or were capable of cultivating a *chift* of land, they used to take one [gold] *eshrefi* as *chift*-tax, one *eshrefi* being worth forty Ottoman aqches. This practice has been confirmed. The season for taking it is in spring, at the vernal equinox.
> They used to take [a tithe] of one-fifth from their cultivated crops. This has been re-established.
> ...
> They used to take a fixed tax of three-hundred gold coins from the inhabitants of the villages in the said district ... The said three-hundred gold coins have been abolished, and nothing entered in the new register.[52]

Since many Ottoman law-books incorporated pre-Ottoman laws, and since feudal custom varied from place to place, there were wide differences between the *qanun*s applicable in different regions or to different groups in the Empire. Furthermore, specialised economic activities gave rise to specific forms of taxation, which were applicable only locally or to a particular community. *Qanun*s, for example, regulating taxes on pigs clearly applied only to Christians, and not to Muslims or Jews; or a clause, for example, in the 'Law-book of the gypsies in the province of Rumelia' of 1530, imposing a monthly fine on gypsy dancers and entertainers, was clearly specific to the gypsy community:

(20) The gypsies of Istanbul, Edirne, Plovdiv and Sofia pay a fixed tax of one hundred aqches per month for each of their women who perform acts contrary to the *shari'a.*[53]

Nonetheless, despite an inevitable diversity, there was also a tendency towards the standardisation of *qanun*, particularly as the sixteenth century progressed.

This was, in part at least, a conscious process. When a cadastral register became obsolete with the passage of time, a new survey was made, together with a new law-book, which inevitably emended some of the statutes in the old one.[54] The purpose of many of the emendations was simply to regulate problems which had arisen. The following clause, for example, from the law-book of the province of Diyarbekir, records the reason for the abolition of the payment of tithes in cash:

(21) Previously, when the subjects' produce was tithed, [the tithe] was not taken in kind, but a cash sum in excess of the daily fixed market-price [for the produce] was levied. Oppression and wrongdoing against the subjects passed all bounds and for this reason many of them fled the district, while others, because they had fallen into bankruptcy and poverty, became unable to till the soil.

When these injustices and tyrannous acts were submitted to the Foot of the [Sultan's] Exalted Throne, the practice of taking [tithes] in cash was abolished, and because it was decreed that wheat be taken from wheat, barley from barley, and that whatever the sort of grain, [the tithe be taken] in kind, this has been entered into the new [cadastral] register.[55]

However, other emendations to the law-books serve not to regulate a particular problem, but to bring local usage into line with standard Ottoman practice. Some taxes or customs the new law-books abolish on the grounds that they are 'contrary to the *qanun*' as, for example, a tax on weavers in an undated law-book for the district of Ergani in the province of Diyarbekir:

(22) Weavers' tax has been abolished because it is contrary to the *qanun.*[56]

In other case, the notion of 'Ottoman *qanun*' led not to the abolition of taxes, but to their standardisation, particularly, it seems, in the rates of fines and incidental dues, such as bride-tax, or the entry fine payable to the fief-holder when a peasant first occupies a tenement. A clause in the 1559 law book of Malatya is typical of many others:

> (23) In the matter of incidental taxes and fines, reference should be made to the Ottoman *qanun*.[57]

In the following clause, from the 1570 law-book of Aleppo, the compiler invokes the Ottoman *qanun* to override what was evidently a local practice of commuting capital punishment for payment:

> (24) For other fines, reference should be made to the Ottoman *qanun*, and no more taken [than specified]. Cash should not be taken from those who merit capital punishment, as payment in lieu of execution. The punishment should be carried out according to their deserts, in the place where they sinned.[58]

References in the district law-books to the 'Ottoman *qanun*', or sometimes to the 'old Ottoman *qanun*', do not relate simply to legal principles in the abstract, but specifically to the general Ottoman Law-Book , a code of laws which has its genesis in the reign of Bayezid II (1481–1512).

What is apparently the earliest attempt to compile a general Ottoman Law-Book survives in a manuscript written probably in the early 1490s, and bearing the heading: 'This is a copy of the Imperial *qanun* of Sultan Mehmed son of Murad Khan'.[59] The heading is misleading in attributing the code to Bayezid's father, Mehmed II (1451–81), since the compilation as it stands is almost certainly Bayezid's.[60] Nonetheless, the linguistic and legal archaism of the text indicates that most of its constituent elements date at least from the time of Mehmed II, and probably earlier. What the compiler has done is to produce a 'general' code by assembling in a single manuscript a code of criminal law, which is, in essence, a tariff of fines and strokes of the lash, together with a section headed '*Qanun* of Sultan Mehmed Khan', a brief statute summarising the military services due from Turkish nomads, and a section headed '*Qanun* of the married infidels'. The latter records 1488 as the year of its enactment. The '*Qanun* of Sultan Mehmed Khan' and the '*Qanun* of the married infidels' list, in the barest outline, the taxes and tolls levied in an unspecified European province of the Empire, and conceivably represent a digest of warrants issued to tax-collectors, governors and other fief-holders, enumerating the taxes to which they were entitled. The purpose of the entire compilation is not at all clear.

The criminal code, however, reappears with very little emendation as the opening section of Bayezid II's general law-book of c. 1500. This contains criminal statutes, the rules which define membership of the military class, a list of the services owed by holders of military fiefs, the obligations of the taxpaying subjects, laws on the relations between the military class and taxpayers, tax regulations, some general and some relating to specific districts, and other matters.

The compilers of the Law-Book drew, it seems, on a large number of sources. The criminal code they took from the earlier general law-book, the 'Qanun of Sultan Mehmed', but added to it a separate set of penal statutes which lists offences which, in the main, incur corporal punishment and a few rules on criminal procedure. This, it seems, was originally an independent text, which the compilers have incorporated as a block into the new Law-Book.[61] The rules on the rates of taxation they clearly drew from cadastral registers and district law-books, as, for example, when they record the non-standard rates of the *chift*-tax:

(25) In the district of Menteshe, the *chift*-tax is thirty aqches, and half of this from someone with half a *chift* ...

In the district of Bolu, the *chift*-tax in some sub-districts is forty or fifty aqches ...

In the dependencies of Gerede, it is thirty-four aqches, of which twenty-four go to the cavalryman and ten to the district governor ...[62]

The section which enumerates the services due from military fiefs is extremely laconic, indicating that the compilers abstracted the material from the cadastral registers, which list this information in a shorthand form against the name of each fief-holder. The sections begins:

(26) The holder of a fief worth 1,000 aqches [is to present] himself [for campaign] in light armour.

The holder of a fief worth 2,000 aqches [is to present] himself [for campaign] in light armour [with] an attendant.

The holder of a fief worth 3,000 aqches [is to present] himself [for campaign] in full armour [with] one armed retainer ...[63]

Some passages clearly incorporate the texts of what had once been Sultanic decrees issued in response to a specific problem. Of the following two clauses, for example, the second very obviously retains the format of a decree. It presumably therefore started its life independently of the first clause, whose format suggests that it conceivably originated as a fatwa, with the protasis representing the question and the apodosis the answer. The compilers have brought the two together, as they relate to the same problem:

(27) If a cavalryman (*su eri*) takes tax from a subject before it is due –

such as sheep-tax or *chift*-tax before the season [for] their [collection] has come – and the cavalryman is dismissed and the fief given to another, the newly-installed cavalryman should take [the tax] from the cavalryman who has been dismissed, and not demand anything from the subject ...

Governors-general have been giving some cavalrymen (*sipahi*) letters stating that 'this person should take such-and-such [a tax] from the subjects before it is due', and sending them to judges.

It is determined that governors-general should not give such letters. If they do give letters that are contrary to the *qanun*, judges will not be censured if they do not act on them.[64]

The compilers of the general Law-Book seem to have aimed to codify and, where possible, to standardise feudal taxes and usages and, to do this, used the most authoritative sources at their disposal. They also clarified some feudal terminology as, for example, in their definition of what is meant by 'incidental taxes' (*bad-i hava*):

(28) What are recorded in the register[s] as incidental taxes are bride-tax, fines, entry fines for [new occupants of] *chift*s, and for the land on which a house is constructed, and smoke-tax [levied] on [nomads] who come from outside and occupy pasture.[65]

Of these imposts, they give a detailed tariff of fines in the opening chapter of the code and, in the same section, the precise rates for the bride-tax:

(29) Bride-tax is sixty aqches for a virgin and forty aqches for a previously married woman ...[66]

The purpose of the general Law-Book was undoubtedly to provide an Empire-wide view of the feudal law, and a source of reference for determining what taxes fief-holders were entitled to collect, at what rates and at what time. It provided a standard for determining what constituted Ottoman *qanun*. Above all, as a written law and as a royal code, it had the effect of increasing the authority of the Sultan by diminishing the discretion of the fief-holders in matters of taxation and feudal services.

Bayezid II's general Law-Book of c. 1500 remained, with subsequent revisions, amendments and additions, in force throughout the sixteenth century. The final recension, dating from about 1540, incorporates much of the original text virtually unamended. The wording, for example, of the clauses dealing with cavalrymen who collect taxes before they fall due, is altered, but the contents remain the same.[67] In some cases, the revision is minimal, as for example in the clause giving the standard rate of the *chift*-tax. The first passage below is from the Law-Book of c. 1500, the second from the recension of c. 1540:

(30) 1. *Chift*-tax is thirty-six aqches for someone registered as holding a full *chift*, and half of this from half a *chift*. In the district of Hamid, *chift*-tax is forty-two aqches for a subject registered as holding a whole *chift* and half of this for half a *chift*.[68]

2. *Chift*-tax is taken from the subjects in March. In some districts, *chift*-tax is thirty-six aqches, but in the district of Hamid, it is forty-two aqches. A half-*chift* is half of this.[69]

The first section of the code, on criminal law, illustrates how the compilers of 1540 proceeded. The Law Book of c. 1500 contains two separate sets of criminal statutes, the tariff of strokes and fines from the so-called '*Qanun* of Sultan Mehmed', and the code on corporal punishment. The redactors of 1540 have amalgamated the two. For example, the first two clauses of the code on corporal punishment read as follows:

(31) A person who abducts a girl or boy; or enters a stranger's house with malice; or who joins [another as an accomplice] in abducting a woman or girl, shall be castrated.

A person who abducts or forcibly marries a woman should be compelled to divorce her. The person who marries [the couple] should have his beard cut off [as a mark of disgrace] and be severely beaten.[70]

In the general Law Book of c. 1540, the compilers have incorporated these two clauses, with some modification of the language, into the first section of the tariff of strokes and fines, dealing with the punishments for fornication. The tariff itself has also undergone some emendation, both in the punishments prescribed and, in some places, in the literary format. Here, for example, are three clauses from the original code, from the section on theft:

(32) If a person steals a goose or duck, the judge shall chastise [him] and a fine of one aqche shall be collected for each stroke.

If a person steals a sheep or beehive, a fine of fifteen aqches shall be collected.

If a person steals a purse or turban – if his hand does not have to be cut off – the judge shall chastise him and a fine of one aqche shall be collected for each stroke.[71]

Here the code, with a greater regard for literary convention than for legal nicety, groups the stolen goods together in pairs. The recension of c. 1540 not only changes some of the penalties but also lists the goods not in pairs but in groups of three:

(33) If [a person] steals a goose, hen or duck, the judge shall chastise him, and a fine of one aqche shall be collected for [every] two strokes.

If a person steals a beehive, sheep or lamb – if the [value] of the stolen property does not reach the legal minimum [which incurs amputation] – the judge shall chastise [him], and a fine of one aqche shall be collected for each stroke.

If a person steals a purse, turban or towels – unless his hand is to be cut off – the judge shall chastise him, and a fine of one aqche shall be collected for [every] two strokes, or one aqche shall be collected for each stroke.[72]

To these emended and rearranged materials, the redactors of c. 1540 have also added new clauses. An example is the prohibition on lending money at a rate of interest higher than 10 per cent:

(34) [Persons] who make [loan] transactions in accordance with the *shari'a* shall not be allowed [to take] more than eleven for every ten [pieces of money lent].[73]

The Law-Book of c. 1540, therefore, is in essence a reworking, with additional clauses, of Bayezid II's code of c. 1500. This, in its turn, represents an effort to systematise material from numerous different sources, some of which goes back at least to the mid-fifteenth century. Both codes, like all *qanun*s, derived their authority from the notion that they represent Ottoman custom, and from their enactment by the Ottoman Sultan.

Ottoman texts clearly distinguish between *qanun* and *shari'a*, that is between the secular and the sacred law, often referring to 'the law' as a general concept with the phrase '*shar'* and *qanun'*. Nonetheless, there is always the sense that the *shari'a*, as the divine law, occupies a superior position, an idea which occasionally finds a reflection in the formulation of *qanun*. Taxes on pigs, for example, are strictly speaking illegal. Since pigs are forbidden to Muslims, they have no commercial value and cannot therefore be subject to taxation. The district law-books, therefore, avoid the word 'pig' with the euphemism *janavar* ('beast') or else refer to this impost not as 'pig-tax', but as 'pig-*bid'a*', the term *bid'a* carrying the sense of an innovation which is contrary to the *shari'a* and therefore forbidden.

In its section on theft, the criminal code also makes a gesture to the *shari'a* by prefixing, to the prescribed penalty for the offence, the phrase 'if the offender's hand is not to be cut off'. A *qanun* of 1498, regulating the distribution of booty from raids into Christian territory, divides raiding parties into three named categories according to their size,[74] in conscious imitation, it would seem, of a similar division which occurs in the works of some jurists. The parallel passage in the 'Fatwas' of Qadikhan begins: 'Abu Hanifa said: The smallest raiding party is one-hundred men; the smallest army is four-hundred men ...'.[75] Very occasionally, the *shari'a* influences the substance of the *qanun*. The penal code, for example, borrows from the *shari'a* the notions that it is a criminal offence to bring a false accusation of fornication, and that cases of fornication should, as far as possible, not come before the courts.[76]

These occasional similarities between *qanun* and *shari'a* are, however, entirely superficial, the result of sporadic efforts by the compilers of the *qanun* to bring it into the sphere of the Holy Law. In reality, the two systems of law had grown up independently of one another. The *shari'a* is the outcome of juristic speculation, and had reached its maturity two centuries before the emergence of the Ottoman Empire. The *qanun*, on the other hand, was a systematisation of specifically Ottoman feudal practice which, in many essential areas of land tenure and taxation, ran directly counter to the doctrines of the jurists. It remained to Ebu's-su'ud to redefine the basic laws of land tenure and taxation in terms which he borrowed from the Hanafi tradition, and it was above all this redefinition which gained him the reputation of having reconciled the *qanun* with the *shari'a*. His statements on Ottoman tenure and taxation came to occupy a central position in the Ottoman legal canon. They acquired a new lease life in the late seventeenth century, in particular with the compilation after 1673 of a new land code, the 'New *Qanun*'. This was to remain in force until the promulgation of a new Ottoman code of land law in 1858.

Legal Documents and Fatwas

The fatwas of the *sheikhu'l-islam*s form one of the three major categories of Ottoman legal documents, the other two being Sultanic decrees and certificates issued by judges.

Sultanic decrees fall into two main groups: those which address specific individuals and those which address the world at large. Letters patent, granting posts, privileges or exemptions, belong to the second group. Despite differences in detail between the various types and subtypes, all decrees have in essence the same format. They are written on scrolls of paper, much longer than they are wide, bearing the Sultan's cipher (*tughra*) at the top, with the date and place of emission as the final elements. The cipher presents, in an elaborately stylised and calligraphic form, the name and honorifics of the reigning Sultan, the cipher of Süleyman I, for example, being made up of the Arabic letters of his title: 'Süleyman Shah son of Selim Shah Khan, may he be ever-victorious'. Below the cipher come the name, titles and honorifics of the addressee or addressees or, in the case of letters patent, a statement that what follows is the command which the Imperial cipher, representing the person of the Sultan, conveys. The main body of the text follows. This divides into two sections: the narration setting out the reasons for issuing the document, and the disposition, setting out the command itself. This section always begins 'I [the Sultan] have commanded that ...'. A warning statement often follows, to the effect that if they disobey the command, the recipient or recipients will be dismissed from office and punished.[77] Although the Sultan clearly never set eyes on the more mundane decrees and letters patent issued in his name, they all have the same first-person format, leaving no doubt that they derive their legal authority from the will of the Sultan.

The certificates which judges issued on all matters which fell within the competence of the Islamic courts form the second category of legal document. Judges acted both as notaries, formally attesting legal transactions such as sale or lease, where there is no dispute between the parties, and as adjudicators in litigation. In both cases, however, the format of the certificates which they issued as an authentic record of the proceedings is identical. The document opens with the formula: 'The reason for writing this legal (*shar'i*) document is as follows ...', or a variation on this, with the first letter elongated to fill over half the top line. A record of the case follows, concluding with some variation of the formula: 'What happened was written down and delivered to the applicant, so that he may produce it as proof whenever there is need', followed by the date. Beneath the main body of the text is the heading: 'Witnesses to the case', with the first letter again extended across almost the whole line. Beneath this are the names of the people, often about ten of them, who were present in the court when the case was transacted, and who presumably would also be available as witnesses if the outcome of the case or the validity of the certificate were ever in doubt. The final stage in drawing up the document was for the judge to authenticate it by adding his signature and seal. He signed usually at the top of the document, above the heading, towards the left margin, using a formula such as: 'The case is as is written herein. The most abject of God's slaves, A son of B, judge in the judicial district of X.'[78] The judge would also make a copy of the certificate in the register (*sijill*) which recorded the daily transactions of the court.

The purpose of judges' certificates was not to provide a transcript of everything that had happened in court, but rather to provide evidence that the case had proceeded exactly according to the requirements of the law, and to furnish proof of its outcome. The texts of the certificates tend, for this reason, to be highly formulaic, with even the statements of the parties and witnesses reduced to essentials and rarely recorded verbatim. In straightforward cases, therefore, a judge could reproduce the format and wording of an existing certificate, altering only the names and other elements specific to the case in hand. The correct drafting of certificates according to recognised patterns came to form a branch of legal literature, to which Ebu's-su'ud contributed with his 'Judge's Merchandise', a collection of certificates arranged under appropriate legal headings, which were to serve as exemplars for practising judges. The collection, he says, arose from his own experience as a judge 'in the law-courts of the cities' and especially, it seems, as a result of his time as judge of Bursa.

The certificates which follow are from the 'Judge's Merchandise', and appear to be copies of documents which Ebu's-su'ud himself had drawn up, with the standard introductory and closing formulae, and some of the names, omitted. The first records the sale of a house:

(35) A son of B avowed and acknowledged with an acknowledgement that is valid in law, that he has sold to the bearer of this document X son of Y, and that the latter bought from him, what belonged to him and [was] his property, [namely] this house, standing in the Protected City of Bursa in the quarter of the late 'Isa Beg el-Fenari, consisting of three ground-floor rooms, one upper room, with a cellar beneath, a well with pitcher, and a privy, [the whole surrounded by] a wall, and bordered by the property of M and the property of the heirs of N son of O, and by the public road on two sides, with all its boundaries and rights, for a specified price which has been received, of 10,000 silver *dirhams* in the current denomination. [The purchaser] confirmed this in his presence. What happened etc.[79]

If a sale is to be valid, the object of the sale must be the property of the vendor. It must be described and a price must be named. The vendor must deliver the object to the purchaser who, in turn, must deliver the price. Here, the certificate is constructed so as to show that the parties have satisfied each of these conditions and confirmed the sale orally in each other's presence. The judge would then deliver the certificate to the purchaser, so that it would serve as a title-deed to the property.

The second example is a record of a contract of marriage:

(36) Praise be to God who made marriage licit and fornication illicit, and blessings be upon Muhammad, the Most Excellent of Souls and Spirits, and on his Family and Companions, every morning and evening.

As for what follows, this is a deed valid in law and a document which is plain and to be observed whose contents concern the [following] matter:

A son of B came to the Court of the Noble *Shari'a* and the Assembly of the Exalted Law, [where] he attested to his agency in the matter of contracting a marriage on behalf of Lady X the daughter of Y, with M son of N and O son of P [acting] as witnesses. He married her to the bearer of this document C son of D, for a deferred dower of 10,000 silver *dirham*s in the current denomination, and an advance dower of a gold-threaded outer garment of red velvet and a gold nuptial bracelet weighing thirty *mithqal*s. The agent of the said spouse, G son of H, accepted on behalf of his mandator, the said C, in the manner set forth, after proving his agency on his behalf, through the testimony of I son of J and K son of L. This was in the presence of witnesses whose evidence is heard and whose words are accepted. The contracting in marriage and the acceptance are valid and accepted in law.[80]

The conditions essential to a valid contract of marriage are that there should be an offer and an acceptance, that there should be two witnesses, and that the husband should pay the wife a dower, the first part usually to be paid on marriage and the second on divorce or the death of the husband. The document shows that there has been an offer and acceptance in the presence of witnesses and that the dower has been named and recorded. A complication arises from the fact that neither party is present in court. Both are contracting the marriage through an agent, and the document has therefore also to record that the agencies are valid.

The third case involves a woman who is seeking a separation from her husband for the non-consummation of the marriage:

(37) The agency of M son of N, on behalf of A daughter of B was established in the following suit, through the testimony of W son of X and Y son of Z. [The agent] brought with him to the suit C son of D, the husband of his said [female] mandator.

He said in the statement of his suit: 'C son of D married my mandator and withdrew with her in a valid privacy. She delivered herself to him and found him impotent and incapable of intercourse.' When the husband was questioned, he acknowledged what the said agent had said and sought a legal postponement from the judge whose signature is above, in expectation of the good will of his God. The judge granted him a legal postponement for a complete year from such-and-such a month. He ordered [the wife] to deliver herself to him, and if he has intercourse with her within the said period, well and good. Otherwise the judge will separate them with a complete and irrevocable divorce, and she will receive her entire dower on account of the valid privacy.[81]

One of the few cases where a woman can obtain a judicial separation from her husband is when, on the first night of the marriage, he turns out to be impotent. In this case, the woman may seek a judicial separation, and if she does so, the judge must grant the husband a year's delay from the date of the application. If he fails to consummate the marriage within this period, then the judge separates the couple. The document makes the steps clear. It also makes it clear that, in the event of non-consummation and subsequent separation, the woman will receive her dower, as Hanafi law requires.

Judicial decrees and notarial acts derive their authority from two sources. The first is the Hanafi juristic tradition, and the second the Sultan. The contents of the law which the judges administered was, for the most part, Hanafi, but it was by virtue of their appointment by the Sultan that they exercised legal power and put the law into effect. They also, on occasions, executed commands which they received directly from the Sultan, or decided cases on the basis of the *qanun*.

The third category of legal document was the fatwa, an authoritative legal opinion which a qualified jurisconsult issues in response to a question. In the Hanafi, as in the other Sunni Schools of law, it is not an executive decree, and, if its ruling is to apply in a particular case, an authority with executive power, either a ruler or judge, must put it into effect. A fatwa, however, has a general validity, whereas a judicial decree is valid only for the case in hand.

This notion of fatwas as having a general rather than a specific validity has affected their literary presentation. A fatwa always has two sections, the Question and the Answer, and it is usual to omit from both of them all specificities which are not immediately relevant to the legal point at issue. A fatwa will almost never, for example, give the name of an individual, only rarely the name of a place and never the exact circumstances in which the case arose. In this respect, the following two fatwas of the Egyptian jurist Ibn Nujaim (d. 1563) are typical:

(38) He was asked about someone who married a woman in a village near to the town. Does he have the right to transfer her to the town without her consent, when he has paid the advance portion of her dower, or not?
He replied: 'Yes, he has the right without her consent'.

He was asked about someone who said to his slave: 'I have freed you', without intending to free him. Is [the slave] freed by this?
He replied: 'Yes, [the slave] is freed by this, even if [the master] did not intend to free him'.[82]

The fatwas of the Ottoman *sheikhu'l-islam*s observe these conventions of anonymity. Instead of the names of real persons, they use a set of conventional names, usually Zeyd, 'Amr, Bekr and Bishr for males, and Hind, Zeyneb and Khadija for females. The Question itself usually takes the form of a conditional sentence; 'If X happens, what happens in law?', with all extraneous details omitted. The task of actually drafting the questions fell not to the *sheikhu'l-islam* himself but to the clerks who worked in his office under the supervision, in the centuries after Ebu's-su'ud, of the Superintendent of Fatwas, who was himself a trained jurist. The applicant for a fatwa would hand the question in at the *sheikhu'l-islam*'s office, where the clerks would redraft it into the form in which it came before the *sheikhu'l-islam* himself, who would then add the answer.

Of the thousands of fatwas which the *sheikhu'l-islam*s issued, very few survive in their original format. The few that do survive have survived largely through the interest of anonymous collectors, who have assembled original fatwas and reduced them in size by cutting closely round the margins of the text and pasting them into albums, with four or sometimes more fatwas to the page.[83]

These, together with other isolated specimens which have survived,[84] show that the basic format of Ottoman fatwas remained intact from the fifteenth to the early twentieth centuries. From the few specimens to survive uncut, it appears that the *sheikhu'l-islam*'s office issued fatwas on rectangular slips of paper, much longer than they are wide, imitating, on a miniature scale, the format of Sultanic decrees. The Arabic word 'He', representing the name of God, appears, as it often does on decrees,[85] at the head of the paper, indicating that He is above all things. Below the name of God is an Arabic prayer, often in the form of a complex calligraphic cipher, invoking God's assistance in answering the question. This occupies a place on the document equivalent to the position of the Sultan's cipher on royal decrees. A typical prayer formula, and one that often appears above Ebu's-su'ud's fatwas, is: 'O God, Lord of protection and good fortune! We ask guidance from you to the right path.' The text of the fatwa comes below the prayer, and begins with the heading to the Question. This normally uses the formula: 'What would be the answer of the Hanafi Imams in elucidating this question?' The word 'question', which in Turkish is the second element in the sentence, occupies almost the whole line, with the remaining words written horizontally or diagonally up the left margin. The invocation of the Hanafi Imams emphasises the authoritative nature of the answer. The text of the Question itself appears below the heading, ending usually with the formula: 'An elucidation is requested. May it be rewarded [by God]!' Beneath the Question is the heading: 'The Answer', written across almost the width of the margins and, following the heading, the formula: 'God knows best!', an avowal that neither the law nor the *sheikhu'l-islam* is infallible.

Up to this point, the text is in the hand of one of the *sheikhu'l-islam*'s clerks. The Answer to the Question follows in the hand of the *sheikhu'l-islam* himself, and below the Answer, at the bottom left of the page, is the *sheikhu'l-islam*'s signature, contained within an almost unvarying Arabic formula: 'The humblest of God's slaves [e.g. Ebu's-su'ud] wrote this. May God forgive him!' A distinguishing feature of some of Ebu's-su'ud's fatwas which survive in their original format is that both the Question and the Answer are in his own hand,[86] an indication perhaps that pressure of business was so great that he had no time to wait for a clerk to formulate and write out every question that came before him, but had to share in this task himself.

A feature of Ottoman fatwas is that, in complex cases, the clerks divided the Question into two or more parts. First, they pose the basic question and then, arising out of it, one or more supplementary questions, each beginning with the formula: 'In which case ...'. It appears from the surviving originals that the opening question and the supplementary or supplementaries were composed and written on the slip at the same time, leaving ample space between the first question and the supplementary for the *sheikhu'l-islam*'s answer and his signature.

Since the surviving original fatwas have been cut and pasted into albums, it is rarely possible to look at the reverse. However, a few eighteenth-century specimens, which are not cut round the margins and which remain loose, have the name of the questioner on the back: "Ali the bun-maker, from Gallipoli', or 'Ahmed Hekimoghlu, for 'Ali Pasha the imam'.[87] This was undoubtedly to enable the clerk to identify the enquirer when he called back to collect the fatwa issued in answer to his question. Presumably this had been the practice in earlier centuries too.

The overwhelming majority of fatwas survive not in the form of original documents, but in collections devoted to the fatwas of either a single or several *sheikhu'l-islam*s. The compilers of these volumes organised the fatwas under legal headings and subheadings, making them a practical source of reference for students, judges, jurisconsults and others with an interest in the law. The fine calligraphy and illuminations of some collections, however, suggest that their owners often valued them for more than merely practical reasons. The albums containing original fatwas give some idea of how the compilers worked. In one of these, several of the fatwas have a rubric indicating the legal heading under which they belong, such as 'marriage', 'lease', 'trusts' or 'lawsuits'.[88] Having thus classified each fatwa, a compiler could then file them under each heading and subheading and then, after arranging them as logically as possible within each category, copy the files, fatwa by fatwa, into the new volume. Most compilers, and all compilers of Ebu's-su'ud's fatwas, where it is possible to identify them, seem to have been employees of the *sheikhu'l-islam*'s office, with easy access to copies of original texts.

The fatwas in these compilations differ from the originals in that they omit the Name of God and the Prayer, and confine the section headings simply to the words 'Question' and 'the Answer'. They usually also omit the formula at the end of the Question. These compilations were copied and recopied, giving the fatwas a general circulation, with individuals frequently copying fatwas which interested them into their private notebooks. Hence, Ebu's-su'ud's fatwas turn up, whether as primary text or as marginalia, in a bewildering number of manuscripts. This at once raises the question of the reliability of the texts, given that they were copied so often over a period of three centuries. This particular point requires investigation, but first impressions at least suggest that copyists had a remarkable respect for the texts and that significant variations are few.[89] There are, however, cases of 'floating answers', where the Answer to a particular Question in one collection becomes attached to a different Question in another. It is common, too, when a fatwa in one collection has one or more supplementary Answers, to find these omitted in another.

Ottoman fatwas in theory derived their legitimacy solely from the tradition of Hanafi jurisprudence, and from the status of the jurisconsult as the expounder of this tradition, with the *sheikhu'l-islam*, the 'Mufti of Mankind', enjoying the greatest prestige. As statements of the Holy Law, they enjoyed an authority which was in theory independent of, and superior to, the will of the Sultan. Indeed, when a Sultan undertook anything which might arouse controversy, such as the attack on Cyprus in 1570, in contravention of a peace treaty, he was usually careful to obtain a fatwa to justify his action in advance. After the sixteenth century, when the deposition of the reigning Sultan became commonplace, those responsible would almost always act with the sanction of a fatwa from the *sheikhu'l-islam*. Nonetheless, the notion of the higher authority and independence of the *sheikhu'l-islam* was always, to some degree, a fiction. Like all members of the higher ranks of the religious-legal profession, the *sheikhu'l-islam* reached his position through direct royal patronage, and relied for his promotion on the support of a family or faction. He was never, in reality, out of and above everyday politics. It was, again, Ebu's-su'ud who sought to reconcile the sovereignty of the *shari'a* with the sovereignty of the Sultan.

Notes

1. See Joseph Schacht, *The Origins of Islamic Jurisprudence*, Oxford: Clarendon Press (1950); Norman Calder, *Studies in Early Muslim Jurisprudence*, Oxford: Clarendon Press (1993).
2. Jonathan Berkey, *The Transmission of Knowledge in Medieval Cairo*, Princeton: Princeton University Press (1992), p. 48.

3. George Makdisi, *The Rise of Colleges: Institutions of Learning in Islam and the West*, Edinburgh: Edinburgh University Press (1981).

4. The probity of the witnesses is not a condition for the formation of a valid contract. A successful prosecution for *qadhf* would render the accused 'unrighteous' and therefore disqualified from testifying in certain cases.

5. Arabic text with French translation in G. H. Bousquet and L. Bercher, *Le Statut Personnel en Droit Musulman Hanéfite*, Tunis: Institut des Hautes Etudes de Tunis, Recueil Sirey (1950), pp. 12–13.

6. al-Sarakhsi, *al-Mabsut*, Beirut: Dar al-Marefah (1982), vol. 4, p. 197.

7. al-Kasani, *Bada'i' al-sana'i' fi tartib al-shara'i'*, Beirut: Dar al-Kitab al-'Arabi (1982).

8. al-Marghinani, *al-Hidaya*, Cairo: Matba'a Mustafa al-Babi al-Halabi (1972), vol. 3, pp. 189–91.

9. Ibid., vol. 6, pp. 305-6.

10. Ebu's-su'ud, *Sharh kitab al-buyu' min al-hidaya*, Topkapı Palace Library, MS A1,541, ff. 409b–410a.

11. Qadikhan, *al-Fatawa al-Khaniyya*, in margins of *al-Fatawa al-Hindiyya*, Bulaq: Imperial Press (1912/13), vol. 3, p. 382.

12. Ibid., vol. 1, p. 2.

13. Katib Chelebi, ed. Gustav Flügel, *Kashf al-zunun 'an asami al-kutub wa'l-funun*, Leipzig: Oriental Translation Fund of Great Britain and Ireland (1835–58), vol. 2, p. 49.

14. Hamidi, *Jami' al-Fatawa*, Topkapı Palace Library, MS R665, f. 2a.

15. See below, Chapter 7.

16. Baber Johansen, 'Der 'isma-Begriff im Hanafitischen Recht', *Actes du VIIIe Congrès International de l'Union Européen des Arabisants et des Islamisants*, Aix-en-Provence: Edisud (1978), pp. 264–82.

17. Chafik Chéhata, *Théorie Général de l'Obligation en Droit Musulman Hanéfite*, Paris: Editions Sirey (1969).

18. Baber Johansen, 'Die sündige gesunde Amme: Moral und gesetzliche Bestimmung (*hukm*) im islamischen Recht', *Die Welt des Islams*, 28 (1988), 264–82.

19. E. Tyan, 'Méthodologie et sources du droit', *Studia Islamica*, 10 (1959), 79–109.

20. Ibn Bazzaz, *al-Fatawa'l-bazzaziyya*, in margins of *al-Fatawa'l-Hindiyya*, Bulaq: Imperial Press (1912/13), vol. 3, pp. 185–6.

21. al-Marghinani, *al-Hidaya*, vol. 4, p. 445.

22. Nabil Shehaby, "*'Illa* and *qiyas* in early Islamic legal theory', *Journal of the American Oriental Society*, 102 (1982), 40–70; Wael B. Hallaq, "'The Book of Juridical Qiyas": a tenth–eleventh-century treatise on a juridical dialectic', *Muslim World*, 77 (1987), 207–28. On the casuistic method of Muslim jurists, see Baber Johansen, 'Casuistry: between legal concept and social praxis', *Islamic Law and Society*, 2/2 (1995), 135–56.

23. Ibn Nujaim, *al-Bahr al-Ra'iq*, Cairo: al-Matba'a al-'Ilmiyya (1893), vol. 5, p. 20.

24. N. J. Coulson, *Succession in the Muslim Family*, Cambridge: Cambridge University Press (1971).

25. See below, Chapter 8.

26. Ignaz Goldziher, trans. S. M. Stern, *Muslim Studies*, London: George Allen and Unwin (1967), vol. 2.

27. Norman Calder, *Studies in Early Muslim Jurisprudence*, chapter 6.
28. al-Marghinani, *al-Hidaya*, vol. 5, pp. 80–1.
29. Ibid., vol. 6, pp. 261–2.
30. Ibid., vol. 9, pp. 58–60.
31. Ibid., vol. 4, pp. 453–4.
32. Ya'akov Meron, 'The development of legal thought in Hanafi texts', *Studia Islamica*, 30 (1969), 73–118.
33. Baber Johansen, *The Islamic Law of Tax and Rent*, London: Croom Helm (1988).
34. Baber Johansen, 'Eigentum, Familie und Obrigkeit im Hanafitischen Strafrecht', *Die Welt des Islams*, (1979) 19, 1–73.
35. J. R. Mandaville, 'Usurious piety: the cash waqf controversy in the Ottoman Empire', *International Journal of Middle Eastern Studies*, 10 (1979), 289–308.
36. Ibn 'Abidin, *Radd al-Muhtar*, Beirut: Dar al-Fikr (1979), vol. 4, pp. 363–4.
37. In the area of land tenure and taxation, custom does seem to have produced some fundamental changes in Hanafi theory, notably in its recognition of the legal validity of share-cropping. See Baber Johansen, 'Coutumes locales et coutumes universelles aux sources des règles juridiques en droit musulman hanéfite', *Annales Islamologiques*, 27 (1993), 29–35.
38. See Chapter 9, no. (3).
39. Wael B. Hallaq, 'Logic, formal arguments and formalization of arguments in Sunni jurisprudence', *Arabica*, 37 (1990), 315–58.
40. Jelalzade Mustafa, ed. Petra Kappert, *Tabakat ül-Memalik ve Derecat ül-Mesalik*, Verzeichnis der Orientalischen Handschriften in Deutschland, Supplementband 21, Wiesbaden: Franz Steiner Verlag (1981), f. 201a.
41. D. Santillana, *Istituzioni di Diritto Musulmano*, Rome: Istituto per l'Oriente, 2 vols (1925, 1938).
42. Joseph Schacht, *An Introduction to Islamic Law*, Oxford: Clarendon Press (1964), chapter 15.
43. Vera Mutafčieva, 'Sur le caractère du timar ottoman', *Acta Orientalia*, Budapest, 9 (1959), 55–61.
44. Heath W. Lowry, 'The Ottoman Liva Kanunnames contained in the Defter-i Hakani', *Journal of Ottoman Studies*, 2 (1981), 43–74.
45. Ö. L. Barkan, *Kanunlar*, Istanbul: Burhaneddin Matbaası (143), pp. 1–2, no. I, section 1.
46. Ö. L. Barkan, 'XV asrın sonunda bir büyük şehirde eşya ve yiyecek fiyatları', *Tarih Vesikaları* 2/7 (1941), p. 15.
47. R. Anhegger and H. İnalcık, *Kanunname-yi sultani ber muceb-i 'örf-i 'osmani*, Ankara: Publications of the Turkish Historical Society, series 11, no. 5 (1956), p. 51; Ahmed Akgündüz, *Osmanlı Kannunameleri*, Istanbul: Fey Vakfı Yayınları, vol. 1 (1990), pp. 460–1, sections 1–2; French translation, Nicoara Beldiceanu, *Les Actes des Premiers Sultans*, Paris and the Hague: Mouton & Co. (1960), pp. 119–20, sections 2–3.
48. R. Anhegger and H. İnalcık, *Kanunname-yi sultani*, pp. 51–2; Ahmed Akgündüz, *Osmanlı Kanunnameleri*, vol. 1, p. 462, section 1; French translation, Nicoara Beldiceanu, *Les Actes*, p. 121, section 1.
49. Ahmed Akgündüz, *Osmanlı Kanunnameleri*, vol. 1, p. 469.
50. Ibid., section 2. Akgündüz misreads this passage, to give the sense of '*Salarliq* should be taken at the rate of one bushel in [each] bushel from their own produce'. For the corrrect reading, see facsimile, p. 473.

51. Text in Ahmed Akgündüz, *Osmanlı Kannunnameleri*, vol. 2 (1990), pp. 307–29.
52. Ö. L. Barkan, *Kanunlar*, pp. 170–1, no. 41, sections 1, 2, 8.
53. Ibid., p. 249, no. 71, section 2.
54. Heath W. Lowry, 'A corpus of extant kanunnames for the island of Limnos as contained in the tapu-tahrir defter collection in the Başbakanlık Archives', *Journal of Ottoman Studies*, 1 (1980), 41–60; Colin Heywood, 'The evolution of the Ottoman provincial law-code (Sancak Kanun-name): the kanun-name-i liva-i Semendire', *Turkish Studies Association of America Bulletin*, 15/2, (1991) 223–51.
55. Ö. L. Barkan, *Kanunlar*, p. 131, no. 31, section 1.
56. Ibid., p. 154, no. 35, section 8.
57. Ibid., p. 117, no. 26, section 13.
58. Ibid., p. 207, no. 57, section 8.
59. Turkish text with German translation, Fr. Kraelitz-Greifenhorst, 'Kanunname Sultan Mehmeds des Eroberers', *Mitteilungen zur osmanischen Geschichte* (1921), repr. Osnabrück: Biblio Verlag (1972), pp. 13–48.
60. Uriel Heyd, ed. V. L. Ménage, *Studies in Old Ottoman Criminal Law*, Oxford: Clarendon Press (1973), p. 13.
61. Uriel Heyd, *Studies*, pp. 15–18.
62. M. 'Arif (ed.), 'Qanunname-yi al-i 'osman', *Tarih-i osmani encümeni mecmuası*, suppl. (1911), p. 28. Ahmed Akgündüz, *Osmanlı Kanunnameleri*, vol. 4 (1992), pp. 365–431, also gives a text of this Law Book. Following 'Arif, Akgündüz wrongly attributes it to Süleyman I.
63. Translation by T. C. Stanley, 'Aspects of Ottoman Kanun in the fifteenth century' (unpublished), emending the 'Arif text which is corrupt at this point.
64. M. 'Arif, 'Qanunname', p. 15.
65. Ibid., p. 38.
66. Ibid.
67. British Library, MS Or. 7,268, ff. 8a–b.
68. M. 'Arif, 'Qanunname', p. 27.
69. British Library, MS Or. 7,268, f. 4b.
70. M. 'Arif, 'Qanunname', p. 7.
71. Fr. Kraelitz-Greifenhorst, 'Kanunname Sultan Mehmeds', p. 21; M. 'Arif, 'Qanunname', p. 5.
72. Uriel Heyd, *Studies*, pp. 73–4, 111–12.
73. Ibid., pp. 84, 122.
74. Ismail Hakkı Uzunçarsılı, *Kapıkulu Ocakları*, Ankara: Turkish Historical Society (1943), pp. 86–9.
75. Qadikhan, *al-Fatawa*, vol. 3, p. 560.
76. Colin Imber, '*Zina* in Ottoman law', *Contributions à l'histoire économique et sociale de l'Empire ottoman*, Collection Turcica III, Louvain: Editions Peeters (1981), pp. 59–92.
77. Jan Reychman and Ananiasz Zajaczkowski, *Handbook of Ottoman Turkish Diplomatics*, Paris and the Hague: Mouton (1968).
78. Klara Hegyi, 'The terminology of the Ottoman Turkish judicial documents on the basis of sources from Hungary', *Acta Orientalia*, Budapest, 18 (1965), 191–203; Vanco Boškov, 'Die *hüccet*-Urkunde – diplomatische Analyse', *Studia Turcologica Memoriae Alexii Bombaci Dicata*, Naples: Istituto Universitario Orientale (1982), pp. 79–87; Colin Heywood, 'An unsolved murder in

the Marmara (Notes on Bodl. MS Turk. d.32)', *Studies in Ottoman History in Honour of Professor V. L. Ménage*, Istanbul: Isis Press (1994), pp. 91–106; Asparouh Velkov, 'Signatures-formules des agents judiciaires dans les documents ottomans à caractère financier et juridique', *Turcica*, 24 (1992), 193–240.

79. Ebu's-su'ud, *Bida'at al-qadi*, Süleymaniye Library, Istanbul, MS Laleli 3,711, chapter 7.

80. Ibid., chapter 3.

81. Ibid.

82. Ibn Nujaim, compiled with Turkish translation by Ref'et b. el-Hajj Ibrahim Rüshdi, *Fatawa Ibn Nujaim*, Istanbul: Sheikh Yahya Press (1862/3), pp. 46, 89.

83. Süleymaniye Library, Istanbul, MSS Şehid Ali Paşa 2,865, 2,867, 2,868; University Library, Istanbul, MSS T2,088, T2,112.

84. *İlmiye Salnamesi*, Istanbul: Imperial Press (1916).

85. V. L. Ménage, 'On the constituent elements of certain sixteenth-century Ottoman documents', *Bulletin of the School of Oriental and African Studies*, 48 (1985), 283–304.

86. For example, University Library, Istanbul, MS T2,088 f. 59b.

87. University Library, Istanbul, MS T2,112 f. 67a.

88. Süleymaniye Library, Istanbul, MS Şehid Ali Paşa 2,867 ff. 88b–90a.

89. A copyist's error can, however, create a tradition. In Kemalpashazade's fatwa on land tenure, the word *hauz*, meaning land rented out by the monarch, was misread by a copyist of the 'New *Qanun*' in the late seventeenth century as the meaningless *khwan*, and appears as such in all subsequent manuscripts. See below, Chapter 5, no. (1).

PART II

The Sources of Legal Authority:
the Holy Law and the Ottoman Sultan

3

The Sultan and Legal Sovereignty

The Hanafi Theory of Rulership: the Legal Basis of Sovereignty

For most Hanafi jurists, questions of rulership and political authority are marginal. It is essential to establish who is a legitimate ruler only because it is from the ruler that judges acquire their authority to execute the law. The ruler has no powers over the formulation or the contents of the law itself, since its transmission and interpretation falls entirely within the competence of the jurists. At a metaphysical level, this view of legal sovereignty reflects the notion that the *shari'a* is the Law of God, which binds the monarch as much as it binds his humblest subjects. At a practical level, it reflects the view that the jurists had of themselves as the guardians of the legal tradition, and the fact that Islamic Law is the law of a community and not of a state. The Islamic community and, within it, the Hanafi community, were subject to frequent political fracture and change of ruler and dynasty but, throughout these political transformations, the law itself remained unchanged. It was the law that gave the Islamic community its identity, and it was the jurists who were the guardians of the law.

The Hanafis do, it is true, recognise the concept of the Caliph (*khalifa*) as the supreme head of the Islamic community, but it is a concept that had almost no influence on the structure or formulation of the law. They also, in referring to the monarch, use the term *imam*, which theorists of Islamic government use to designate the Caliph. But in Hanafi usage, *imam* means no more than *de facto* ruler or military commander. It rarely carries the sense of supreme head of the Muslim community. In fact, in the mainstream Hanafi tradition, the legitimate authority is simply a person who successfully seizes and holds power. This becomes clear in the jurists' discussions of Friday prayer.[1]

Friday prayer is a congregational prayer which is valid only if it is held in a town with a judge and, more importantly, where the prayer-leader is the ruler himself or his appointee. Legitimacy of the prayer therefore depends on the legitimacy of the ruler, and it is this rule that forces jurists into defining rightful political sovereignty. In facing this question, Qadikhan (d. 1196) presents a case which is perhaps typical of the Hanafi tradition as a whole: 'A usurper has no commission: that is, he has no diploma of appointment from the Caliph. If his conduct towards the subjects is the conduct of governors, and he passes judgement in their affairs with the authority of a ruler, then it is licit to perform Friday prayer in his name.'[2] Three centuries later, the Egyptian jurist, Ibn Humam (d. 1457), slightly adapted Qadikhan's words to express the same general opinion. Unlike Qadikhan, however, he omits any reference to the Caliph and refers simply to 'the usurper who has no diploma of appointment'. If such a man behaves towards the people as a governor, 'Friday prayer is permissible in his presence, because rulership (*saltana*) is thereby realised'.[3] Qadikhan, 'in a case of dire need', would even recognise a ruler whom the common people had promoted, although this was a view which Ibn Humam would not accept.

To Qadikhan and Ibn Humam, therefore, the ruler is a person who effectively seizes and holds power, and this, it seems, is the opinion of the majority of Hanafi jurists. When they refer to the ruler, whether calling him 'Imam' or 'Sultan', the term means no more than the *de facto* political authority. Nor even was justice a necessary quality for a legitimate sovereign. On the crucial question of whether a judge can accept office from an unjust ruler, Marghinani (d. 1197) clearly states the rule: 'Investiture [as judge] by an unjust sovereign is permissible, just as it is by a righteous one', a view which he supports with a Tradition concerning the practice of the Companions of the Prophet.[4] The reasoning behind this rule, unless one accepts that it really did derive from Prophetic precedent, appears to be entirely practical. If a ruler, however unjust, is sufficiently powerful, it is simply not possible to overthrow him.

It is again Qadikhan who makes this point most clearly. He explains first that a Sultan comes to power either as a result of a compact with the nobles of the realm, or simply 'by executing his commands among his subjects by means of fear and overwhelming power'. However, even if the people have paid him their allegiance, he does not become Sultan unless he is able to subdue them by force. Next Qadikhan raises the question of the unjust Sultan: 'A man becomes Sultan by compact and acts unjustly. If he possesses overwhelming power, he is not deposed, because if he were deposed, he would [simply] become Sultan again by [means of the same] overwhelming power, and [the deposition] would be of no use. If he has no overwhelming power, then he is deposed.' In this view of rulership, a compact with the nobility and justice are desirable qualities in a Sultan but, in the last analysis, the only indispensable quality is the ability to exercise force. It is power and not justice that legitimises rulership.

The ruler is essential mainly because it is from him that judges acquire their authority, and it is through his coercive power that the law is able to offer protection of life and property. Without a ruler, the law is ineffective. Nevertheless, he cannot make or modify the law, and, in the formulation of Sarakhsi (d. 1097), he is exclusively responsible for its implementation in only four areas: Friday prayer, the infliction of the fixed penalties (*hudud*), alms, and the levying of the fifth (*khums*), a tax at the rate of one fifth, levied on war booty.[5] These, Sarakhsi says, are 'claims of God, which the ruler (*imam*) fulfils, and in whose fulfilment no one else has a share, as in tribute (*kharaj*), poll-tax (*jizya*) and alms'.[6]

However, even in these four areas, the jurists severely restrict the ruler's powers. Friday prayer clearly did have a great practical importance, since it was through this prayer that Islamic monarchs broadcast their claims to sovereignty. The fixed penalties, however, had little bearing on everyday reality. Despite their insistence on the execution of these penalties as being a primary duty of the ruler, and essential for the well-being of the Muslim community, the jurists limit these punishments to five offences: fornication, false accusation of fornication, wine-drinking, theft and highway robbery. Furthermore, in the case at least of fornication and theft, by erecting insurmountable procedural barriers to a successful conviction, they relegate the penalties to the realm of fiction. In referring to 'alms' as falling within the direct authority of the ruler, Sarakhsi is referring to the alms-tax (*zakat*), a theoretical impost payable by all Muslims possessing a specified minimum wealth. In his commentary, he makes it clear that the ruler's powers also extend to the collection of the other canonical taxes – tribute payable on land, poll-tax payable by non-Muslim subjects, and the fifth on war booty. The jurists thus accord the ruler the power to raise taxes, but, by defining what taxes are to be raised, at what rate, and for what purposes they are to be spent, leave him no powers of discretion.

The Hanafi Theory of Rulership: The Conduct of Government

In Hanafi theory, therefore, a ruler is a person who successfully takes and holds power, and whose unmediated authority is effective only in four areas of the law. The same highly restrictive view of the ruler's powers is evident in the treatment of 'the conduct of government' (*siyar*), a topic which occupies an independent chapter in most Hanafi texts. Here, the concern of the jurists is not to establish a theory of government, but rather to erect a theory which explains the legal status of persons, land and taxation in an Islamic sovereignty.

The basis of this theory is holy war (*jihad*). This the jurists present as an act of worship (*'ibada*), like prayer or fasting in Ramadan, except that it is incumbent not on every individual, but on the Muslim community as a whole. However, a group of Muslims must be fighting at all times, and if the holy war ever ceases, then it is a sin which the entire community must bear. It becomes an individual obligation only when there is a general mobilisation following an enemy invasion. Holy war must last until the end of time, in order, in Ibn Humam's formulation, 'to exalt the Word of God Most High' and to 'remove corruption from the world'.[7] Since warfare, like prayer, is a continuous obligation which the Muslim community owes to God, peace with the infidels is an impossibility. The Muslim ruler or army commander may make a temporary truce if it is in the interests of the Muslim community to do so, but such a truce is not legally binding: 'If a ruler (*imam*) makes a truce [with the infidels] for a while, but then sees it to be more beneficial to break the truce, he should default and fight against them. This is because the Prophet (peace and blessings be upon him) defaulted on the truce between himself and the Meccans; and because, when the interests of Muslims change, to default is [to wage] holy war, and to keep the treaty is to abandon holy war, both in form and spirit.'[8] In other words, peace is conceivable only if it promotes the cause of Islam.

Holy war is an obligation which the Muslim community owes to God. Its purpose is to promote Islam and to subdue infidelity, and, to this end, the jurists formulated specific rules of warfare. The Muslims must not attack the infidels without first calling on them to accept Islam, or to pay the poll-tax (*jizya*) as a mark of their tributary status. In Hanafi opinion, it is permissible to kill infidel warriors, but not women, children, old men, the blind or lunatics, unless they are adepts at war. An old man may, for example, be able to give advice on the conduct of war, or a woman might be a queen, in which case they should be killed. When Muslims take prisoners, the Muslim ruler or commander may kill them if they are adult males, enslave them, or leave them free as tributary infidels, but he may not return them to the infidel realms, as this would strengthen the power of the unbelievers. An opinion attributed to Abu Hanifa even disallows their ransom against Muslim prisoners, since they would return to make war on Islam, which is more harmful than the release of Muslims is beneficial.[9]

The jurists, in short, present a theory of religiously justified warfare and its conduct. It is a theory which has a central position in the general structure of Hanafi law, since it is holy war that determines the legal status of individuals, of land and of taxation. It is also a legitimate mode of acquisition.

So far as individuals are concerned, the law divides the world into two realms, the realm of Islam (*dar al-Islam*) and the non-Muslim world, the realm of war (*dar al-harb*). A dweller in the realm of war is an enemy (*harbi*) to whom the law offers no protection. It is an obligation on Muslims to attack him in his own realm, and if he enters the realm of Islam and is killed, his blood is unavenged. There are, however, ways in which a free non-Muslim can acquire the right of residence and legal protection in the realm of Islam. In the first place, he can abjure infidelity and accept Islam. Or, he can accept to pay the poll-tax and acquire the status of a tributary subject (*dhimmi*), in which case the law protects both his life and his property. Or, as a slave, he may become a chattel of a free Muslim. Finally, the ruler may grant an enemy a temporary safe-conduct, which gives him the status of protected resident (*musta'min*). The jurists grant this concession, because without it, food supplies would be cut off and 'the door of trade blocked'.[10] Nonetheless, if a protected resident stays more than a year, he loses his status, since an enemy cannot reside permanently in the realm of Islam, except as a slave or tributary subject.

Thus, between the two extremes of the free Muslim and the legally dead enemy, the jurists categorise individuals as slaves, tributary subjects or protected residents. It is a division of humanity which finds its justification in the theory of holy war.

So too does the juristic scheme of taxation. The jurists recognise five forms of taxation – poll-tax (*jizya*), tribute (*kharaj*), tithe (*'ushr*) the fifth (*khums*) and alms-tax (*zakat*) – of which all but the last relate to holy war. The poll-tax is an impost on all adult, non-Muslim males in the realm of Islam. The jurists sometimes explain it as a 'punishment' (*'uquba*) on the conquered peoples for their failure to accept Islam, and as a symbol of submission and humiliation. Qadikhan, in answering the question of how it should be collected, says: 'Some maintain that the collector should seize [the poll-tax payer] by the collar, mock him and say, "Pay poll-tax, O enemy of God!"'[11] Tithe and tribute were both land taxes. If, at the time of the Muslim conquest, the ruler allocates land to the Muslim conquerors, they pay tithe at the rate of one tenth of the produce. If the Muslim ruler leaves the land in the ownership of the conquered infidels, then they pay tribute at a discretionary rate of up to half the produce. The jurists classify the payment of tithe as an act of worship, and the tribute as a 'burden' (*ma'una*) on the conquered people. Finally, there is the fifth, the levy which the ruler makes on moveable goods which the Muslim troops seize as spoils of war. These four juristically-conceived taxes arise out of the conquest of infidelity. It is the holy war which forms the basis of their legitimacy.

Finally, holy war is as much a legitimate means of acquiring property as, say, purchase or gift. The distribution of immoveable property is dependent on the will of the ruler or commander at the time of the conquest. He can reinstate the existing owners or redistribute it to the Muslims. The owners then have the absolute power to dispose of the property as they wish. The case of moveable property is much more complex. Ownership is again dependent on the will of the ruler, but the question is to establish the precise moment at which the warrior acquires ownership of the booty which falls to his lot. In the ideal Hanafi model, the warriors do not receive their portion of the spoil until the Muslim commander has taken it into the custody (*ihraz*) of the realm of Islam, since it is only when it is within the boundaries of a Muslim sovereignty that property acquires the protection of the law and becomes subject to full legal ownership.[12] Here, the commander should take out 'God's share' of one fifth and divide the remainder among the warriors, according to fixed rules whereby, for example, a cavalryman receives two shares to an infantryman's one. It is at the moment of distribution that the spoil becomes property, and it is at this point that the authority over it of the ruler or commander ceases. Acquisition of ownership is thus dependent on three conditions: removal of the booty to the realm of Islam, the removal of the fifth, and distribution by the ruler or commander. It is not permissible to sell plundered goods in the realm of war, because there is no ownership before division. It is also permissible, if less meritorious, for the ruler or commander to distribute booty before battle (*tanfīl*) – in effect, to allow warriors to keep what they take – as a means of goading the troops to fight. But here too, the acquisition of ownership is dependent on the authority of the ruler or commander.

The jurists deal with two further topics in the same chapter as they deal with holy war. These are apostasy, where a Muslim abjures the faith, and rebellion, where he renounces allegiance to a legitimate Muslim sovereign, but without renouncing his faith.

The penalty for the male apostate is death. Before the execution of the sentence, however, the jurists grant a three-day delay. If, during this period, the apostate repents and accepts Islam, he is reprieved. The penalty for a female apostate is imprisonment until she accepts Islam. The difference is that a woman does not possess the physique for fighting, and so a female apostate, like a female enemy, does not pose an imminent threat to the Muslim community. For this reason she escapes death.[13]

These rules are simple. The greatest concern of the jurists, however, is to establish the legal status of an apostate and his property when he is alive. So far as concerns offences committed against his person, he loses the legal protection ('*isma*) arising from his subjection to a Muslim sovereignty: 'A man's apostasy cancels the legal protection owing to his person. If [a person] kills him without an order from the judge, whether deliberately or by mistake; or without an order from the political authority (*sultan*); or if [a person] destroys one of his limbs, then [that person] is not liable.'[14] The status of his property, however, is subject to dispute. In the view which the jurists attribute to Abu Hanifa, his ownership lapses on apostasy and returns immediately he accepts Islam. In the opinion which they attribute to Abu Yusuf and Shaibani, it does not lapse. For Abu Hanifa, therefore, certain of his transactions, such as sale, lease, manumission or testamentary bequest are in suspense until he accepts Islam. For Abu Yusuf and Shaibani, they are valid. However, opinion is unanimous in, for example, forbidding an apostate to marry, since adherence to a religion is a necessary element in marriage; or, for example, in permitting him to accept gifts.[15]

An apostate, in fact, lives in a legal twilight. If he migrates, and a judge rules that he has reached the realm of war, he becomes legally dead: 'By reaching the realm of war, he becomes [an enemy], one of the people of war, and they are dead with respect to the ordinance of Islam, because of the cessation of authority and obligation'.[16]

The laws relating to rebels, which in effect regulate warfare against fellow Muslims, are simpler than the laws of apostasy, since questions of ownership and of the validity of legal acts are less complex. The just ruler should not attack the rebels until they invade his land or, in a more realistic ruling, until they assemble an army. Before attacking them, in parallel to the summons, in a holy war, to the infidels to accept Islam, he should call on them to 'return to the [rightful] congregation, and investigate the cause of the rebellion'. In contrast to holy war, their women and children should not be enslaved, nor their property divided, 'because they are Muslims, and Islam protects life and property'.[17] This punctiliousness over property raises the question as to whether the ruler's troops may fight with weapons captured from the rebels. They may do so as a result of need, but not as a result of the transfer of ownership. Since a ruler may make use of a just subject's property in case of need, *a fortiori* he may make use of a rebel's.[18] What the ruler and his warriors cannot do is to acquire ownership of the rebels' property. Instead, the ruler detains it, and does not return it until they repent. The right to retain their property is simply in order to break their power. It does not imply a transfer of ownership, as does the division of spoil in a holy war. War against rebels, unlike holy war, is not a legal mode of acquisition.

There remains, however, the question of legal liabilities which arise when a ruler's authority has lapsed. First, there is the question of taxation. If the rebels levied tribute and tithe, the just ruler does not have the right to levy it a second time. In Hanafi doctrine, taxation is an element in a reciprocally binding contract between the ruler and people: there is no taxation without protection (*al-jibaya bi'l-himaya*). In allowing the rebels to prevail, the just ruler did not protect his subjects, and so loses the right to taxation.[19] Second, there is the question of whether the ruler can execute the claims of subjects which arose under the jurisdiction of the rebels. The jurists bring the case of a claim for talion. If the killer and his victim belong to the rebel army, which the just ruler subsequently conquers, there can be no claim for talion 'because the just ruler had no authority at the time of the killing, and the obligation does not come into effect'.[20] The case is different when there is a deliberate homicide in a town which the rebels have conquered and the just ruler has subsequently recaptured. In this case, talion is inflicted if the ruler expelled the rebels before his own authority ceased to be effective. But, says Ibn Humam, commenting on this rule, 'if the rebel ruler's decrees come into force to the extent that they form the basis of his authority, there is no talion and no blood-vengeance. [The killer], however, merits punishment in the Other World.'[21] Again, it is *de facto* power that underpins legal authority.

What is perhaps most striking about the rules for the conduct of government, apart from their general air of unreality, is the minimal role which they assign to the ruler. The most important topic under this heading is the conduct of holy war. The holy war, however, is an obligation on the Muslim community as a whole, and not on the ruler in particular. In the context of juristic discussion of holy war, the term 'imam', usually reserved for the ruler, need mean no more than simply the 'commander of the army', and this is in fact the term that Qadikhan uses. Furthermore, since holy war is a communal and not an individual obligation, the ruler has no authority to coerce individuals to fight. Participation is voluntary, and the question of authority arises only in the context of the family: 'A man cannot depart for the holy war, except with the permission of both parents together. If one permits him and the other does not, it is not fitting that he should depart.'[22] In this area, even a woman has moral, although not coercive authority: 'A woman prevents her son from [departing to the holy war.] If her heart cannot endure the pain of separation ... she may restrain him from the holy war without committing a sin.'[23] Equally, a slave may not fight without the permission of his master, or a woman without the permission of her husband. The only case in which the ruler's call to arms overrides the authority of parent, husband or master is when there is a general levy following an enemy invasion. The source of this overriding authority is not, however, the ruler, but the overwhelming need of the Muslim community.

The Hanafi jurists assign to the ruler or army commander an essential role in establishing the individual ownership of goods and lands acquired as booty. However, once ownership is established, the ruler's interest in the property ceases, except in the case of land as a source of revenue. The right to levy taxes is clearly the first essential of rulership. It is, nevertheless, a right which the jurists carefully circumscribe.

The taxes which a ruler may legitimately raise are tribute, tithe, the fifth, poll-tax and alms-tax. All but the last, as has been said, have the holy war as their source of legitimacy. A ruler may not, however, dispose of these taxes freely. He should instead place them in four separate treasuries, each of which has its separate function. The first treasury is for the receipt of the fifth, which the ruler, in accordance with a Quranic injunction, should expend on 'orphans, the destitute and travellers'.[24] The second is for the receipt of the alms-tax. This the ruler should expend on the poor, the destitute, bondsmen, and other categories imprecisely specified in a Quranic verse.[25] The third treasury is for the receipt of tribute, poll-tax and tithes. The ruler should spend this on fighting men:

'It is wealth that accrued through their power, and so it is spent on them'. The fourth treasury is for the receipt of ownerless properties 'such as estates to which there is no heir'. These the ruler should use on the upkeep of roads, bridges and hospices which have no income from endowments. The function of the ruler is, in short, to collect the juristically-determined taxes, and to disburse them for juristically determined charitable purposes.

The Ottoman Practice of Rulership: The Legitimisation of the Dynasty

Where the Hanafi theory of rulership is most realistic is in its simple definition of a legal sovereign as a person who seizes and effectively exercises power. Although this was the real basis of Ottoman rule, it was not something to which the Sultans could admit. Instead, they made elaborate claims to rightful sovereignty which, from modest beginnings in the fourteenth century, culminated in Ebu's-su'ud's formulation of a claim to universal sovereignty in the sixteenth. ·

The earliest claim, which the Sultans made as early as the fourteenth century and continued to make until the twentieth, was that they were leaders of the Muslims in a holy war against the infidels. This is a concept which derives directly from the rules for 'the conduct of government' in the *shari'a* and which, by the late fifteenth century, had come to form a basis for Ottoman claims to territorial legitimacy. The Ottoman Sultans, the argument ran, had acquired their lands by conquest from the infidels and not by usurpation from the Muslims, and so they ruled in these lands as legitimate monarchs. This argument was, however, inadequate, since the Ottomans had also acquired extensive territories in Anatolia, which they had taken from Muslim rulers. To meet this problem, Ottoman chroniclers in the late fifteenth century devised a story about how the last Sultan of the Seljuk dynasty, the rulers of central Anatolia from the late eleventh century until about 1300, had appointed the first Ottoman Sultan as his successor. This story made the Ottoman Sultans legal heirs to the Seljuk territories and 'proved' that the Muslim sovereigns whom they had displaced were 'usurpers'. Thus their claims both to be leaders of a holy war and to be heirs to the Seljuk dynasty gave legitimacy to their rule in lands conquered from Christians, and in lands in Anatolia conquered from Muslims. Alongside these devices for claiming rights to territory, the Ottomans, during the course of the fifteenth century, created a dynastic genealogy going back to Noah. They assembled the materials for this from the Turkish epics of Oghuz Khan, the legendary ancestor of the western Turkish peoples. The genealogy shows, in all its different versions, that the Ottomans descended in the senior line from Oghuz Khan himself, and so were the rightful leaders of all the Oghuz peoples and, in particular, senior in descent to neighbouring Turkish monarchs.

By about 1500, these were the most important elements in Ottoman claims to sovereignty. They amounted, in effect, to a claim to rightful sovereignty in Anatolia and the Balkan peninsula, and to supreme rulership of the western Turks. Half a century later, Ottoman pretensions were far less modest. Selim I's defeat of the Mamluk Sultanate of Cairo in 1517 made him *de facto* the most powerful monarch in the Islamic world, and gave him, as possessor of the holy cities of Mecca and Medina, the right to the coveted title of 'Servitor of the Two Sacred Precincts'. This gave him a spiritual pre-eminence among Muslims. Selim's reign also saw the beginning of hostilities with the Safavid Shahs of Iran. Since the Safavids were Shi'ites and, by virtue of their headship of a mystic Order, claimed peculiar spiritual authority, the Sunni Ottoman Sultans regarded them as heretics, and presented their own wars against them as the defence of orthodox Islam. The possession of the holy cities and the wars against the heretical Iranians led Selim I (1512–20) and especially his successor Süleyman I (1520–66) to present themselves, above all, as defenders of the faith, who waged war against infidelity and heresy, and without whose aid the faith and the holy law could not survive. In this formulation, the defence and implementation of the *shari'a* was dependent on the rule of the Ottoman Sultan.[26]

This was the core of the Ottoman claim to sovereignty in the sixteenth century. The reign of Süleyman I, however, saw a further aggrandisement of Ottoman pretensions. The occupation of Algiers in 1519 and the victory over the king of Hungary in 1526 brought Süleyman directly into conflict with the two Habsburg monarchs: the Holy Roman Emperor and King of Spain, Charles V, and his brother, Ferdinand of Austria, who claimed the title 'King of the Romans'. Rivalry with the Habsburgs in Hungary and the Mediterranean was a major theme of Süleyman's forty-six-year reign. In the Habsburgs, the Ottomans encountered a dynasty which was their equal not only in military strength but also in the grandeur of their claims. Charles V, as Holy Roman Emperor, was both the secular head of Christendom and the heir to Roman sovereignty. These were pretensions which Süleyman was to match.[27]

In 1547, he concluded a treaty with Charles and Ferdinand, granting peace on the condition that they pay tribute for the lands which they held in Hungary. The texts refer to Charles not as 'Emperor' but simply as 'King of Spain', and to his brother simply as 'King of Germany'.[28] It was, it seems, from this moment that Süleyman began to conceive of himself as having wrested the Roman Imperial title from Charles, and to see himself without question as Caliph of all the Muslims, as a counterpart to Charles' role as Emperor of all the Christians. It was also, it seems, immediately after the treaty that Süleyman laid the plan for the construction of his great mosque in Istanbul,[29] whose completed span equals the dimensions of the Emperor Justinian's great church of the Hagia Sophia, which stood in the Ottoman capital as a symbol of Roman imperial power. The mosque remains as a monument to Süleyman's claim to universal sovereignty.[30]

It was Ebu's-su'ud who most successfully formulated this claim, which he encapsulated in the words of the inscription over the portal of the mosque:

(1) [Sultan Süleyman] has drawn near to [God], the Lord of Majesty and Omnipotence, / the Creator of the World of Dominion and Sovereignty, / [Sultan Süleyman] who is His slave, made mighty with Divine Power, / the Caliph, resplendent with Divine Glory, / Who performs the Command of the Hidden Book / and executes its Decrees in [all] regions of the inhabited quarter: / Conqueror of the Lands of the Orient and the Occident / with the Help of Almighty God and His Victorious Army, / Possessor of the Kingdoms of the World, Shadow of God over all Peoples, Sultan of the Sultans of the Arabs and the Persians, / Promulgator of Sultanic *Qanun*s, / Tenth of the Ottoman *Khaqan*s, / Sultan son of the Sultan, Sultan Süleyman Khan / ... / May the line of his Sultanate endure until the End of the Line of the Ages!/ ...[31]

Restricted as he was by the space available above the mosque portal, Ebu's-su'ud has in fact provided a relatively modest catalogue of Sultanic attributes. He had already composed a more extensive list in the preamble to the law-book of Buda in 1541, which he was to repeat almost verbatim in the law-book of Skopje and Thessaloniki in 1568. Even these lists, however, were modest in comparison with those which appear in the prefaces to his commentary on the Quran and his treatise on ritual ablution, which he completed at about the same time.

By its brevity, however, the Süleymaniye inscription serves to emphasise the relative importance of the constituent elements of the claims which Ebu's-su'ud made on the Sultan's behalf. Süleyman was ruler by both secular and divine right. He had, through conquest, become 'possessor of the kingdoms of the world' and, in the longer versions, Sultan not simply of the Arabs and the Persians, but also of the Greeks (*Rum*). Already in 1541, Ebu's-su'ud had given him the epithet 'Chosroes of Chosroeses',[32] a reference to the pre-Islamic monarchs of Iran whose title he had acquired through victory over the Safavids. After 1547, he adds the Roman title 'Caesar of Caesars'[33] and, in order to emphasise Süleyman's humiliation of both the Habsburgs and the Safavids, he describes the Sultan as the 'breaker of Caesars'[34] and as the 'one who casts dust in the faces of Chosroes and Caesar'.[35] At the same time, the Sultan retains the originally Turkish title of 'Khaqan', a reference perhaps to his alleged descent from Oghuz Khan, the legendary ancestor of the Ottoman dynasty.

The inscription nevertheless makes it clear that, however grandiose were Süleyman's claims to secular sovereignty, they were secondary to his claim to rule by divine right. It omits one element which appears in the other lists of royal epithets, and this is the title 'servitor of the Two Venerated Sacred precincts'. Another, 'leader of holy wars, famous among mankind'[36] emphasising the Sultan's role as a holy warrior, it refers to only obliquely. Instead it emphasises Süleyman's position as Caliph, the supreme head of the entire Muslim community. It is through the Caliph, the Shadow of God on earth, that the Almighty executes the commands of the 'Hidden Book', a reference to the celestial prototype of the Quran, the uncreated Word of God. This idea is already present in the law-book of Buda, where Ebu's-su'ud designates the Sultan as the one 'who makes smooth the path for the precepts of the manifest *shari'a*' and who 'makes manifest the Exalted Word of God'.[37] By the time of the treatise on ritual ablution and the Quran commentary, the Sultan has become the one 'who expounds the signs of the luminous *shari'a*'. In short, it is the Sultan who, as Caliph, is the interpreter and executor of God's law.

What the inscription does, above all, is to emphasise Süleyman's role as law-giver. As Caliph, he is both the interpreter and executor of God's Law, the *shari'a*, and as 'possessor of the kingdoms of the world', the promulgator of secular Sultanic law, the *qanun*. These themes are present in all Ebu's-su'ud's lists of royal titles, but it is above all the Süleymaniye inscription that makes it clear that they are of paramount importance, and explains why, in Ottoman tradition, Süleyman I acquired the epithet 'the Law-giver'.

The Ottoman Practice of Rulership: The Conduct of Government

The claims which Ebu's-su'ud made for the legitimacy of the Ottoman dynasty owe little to the Hanafi concept of coercion as the basis of legitimate sovereignty. The powers which the Sultans enjoyed derived, in Ebu's-su'ud's formulation, above all from their election by God to universal rule, and their accession by conquest to secular sovereignty. They ruled by divine right, and not by simple coercion. Furthermore, in adopting the title of Caliph, the Sultan was laying claim to an authority over the interpretation and implementation of the *shari'a* which is very much wider than the strictly limited powers which the Hanafi jurists accord the ruler.[38]

This was in the realm of theory. In its practice too, Ottoman government was equally at odds with Hanafi theory. To begin with, however much the Sultans sought to project their military campaigns as holy wars, their real motive was always dynastic aggrandisement or the defence of dynastic interests. Furthermore, the troops who fought in the Sultans' armies were not the religiously-enthused volunteers of Hanafi theory. Military service was a contractual obligation which holders of military fiefs or salaries owed to the Sultan. The military structure of the Empire also produced a legal classification of persons which is purely Ottoman. This was the distinction between the military class who paid no taxes, and received fiefs or salaries in return for military or other services, and the subject class who paid taxes. Thus the basic legal divide was not, as in Hanafi law, between Muslim and non-Muslim, but between taxpayers and non-taxpayers. Most of the military class were, in fact, Muslim, but so too was a large proportion of the subjects. The two classes were also subject to a separate jurisdiction, which was unknown to the Hanafi jurists. A fatwa of Ebu's-su'ud makes it clear that he accepted this legal distinction without demur:

(2) The defendant Zeyd is [a member of the] military [class]. Can he say to his opponent, 'Amr: 'I am not going to the judge. Let our case be heard before the military adjudicator (*qassam*)'?
Answer: Yes. [*Ch*, f. 46b]

In more important matters, cases involving the military class went before the Sultan's Imperial Council in Istanbul.

Nonetheless, despite the dichotomy in this area between Ottoman reality and Hanafi theory, the juristic notions of the 'conduct of government' and of the four areas where the ruler exercises direct authority did have a strong influence on Ottoman law, politics and ideology.

This is most evident perhaps in the pervasive ideology of the holy war, which the Sultans projected as a raison d'être of their rule, and as a legal justification for all their wars against Christian enemies. It was an ideology which derived ultimately from the juristic theory of holy war which, in the Ottoman Empire, became a vehicle for imperial propaganda. For the jurists, holy war is an obligation on the entire community, and not on individuals or rulers. The Ottoman Sultans, however, arrogated the merits of holy war to the dynasty, presenting themselves, by the end of the fifteenth century, as the greatest holy warriors since the Prophet himself.[39] It is therefore the Sultan and not the community, who is, in Ebu's-su'ud's words, 'the mighty annexer of the realm of war to the realm of Islam'.[40] In this way, the ruler came to personify the holy war, transforming a juristic theory into a prop of dynastic legitimisation.

The holy war was important as ideology. By contrast, the gradations in personal status which, in Hanafi theory arise from conquest in holy war, were important in practice. The most significant legal distinction in the

Ottoman empire was perhaps between the subject class and the military class, the former supporting the latter with their taxes, and the latter, in exchange for this income, providing the Sultan with military and other services. However, superimposed on this division was the legal distinction, deriving from Hanafi theory, between free Muslim, tributary infidel, protected resident and slave. This had important consequences in law. Free Muslims were subject to the jurisdiction of the Muslim courts, although with a separate jurisdiction for members of the military class. Tributary infidels, most of whom were members of the Orthodox, Armenian or Jewish communities, could bring cases before a Muslim judge, but in intra-communal cases could go to their own communal courts. The authorities in the Christian and Jewish communities held their positions, like the Muslim judges, by virtue of a royal warrant. In this sense, all legal authority flowed from the Sultan. Foreign ambassadors and residents enjoyed the status of protected residents, although in practice it tended to be treaty relationships with the Sultan, rather than strict Hanafi law, that defined their status. The numerous domestic and agricultural slaves in the Empire were subject to the Hanafi statutes of slavery and manumission. This was, it seems, an area of the law where the precepts of the jurists generally applied in practice.

There was, however, a category of slave to whom the normal statutes did not apply. These were the slaves of the Sultan's household. Some of these may have been simple menials but, more significantly, many of the provincial governors and viziers serving on the Imperial Council were, in the sixteenth century, household slaves who had received their education and training in the Palace. The powerful and privileged military corps attached to the royal household, most famously the Janissaries, were also composed of slaves. It was in fact largely through household slaves that the Sultan governed his Empire, and such persons, through their proximity to the monarch, enjoyed privileges which free men did not possess. Legally, they differed from ordinary slaves in two important respects. First, prisoners-of-war were the normal source of slaves, and these were particularly abundant in a period of successful warfare. However, from as early, it seems, as the late fourteenth century, the Sultans began to make regular levies of slaves from among the Christian populations of their own Empire, a practice which Hanafi law forbids. Christians in the realm of Islam have the status of tributary infidels. It is only enemies in the realm of war whom Muslims may enslave. Second, slaves cannot, in law, own property. Many of the Sultan's slaves, however, acquired enormous wealth, which reflected both the opportunity for enrichment provided by high office, and their elevated status in society.

In the sixteenth century, some people did have doubts about the strictly illegal practice of enslaving the Sultan's subjects, and found ingenious ways to justify it in law,[41] but this was not a problem which engaged the attention of Ebu's-su'ud. The spectacle of slaves disposing of great riches was probably less disquieting, since servants of great households often enjoyed a privileged and trusted status. The exalted position of the Sultan's slaves was simply a reflection of the status of their master. Ebu'-su'ud, however, makes no concessions to their *de facto* status as property-owners. To do so would have been to admit publicly that the Sultan did not have absolute power over his own bondservants. He simply applies the Hanafi rule that slaves cannot own property. A slave cannot therefore own another slave:

(3) His Excellency the Sultan, the Refuge of the World, sends his wholly-owned slave Zeyd [to a post] outside the Palace for a salary. Is it permissible for Zeyd to buy and to have intercourse with slave girls? *Answer*: It is not possible. [*D*, 552]

This ruling, however, had no general effect. The slaves of the Sultan continued to use their rank to accumulate personal wealth, including slaves.[42]

The Hanafi theory of the 'conduct of government' did, therefore, play an important part in shaping Ottoman dynastic ideology and in moulding the legal order in the Ottoman Empire. It did so, however, without seriously modifying the essentially feudal political structure, and it did so without diminishing the Sultan's claim to a sovereignty that was not merely legitimate but, in its sixteenth-century manifestation, universal.

The Ottoman Practice of Rulership: The Four Areas of Exclusive Royal Authority

Sarakhsi gives the ruler direct legal authority only in the areas of Friday prayer, taxation, the fifth on war booty and the fixed penalties. In reality, the scope of the Sultan's legal powers was much wider, since fiscal, criminal and land law came largely within the sphere of the *qanun*, which he could enact *ab initio*, or modify by royal decree. Nonetheless, it becomes clear from Ebu's-su'ud's fatwas that these four areas did in his time, and sometimes under his influence, play an important if often symbolic role in the exercise of government.

Friday Prayer

The importance of the Friday prayer is self-evident. It is through this obligatory congregational prayer, where the prayer-leader is the ruler himself or his delegate, and where the preacher mentions the ruler's name in his address, that Islamic monarchs proclaim their sovereignty to their subjects. Hence the imams and preachers of the congregational mosques in Ottoman towns and cities were government appointees. This the fatwas of Ebu's-su'ud make clear, while also indicating that, during his period as Military Judge of Rumelia, there had been a rationalisation of the appointment procedure:

> (4) The preacher Zeyd does not have permission to appoint a deputy. Is it permissible [for him] to appoint a deputy [to preach] the sermon and to lead the Friday prayer?
> *Answer*: Yes, there was a general permission in the year 945/1538. [*H*, p. 25; *D*, 267]

The problem here is whether a preacher, who is a government appointee, has the authority to appoint as preacher someone who is not. To forbid the practice would have been impractical, leading to interruptions in the performance of Friday prayer when the regular preacher was ill or absent. To have allowed it without qualification would have led to the appointment of preachers and prayer-leaders who had not received Sultanic authority. The solution was therefore to issue a Sultanic decree giving preachers the general authority to appoint deputies, who then, by virtue of this general decree, could perform the Friday prayer in the Sultan's name.

The same problem arises when a preacher leaves his post or dies:

> (5) Zeyd, the preacher at a mosque, dies. The judge gives the position to 'Amr, and gives him a petition [requesting the post from the Sultan]. Is it permissible for him to preach before [the petition] for the post of preacher has been submitted?
> *Answer*: Yes. [*D*, 242]

In answer to an almost identical question, Ebu's-su'ud amplifies this reply:

> In cases like this, the permission of the Sultan occurs [with the] permission of the judge. [The preacher] has a dispensation until a diploma [of appointment] is issued. [*D*, 267]

This rule prevented any interruption in the performance of Friday prayer. If a preacher died, the judge of the town, who was himself a royal appointee, immediately chose his successor. At the same time, he wrote a petition to the Sultan requesting the post for his nominee who, in the meantime, took up the position. He enjoyed a general Sultanic dispensation, allowing him to preach, until his personal diploma of appointment arrived from the capital. This meant that there was no break in the Friday prayer, and no cessation of royal authority.

The Sultan also maintained control of where the Friday prayer could be performed. The law made it compulsory in towns with a congregation and a Muslim judge, and forbade it in villages. The outskirts of towns and places where Muslims congregate on pilgrimage were matters for juristic dispute. In the Ottoman Empire, what determined its legality was royal permission:

> (6) For more than thirty years, the Festival Prayer has been held in an oratory outside the town. Is it still permissible for the Festival Prayer to be performed, when it is not known whether or not it has been performed with the Sultan's permission?
>
> *Answer*: It is permissible. In the year 944/1537, there was a general Sultanic permission to let the preachers of the great mosques perform prayers at the oratories of those towns that have them. However, oratories created [after the date of the decree] require [a separate] permission. [*H*, p. 26]

Festival prayer is subject to the same rules as Friday prayer. By insisting that it takes place only in places which he has authorised, and that the prayer-leaders are the preachers of great mosques, whom he has licensed, the Sultan is here bringing its performance under his direct authority. The date of the decree is the same as Ebu's-su'ud's accession to the post of Military Judge, suggesting that he was its initiator.

In this case, permission to perform the prayer was general. In other cases, it might be necessary to seek a specific authorisation:

> (7) A mosque in a town has no congregation, and so ordinary prayer is not performed there. On Friday, the people of the surrounding villages gather and perform Friday prayer in the said mosque. Is this permissible in law?
>
> *Answer*: Some authorities have considered it permissible, so long as the Sultan allows it. [*D*, 287]

Here, Ebu's-su'ud invokes a minority juristic opinion to permit the prayer, so long as it has the consent of the Sultan. For him, as for the Hanafi jurists, the essential thing is to ensure that the Friday prayer, as the symbol of sovereign power, always remains under the control of the monarch.

Taxation

No government can survive without revenue, and it is for this reason that Sarakhsi identifies taxation as one of the areas which are subject to direct royal control. The problem was that, apart from the poll-tax, the revenues which the Sultans raised did not correspond with the theoretical imposts of the Hanafi tradition. This dichotomy between juristic theory and Ottoman practice became an issue in the late fifteenth century, and was to remain so in succeeding ages. A treatise on customs revenue, dedicated to Bayezid II (1481–1512), exemplifies this new-found concern. The Turkish term for customs, *gümrük*, derives from the Greek word *kommerkion*, suggesting that the Ottomans, in levying customs duty, simply adapted pre-existing practices. The author of the treatise, however, uses the Arabic term for customs which was current in Hanafi texts and, in his introduction, bemoans the fact that 'not one of the learned class has instructed the just Sultan [Bayezid] in the lawful method' of collecting customs dues. In the treatise, he intends to do this, using 'respected books, like the *Hidaya* and the *Wiqaya*'.[43] The treatise had no effect whatever on Ottoman practice, but is important in that it signals a wish to bring taxation into conformity with Hanafi ideals. It was in the end Ebu's-su'ud who redefined Ottoman taxation and the system of land tenure on which it largely depended, in terms which he borrowed wholly from the Hanafi tradition. It is above all for this achievement that Ottoman tradition credits him with having reconciled the *shari'a* with the *qanun*. This will be the subject of a separate chapter.[44]

He shows the same concern to reconcile juristic theory with reality in a reply to a letter from the Khan of the Crimea, Devlet Girey (1551–77), who had enquired whether the law obliged him to pay alms-tax (*zakat*) on the wealth in his treasury. The scholars of the Crimea had disagreed on this point. The Khan's request was admirably pious but, to say the least, eccentric. Not only is it unusual to find rulers wondering whether they should pay tax, but the alms-tax had no real existence outside the pages of the jurists. It is a theoretical impost on Muslims owning property of more than a fixed minimum value, destined for the support of the indigent, and classified as an act of worship. Ebu's-su'ud nonetheless gave a detailed reply:

(8) ... The performance of acts of worship, whether physical [such as prayer or fasting] or financial [such as the payment of alms-tax], is a binding decree and obligatory order imposed on all individuals. [Revenue raised through the canonical taxes] is property that does not enter into your noble ownership. It is a claim of the Muslim public, which is at the disposal of Sultans, the income and expenditure of which is entrusted to their sound judgement.

There are four categories [of tax], each of which has a separate depository, each called a treasury (*bait al-mal*). One is the depository for the fifth, the alms-tax and tithes. One is the depository for the tribute from Russia. The fixed and proportional tribute on land (*kharaj muwazzaf, kharaj muqasama*) is also in this treasury. One is the depository for the estates of those who die without heirs. One is the depository for treasure trove.

The wealth in these four depositories is not the property of the Sultans. Each one [is reserved for] specific expenditures, and the Sultan needs do no more than to expend [the income] in its proper place. Wealth which legally accrues to the Sultan by other means is his [personal] property, on which the alms-tax is an obligatory impost.

The revenue of the salt-pans, as set forth in the letter – that is the selling price of the salt which is extracted – is property. The adjunction of Sultanic coercion in extraction and [revenue-]collection does not impair its quality as property. As for the revenues of the mint, so long as they do not accrue from metal, or from the fifth [portion of minerals extracted from the ground and in law due to the sovereign], but consist of the rent from workshops held in ownership, these too are property. There is absolutely no ambiguity about the quality as property of the Sultan's annual income (*salyane-yi sultaniyye*).

In these and similar things, there is no room for hesitation or doubt about the necessity of [paying] the alms tax [on them]. [*K*, f. 67b]

In making a distinction between the wealth of the treasury and the privately-owned wealth of the ruler, Ebu's-su'ud is here following the juristic tradition precisely. For the jurists, the treasury (*bait al-mal*) is property in the joint ownership of all members of the Muslim community. He is also following the tradition in postulating that there are four treasuries, each responsible for specific expenditures. He defines the Crimean revenues as far as possible in terms which he borrows from the jurists as, for example, in his definition of taxes on land as fixed and proportional tribute. He is careful, however, not to specify the expenditure of each treasury, stating merely that the revenues should be spent 'in their proper place'. To stipulate, as did the jurists, that the income was for the support of orphans, the destitute and bondsmen, would have been to stretch reality too far. The definition of revenues from the salt-pans as the Khan's private property must reflect the status of salt-extraction as a royal monopoly.

Once he has made the distinction between what belongs to the Muslim public in joint ownership and what belongs to the Khan as private property, Ebu's-su'ud is able to answer the Khan's question. The alms-tax is theoretically payable by persons of full legal capacity on property above a certain minimum value, consisting either of gold or silver, trade goods or cattle. So any revenue coming to the Khan as private property is liable to the tax. Whether he duly disbursed the tax to the poor, whom the law identifies as its rightful recipients, is another matter. The interest of the text is as an example of Ebu's-su'ud's attempting to adapt juristic theory to reality.

The Spoils of War

The third area where, in Hanafi theory, the monarch exercises exclusive authority is the spoils of war. The law entitles the ruler to a fifth share of all plunder taken in a holy war, and assigns the ownership of booty to individuals only after distribution by the ruler. War booty, particularly in the form of slaves, provided an important source of income for both the Ottoman Sultans and their subjects. For the troops in the Ottoman armies, the opportunity for rapine and pillage was the major consolation for the miseries of warfare, and the formalistic Hanafi rules were hardly relevant to their activities. Nonetheless, from the late fifteenth century onwards, the Sultans in particular, and some of their more pious subjects, clearly wished to establish a legitimate basis for the ownership of slaves and goods taken in war. This is again an area where Ebu's-su'ud tried to harmonise theory with reality.

The first question was whether the conflict which produced the booty was a legitimate holy war. Hostilities against fellow Muslims, for example, are not holy war, and not, therefore, a lawful mode of acquisition. Campaigns against Christians are, but even here there could be doubts. A case in point is when the Muslim ruler has a treaty with the enemy. This problem arose notoriously in 1570, when Sultan Selim II (1566–74) planned to attack the Venetian island of Cyprus in contravention of a treaty with Venice. The question of legality was put to Ebu's-su'ud:

(9) A land was previously in the realm of Islam. After a while, the abject infidels overran it, destroyed the colleges and mosques, and left them vacant. They filled the pulpits and the galleries with the tokens of infidelity and error, intending to insult the religion of Islam with all kinds of vile deeds, and by spreading their ugly acts to all corners of the earth.

His Excellency the Sultan, the Refuge of Religion, has, as zeal for Islam requires, determined to take the aforementioned land from the possession of the shameful infidels and to annex it to the realm of Islam.

When peace was previously concluded with the other lands in the possession of the said infidels, the aforenamed land was included. An explanation is sought as to whether, in accordance with the Pure *shari'a*, this is an impediment to the Sultan's determining to break the treaty.

Answer: There is no possibility that it could ever be an impediment. For the Sultan of the people of Islam (may God glorify his victories) to make peace with the infidels is legal only when there is a benefit to all Muslims. When there is no benefit, peace is never legal. When a benefit has been seen, and it is then observed to be more beneficial to break it, then to break it becomes absolutely obligatory and binding.

His Excellency [Muhammad] the Apostle of God (may God bless him and give him peace) made a ten-year truce with the Meccan infidels in the sixth year of the Hegira. His Excellency 'Ali (may God ennoble his face) wrote a document that was corroborated and confirmed. Then, in the following year, it was considered more beneficial to break it and, in the eighth year of the Hegira, [the Prophet] attacked [the Meccans], and conquered Mecca the Mighty.

His Excellency the Caliph of the Lord of the Worlds [Selim II] (may God Most High make the shadow of his sultanate eternal over the heads of Muslims, and support him with mighty assistance and clear victory) has, in his imperial actions, been guided by the noble acts of His Excellency the Bearer of Prophecy (may God bless him and give him peace). With the grace of God, the King and Helper, it will be the precursor to a clear victory. [*D*, 478]

Here, Ebu's-su'ud gives the answer which the Sultan requires while, at the same time, ignoring the questioner's tendentious line of reasoning. Cyprus, Islamic tradition asserts, had been a Muslim island which the infidels had reconquered, and therefore properly belongs to the realm of Islam. The implication of the question is that a treaty which allows the infidels to remain in occupation is for this reason invalid. Ebu's-su'ud takes no account of this argument, citing instead the basic Hanafi rule that treaties with infidels are valid only when they are beneficial to Muslims, who should break them when they cease to be so. In a manner typical of the Hanafi jurists, he supports the rule with a precedent from the career of the Prophet. In invading Cyprus therefore, the Sultan was simply taking the Prophet as his model, and the invasion was a legitimate holy war.[45]

In the sixteenth century, however, Cyprus was a unique case of a broken treaty. A more common legal and ideological problem which the Ottomans faced was to justify warfare against fellow Muslims. The most obvious strategy which the law had to offer was to present the enemy as 'rebels' against the just ruler, that is, against the Ottoman Sultan. This justified warfare. It did not, however, justify the seizure of booty. The sultan could not levy the fifth on what his warriors captured, nor could his warriors acquire ownership since, after the defeat of rebels, the booty returns to its original owners or their heirs.

The only large-scale and prolonged wars which Süleyman I and his successors waged against Muslims were against the Safavid dynasty of Iran, with one major campaign between 1549 and 1555 coinciding with Ebu's-su'ud's period of office as Mufti. The first Safavid Shah, Isma'il I, had come to power in 1501 as the charismatic leader of a mystic Order, which had a wide following among the Ottoman Sultan's subjects in Anatolia. Furthermore, Isma'il and his successors had established Shi'ism as the dominant form of Islam in Iran, and carried out an active campaign of proselytisation in the Ottoman realms. To counter this mortal danger to their rule, the Ottoman Sultans from early in the century not only waged war against the Safavids, but also developed a counter-propaganda.[46] This presented the Iranian Shahs as arch-heretics, who arrogated to themselves claims of divinity and who, as Shi'ites, abjured true Sunni Islam and cursed the Rightly Guided Caliphs whom the Sunnis revere. It was only the Ottoman Sultan who stood as a bastion in defence of orthodox Islam. This view of the Sultan as the defender of the faith against Safavid heresy not only became a major prop in the legitimisation of Ottoman rule, it also allowed Ebu's-su'ud to present hostilities against the Safavids as holy war:

(10) Is it licit according to the *shari'a* to fight the followers of the Safavids? Is the person who kills them a holy warrior, and the person who dies at their hands a martyr?
Answer: Yes, it is a great holy war and a glorious martyrdom.

Another question: Assuming that it is licit to fight them, is this simply because of their rebellion and enmity against the [Ottoman] Sultan of the People of Islam, because they drew the sword against the troops of Islam, or what?
Answer: They are both rebels and, from many points of view, infidels. [D, 479]

By thus declaring the Safavids and their followers to be infidels, Ebu's-su'ud is defining war against them as holy war, and therefore not merely licit but obligatory.

By these and similar means, the Ottoman Sultans were able to present all their campaigns as holy wars. In a holy war, the law permits the troops to take plunder, and the ruler to tax their spoil, and it is clear that the Ottoman Sultans did in fact claim a percentage of war booty. What is probably the earliest attempt to codify the practice survives in a decree of 1493, which lays out, in over optimistic detail, the rules governing the royal levy on youths and cattle captured on the European frontier of the Empire.[47] A parallel decree which survives in a copy of 1511 sets out the rates at which the Sultan took a toll on slaves being brought across the Bosphorus at Istanbul.[48] Neither tax is levied at the rate of one fifth, and so neither in practice corresponds to the fifth of the holy law. Nonetheless, a popular etymology served to appease the consciences of the pious. The Turkish term for both the direct levy of slaves and cattle, and for the transit toll, is *penjik*, a word of obscure origin which, in Arabic script, has precisely the same form as the Persian *panj-yak*, meaning 'one fifth'. This etymology was enough to show that the tax was indeed the canonical fifth.

In legal theory, an individual can acquire ownership of booty only after the extraction of the fifth, and only after distribution by the ruler or commander, preferably in the realm of Islam. This rule is clearly quite impractical, and it is unlikely that, before the mid-sixteenth century, the Sultans concerned themselves with anything except their own share of the spoil. By about 1540, however, the question of how individuals acquire rightful ownership had clearly become an issue:

> (11) There is doubt as to whether the booty was distributed among the warriors of Islam in the legal manner. In this case, is it in any way blameworthy, without marriage, to have intercourse with slave girls bought from them?
> *Answer*: [In our time] there is no canonical division of spoil. In the year 948/1541–2, there was a general pre-distribution of spoil (*tanfil*). After paying the *penjik*, no doubt remains. [*H*, p. 31]

The question here involves legal ownership. A man may not have intercourse with a woman without ownership, which he can acquire by purchasing her as a slave, or by marrying her and paying her a dower.[49] In the case of purchase, the sale is valid only if the goods were the property of the seller. If the vendor of a female slave acquired her as booty, but without the division of spoil as the law requires, he is not her owner. The sale of the slave is therefore invalid, the purchaser does not become her owner, and intercourse with her is illegal. In answer to the question, Ebu's-su'ud points to a Sultanic decree of 1541–2, giving Ottoman soldiers a general permission to keep their plunder. It became their fully-owned property immediately after the levy of the *penjik*. In reality, the decree was doing no more than to legitimise what had always been the practice. Its importance is that it did it with reference to Hanafi law. The jurists somewhat reluctantly permitted the ruler to pre-distribute booty before battle, and the decree of 1541–2 generalised this rule, making it effective for all campaigns and, in so doing, bringing Ottoman practice within the scope of the *shari'a*. The decree again dates from Ebu's-su'ud's period as Military Judge and, again, he was very probably its instigator.

The decree was clearly applicable in all wars against Christian adversaries, confirming that, after the levy of the *penjik*, all booty became the property of the looter. The legal status of plunder from war against the Safavids was more problematical. Ebu's-su'ud and Muftis before him had declared the Safavids to be infidels and campaigns against them to be holy wars, but a problem remained. Since they claimed to be Muslims, the Safavids were clearly not infidels in the same sense as Christians and Jews, to whom the term usually applied. As a result, the normal legal rules governing the spoils of war did not apply. The following case makes this clear. The Sultan had ordered that the followers of the Safavids, evidently meaning adult males, should be killed. The question then was whether their children could be enslaved:

(12) Can the children of Safavid subjects captured in the Nakhichevan campaign be enslaved?
Answer: No. [*D*, 482]

Had Ebu's-su'ud regarded the Safavids as straightforward infidels, the answer would have been yes. The reason for his refusal to allow enslavement becomes clear when he answers a question on female captives:

(13) According to a tradition related from Abu Hanifa, it is permissible to take captive a female apostate before she reaches the realm of war ... Is it permissible to act according to this tradition?
Answer: Yes. [*D*, 484]

If women are taken prisoner in accordance with this tradition, are their services licit, and is intercourse with them licit according to the *shari'a*?
Answer: All their services are licit, but they are apostates. Intercourse with them is not licit until they accept Islam. [*D*, 485]

The Safavids then were apostates. By the laws of apostasy, it was obligatory to kill their adult males and to imprison their women. An apostate, however, man or woman, cannot marry, and an apostate woman is a prisoner but not a slave, and so not subject to ownership. The law forbids sexual intercourse without ownership acquired through marriage or enslavement, and so intercourse with a captured Safavid woman is forbidden.

Nor did Ebu's-su'ud permit the enslavement of Christian subjects of the Safavids:

(14) The followers of the Safavids are killed by order of the Sultan. If it turns out that some of the prisoners, young and old, are Armenian, are they set free?
Answer: Yes. So long as the Armenians have not joined the Safavid troops in attacking and fighting against the troops of Islam, it is illegal to take them prisoner. [*D*, 483]

Since the Armenians were not subject to a Christian sovereignty, they were not technically enemies dwelling in the realm of war, and since they were not, in a religious sense, followers of the Safavid Shah, they were not apostates. To kill, imprison or enslave them was, for this reason, illegal.

In Ebu's-su'ud's view, therefore, prisoners captured in the wars with Iran were not subject to the same statutes as prisoners taken in the Sultan's campaigns in Europe. The difference arises from the definition of European foes as 'enemies' in its conventional legal sense, and the Safavids as 'apostates', to whom different laws apply. In both cases, however, Ebu's-su'ud is clearly anxious to bring Ottoman practice more or less into harmony with Hanafi precepts.

The Fixed Penalties

The last area of the law which Sarakhsi assigns to the exclusive authority of the ruler is the fixed penalties. These are the punishments for fornication, false accusation of fornication, wine-drinking, theft and highway robbery. The punishment for fornication is, according to the status of the offender, stoning or the lash. For false accusation of fornication, and for wine-drinking, it is the lash. Theft incurs the amputation of a hand, and highway robbery the amputation of a hand and foot for stealing, and crucifixion for killing. These penalties differ from the punishments for homicide, wounding, misappropriation and damage to property, in that they do not depend upon the principle of compensation, and in that the victim of the offence or his heirs do not have the right to waive the claim to the punishment. The punishment is a 'claim of God' and its infliction a duty that belongs solely to the ruler. To this extent, the concept of the fixed penalties resembles the concept of a criminal law.

To equate the fixed penalties with criminal law is, however, misleading. Of the offences which incur fixed penalties, only highway robbery satisfies the strict definition of a crime. For most offences of violence committed within a community, Hanafi law makes the community itself responsible for bringing assistance and, in cases of homicide where the killer is unknown, for defraying the blood-money paid to the heirs of the victim. Responsibility for law and order therefore falls on the community, and responsibility for taking blood-money falls on the deceased's next-of-kin.[50] Highway robbery, however, occurs on the open road, far from any community that could bring assistance to the victim. Responsibility for maintaining order there, and for punishing offenders, therefore falls on the public authority. In this sense, highway robbery is a criminal offence.

This is not, however, strictly true of fornication, false accusation, theft and wine-drinking. The classification of these offences and the penalties for them does not in any sense arise out of the structural logic of the law, but solely out of scriptural authority. With the exception of stoning for fornication, the Quran itself specifies the penalties, which it is then the duty of the ruler to execute. This, at least, is the theory. In practice, the infliction of the punishments for fornication and theft is impossible, since the rules of procedure are so strict. A successful prosecution for fornication, for example, requires four male eyewitnesses to the act, whose probity the judge has 'publicly and secretly' to investigate. The procedure in cases of false accusation is less rigorous, but this is simply because the punishment acts as a further deterrent to anyone trying to bring to law cases of fornication. A successful prosecution for wine-drinking is difficult, although not quite impossible. With the exception of highway robbery, therefore, the fixed penalties are not legal realities. The jurists have a theological explanation for this phenomenon. The fixed penalties, they argue, are claims of God, and God has no need of a human agency to execute his will.[51]

In rendering the execution of the fixed penalties difficult or impossible, the jurists create a paradox. They declare that the punishments are an area of the ruler's sole authority, and essential for the well-being of the Muslim community, and then remove them from the realm of practical law. Nonetheless, the theory of the fixed penalties did have important effects, both practical and symbolic, on Ottoman government.

The area where the theory corresponds most closely with reality is highway robbery. Public security is obviously the first duty of any government, and, since brigandage was endemic in the Ottoman countryside, it was a constant concern to the Ottoman Sultans. The innumerable decrees ordering provincial authorities to execute or otherwise punish highwaymen and brigands in practice owes nothing to the juristic prescriptions for highway robbery, but Ebu's-su'ud had no difficulty in equating acts of lawlessness in the countryside with highway robbery in a technical juristic sense. In replies to questions on the subject, he lays out in detail the juristic scheme of punishment:

(15) There are some brigands in a province, masquerading as college students. They abduct certain Muslims' sons and then, when their guardians come to seek them, they refuse to give them up or, in some cases, give back their sons for money. They unlawfully seize the sheep belonging to certain Muslims. Others they seize and, hanging them by the arms, subject them to severe beating and torture. They seize large sums of money and divide it among themselves. Their wrongdoing and oppression exceed all bounds. What should be done to them?
Answer: If the aforenamed are not between two villages or towns; if they are a group capable of force and violence, who gather in a cave at least a journey's distance from a town; if they waylay Muslims and seize their property; and if [the stolen property] amounts to ten *dirham*s for each of them [when divided]; in this case, those whose hands and feet are sound, have their left hand and right foot amputated.

If they waylay a man and kill him, then, as the fixed penalty, the ruler executes them. If the heirs of the dead man forgive [them, their pardon] is disregarded.

If each took the [minimum] sum of [ten *dirhams* for which the penalty becomes due] and also killed a person, then the ruler has a choice. If he wishes, he may amputate their left hands and right feet, and then crucify them; or he may crucify them immediately. If he wishes, he may crucify them and split their sides with a spear.

After the punishment [has been inflicted], if any of the property which they took remains, it is given back to its owners. If it has been lost, they are not compensated ...[52] [*D*, 735]

It is hardly likely that Ebu's-su'ud would have expected anyone to take literally either the precise definition of highway robbers, or the prescription for their punishment. All he is doing by his answer is to bring the everyday government activity of pursuing bandits within the scope of the *shari'a*. Having done this, in answer to a supplementary question, he cites a Hanafi tradition which gives a much less restrictive definition of a highwayman:

(16) There is a tradition from Abu Yusuf. If they intend to waylay with a weapon within a town, they are highway robbers. Similarly, if they intend to kill someone with sticks or stones outside a city, in a place where no assistance is available; or in the city itself at night, they are also highway robbers. If they intend to kill with sticks and stones by day [in a town], the law for highway robbery does not apply. [*D*, 736]

With some elasticity of interpretation, this ruling brings most acts of armed robbery and affray under the authority of the ruler, and offers a canonical justification for the Sultan's peacekeeping activities.

Highway robbery, however, is the area where the laws of the fixed penalties engage most closely with reality. Fornication and wine-drinking are different, since the clear intention of the jurists is that the penalties should never be inflicted. These punishments are therefore not so much real, as symbolic of the enormity of the offence in the eyes of God, and it is as symbols that they came to play a role in the Ottoman practice of government. They came, above all, to form a standard ingredient in the indictment of heretics.

In the sixteenth century, heresy was a major concern of the Ottoman government. As the Sultans, especially in response to Safavid propaganda, began to project an image of themselves as the leaders and sole defenders of Sunni Islam, any challenge to the tenets of orthodoxy became, in effect, a challenge to the legitimacy of Ottoman rule. Loyalty to the Sultan and loyalty to Sunni Islam became one and the same, and the Sultan's role as defender of the faith obliged his government to identify and eliminate heretics.

The task was not easy, since the variety of beliefs and practices in the Ottoman Empire was as heterogeneous as the Muslim population itself. Above all, the theology and rituals of the numerous mystic Orders often ran directly counter to orthodox belief, and did at times arouse controversy and the hostility of the orthodox pious. Nonetheless, for the Sultan to attack the Orders and ban the many varieties of folk Islam would have served no purpose. For the most part, they posed no threat to the established political order and to declare them illegal would simply have stirred up opposition. Instead, the Ottoman government applied to suspected heretics a very simple loyalty test. The jurists divide human acts into two categories, the licit (*halal*) and the forbidden (*haram*), with licit acts further subdivided into the categories of obligatory (*wajib*), morally indifferent (*mubah*) and reprehensible (*makruh*). The obligatory acts comprise, above all, the acts of worship, such as formal prayer and fasting in Ramadan. The forbidden acts include fornication and wine-drinking. The test for heresy was by examination of the suspect's views on the licit and forbidden. If he held illicit acts to be permissible, or obligatory acts to be voluntary, then he had abjured the *shari'a* and was a heretic. In a letter giving guidance for the conduct of a heresy trial in the 1560s, Ebu's-su'ud began his instructions: 'Let it be clear that if the words attributed to the aforenamed concerning ... the licit and the forbidden are proven ... then his heresy and unbelief are certain'.[53]

The licit and the forbidden thus became the touchstone of belief. If a person declared, for example, that fasting was not obligatory or that wine-drinking was licit, he was a heretic. If a person actually drank wine, this was, in general, a matter between himself and God, but if he openly declared wine to be licit, this was a public offence. The declaration made him an apostate who no longer enjoyed the protection of the law and whom the ruler could therefore execute:

(17) Zeyd is a wine-drinker. While he is drinking wine, he – we take refuge in God – curses, using the f. word, and says: 'Wine's a brilliant thing. It's a lovely thing. I'll so-and-so anybody's wife who doesn't drink it!' 'Amr applauds Zeyd, saying: 'You're right!' What should happen?
Answer: They are both infidels. It is permissible to kill them. [*D*, 509]

Of the illicit acts, wine-drinking and fornication were the most potently symbolic, and it unsurprising therefore to find that they often appear among the accusations which the Ottoman authorities laid against heretical groups whom they suspected of disloyalty to the Sultan. These acts were especially shocking to orthodox Muslims, and, by claiming that suspected heretics regularly indulged in them, the authorities could 'prove' that they had declared the forbidden to be licit, and so justify their execution. The following fatwa of Ebu's-su'ud is typical:

(18) When some members of the Semavetlü sect drink wine, they permit each other to have disposal of one another's wives. What should happen to them?
Answer: It is legally binding to kill them. [*D*, 970]

It is most unlikely that heretics really behaved in this way, but the fact that people were prepared to believe that they did is an indication of the important place which wine-drinking and fornication, both offences which incur fixed penalties, occupy in Muslim belief, and an indicator of how these offences were of direct concern to the ruler.

The canonical prohibition on wine-drinking had another effect on public policy when, from time to time, the Ottoman Sultans issued decrees closing wine-shops as 'tokens of unbelief' in the Ottoman capital. This they usually did at the outset of major military campaigns in an effort to elicit divine support for their army, although the repetitions of the commands indicate that they never had more than a temporary effect. Süleyman I, under Ebu's-su'ud's influence, even extended the ban to coffee-houses, the first of which had opened in Istanbul in 1554. Ebu's-su'ud, presumably on the grounds that coffee, like wine, is an intoxicant, had declared it to be morally reprehensible:

(19) Zeyd drinks coffee to aid concentration or digestion. Is this licit?
Answer: How can anyone consume this reprehensible [substance], which dissolute men drink when engaged in games and debauchery? [*D*, 722]

There was, furthermore, a fear that coffee-shops, like wine-shops, would lead to a collapse of public order:

(20) The Sultan, the Refuge of Religion, has on many occasions banned coffee-houses. However, a group of ruffians take no notice, but keep coffee-houses for a living. In order to draw the crowds, they take on unbearded apprentices, and have ready instruments of entertainment and play, such as chess and backgammon. The city's rakes, rogues and vagabond boys gather there to consume opium and hashish. On top of this, they drink coffee and, when they are high, engage in games and false sciences, and neglect the prescribed prayers. In law, what should happen to a judge who is able to prevent the said coffee-sellers and drinkers, but does not do so?

Answer: Those who perpetrate these ugly deeds should be prevented and deterred by severe chastisement and long imprisonment. Judges who neglect to deter them should be dismissed. [*D*, 724]

Wine and coffee-drinking in public came, for the Ottoman authorities, to symbolise defiance of the ordinances of the *shari'a* and therefore by extension, a defiance of the will of the Sultan and a threat to public safety.

In certain senses, therefore, the offences which incur fixed penalties did form an area of the law which came under the direct authority of the ruler, although clearly not in a manner that Sarakhsi had envisaged. First, Ebu's-su'ud was able to invoke the rules on highway robbery to justify the Sultan's actions against highwaymen and brigands. Second, the classification of wine-drinking and fornication as offences against God gave them a unique power to shock the pious, providing the authorities with a potent accusation to lay against heretics whom they suspected of disloyalty to the Sultan. Finally, and again in the sphere of public order, Ebu's-su'ud used the canonical ban on wine to justify the closure of taverns and coffee-houses. Such pious measures, apart from securing divine approval, provided a legal focus and an illusion of firm action in the face of panics over the imagined breakdown of public morality.

What the Sultans did not do was actually to impose the fixed penalties for the offences, since the rules of procedure were too strict to make this a possibility. Ironically, however, this had the effect of greatly extending the ruler's authority. In addition to the fixed penalties, the jurists recognise the power of the executive authorities to exercise discretionary punishment, which they usually understood to mean flogging, imprisonment or, with the greatest reluctance, money fines. The jurists reserve discretionary punishment for a residual category of offence that does not incur talion, blood-money, compensation for damage, or one of the fixed penalties. In practice, however, the unreality of the canonical rules governing the fixed penalties and related areas of the law had the effect of pushing most punishments into the discretionary category. The jurists do not define what constitutes a discretionary offence. Ebu's-su'ud, for example, was able to bring coffee-drinking into this category. Nor do they lay down rules of procedure. The result was to bring the punishment of most offences under the authority of the ruler to deal with as he wished, with no juristic restraints.[54] This was also the case in the Ottoman Empire, where criminal law was subject to the secular jurisdiction of the Sultans.

Hanafi Theory and Ottoman Practice: A Summary

The Hanafi view of legal authority had an important effect on the Ottoman practice of government, most notably in limiting the power of the Sultan. Except in the admittedly vital areas of land tenure, taxation and crime, which fell within the scope of the *qanun*, it was Hanafi law that the courts applied, and which the Sultan himself had no competence to abrogate or modify. The *qanun* he could regulate by decree, but even here the force of custom set narrow limits on his authority. In the legal sphere, therefore, the scope of the Sultan's practical influence was modest, and far removed from the image of the centralising, absolute monarch on which modern historiography insists.

In practice therefore, the *shari'a*, and to some extent also the *qanun*, were factors limiting the authority of the monarch. What the Sultan did, however, and especially through the formulations of Ebu's-su'ud, was to co-opt the *shari'a* and, to a lesser extent, the *qanun*, to bolster his own claim to political legitimacy. This mirrored, on a larger scale, what the Sultans had always done, when they arrogated to the dynasty the merits of Holy War, which the jurists define as a communal and not as a royal or individual obligation. The Hanafi jurists themselves clearly demarcated political and juristic authority, defining a rightful ruler as anyone who successfully seizes and holds on to power, while jealously preserving their own role as guardians of the substance of the law, independent of the authority of the governor. Ebu's-su'ud, however, presented the rule of the Ottoman Sultan as a necessary precondition to the rule of the *shari'a* and, more boldly still, projected an image of the person of the Sultan as the agent through whom God put into effect the *shari'a* on this earth. This notion that it is the Sultan who 'makes manifest the Exalted Word of God' and 'expounds the signs of the luminous *shari'a*' has the effect of undermining the juristic notion that the sovereign has unmediated authority only in four areas of the law.

Nonetheless, under Ebu's-su'ud's influence, these 'four areas' came to occupy an important place in Ottoman imperial consciousness and, to some extent, on the actual functioning of government, despite the fact that, with the exception of Friday prayer, they are the areas of Hanafi law that had least application in practice. The Sultanic decree ordering the 'general pre-distribution' of booty, and the redefinition of Ottoman taxes in Hanafi terms, may not have made much difference to what the government did in reality, but both measures created an image of rule by the *shari'a*, and of the harmonisation of secular administration with divine law. Again, the offences which incur fixed penalties, while having no applicability in practice, acquired a great symbolic importance in defining loyalty to the *shari'a*, which, with Ebu's-su'ud's identification of the rule of the Sultan with the rule of the *shari'a*, came to be identified with loyalty to the Ottoman dynasty.

Notes

1. Norman Calder, 'Friday prayer and the juristic theory of government: Sarakhsi, Shirazi, Mawardi', *Bulletin of the School of Oriental and African Studies*, 49 (1986), 35–47.
2. Qadikhan, *al-Fatawa al-Khaniyya*, Bulaq: Imperial Press (1912/13), vol. 1, p. 173.
3. Ibn Humam, *Fath al-Qadir*, Cairo: Matba'a Mustafa al-Babi al-Halabi (1972), vol. 2, p. 53.
4. al-Marghinani, *al-Hidaya*, Cairo: Matba'a Mustafa al-Babi al-Halabi (1972), vol. 7, p. 263.
5. Baber Johansen, 'Sacred and religious element in hanafite law – function and limits of the absolute character of government authority', in Ernest Gellner and Jean-Claude Vatin (eds), *Islam et Politique au Maghreb*, Paris (1981), pp. 281–303.
6. al-Sarakhsi, *al-Mabsut*, Beirut: Dar el-Marefah (1982), vol. 9, p. 81.
7. Ibn Humam, *Fath*, vol. 5, p. 434.
8. al-Marghinani, *al-Hidaya*, vol. 5, p. 457.
9. Ibid., pp. 473–4.
10. Ibid., vol. 6, p. 22.
11. Qadikhan, *al-Fatawa*, vol. 3, p. 589.
12. Baber Johansen, 'Der *'isma*-Begriff im hanafitischen Recht', *Actes du VIIIe Congrès International des Arabisants et Islamisants*, Aix-en-Provence: Edisud (1978), pp. 97–101.
13. al-Marghinani, *al-Hidaya*, vol. 6, p. 72.
14, Qadikhan, *al-Fatawa*, vol. 3, p. 581.
15. Ibid., p. 580.
16. al-Marghinani, *al-Hidaya*, vol. 6, p. 70.
17. Ibid., p. 104.
18. Ibid.
19. Ibid., p. 105
20. Ibid., p. 106.
21. Ibn Humam, *Fath*, vol. 6, p. 106.
22. Qadikhan, *al-Fatawa*, vol. 3, p. 558.
23. Ibid.
24. Quran 8:41.
25. Quran 9:60.
26. Colin Imber, 'The Ottoman dynastic myth', *Turcica*, 19 (1987), 7–27.
27. Gülru Necipoğlu, 'Süleyman the Magnificent and the representation of power in the context of Ottoman–Hapsburg–Papal rivalry', in H. İnalcık and Cemal Kafadar (eds), *Süleyman the Second and his Time*, Istanbul: Isis Press (1993), pp. 161–94. M. Köhbach, *'Çasar oder imperator?* Zur Titulatur der römischen Kaiser durch die Osmanen nach dem Vertrag von Zsitvatorok (1606)', *Wiener Zeitschrift für die Kunde des Morgenlandes*, 82 (1992), 223–34.
28. Anton C. Schaendlinger and Claudia Römer, *Die Schreiben Süleymans des Prächtigen an Karl V., Ferdinand I und Maximilian II*, Vienna: Verlag der Österreichischen Akademie der Wissenschaften (1983), pp. 11–18.
29. Stephane Yérasimos, *La Fondation de Constantinople et de Sainte Sophie*, Bibliothèque de l'Institut Français d'Etudes Anatoliennes d'Istanbul, 31, Paris: Librairie d'Amérique et d'Orient, (1990), p. 221.

30. Gülru Necipoğlu, 'The Süleymaniye complex in Istanbul: an interpretation', *Muqarnas*, 3 (1985), 93–117.
31. Cevdet Çulpan, 'Istanbul Süleymaniye Camii kitabesi', *Kanunî Armağanı*, Ankara: Turkish Historical Society, Series 7, no. 55, pp. 291–9.
32. Ö. L. Barkan, *Kanunlar*, Istanbul: Burhaneddin Matbaası (1943), p. 296.
33. Ebu's-su'ud, *Risala fi mas'alat al-mash 'ala'l-khuffain*, Library of the Topkapı Palace, Istanbul, ms A1,541, f. 371b.
34. Ebu's-su'ud, *Risala*, f. 371b.
35. Ebu's-su'ud, *Irshad al-'aql al-salim ila mazaya al-kitab al-karim*, in margin of Fakhr al-Din Razi, *Mafatih al-ghaib*, Istanbul: Imperial Press (1872/3), p. 26.
36. Ö. L. Barkan, *Kanunlar*, p. 296.
37. Ibid.
38. See below, Chapter 4.
39. Colin Imber, 'The Ottoman dynastic myth'.
40. Ö. L. Barkan, *Kanunlar*, pp. 296, 297.
41. V. L. Ménage, 'Sidelights on the devshirme from Idris and Sa'duddin', *Bulletin of the School of Oriental and African Studies*, 18 (1956), 181–3.
42. On the question of the legal status of the Sultan's slaves, see V. L. Ménage, 'Some notes on the devshirme', *Bulletin of the School of Oriental and African Studies*, 29 (1966), 64–78; R. C. Repp, 'A further note on the devshirme', *Bulletin of the School of Oriental and African Studies*, 31 (1968), 137–9; İ. Metin Kunt, 'Kulların kulları', *Boğaziçi Üniversitesi Dergisi*, 3 (1975), 27–42.
43. Bunyad b. Maulana Muhammad, *al-Risalat al-'ashiriyya*, Library of the Topkapı Palace, Istanbul, ms Koğuşlar 770, f. 2a.
44. See below, Chapter 5.
45. On this fatwa, see V. L. Ménage, 'The English capitulations of 1580: a review article', *International Journal of Middle Eastern Studies*, 12 (1980), 373–83.
46. Elke Eberhard, *Osmanische Polemik gegen die Safawiden im 16. Jahrhundert nach arabischen Handschriften*, Islamkundliche Untersuchungen 3, Freiburg-im-Breisgau: Klaus Schwarz Verlag (1970).
47. İsmail Hakkı Uzunçarsılı, *Kapıkulu Ocakları*, Ankara: Turkish Historical Society (1943), pp. 86–9.
48. Ibid., pp. 89–90.
49. See below, Chapter 7.
50. See below, Chapter 9.
51. Baber Johansen, 'Eigentum, Familie und Obrigkeit im hanafitischen Strafrecht', *Die Welt des Islams*, 19 (1979), 1–73.
52. This is a floating answer. The same answer appears in Chetham's Oriental ms 7,979, f. 88a, appended to a different question.
53. 'Ata'i, *Hada'iq al-haqa'iq fi takmilat al-shaqa'iq*, Istanbul: Imperial Press (1851–2), p. 87. The reference is to the trial of Gazanfer Dede.
54. Baber Johansen, 'Eigentum'. See below, Chapter 8.

4

The Caliphate

In his lists of honorific titles, Ebu's-su'ud implies that the Sultan is both the interpreter and the executor of the *shari'a*. This is a view for which the Hanafi jurists provide no justification since, in their opinion, they are themselves the sole interpreters of the *shari'a*, and only in four areas of the law does the monarch exercise unmediated authority. Ebu's-su'ud had, therefore, to seek a justification outside the juristic tradition.

The jurists do, it is true, concede to the ruler the authority to exercise *siyasa*, a term which, in jurisprudence, has the general sense of punitive action falling outside the scope of the *shari'a*, which the legitimate sovereign exercises for the good order of society. Ibn Nujaim, for example, invokes the ruler's right to exercise *siyasa* in order to justify the execution of habitual sodomites.[1] In Ottoman usage, the term came to have the primary sense of capital punishment. In the nineteenth century, with the introduction of European political concepts into the Islamic world, it acquired the sense of 'politics', which is the meaning it has today. The jurists do not define or set limits on *siyasa*, conceding in effect that rulers have unfettered power outside the confines of the *shari'a*. Nonetheless, it was a power which Sultans had to justify. They did this usually by proclaiming that their rule – that is, their exercise of *siyasa* – creates the good order in the world which is a precondition for the rule of the *shari'a*. This claim was a commonplace, and one which Ebu's-su'ud makes in the Law-Book of Buda of 1541, where he describes the Ottoman Sultan as the one 'who makes smooth the path for the precepts of the manifest *shari'a*'.[2] Ebu's-su'ud, however, goes much further than this. In his formulation, the Sultan is also the one who himself 'makes manifest the Exalted Word [of God]', 'expounds the signs of the luminous *shari'a*'[3] and 'performs the command of the Hidden Book / And executes its decrees in all regions of the inhabited quarter'.[4] In other words, the Sultan has powers not only of *siyasa*, but also of interpreting and executing the *shari'a*, which go far beyond the strict limits which the Hanafi jurists prescribe. It was in order to justify this sweeping extension of the ruler's authority that Ebu's-su'ud invoked the theory of the Caliphate and bestowed on the Ottoman Sultan the title of Caliph.

The Caliphate in Islamic Tradition

This bold assertion of the ruler's authority is alien to mainstream Hanafi jurisprudence, theories of the Caliphate belonging to the traditions of Islamic historiography and theology rather than to the tradition of law. According to the Sunni theologians and historians, the Four Rightly Guided Caliphs, Abu Bakr, 'Umar, 'Uthman and 'Ali, were the legitimate successors to the Prophet Muhammad; and, for Sunnis, the period of their rule represents the ideal model of the Caliphate. A number of rulers and dynasties were to adopt the title Caliph, most notably the 'Abbasid rulers of Baghdad between 750 and 1258, under whose auspices Sunni theories of the Caliphate came into being.

For the Sunni theologians, the concept of the Caliphate (*khilafa*) or, to give it its alternative designation, the Imamate (*imama*), first became important when there was a need to counter the claims of the Shi'a and other heretical sects. The central tenet of the Shi'a, which distinguishes them from the Sunnis, is the belief that the first three of the Rightly Guided Caliphs were usurpers, that the Prophet himself had designated his son-in-law 'Ali, as his successor, and that thereafter the true line of succession from the Prophet was in the descendants of 'Ali. In order to counter these heretical claims, the Sunni theologians developed a theory of the Imamate which asserted the legitimacy of the first three Caliphs. That the function of the Sunni theory of the Caliphate was originally to defend the Sunni account of the succession to the Prophet is especially evident in the works of Baqillani[5] (d. 1013) and Baghdadi[6] (d. 1037). Baqillani lays out the 'true' doctrine of the Caliphate in a series of answers to questions which a heretical interlocutor might raise, and devotes much of his space to a proof of the validity of the Caliphates of Abu Bakr, 'Umar and 'Uthman. Baghdadi usually presents each item of the 'true' doctrine against a list of the erroneous views of heretics.

Since the crucial point of the Sunnis' dispute with the Shi'a is the mode of succession to the Caliphate, this is the issue which is central to the theory. The choice is between designation and election. The Shi'a maintain that the Prophet designated 'Ali as his successor. The Sunnis maintain that he designated no-one, but that his Companions elected Abu Bakr from among their number. In the Sunni tradition, the third Caliph, 'Uthman, similarly assumed the Caliphate after election. In Sunni dogma, therefore, election is the preferred mode of succession. The problem then is to determine the method.

This the theologians did by borrowing from the jurists the concept of contract. A contract (*'aqd*) in Islamic law is an agreement between two parties which changes the legal status quo, usually by effecting a transfer of property. Contracts are not, however, negotiable. Their validity depends on the fulfilment of fixed and predetermined conditions. In

order, therefore, to present the succession to the Caliphate as the outcome
of a contract between the candidate for office and the electors, the
theologians had to establish the conditions necessary for the validity of
the contract.

For Baqillani, validity was dependent essentially upon determining
the minimum number of electors and the qualifications of the candidate.
The contract, he concluded, was valid when it was 'contracted and
completed by [even only] one "man of loosing and binding"'[7]... when he
contracts it with a man who possesses the qualities obligatory to Imams'.
It was essential, too, as in a contract of marriage, that there should be
witnesses.[8] To qualify as Imam, a man had to fulfil five conditions. First,
he had to be a descendant of the Quraish, the tribe to which the Prophet
belonged. Second, he had to possess knowledge to a degree which would
qualify him to be 'a judge among Muslims'. Third, he had to be skilled in
the arts of war. Fourth, he should be a person who shows no leniency in
the infliction of the fixed penalties of the *shari'a*, or in 'striking off heads
and skins'. Fifth, he should be the most perfect of the candidates in
knowledge of things in which superior knowledge is possible.[9]

Baghdadi's view of what constitutes a valid contract is essentially the
same as Baqillani's, except that he gives a list of the various opinions on
the number of electors necessary to make the contract,[10] and his list of the
candidate's necessary qualifications is not absolutely identical.[11] Like
Baqillani, he states that there may be no more than one Imam at any one
time 'unless there is a sea between them',[12] thus invalidating any contract
with a second candidate. Again like Baqillani, he refutes the notions of
the Shi'a, that the rightful Imam is hidden and that the Imam must be
free from sin. For both Baqillani and Baghdadi, the Imam must be
present in the community and need not be sinless. If he deviates from
righteousness, the rebuke of the community will guide him to virtue.[13]

The effect of the contract with the elector or electors is to transfer the
Imamate to the candidate and to create an obligation on the community
of obedience and assistance. On the conclusion of the contract, it becomes
impossible, Baqillani says, to depose the Imam, unless he loses his
judgement or becomes insane for a sufficient period to harm the Muslim
community.[14]

Thus, in the construction of the Sunni theologians, the normal mode of
succession to the Caliphate is through a contract formed between the
candidate and one or more electors. Their analogy was clearly with the
mode of succession to property. A person can, however, acquire property
without a contract, by inheritance or testamentary bequest, and Baghdadi
therefore raises the question of whether the Imamate can descend in this
way. On the question of inheritance, he concludes that 'all who uphold
the Caliphate of Abu Bakr (i.e. the Sunnis) maintain that it is not
inherited'. Abu Bakr, in Sunni tradition, did not inherit the Caliphate.

On the question of testamentary bequest, however, Baghdadi does concede that this is permissible: 'If the Imam disposes of [the Imamate] by testament to someone who is qualified for it, the execution of the testament is incumbent on the community'.[15]

The purpose of this theory of the Caliphate was to defend Sunni dogma and, in an unspecified way, to defend the legitimacy of Sunni rule against heretics, and especially against the Shi'a. It had little connection with political reality in the Islamic world, where rulers came to power by usurpation or dynastic succession, and where by this period the titular Caliphs, the 'Abbasids of Baghdad, had no real power. The only concession to contemporary reality is perhaps Baghdadi's view that the Imamate could descend by testamentary bequest, a theory which might serve to justify descent within a dynasty.

Once the theologians had established the theory of the Caliphate, it remained intact, even when the concern of the author was with politics rather than religious dogma. In a treatise on government addressed to an 'Abbasid Caliph, Mawardi (d. 1058) devotes the first chapter to the Imamate.[16] His account of the institution is essentially an elaborate reworking of the theory of a contract between the electors and the candidate for office. He too makes the presence of certain qualities in the candidate, but now also in the electors, a condition for the validity of the contract. The electors must possess justice, knowledge and judgement. The candidate must possess justice, knowledge, soundness of his senses and limbs, the judgement necessary for disciplining his subjects and managing affairs, courage in war and, finally, descent from the Quraish.[17]

However, in parallel with contract as a mode of succession, Mawardi also permits investiture by the previous Imam,[18] a view which he justifies by citing a Sunni tradition according to which the first Caliph, Abu Bakr, nominated his own successor, 'Umar. In a case of investiture, the consent of the electors is not necessary, unless the Caliph vests his own son. In this case, 'in the opinion of some', it is preferable that the electors should 'consult among themselves and see that he is fit [for office] ... because this is an attestation of [the suitability of] his character, [a father not being legally competent to attest on behalf of his son], and stands as evidence, and his appointment over the community stands as a [judicial] decree'.[19] Here, Mawardi's language is quasi-judicial, requiring the 'testimony' of the electors to validate the Caliph's 'decree' appointing his son. His real purpose was presumably to establish a formal procedure for validating dynastic succession. If this is the case, it represents a concession to political reality.

In another area, too, reality intrudes upon Mawardi's scheme. Like his predecessors, Mawardi insists that there cannot be more than one Imam at any one time, and the Imam to whom he addressed the work was an 'Abbasid Caliph of Baghdad. By Mawardi's time, however, the 'Abbasid

Caliphate was a titular institution. Effective power in Baghdad was in the hands of the Buyid dynasty, and political power in the Islamic world as a whole was fragmented between competing sovereigns. Mawardi had to reconcile this fact with the theory which he had inherited from the Sunni theologians. He did this by introducing the notion of 'governorship' (*amara*). There are, he says, two types of governorship, 'governorship by trust, [formed by] an elective contract', and 'governorship by usurpation, [formed by] a coerced contract'. The first type was where the Imam voluntarily 'delegated to [the governor] the governorship of a country or clime'.[20] The second was where the governor 'forcibly seizes the lands, whose governorship the Caliph [then] bestows on him, and whose management and ordering he delegates to him, so that the governor through his usurpation becomes independent in ordering and management'.[21] The notion that a governor, who may well be an independent sovereign, rules by powers which the Imam has, voluntarily or involuntarily, delegated to him, served to maintain intact the inherited theory of the Caliphate in the face of political reality.

At the end of the same century, the theologian al-Ghazali (d. 1111) solved the same problem of reconciling theory with reality in a different way. He too maintained intact the notion of the Caliph's coming to office as the outcome of a contract with the electors,[22] and he too, like Mawardi, had to face the fact that the 'Abbasid Caliph of his own day possessed no political power. He did not, however, adopt Mawardi's idea of the Imam's delegating power to the secular ruler. He instead made secular power one of the qualities which the candidate for the office of Caliph must possess, if his contract with the electors is to be valid. A necessary qualifications for the Imamate is, Ghazali says, the means to call on the power of armies. This the 'Abbasid Caliphs could do by summoning the 'Turks',[23] a reference to the forces of the Great Seljuk Sultan who, in Ghazali's time, was the *de facto* ruler of Baghdad.

An inevitable effect of the theses of Mawardi and Ghazali is to create two forms of rulership: Imamate or Caliphate, and Sultanate. Spiritual and moral authority remains with the Caliph, but secular power, whether by delegation from the Caliph or exercised in his support, remains with the Sultan.

The Hanafi jurists, for the most part, ignored these theories of the Caliphate. An exception, however, is the Syrian jurist Kasani (d. 1189), who appends to his discussion of the fixed punishments what amounts to a theory of caliphal power. His starting point is the rule that, in the infliction of these penalties on slaves, the authority of the ruler overrides the authority of the slave's owner. From here, he moves the argument on to the question of whether he may delegate his authority in the area of the fixed penalties. Clearly he can, 'because he cannot exercise them entirely on his own. The causes necessitating [the fixed penalties] are present in

[all] districts of the realm of Islam, and it is not possible for him to go to all of them; and to bring [the miscreant] to the place of the ruler would cause great difficulty.' The ruler must therefore delegate his powers.

It is at this point that Kasani provides what is, in effect, a theory of the Caliphate. In justifying the ruler's right to delegate the power to inflict the fixed punishments, he writes: 'It is for this reason that the Prophet (blessings and peace be upon him) entrusted to Caliphs (*khulafa*) the execution of decrees and the infliction of the fixed penalties'. He continues by identifying two forms of delegation, the specific and the general. Specific delegation is the delegation of power for a particular purpose 'such as collecting taxes'. General delegation is where he appoints a man with general authority, 'such as the governorship of a clime or of a large land. [In this case] the appointee possesses [the power] to inflict the fixed punishments, even if this was not specified, because when [the Caliph] bestowed the governorship of the land, he delegated to him [the power] to act in the public interest, and the execution of the fixed punishments is greatly in the interests of the public.'[24]

In this discussion, Kasani is proposing a theory of rulership. The function of the ruler is to exercise authority in the interests of the Muslims, which Kasani characterises, following Sarakhsi, as the execution of the fixed penalties. In areas involving the public interest, the authority of the ruler overrides the authority of the individual. The next question is to establish the source of the ruler's authority. God revealed the law through His Prophet, Muhammad. The Prophet in turn delegated the execution of the law to the Caliph, who in turn delegates it to governors. Ultimately, therefore, the Caliph rules and executes God's law by virtue of Prophetic authority.

This view of the ruler is not typical of the Hanafis. Qadikhan's view that, in the end, it is effective power that is the sole basis of legitimate authority, is more usual. In the respect, however, that he gives the Caliph no powers to make or modify the law, Kasani belongs to the juristic mainstream.

Ebu's-su'ud and the Ottoman Caliphate

These were the traditional concepts which Ebu's-su'ud inherited. They had not, it seems, developed in any way since the extinction of the 'Abbasid Caliphate in 1258. In fact, the theologian al-Taftazani (d. 1389) commented that 'after the 'Abbasid Caliphate, the Caliphate is a difficult matter'.[25] Caliph became, above all, a title which Muslim sovereigns adopted for rhetorical effect without making any specific claim to divine right or to supreme sovereignty over the entire Muslim community. The Ottoman Sultans began to use the title from at least as early as 1421. A list of royal titles in an Almanac of this year, dedicated to Mehmed I (1413–21), includes, among other honorifics, the epithet 'Shadow of God in the Two Worlds, Caliph of God on the Two Earths'.[26] Thereafter, Caliph continues to appear sporadically among the honorific titles of the Ottoman Sultans.

It was not, however, until the reign of Süleyman I (1520–66) that the Ottoman use of the title acquired a doctrinal as well as a rhetorical significance. Süleyman was, it seems, the first Ottoman Sultan to claim not merely the title but also the office of the Caliphate, with its implications of universal sovereignty. His chief spokesman in this was Ebu's-su'ud, although Ebu's-su'ud was not alone. The major weakness in the Ottoman claim to the Caliphate was that in traditional Sunni theory, a necessary qualification for the office was descent from the Prophet's tribe of Quraish. However, the genealogy which the chroniclers had created for the Sultans in the fifteenth century, and which had become canonised by the sixteenth, did not trace the line back to the Quraish, and so, in mainstream Sunni theory, the Ottoman Sultan could not be Caliph. It was to overcome this difficulty that a former Grand Vizier and son-in-law of the Sultan, Lutfi Pasha, composed a treatise proving that descent from the Quraish was not a necessary legal qualification for the Caliphate, and that the Ottoman Sultan was therefore rightful Caliph.[27] Ebu's-su'ud, who must have discussed the question with Lutfi Pasha on many occasions, was wiser and simply bypassed the problem.

Ebu's-su'ud, however, did not support the Sultan's claim by writing justificatory treatises. He simply asserted it through the medium of the honorific titles which he accorded to the Sultan. These he made public in inscriptions, notably over the portal of the Süleymaniye, and in the dedicatory prefaces to works written for the Sultan, which circulated in manuscript among the literate élite.

The caliphal claims which he made accord only in part with the Sunni tradition. The form of the title which Mawardi prefers is 'Caliph (literally, 'successor') to the Messenger of God (i.e. the Prophet)', and this Ebu's-su'ud adopts in the law-books of Buda (1541) and of Skopje and Thessaloniki (1568), where he describes the Sultan as 'Caliph of the Messenger of the Lord of the Worlds'.[28] An alternative title is 'Caliph of God', although this is one that Mawardi does not admit, on the grounds that 'Caliph' means 'successor' and God, who is eternal and omnipresent, cannot have a successor.[29] Despite Mawardi's strictures, Ebu's-su'ud adopts this title in the preamble to his treatise on ritual ablution, where the Sultan is 'Caliph of God Most High on His Earth',[30] and also, by implication, in the Süleymaniye inscription. A feature of both Mawardi's and Ghazali's theories of the Caliphate is a distinction between the sacred office of Caliph and secular rulership, the secular monarch, in Mawardi's opinion, holding office by delegation from the Caliph. Ebu's-su'ud maintains the distinction, but combines both forms of rulership in the person of the Ottoman Sultan, who is both 'pre-eminent Sultan' and 'possessor of the mighty Imamate'.

A central feature of the 'classical' Sunni theory of the Caliphate is the mode of succession. This, the theologians insist, is by a contract with the electors. In his lists of honorifics, Ebu's-su'ud ignores their view entirely, although it does seem to have had some influence on Ottoman ceremonial. The contemporary chronicler, Selaniki, describes how, on the accession of Süleyman I's son Selim in 1566, Ebu's-su'ud and other dignitaries stood in ranks and proclaimed: 'He is worthy and fitting', as the new Sultan entered the city on horseback.[31] This ceremony appears to derive from Mawardi's rule that, if a Caliph designates his son as successor, the electors should testify to his suitability for office. There had, however, been no such formal validation of Süleyman's own Caliphate, since he had been the first of his line to lay claim to the office, and had not done so, it seems, until about two decades after his accession to the throne. Süleyman could not, therefore, declare that he was Caliph by contract.

To justify Süleyman's claim, Ebu's-su'ud instead made a bold assertion. The Sultan, he announced in the Law-Book of Buda and in his subsequent lists of honorifics, was the 'inheritor of the Great Caliphate from father to son', a statement which ignores entirely the 'classical' theory of appointment and succession. The phrase 'Great Caliphate', which he uses in conjunction with the, in Arabic, rhyming phrase 'Mighty Imamate', must refer to the four Rightly Guided Caliphs who succeeded the Prophet, the implication being that the Sultan is the heir to the Caliphs of the Islamic golden age. The assertion that the Sultan is 'inheritor' of the Caliphate directly contradicts the 'classical' theory, according to which the office is not hereditary (*mauruth*). Ebu's-su'ud, by contrast, not only states that it is, but also gives the Ottoman Caliphate a historical legitimacy by asserting that it is inherited from 'father to son', thus projecting the claim backwards to Süleyman's ancestors and forward to his successors.

The hereditary principle makes the Caliphate a monopoly of the Ottoman Sultans. This, however, leaves open the question of how they had acceded to the office in the first place, and in what sense they were the 'inheritors of the Great Caliphate'. This Ebu's-su'ud answers once again with a bold assertion, which he expresses most clearly in the dedicatory preface to his commentary on the Quran. Here, the Ottoman Sultan is the person upon whom 'God Most High has bestowed the Caliphate of the Earth' and whom 'He has chosen for its Sultanate throughout its length and breadth'.[32] In this formulation, the Ottoman Sultan did not become Caliph by contract with the electors, but through direct appointment by God. He was, as the inscription of the Süleymaniye proclaims 'made mighty with divine power' and 'resplendent in divine glory'. God, in short, had bestowed the Caliphate as a hereditary office on the Ottoman dynasty, in direct succession to the Rightly Guided Caliphs who had succeeded the Prophet.

Ebu's-su'ud gives no scriptural justification for this claim, obviously because he did not have to and could not. In the middle decades of the sixteenth century, the Ottoman dynasty appeared invincible and destined to rule until the end of time. Each Sultan in turn had added new territories to the Empire, subduing infidel Christians in the West and usurpers and heretics in the East. Such unbroken success was a clear sign of divine favour. The imperial magnificence of the Ottoman Empire at its height was itself proof that God had appointed the Ottoman Sultan as Caliph on earth. Despite the vicissitudes of the following centuries, this was a claim which the dynasty did not finally abandon until the abolition of the Caliphate in 1924.

The Caliphate and the Law

The main purpose of the Ottoman claim to the Caliphate was to enhance the Sultan's authority over his subjects and to assert his primacy over other Islamic rulers. In this respect, it was simply an extravagant addition to a series of devices through which the dynasty sought to legitimise its rule. For Ebu's-su'ud, however, it also had a juristic function. At several points in his lists of honorific titles, he emphasises the Sultan's role as the executor of God's law. It is the Sultan who is responsible for establishing the good order which is a precondition for the rule of the *shari'a*, and it is the Sultan who expounds the *shari'a* and puts it into effect.

These functions to some extent reflect the views of the 'classical' theorists of the Caliphate. An attribute which the Caliph must possess, if his contract with the electors is to be valid, is the ability to order affairs (*tadbir al-masalih*) and to exercise power over his subjects.[33] The Ottoman Sultan displayed this quality above all in his role as a secular law-giver. He was, in Ebu's-su'ud's phrase, the 'promulgator of Sultanic *qanuns*'. Another necessary qualification is learning, which in its Islamic sense means, above all, knowledge of the law. In Baqillani's formulation, the Caliph must have knowledge 'such as qualifies him to be a judge among the judges of the Muslims'.[34] Baghdadi and Mawardi go further and claim that it must be sufficient to qualify him to exercise *ijtihad*,[35] that is, to exercise his discretion in using legal sources. This gives the Caliph a scope, albeit limited, in interpreting the law, and in choosing between the various solutions to legal problems which the juristic tradition has to offer. The Caliph could not therefore change the law, but he could exercise his discretion in its application.

These were powers which Süleyman, as Caliph, exercised in a series of decrees which aimed to regularise legal practice, either by introducing new laws or, more often, by restricting in certain cases the powers of judges to choose between the range of solutions which were permissible within the *shari'a*. The Sultan's partner in this exercise was Ebu's-su'ud who, in his day-to-day work of issuing fatwas, constantly found uncertainties and anomalies in the law. When he encountered such a difficulty, he would make a written submission to the Sultan, stating the problem, offering a solution, and requesting the Sultan to issue a decree putting his solution into effect. This partnership between Sultan and jurist was something that caught the attention of the literary commentators, one of whom admirably demonstrated how it worked.

In his anthology of writings by Hanafi jurists, the scholar and judge, Mahmud of Caffa (d. 1582), wrote of Ebu's-su'ud: 'He had great renown in doctrine and variant [legal] opinions. In certain cases he followed the path of [independent] judgement (*ra'y*). Then he took counsel with Sultan Süleyman ... on whether he could give fatwas according to what he saw fit, and to whichever he preferred of the solutions which occurred to him. A decree was issued accordingly.'[36] In other words, the Sultan was delegating to Ebu's-su'ud some of the powers of legal discretion which belonged to him as Caliph. Molla Mahmud follows this statement with the texts of three petitions which Ebu's-su'ud submitted to the Sultan on 27 April 1550, with a note in each case of the Sultan's response. The texts of the petitions are well known, since they appear, rather misleadingly, in most collections of Ebu's-su'ud's fatwas.

In the first of the petitions, Ebu's-su'ud presents the case for the enactment of a statute of limitation:

(1) A plaintiff has delayed his case for a while without a legal excuse. Now there is no tradition from the great Imams, specifying the period beyond which a case may not be heard. In cases which have been enquired about up until now, [I] have given the following reply: 'If the time [lapse] is not excessive, if the plaintiff is not a fraudster, and if there are just witnesses, it should be heard'. The fear is that if [cases] are not heard on the grounds that the time has lapsed, many rights will be lost. [On the other hand] there is a fear that, if they are heard, this will open the door to fraud.

[I] have therefore petitioned the Threshold of Felicity [as follows]:

It is understood to be reasonable that a time limit be set, that judges should be permitted to hear cases within this limit, and that, beyond this limit, they should hear them only [if authorised to do so] by a special Imperial decree. When questions are put about actual cases that occur, the answer should be given accordingly.

What had clearly happened is that, in his daily work at the Fatwa Office, Ebu's-su'ud had received numerous queries about the time limit for hearing cases. There is no ruling on this point in Hanafi law, and Ebu's-su'ud therefore asked the Sultan for legislation. A note appended to the text of the petition records the outcome:

> It has been decreed that, when there is no Noble [Sultanic] Command, cases which have been delayed for ten years without a legal excuse should not be heard. This is in cases involving land. In other cases, fifteen years has been specified. A Noble Command to this effect was issued in the year 1550. [*H*, p. 56]

Here, the Sultan's decree following Ebu's-su'ud's petition made up for a lacuna in the Holy Law.

The second petition serves, by the same process, to enact as law a particular opinion within the Hanafi tradition, and to forbid judges to act according to the contrary view. The question is whether, when there is a homicide on rented property and the killer is unknown, it is the owner of the property or the lessee who is liable to pay the blood-money. The Hanafi jurists took opposing views on the subject. Ebu's-su'ud petitioned the Sultan that the occupant or lessee should be responsible and not the owner, and an Imperial decree followed giving this recommendation the force of law.[37]

Molla Mahmud's third example, like the first two, arose from Ebu's-su'ud's work as Mufti, and his wish to give clear and precise answers in areas where the law was non-existent, or where legal opinions are contradictory:

> (2) A tributary infidel dies, and the Treasury Commissioner detains his property [until claimed by an heir]. If the heir appears, bringing non-Muslim witnesses to his claim [to be rightful] heir, by [strict] analogy, his claim is not accepted. It is, however, accepted by equity (*istihsan*). In cases of property in the custody of the Treasury Commissioner, the judges in the provinces have always acted according to this [ruling], giving judgements and issuing certificates.
>
> However, in the year 1543, in the case of the Ragusan merchant, there was a petition to the Foot of the Throne, and an Exalted Decree was issued to the effect that there should be an investigation to see whether there were Muslim witnesses. From this, it is understood that there is no Imperial permission to act according to equity [and to permit the evidence of non-Muslims].
>
> In this matter, judges pass judgement [on the evidence of] non-Muslims and bring the certificates which they issue, enquiring, before adding their signatures to confirm [the documents'] validity, whether

or not the certificates are valid. [In these cases] it is not possible to give a clear-cut answer. The reply given is as follows: 'The judge who has been commanded to act according to equity is able to accept [the evidence of non-Muslims]'. In this matter, is there a general permission to the judges of Islam to act according to equity? A clarification is requested.

The problem which Ebu's-su'ud faced was whether an Imperial decree, requiring Muslim witnesses in an incident involving a non-Muslim, was intended as a precedent in all similar instances. The matter had clearly caused confusion among judges, and Ebu's-su'ud had been unable to give satisfactory answers to their queries. He therefore sought clarification from the Sultan, who confirmed that the decree of 1543 had applied only to the case of the Ragusan:

> When the petition was presented, [the Sultan] decreed: 'They should act according to equity'. The phrase: 'Let Muslim witnesses be found' was specific to the Ragusan because, in this claim, there was understood to be fraud. [*H*, pp. 53–4]

Molla Mahmud gives only these three examples of Ebu's-su'ud's petitions. Other anthologies give more. For example, a list bearing the heading: 'Copies of what was commanded when His Excellency, the *sheikhu'l-islam* Ebu's-su'ud petitioned His Excellency, the late Sultan Süleyman Khan in the first decade of the month Rabi' al-akhir, 957 (April 1550)' contains, in addition to Molla Mahmud's items, summaries of petitions and subsequent decrees dealing with the reappointment of deputy judges who have been dismissed for misconduct, the sale of escaped slaves, the transfer of evidence from one court to another, the prohibition of marriages which do not have the consent of the bride's guardian,[38] and a prohibition on charging interest at more than 15 per cent.[39] The full texts of these and other items appear in a late seventeenth-century anthology of Ebu's-su'ud's fatwas and petitions, known as the 'Submissions' (*Ma'ruzat*).

What Ebu's-su'ud was doing was to bring about a piecemeal rationalisation of the law by making use of the royal authority. In so doing, he was also extending the Sultan's power at the expense of the judges who, in certain areas, lost the right to choose between the entire range of opinions available within the Hanafi tradition.

This capacity to regulate the application of Hanafi law was perhaps the most practical consequence of the Ottoman Sultan's claim to the Caliphate. What it did not do, however, was to give him the power to change the law in its essence. This Ebu's-su'ud makes clear in an answer which amounts to a ruling that there is no appeal against the decision of a court without a Sultanic decree, and that even this is ineffective when the court's decision is valid according to the *shari'a*:

(3) A matter has been decided once by the Noble *shari'a*, and another judge has put it into effect and signed [the certificate]. Is it lawful for the case to be heard again from the beginning?
Answer: No, so long as there is no Sultanic decree. But even if there has been a decree, if what was previously established by the *shari'a* is settled, it cannot be changed. [*H*, p. 52]

A Sultanic decree cannot therefore overturn a verdict which is valid according to the *shari'a*. Even as Caliph, the Sultan's authority over the substance and application of the law remains limited.

Notes

1. Ibn Nujaim, *al-Bahr al-Ra'iq*, Cairo: al-Matba'a al-'ilmiyya (1893), vol. 5, pp. 16–17.
2. Ö. L. Barkan, *Kanunlar*, Istanbul: Burhaneddin Matbaaası (1943), p. 296.
3. Ebu's-su'ud, *Risala fi mas'alat al-mash 'ala'l-khuffain*, Library of the Topkapı Palace, Istanbul, ms A1,541, f. 371b.
4. Süleymaniye inscription. See Cevdet Çulpan, 'İstanbul Süleymaniye Camii Kitabesi', *Kanuni Armağanı*, Ankara: Turkish Historical Society, series 7, no. 55, pp. 291–9.
5. Ibn al-Baqilani, *al-Tamhid fi radd 'ala'l-malhadat al-mu'attala*, Cairo: Dar al-fikr al-'arabi (1947).
6. Abu Mansur al-Baghdadi, *Usul al-Din*, Istanbul: Devlet Matbaası (1928).
7. 'The representatives of the community of Muslims, who act on their behalf in appointing and deposing a Caliph or other ruler', *Encyclopaedia of Islam*, 2nd edn, Leiden: E. J. Brill (1966), vol. 1, pp. 263–4.
8. Ibn al-Baqillani, *al-Tamhid*, pp. 178–9.
9. Ibid., pp. 181–2.
10. Abu Mansur al-Baghdadi, *Usul*, p. 281.
11. Ibid., p. 278.
12. Ibid., p. 274.
13. Ibn al-Baqillani, *al-Tamhid*, p. 182; Abu Mansur al-Baghdadi, *Usul*, p. 278.
14. Ibn al-Baqillani, *al-Tamhid*, p. 178.
15. Abu Mansur al-Baghdadi, *Usul*, p. 284.
16. al-Mawardi, *al-Ahkam al-sultaniyya*, Cairo: Matba'a Mustafa al-Babi al-Halabi (1973). Translated by E. Fagnan as *Les Statuts Gouvernementaux*, Algiers: Typographie Adolphe Jourdan (1915); Comte Léon Ostrorog, *Le Droit du Califat*, Paris: Editions Ernest Leroux (1925). H. A. R. Gibb, 'Al-Mawardi's theory of the Khilafa', *Islamic Culture*, 11 (1937), 291–302. Orientalists have tended to move Mawardi's theory of the Caliphate from the margins of the Islamic legal tradition, where it belongs, to the centre.
17. al-Mawardi, *al-Ahkam*, p. 6.

18. Ibid.
19. Ibid., p. 10.
20. Ibid., p. 30.
21. Ibid., p. 33
22. al-Ghazali, *Ihya 'ulum al-din*, Cairo: al-Matba'a al-'amira al-sharafiyya (1908), vol. 1, pp. 88–9.
23. al-Ghazali, ed. I. Goldziher, *Kitab Fada'ih al-Batinijja: Streitschrift des Gazali gegen die Batinijja-Sekte*, Leiden: E. J. Brill (1916), pp. 67–8. On Ghazali, see Henri Laoust, *La Politique de Gazali*, Paris: Librairie Orientaliste Paul Geuthner (1970).
24. al-Kasani, *Bada'i' al-sana'i' fi tartib al-shara'i'*, Beirut: Dar al-kitab al-'arabi (1982), vol. 7, p. 58.
25. al-Taftazani, trans. E. E. Elder, *A Commentary on the Creed of Islam: Sa'd al-Din Taftazani on the Creed of Najm al-Din Nasafi*, New York: Columbia University Press (1950), p. 146.
26. Ç. N. Atsız, *Osmanlı Tarihine ait Takvimler*, Istanbul: Küçükaydın Matbaası (1961), p. 91.
27. H. A. R. Gibb, 'Lutfi Pasha and the Ottoman Caliphate' *Oriens*, 15 (1962), 287–95.
28. Ö. L. Barkan, *Kanunlar*, pp. 296, 297.
29. al-Mawardi, *al-Ahkam*, pp. 14–15.
30. Ebu's-su'ud, *Risala*, f. 371b.
31. Selaniki Mustafa, ed. Mehmet Ipşirli, *Tarih-i Selânikî*, Istanbul: Istanbul Üniversitesi Edebiyat Fakültesi Yayınları 3,371 (1989), p. 54.
32. Ebu's-su'ud, *Irshad al-'aql al-salim ila mazaya al-kitab al karim*, in margins of Fakhr al-Din Razi, *Mafatih al-ghaib*, Istanbul: Imperial Press (1872/3), vol. 1, p. 24.
33. Abu Mansur al-Baghdadi, *Usul*, p. 278; al-Mawardi, *al-Ahkam*, p. 6.
34. Ibn al-Baqillani, *al-Tamhid*, p. 181.
35. Abu Mansur al-Baghdadi, *Usul*, p. 278; al-Mawardi, *al-Ahkam*, p. 6.
36. *K*, f. 69a; R. C. Repp, *The Müfti of Istanbul*, Oxford: Ithaca Press (1986), p. 279.
37. See below, Chapter 9, no. (37).
38. See below, Chapter 7, no. (5).
39. Süleymaniye Library, Istanbul, MS Laleli 706, ff. 148b–151b.

PART III

The Law in Detail

5

Land Tenure and Taxation

Feudal Tenure

The Ottoman Empire had an agricultural economy, with land as its most important asset. Control of the land gave access to most of its wealth, and so to the source of most of its tax revenues. Land tenure was a vital issue since, in determining who had control of the land and its revenues, it also determined the locus of economic and ultimately political power.

A small minority of lands in the Empire were allodial (*milk*), in the ownership of individuals. Many more belonged to trusts in mortmain (*waqf*), with their revenues assigned in perpetuity to whatever purpose the original donor had stipulated. The majority were subject to feudal tenure, of which the essential institution was the military fief (*timar*), where the Sultan assigned the revenues from an identified parcel of land to a cavalryman (*sipahi*). Occupancy of a fief carried with it a contractual obligation to serve in the Sultan's army with horse, weapons, armour and armed retainers, whose number was in proportion to the value of the fief. The cavalryman lived on the land, collecting the revenues directly from the peasant occupiers. The collectivity of fief-holdings in a particular area formed a district (*sanjaq*) under the command of a district-governor (*sanjaq beyi*), who also drew his livelihood from a fief proportionate in value to his status. In times of war, he commanded the cavalrymen in his district, who fought under his banner. The districts in a particular territory of the Empire together formed a province, whose governor-general (*beylerbeyi*) was again a fief-holder on a grand scale, and again, in times of war, commander of the units made up from the cavalrymen in the districts under his jurisdiction. Most fiefs carried with them an obligation to perform military service. Others were fiscal fiefs, where the holder contracted to remit an agreed sum to the treasury, in return either for a salary or for the right to retain any surplus revenue.

Most fief-holders exercised their privileges by virtue of letters patent (*berat*) from the Sultan, which the Sultan could (and did) withdraw if the fief-holder failed to perform his military or other obligation. Fiefs were not, as a rule, hereditary. What a person inherited was an entitlement to a fief, and it is this – in effect, an entitlement to collect taxes, and an exemption from paying them – that was perhaps the most important marker of legal status in the Ottoman Empire. The taxpaying peasants, in their turn, received the right to cultivate the soil by virtue of an entry fine (*tapu* tax) which a new occupant of a piece of land paid to the fief-holder and which gave him legal title. The peasant occupier had limited rights of tenure. The fief-holder could not evict him unless he failed to cultivate the land for three successive years, and a son could inherit a plot from his father without having to pay an entry fine to the fief-holder.

This system of feudal tenure divides interest in the land between the Sultan, the fief-holders and the peasant occupiers, but does not, strictly speaking, assign ownership. It was a system which pre-dates the Ottomans, having been in force in the late Byzantine Empire and its successor principalities in the Balkan peninsula and western Anatolia.[1] Indeed, the basic administrative vocabulary of Ottoman feudalism seems to derive from the corresponding Greek terms. A very similar system, but one where a portion of the revenues from the land belonged to a private owner, was in force in the Seljuk Sultanate in central Anatolia during the thirteenth century. The Ottomans retained this system in those provinces which were within the boundaries of the former Seljuk realms.[2] The basic principles of Ottoman land tenure and taxation were thus an inheritance from pre-Ottoman régimes, and their function was to provide troops for the Sultan's army and cash for his treasury. It is clear that in their origin and development they owed nothing to the Hanafi doctrine of land and tax. Ottoman tradition nonetheless credits Ebu's-su'ud with having harmonised these two apparently irreconcilable systems.

The Hanafi Doctrine of Land and Tax

The Hanafi jurists usually deal with land and taxation under the general heading of 'the conduct of government' (*siyar*), immediately after the opening section which lays out the rules for prosecuting a holy war. This juxtaposition is logical since, in Hanafi theory, the tax status of the land depends on its status at the time of the Islamic conquest.

The essential distinction which the jurists make is between tithe (*'ushr*) lands and tribute (*kharaj*) lands. Tithe land is land which the ruler (*imam*) divided as spoil among the Muslim soldiers at the time of the conquest, or whose infidel owners voluntarily accepted Islam. A ruler may not levy tax on these lands at a rate higher than one tenth of the produce, and the jurists categorise the payment of this tithe as a 'act of worship'. Tribute land, by contrast, is land which the Muslims conquered by force, but whose inhabitants the Islamic ruler permitted to remain in occupation, in return for the payment of tribute. The ruler may tax these lands according to their capacity, which some texts define as meaning up to half the produce.[3] Tribute itself is of two kinds, proportional tribute (*kharaj muqasama*), levied as a fraction of the produce of the land, and fixed tribute (*kharaj muwazzaf*), payable as an annual fixed sum. The jurists define the cultivation of these lands and the payment of tribute as a 'burden'. Ibn Humam goes further, stating that tribute 'carries with it the sense of punishment (*'uquba*)'.[4] When a country surrenders by treaty, there is a disagreement as to whether the inhabitants should pay tribute or the amount stipulated in the treaty. Marghinani (d. 1197) rules in favour of tribute.[5]

Tithe and tribute lands are the property of their occupiers and subject to the normal property transactions. So although tribute lands begin as the property of infidels, these can sell them to Muslims, and their new Muslim owners become liable to pay tribute. Taxation is thus dependent on the status of the lands at the time of the conquest, and not on the status of the occupier. The essential point, however, is that taxpayers, whether on tithe or tribute lands, are the actual owners of the land. What Ebu's-su'ud had to do, therefore, was to reconcile a theoretical system of land ownership with an actual system of feudal tenure, where there were no real owners.

Hanafi Doctrine and Feudal Tenure

In seeking a solution to this problem, Ebu's-su'ud was not working entirely in the dark. The notion of land as being subject to individual ownership and to the payment of tribute and tithe always remained central to the juristic accounts of land law. Nonetheless, it was a theory which had never fully accorded with reality, since feudal tenure had always been widespread in the Islamic world, and forms a topic which appears sporadically in juristic texts from the ninth century onwards. One of the earliest to deal with it is the 'Book of Tribute', whose authorship the tradition optimistically ascribes to Abu Yusuf. This work describes fiefs in Iraq, taking as a starting point a story about how the second Caliph, 'Umar, granted ownerless lands as fiefs after the Muslim conquest: 'A person of Medina reported to me from the *sheikh*s of previous generations, that it was found in the Register that 'Umar took [?] the property of Chosroes and the family of Chosroes, and of everybody who fled from his land or was killed in battle, all dried-out places and thickets. With these 'Umar enfeoffed those whom he enfeoffed.' This story provides an explanation of how land came to be ownerless and at the disposal of the sovereign. The author next has to establish the legal status of the land which 'Umar granted as fiefs: 'Abu Yusuf said: This [land] is in the position of property which belongs to nobody, and which is not in the possession of an heir. The just Imam may ... give it to a person who has benefited Islam. He puts him in his [proper] place without partiality. In my opinion this is the manner of fiefs in Iraq.'[6] What the ruler grants, therefore, is the land itself, on which the fief-holder must pay the tithe. There is also a hint that the land is granted in return for a service.

This description of a fief which, in effect, makes the fief-holder an owner, is very different from the account of the ninth-century jurist al-Khassaf (d. 874): 'I said: "How is something made a fief (*iqta'*) on behalf of the Treasury (*bait al-mal*)?" He said: "This is land belonging to a person, which is tribute land and owned. The Sultan takes from the arable half of what God Almighty produces. The Sultan makes a fief of this half, part of which he takes for the Treasury. He says to the person to whom he allocated the fief: I have given four fifths of this half to you as a fief, and I have imposed on you one fifth for the Treasury, this being a tenth of everything the earth produces."'[7] This looks like a description of a tax-farm on very favourable terms, where the farmer is obliged to remit only a fifth of what he takes. Al-Khassaf describes the occupants of the lands as owners, and the fief consists of the revenues only. The law permits the ruler to raise up to half the produce as tribute. Of this he gives four fifths to the feoffee, keeping a tenth of the produce for the Treasury.

The 'Book of Tribute' and al-Khassaf thus provide two separate definitions of a fief. Either it is land without an owner, which the sovereign has allocated to a feoffee; or it is a proportion of the tribute which proprietors pay on their land, and which the sovereign has allocated to the fief-holder.

In the twelfth century, Qadikhan (d. 1189) was to take up the problem again. In explaining how feudal tenure arose, he adopts the fiction, similar to that of the 'Book of Tribute', that the owners have either died out or fled: '[It is reported] from Abu Yusuf (may God have mercy on him) that, when the tribute-payers die out, the ruler (*imam*) takes the land and cultivates it, or rents it out and places [the proceeds] in the treasury'. In this formulation, the ruler becomes the *de facto*, if not the *de jure*, owner of the land, and the occupants become tenants, paying rent rather than tribute. He continues: 'If the tribute payers did not die out, but fled, then the ruler leases the land, taking the value of the tribute from the rent and keeping the rest'. In this formulation, the tribute does not drop, because the tribute-payers, although absent, are still alive. A formula somewhat similar to Qadikhan's appears in the 'Fatwas' of Ibn Bazzaz (d. 1414), who refers to lands at the disposal of the sovereign as 'royal demesne' (*aradi'l-mamlaka*), a term which begins to appear in Ottoman texts in the sixteenth century. Like Qadikhan, he offers two explanations as to how the land had passed into the control of the ruler:

There are two ways to elucidate royal demesne. Either it is land with no owner, which the ruler (*imam*) had given to a man to tend as owner, and who pays tribute. Or secondly, it is land with an owner who is unable to pay tribute, which the ruler gives to a man, who stands in place of an owner in [the matters of] paying tribute and cultivation. He does not possess [the right] to sell [the land], because the ruler did not make him owner, but only put him in the position of owner as a special case. However, [the ruler] takes the tribute from what is due as rent (*dahqaniyya*).[8]

Qadikhan and Ibn Bazzaz are both attempting to describe feudal land, which is not in the ownership of its occupiers, but at the disposal of the sovereign. Their descriptions do not, however, explain the position of the fief-holders. This, however, is a subject which Qadikhan raises rather guardedly: 'When the tribute-payers flee, the ruler may, if he wishes ... turn over (*dafaʿa*) [the land] to people as fiefs (*muqataʿatan*) for a consideration (*ʿala shayʾ*). What he takes [from them] belongs to the Muslims.'[9] This looks like a juristic description of fief-holding, where a ruler grants land in exchange for a service, military, fiscal or otherwise. If the tribute-payers flee, tribute is still due, and the sovereign can therefore assign the lands to a nominee, who can collect the tribute directly in return for an unspecified service which benefits the Muslim community.

Tribute, however, is due to the sovereign, who disburses it on behalf of the Muslim community, and Qadikhan's formula therefore raises the question of whether the fief-holders may collect it directly for themselves. Qadikhan rules that they may, on one particular condition: 'When the Sultan allocates land to a landlord (*sahib al-ard*), and leaves him with it, this is permissible in the opinion of Abu Yusuf. It is not permissible in the opinion of Muhammad [al-Shaibani]. Fatwas should be given in accordance with the opinion of Abu Yusuf, if the landlord is a legitimate recipient of tribute (*masraf*).' The condition, therefore, of the fief-holder's receiving tribute, is that he should be a legitimate recipient. This is something which Qadikhan then defines: 'When the Sultan gives a man the tribute from his land, it is mentioned in the *Siyar* that it is not fitting that he should have it, that is, he should not accept it, because it is a right of the community. But if he is a legitimate recipient, he may accept it. The legitimate recipients of tribute from the land, and of poll-tax (*jizya*), are fighting men and their descendants.'[10] Fighting men, alongside muftis, preachers and others who promote Islam, are legitimate recipients, because they pursue holy war on behalf of the community, and for this reason are entitled to receive tribute. With this formula, the jurists eventually arrived at a definition and justification of the military fief.

The formulations of both Qadikhan and Ibn Bazzaz are remarkably favourable to the ruler, as against the cultivators of the land. They make him the *de facto* owner of the land on behalf of the Muslim community, reducing the occupants to the status of tenants. The statement that the ruler, in a case where the tribute-payers have fled, deducts the tribute from the rent, implies that the rent is greater, in effect giving the sovereign absolute discretion over what he charges for the land. Furthermore, as tenants, the cultivators have no right to sell the land. What lies behind this formulation is the Hanafi concept of ownership, which distinguishes between the ownership of the substance (*raqaba*) and ownership of the usufruct (*tasarruf*), and which defines lease as the sale of the usufruct. The ruler in effect owns the substance of the land, while the occupants own the benefits. This was a fiction, but one which was later to underpin Ebu's-su'ud's analysis of Ottoman feudal tenure.

Ebu's-su'ud was not the first Ottoman jurist to attempt such an analysis. The first to do so was his greatest predecessor in the office of Mufti, Kemalpashazade (d. 1534). Kemalpashazade opens his account with a summary of tithe and tribute lands, and then moves on to the substantive issue of the prevailing Ottoman system of land tenure and taxation:

(1) Leasehold (*hauz*) land and royal demesne (*aradi al-mamlaka*) are lands where no one knows from whom they were seized at the time of the conquest, or to whom they were given, or whose owners have died out. Because the status [of the lands] and [their] owners are unknown, they were taken for the treasury.

When the Sultan's agents registered the provinces, they assigned the land as fiefs (*iqta'*). The right to settle on and enjoy the usufruct of the fiefs was given to cavalrymen (*sipahi*) in the form of *timar* revenue. In these realms, this category of land is called *miri*. The holder of the fief (*timar*) is entitled to the right of settlement by letters patent (*berat*) or licence (*tezkere*). He sells the use of this land to his peasants (*re'aya*) and cultivators, taking from them his customary dues and canonical taxes.

Since neither the fief-holders nor the occupiers own the essence (*asl*) or the substance (*raqaba*) of the land, sale, gift and conversion to trust are not permissible, although lease and loan are.

Nevertheless, in accordance with the feudal law (*qanun*), sale and inheritance by male children has been permitted. [*Ch*, ff. 24a–25b]

In Ottoman usage, the standard term for land subject to feudal tenure was '*miri* land', the word *miri* being simply an Arabic calque on a Turkish term *beglik*, meaning 'belonging to / at the disposal of the lord'. Its literal meaning was therefore close enough to the sense of 'royal demesne' (*aradi al-mamlaka*) in the juristic texts for Kemalpashazade to equate the two terms, and to define *miri* land as royal demesne owned by the Treasury. The Treasury in Hanafi theory is the joint property of the Muslims, but at the disposal of the sovereign to administer on behalf of the community. The land, therefore, was *de jure* the property of the Treasury, and *de facto* under the control of the Sultan. Like Qadikhan and Ibn Bazzaz before him, he uses fictions to explain how the Treasury had acquired ownership but, unlike them, does not describe the land as tribute land. Instead, he states simply that the Sultan had distributed it as fiefs. He lends historical dignity to this concept of feudal tenure by using the term *iqta'*, an Arabic word for fief which he derived from classical jurisprudence and historiography. By equating this Arabic term with *timar*, the standard Ottoman word for fief, he is implying that the Ottoman system of land tenure had venerable Islamic precedents. The Sultan gives the fief-holders the right to settle and enjoy the usufruct of the land, and they in turn sell on the usufruct to the occupiers, the taxes which they receive representing the sale price. Thus the Ottoman fief-holder had the right to reside on his fief and to collect taxes from the peasant cultivators, which is what happened in practice. Like Ibn Bazzaz, Kemalpashazade uses the Treasury's ownership of the land to explain why all property transactions involving land are forbidden, except for loan and lease, which involve only a transfer of the usufruct and not of the substance.

It is at this point that Kemalpashazade's definition breaks down. He knew perfectly well that, in reality, peasants did buy and sell land as though they were its owners, and, in fact, he reaffirms the validity of such sales in a separate fatwa:

(2) When Zeyd leaves the land, is it permissible for him to sell the land which he occupied to someone else?
Answer: Yes. [*Ch*, f. 28v]

To explain why peasants could buy and sell land when they were not its owners, Kemalpashazade could at first do no better than to state simply that it was permissible by feudal law. Later, however, he overcame the problem more satisfactorily by devising a new formula according to which it was not the ownership of the land that the peasant was selling, but the right to settle there:

(3) Zeyd and 'Amr are cavalrymen holding a fief jointly. Bekr is one of their peasants. With Zeyd's permission, he sells to Khalid the right of settlement (*haqq-i qarar*) on the land which he occupies. If 'Amr then says: 'You sold it without consulting me', can he cancel the sale?
Answer: Not according to the *shari'a*, but he can prevent it by feudal law (*'urf*). [*Ch*, f. 27b]

Kemalpashazade clearly regards the transaction on the land as a valid sale. The cavalryman has no right to intervene 'according to the *shari'a*', because Hanafi law does not permit a third party to cancel a sale. His right of cancellation derives from feudal law, but does not affect the validity of the original transaction. However, the central point in Kemalpashazade's formulation is that the peasants do not buy and sell the land itself, but the right to settle on the land. This formula kept the Treasury as *de jure* owner of the land, while allowing *de facto* sale and purchase to continue.

This was a concept which Ebu's-su'ud was later to adopt in his own solution to the problem of the sale of feudal land.

Ebu's-su'ud and Feudal Tenure

The Ownership of Land

Three years after Kemalpashazade's death in 1534, Ebu's-su'ud succeeded to the post of Military Judge of Rumelia. As a member of the Sultan's Imperial Council and *de facto* the most powerful judicial figure in the Empire, he too faced the problem of constructing a theory of land tenure and taxation that would reconcile 'what is written in the books' with what actually happened in practice. It was a problem that was to preoccupy him for the rest of his career.

The impetus to describe and systematise Ottoman land tenure came, above all, from the annexation of Hungary. The Hungarian king had been a tributary of the Ottoman Sultan since 1526. When he died in 1541, Sultan Süleyman annexed the Kingdom, converting it to a province under the direct rule of an Ottoman governor-general and subject to Ottoman law. This meant the introduction of Ottoman land tenure and taxation as it existed in Rumelia, that is in the Balkan peninsula south of the Danube. The problem was that the system of feudal tenure in the Balkans had come into existence through custom and piecemeal legislation. Practice was not absolutely uniform, and there was no description of its underlying norms. Legislation to introduce the system into Hungary was therefore impossible without a systematic account of its general principles. Such an account is what Ebu's-su'ud provided for the Sultan in the 'Law-Book' of Buda, for enactment as an Imperial decree. It remained, subsequently through the medium of the 'New *Qanun*', the standard text on land tenure until 1858:[11]

> (4) ... The inhabitants of the said province [of Hungary] are to remain where they are settled. The moveable goods in their possession, their houses in towns and villages, and their cultivated vineyards and orchards are their property to dispose of as they wish. They may transfer ownership by sale, gift or other means. They should pay the

dues on their vineyards and orchards. When they die, ownership of these properties descends to their heirs. No one should intervene or interfere.

The fields which they have from old cultivated and tilled are also confirmed in their possession. However, whereas their goods in the categories mentioned above are their property, their fields are not. [Instead] they belong to the category of royal demesne (*aradi al-mamlaka*), known elsewhere in the Protected [Ottoman] Realms as *miri* land. The real substance (*raqaba*) is reserved for the Treasury of the Muslims, and the subjects (*re'aya*) have the use of it, by way of a loan. They sow and reap whatever cereals and crops they wish, and pay their proportional tribute (*kharaj muqasama*) under the name 'tithe' (*'ushr*), and benefit from the land however they wish.

So long as they do not let the land lie fallow, but cultivate, till and tend it as required, and pay their dues in full, no one may intervene or interfere. They should have the use of it until they die, and when they die, their sons should occupy their positions and have disposal [of the land] in the manner set forth. If they have no sons, then, as in the rest of the Protected Realms, advance rent should be taken from outsiders who are capable of cultivating, and the lands given to these by *tapu*, in the established manner. These too should have the use of them in the manner set forth above.

The plots [where] their vineyards and orchards [are planted] also belong to this category. When their vineyards and orchards fall into a state of neglect, the land [on which they were planted] is like other fields and cultivated places which they occupy. It should not be thought that it is their property.

Ebu's-su'ud's juristic theory of land and tax owes something to Kemalpashazade, and something to Qadikhan and Ibn Bazzaz. Like Kemalpashazade, he identifies Ottoman *miri* land with the 'royal demesne' (*aradi al-mamlaka*) of the jurists; and, again like Kemalpashazade, he distinguishes between the real substance of the land and the usufruct. The real substance is *de jure* the property of the Treasury, and therefore *de facto* at the disposal of the Sultan. The peasants have it merely as a loan (*'ariyya*), which the law defines as a gratuitous transfer of the ownership of the usufruct. Like Qadikhan and Ibn Bazzaz, he defines the land as 'tribute land' and the tax on it as 'tribute', and is at pains to point out that the Ottoman tithe (*'ushr*) is in fact proportional tribute (*kharaj muqasama*) and not the canonical tithe of the jurists. Finally, he refers to the entry fine (*tapu*), which a new occupant of the land must pay to the fief-holder, as 'advance rent'. The 'rent' is presumably for the occupancy rather than the use of the land, since the peasant has the use of it as a loan from the Sultan.

This juristic formula gives the Sultan almost unlimited powers over agricultural land. He administers it on behalf of the Treasury, which is its nominal owner. The peasants are merely borrowers, and since, in Hanafi law, a lender may demand the return of the loan whenever he wishes, the Sultan may dispossess the peasants at will. At the same time, the redefinition of the tithe as proportional tribute increased the Sultan's legal powers to raise taxes. A tithe is merely a tenth of the produce or thereabouts, whereas the Hanafi tradition permits the ruler to levy proportional tribute at a rate of up to one half. The last paragraph, on vineyards and orchards, aims to prevent the peasants from using a legal ruse to acquire ownership of the soil. Fruit trees and vines are the property of the cultivator who, by planting them sufficiently densely to prevent any other crop from growing beneath or between them, gains the *de facto* ownership of the ground. This led to the popular belief that, by planting vines or fruit trees, a person gained permanent, *de jure* ownership of the land beneath. Ebu's-su'ud states categorically that this is not the case. A person who cultivates orchards and vineyards never enjoys *de jure* ownership of the ground, and when the trees and vines are removed the soil returns to the status of *miri* land, fully at the disposal of the Sultan.[12]

Ebu's-su'ud, in short, is concerned with practicalities. He does not bother with the legal fictions which his predecessors had used to explain how tribute land had come into royal ownership. When he did so, over twenty years later, in the Law-Book of Skopje and Thessaloniki, even his fiction reflects a thoroughly practical concern. 'Royal demesne', he wrote, 'is in origin tribute land. However, if [at the time of the conquest] it had been given to its owners, it would have been divided on their deaths among many heirs, so that each one of them would receive only a tiny portion. Since it would be extremely arduous and difficult, and indeed impossible to distribute and allocate each person's tribute, the ownership of the land was kept for the Muslim Treasury, and [the usufruct] given to the peasants by way of a loan.'[13] In other words, it was impossible to give the occupants ownership of the land since, by the laws of inheritance, it would have become excessively fragmented.

The principles which Ebu's-su'ud laid out in his statements on Hungarian land emerge in greater detail in his fatwas. The notion of the land as being on loan from the Sultan emerges only in his general statements. The notion of the entry fine as an advance rent payable to the fief-holder receives some amplification. In a hurriedly-written fatwa, which survives in Ebu's-su'ud's own hand,[14] he describes *miri* land as being 'in essence tribute land, the ownership of which has not been made over to those in possession', adding that the occupiers have the use of it by defective lease (*ijara fasida*). In another fatwa, which the compilers of the 'New *Qanun*' have preserved, he explains why the peasant's lease of the occupancy is defective: 'The cash paid under the name of *tapu* is advance rent. Because the term of occupancy is not [fixed], it is a defective lease ...'[15] The problem here is that, in Hanafi law, a lease is valid only when 'the beneficial uses are known and the rent is known'. In the case of land, the benefits are known 'by the [fixed] term, as in renting ... land for cultivation'.[16] Feudal tenure, however, had no fixed term. It lasted, if the peasant did not leave the land, until the extinction of the male line. To redefine *tapu* tax, which simply granted entry to the land, as advance rent did not therefore conjure into existence a valid contract of lease. The best that Ebu's-su'ud could do was to call it defective lease.

The Taxation of Land

This matter was, however, unimportant, insofar as it had no practical consequences. Far more significant was his redefinition of *miri* land as being, in essence, tribute land. Since tax follows the status of the land, this made the peasant cultivators liable to pay tribute, and required a redefinition of Ottoman taxation in terms of Hanafi theory. The two most important Ottoman agricultural taxes were the *chift*-tax, a fixed sum payable annually on each peasant's holding (*chift*), and tithe, a tax payable as a proportion of the crop. These taxes Ebu's-su'ud identified respectively with the fixed tribute (*kharaj muwazzaf*) and proportional tribute (*kharaj muqasama*) of the Hanafi jurists: 'The peasants sow and reap and pay their fixed tribute under the name "*chift*-tax", and their proportional tribute under the name "tithe"'. The redefinition of the tithe as proportional tribute was particularly important, since it gave the Sultan the option of altering the rate at which it was levied, and met the objections of those who complained that they were paying the tithe at a rate higher than one tenth. The Ottoman tithe, Ebu's-su'ud explained in answer to numerous questions on the matter, was not the canonical tithe of the jurists, which the ruler can levy only at the rate of one tenth:

> (5) The [Ottoman] tithe is not the [canonical] tithe (*'ushr*). To call it 'tithe' is a gross deception by the common people. *Miri* is tribute land: it cannot possibly be tithe land. The share that is paid is proportional tribute. It is the cavalryman's canonical right.
> Tithe land are the districts [around] the Mighty Ka'ba. The tithe from there is given to the poor. [*D*, 839].

It was therefore useless to complain if the rate of the tithe was more than 10 per cent:

> (6) The cavalryman Zeyd takes two bushels in fifteen as tithe. Is this lawful?

Answer: to call what a cavalryman levies 'tithe' is ignorance. If it were tithe, it would be given to the poor. It is proportional tribute. It is not necessary that it be levied [at a rate of] one tenth. It is imposed according to what the land can support and is licit up to a half. [*D*, 45]

This redefinition of tithe seems, at first, to grant the fief-holders who were, in practice, its recipients, the right to increase taxes at will. This was not, however, Ebu's-su'ud's intention, and he makes clear that, in practice, the fief-holders had no discretion over the rates of taxation. The first principle that determined rate of the tithe was custom:

(7) If cavalrymen have, from ancient times, taken one tenth from the people of a village, can the present cavalryman say: 'I am taking one eighth'?
Answer: It is taken at whatever rate was customary. [*Ch*, f. 30a]

The second and more important arbiter of taxation was the rate entered in the cadastral register, which contained the record of the fief-holding in which the dispute arose:

(8) ... The said peasants pay [the fief-holder] Zeyd two aqches each, for each of the olive-trees at their disposal. This is in accordance with the Sultanic register. If Zeyd is not satisfied, can he take more, contrary to [what is recorded in] the register?
Answer: No. [The 'New *Qanun*']¹⁷

These two examples show the principle operating in favour of the peasants, but it could equally well operate in favour of the fief-holder:

(9) In places where a rate of one eighth has been determined, Zeyd pays a tithe not of one eighth, but of one tenth. Is this licit?
Answer: If its rate is one-eighth, no. [*D*, 846]

In fact, neither peasant nor fief-holder had any authority to fix the rate of taxation. This was the prerogative of the Sultan, who should tax the land according to its capacity.

In order to maintain tax revenue, the Sultan also had an unlimited right to confiscate and reassign land. Ebu's-su'ud makes this clear in his statement that the occupants receive the land as a loan, but he also uses another juristic concept to arrive at the same conclusion:

(10) Some [arable] fields which the peasants occupy are capable of [conversion to] meadow. [For this reason] they do not cultivate them, but leave them as meadowland. For one year, they cut the hay which is

produced. If the fisc (*miri*) is in need, is it permissible in law for the fields to be taken from the peasants for the fisc?

Answer: The peasants do not own the lands in their possession. They are royal demesne. At the time of the conquest, they were not given to anybody as [private] property. It was commanded that [the occupants] should cultivate and till them, and pay proportional tribute under the name of tithe, and fixed tribute under the name of *chift*-tax.

The right of the peasants is simply to bear the burden of the land by cultivating and tilling and, after paying the said dues on the produce, to keep the remainder. If they leave the land fallow for three years, it is lawful to take it from them and to give it to someone else.

To convert an [arable] field to meadow is to leave it fallow. The rent (*muqata'a*) due from it is not equal to the tithe which would accrue from cultivation. The remainder of the crop that belongs to the peasant after the deduction of the tithe is the yield of what is produced by labour. If a tithe is taken on what has been produced without the peasant's labour, then the remainder is not due to the peasant.

However, when the fisc has need of the produce of the land which yields through their labour, it is not lawful that it should be given to another person. Instead, in exchange for the fields in their possession, some of the fixed tribute assigned to each holding should be reduced. [*MTM*, p. 55–6]

The law which Ebu's-su'ud is stating here is quite simple. If the peasant lets the land lie fallow for three years, it is liable for confiscation. This was a standard rule of feudal law. Also, a peasant may not convert arable to meadow land, as this results in a loss of revenue. If he does so, he may lose the land. This too is a rule of feudal law, and one which emerges in a fatwa of Kemalpashazade:

(11) Month by month, Zeyd pays the cavalryman the customary taxes due on part of the cavalryman's holding. When Zeyd wishes to create a pasture, can the cavalryman say: 'You must cultivate it, or else I shall give it to someone else'?
Answer: Yes. [*Ch*, f. 29b]

Finally, Ebu's-su'ud makes it clear that the fisc may appropriate the land at any time, but if the land in question is under cultivation, it must compensate the occupier with a corresponding reduction in taxation.

The purpose of these rules was to maintain the flow of revenue, and to maintain the Sultan's powers of discretion over the land. What Ebu's-su'ud does is to justify them in Hanafi terms. Tribute lands are, in Hanafi theory, a 'burden' (*ma'una*) on their owners (or occupiers), and it is this burden of cultivation that entitles them to keep the residue of the produce after the deduction of the tribute owing to the ruler. Ebu's-su'ud's argument is that, if the land lies fallow, there is no burden, and so the cultivator loses his right of occupation. In this argument, meadowland is an analogue of fallow. It produces, provided that one ignores the effort of mowing it, a crop without labour, with the result that the peasant forfeits his tenure. Ebu's-su'ud, in this fatwa, provides no special justification for the rule that the Sultan may confiscate land when the treasury is in need, merely mitigating its effects with the principle that the occupant must receive tax-relief against the loss. In the Law-Book of Hungary, however, he states that the peasants hold the land 'by way of a loan', implying that the Sultan may take it back at will.

The Transfer of Land

Ebu's-su'ud's rulings on land tenure not only justified at least the major features of Ottoman feudal tenure in Hanafi terms, but also defined them in such a way as to give the Sultan absolute power to dispose of the lands as he wished, and to impose taxes, in keeping with Hanafi principles, 'according to what the land can bear'. Equally important was his reworking of the rules for the transfer of land.

In Ebu's-su'ud's scheme, the occupants of the land were not its proprietors, and so could not engage in sale or any other transaction which resulted in a change of ownership. However, since the peasants did in practice buy and sell land, this was a rule which was very difficult to enforce. To put it into practice required first of all a clear distinction between land held as private property and land held by feudal tenure. This Ebu's-su'ud provided, together with a distinction in the status of the two types of land:

(12) What lands are private property (*milk*), and what lands are held by feudal tenure (*miri*)?
Answer: Plots of land within towns are private property. Their owners may sell them, donate them or convert them to trust. When [the owner] dies, [the land] passes to all the heirs. Lands held by feudal tenure are cultivated lands around villages, whose occupants bear the burden of their services and pay a portion of their [produce in tax]. They cannot sell the land, donate it or convert it to trust. When they die, if they have sons, these have the use [of the land]. Otherwise, the cavalryman gives [it to someone else] by *tapu*. [D, 825]

In short, urban land was subject to ownership, rural land was subject to feudal tenure. The only way that a person could acquire ownership of feudal land was through alienation by the Sultan:

(13) Can the Sultan transfer royal demesne (*ard al-mamlaka*) into ownership?
Answer: Yes, he can. [*D*, 824]

The main purpose of this rule was undoubtedly to prevent the alienation to trusts of taxes from rural lands, since this would result in the diminution of the revenue available to the Sultan for distribution as fiefs. A person could not use rural land to endow a trust unless he was also its owner, and, since only the Sultan could grant ownership of such lands *ab initio*, the conversion of rural land to trust was dependent on the authorisation of the sovereign.

Without such authorisation, a person could gain possession, but not ownership, and the normal routes to possession were by payment of an entry fine to the fief-holder, or by inheritance. The feudal law disregarded the Hanafi rules of succession, and restricted the inheritance of the land to sons, although Ebu's-su'ud was willing, on the fulfilment of two conditions, to admit daughters:

(14) If one [of the peasants] dies, leaving a son, [the son] has the use of the land, just as his father did, and no one may interfere. Otherwise, the cavalryman gives it to another person by *tapu*. If he leaves a daughter, [the cavalryman] gives it to her for the [same] *tapu* [tax] that an outsider would give. [*MTM*, p. 62]

The first condition for the succession of a daughter is that she must pay the same entry fine as a new occupant. Ebu's-su'ud reiterates this point in many fatwas. The second condition, which he is less insistent on repeating, is that she must be capable of cultivating the land. The concern, as usual, is to maintain the flow of revenue. Brothers may also succeed to plots of land on the same condition as daughters.

Sons, therefore, have an absolute right of inheritance. In the absence of sons, daughters and brothers have a conditional right. Other relatives have no right at all:

(15) Zeyd dies and his lands require [allocation by] *tapu*. His paternal uncle 'Amr pays what an outsider would pay and says: 'I'll have the lands'. Can the cavalryman allocate them to someone else?
Answer: Yes. [*Ch*, f. 29b]

These rules of succession represent no more than a systematic restatement of the feudal law. They give only the possession but not the ownership of the land.

Succession comes into effect only on death, and the rules in Ebu's-su'ud's time were well established. Other property transfers, during the lifetime of the occupants, were more of a problem. Theoretically, they were impossible because the Treasury and not the peasants owned the land, but in practice they happened, as Kemalpashazade's fatwa permitting sale testifies.

This did not satisfy Ebu's-su'ud. The only transactions which he permitted were loan (*'ariyya*) and deposit (*wadi'a*), in other words any transfer which is temporary and gratuitous and does not require judicial validation:

> (16) To place on deposit and give on loan are not things which require a judicial decree. The peasants can give their land to someone to use or keep watch over, and take it back whenever they wish. [*MTM*, p. 51–2]

Other transactions he banned:

> (17) In Rumelia, Muslim judges give certificates and make entries in their records, [confirming] the validity of the sale and purchase, deposit and loan, and pre-emption and exchange of lands in the possession of the peasants. Does this accord with the Noble *shari'a*?
> *Answer*: It is contrary [to the *shari'a*]. Regard is paid only to the cavalryman's giving the land by *tapu*. It is a mistake for the judges to write 'sale and purchase'. They should write [instead]: 'Zeyd delegated (*tafwid*) the use of the fields which he occupied to 'Amr. In exchange, he received so-and-so many aqches, and gave [the fields] to 'Amr.' [*Ch*, f. 24a]

The enquirer should perhaps have added pledge and lease to his list of dubious transactions, and Ebu's-su'ud, who was obviously answering the question in a hurry, should have added that deposit and loan are permissible. However, the contentious issue was obviously sale, which Ebu's-su'ud, here and elsewhere, forbids absolutely:

> (18) If judges give certificates of sale and purchase, they are absolutely void. [*MTM*, p. 51]

However, the fatwa also makes it clear that this strict prohibition of sale was a legal fiction. Peasants retained the right in practice to buy and sell land, and what Ebu's-su'ud prohibited was the terminology of sale rather than the reality. His starting point in redefining the law of land sale is the notion which Kemalpashazade had developed, that what is being transferred is not the ownership of the land, but the right to settle there:

> (19) When this kind [of transaction] occurs, the judge must record the purchaser's right of settlement (*haqq-i qarar*), stating: '[A], with the

cavalryman's permission, received *x* aqches from B to delegate [to him] the use of his land, and the cavalryman gave it to B by *tapu*'. [*MTM*, p. 51]

Unlike Kemalpashazade, Ebu's-su'ud no longer refers to the transaction as a sale, and in a sense he was correct. Since the 'right of settlement' is a benefit and not a tangible property, it cannot, in Hanafi law, be the object of a sale. It could be the object of a lease; but, in Ebu's-su'ud's theory, the peasant acquires the lease of the land by payment of an entry fine – the *tapu* tax – to the fief-holder. Since neither 'sale' nor 'lease' describes the transaction, Ebu's-su'ud falls back on the notion of 'delegation' (*tafwid*), the only other suitable term which the juristic tradition had to offer. Since the term 'right of settlement' also carries the sense of 'settlement due', that is, the sum paid to acquire the right, Ebu's-su'ud uses the term to represent the price paid for feudal land by the new occupant. By referring to the transfer of land as 'delegation' and the price paid as 'settlement due', he disguises the fact that the transaction is in reality a sale.

This redefinition of the transaction may at first seem pointless, but Ebu's-su'ud's rulings are rarely without a practical purpose, and here his goal is obvious. The formula which he devised for judges to record the transfer of feudal land ends with the statement: 'and the cavalryman gives it to him by *tapu*'. In other words, when a peasant purchased a plot of land, he still had to receive the fief-holder's authorisation to settle on it, and to pay him the usual entry fine. This had the effect of maintaining the fief-holder's flow of income and his control over who settled on the land. Since the fief-holders were themselves appointees of the Sultan, this, in theory, gave the Sultan the ultimate control over the land and its occupants. In sum, therefore, Ebu's-su'ud's rulings allowed the peasants to continue to buy and sell land, but only with the fief-holder's permission, while his forbidding the terminology of sale allowed him to maintain the fiction that the Treasury owned the land.

Other transactions which effect the conveyance of land he banned altogether, as the following makes clear:

(20) Zeyd dies after giving his field to 'Amr as a pledge for a debt. Assuming that [Zeyd] has no children, 'Amr receives the field by *tapu* from the cavalryman, and has the use of it for seven or eight years. Can the said Zeyd's brother pay [the entry fine] that an outsider would pay, and take the field from 'Amr?

Answer: If he was absent [when the cavalryman allocated the field to 'Amr] and has [only] now returned, yes. Otherwise, no. [*Ch*, f. 29a]

The crux of the question is whether the field passed into the possession of the pledgee by virtue of the non-payment of the debt, or by virtue of the cavalryman's allocating it by *tapu*. If it were the first, the pledger's brother could not reclaim the field unless he also repaid the brother's debt. The answer therefore makes it clear that the pledge is invalid, and he can make good his claim provided that he was absent at the time of his brother's death, and so unable to claim his right of succession. Ebu's-su'ud ignores the question of the pledge altogether since, in his view, the transaction was void.

Feudal Practice and Hanafi Doctrine

In practical terms, the most important effect of Ebu's-su'ud's statements on land and taxation was to increase the Sultan's powers over both. In juristic terms, what he did was to redefine a system of feudal tenure as a system of land ownership. In ideological terms, his achievement was to bring Ottoman practice, in appearance at least, into some sort of conformity with the Holy Law of Islam. It was this ideological aspect of the problem that developed a life of its own, with the result that Ebu's-su'ud found himself having to answer innumerable questions on the validity or otherwise of specific feudal taxes and practices.

So far as taxation is concerned, he had already redefined the Ottoman *chift*-tax and tithe as the fixed and proportional tribute of the Hanafi jurists. Sheep-tax he unconvincingly defined as alms-tax (*zakat*), a canonical levy on domestic livestock and other items, the proceeds of which go to support the Muslim poor. Alms-tax is, in Hanafi theory, an 'act of worship' and, as with other acts of worship, intention is a condition for its validity:

(21) The fisc levies cash on sheep belonging to Zeyd, who qualifies [to pay] the alms-tax. Is [this levy] alms-tax?
Answer: If he gives it with this intention, yes. [*D*, 217]

Other taxes, Ebu's-su'ud freely admitted, had no immediate justification in the *shari'a*:

(22) If a bachelor or married person possesses very little land, there is no sanction in the *shari'a* for what is taken from them [in tax]. Bride-tax is similar. [*D*, 838]

However, since Hanafi theory recognised custom (*'urf*) as a source of law, it was custom that Ebu's-su'ud called into service:

(23) Taxes such as *jaba bennak*, taken from peasants with no land, and such-like levies, are what are known as customary (*'urfi*) taxes. [MTM, p. 54]

This device could legitimise any tax that did not directly contravene the canonical texts.

Other pious questioners even worried about the canonical validity of Ottoman measures, in particular of the *dönüm*, a standard unit of land measurement. Ebu's-su'ud, in answer to this, was able to equate the *dönüm* with the fictitious *jarib*, a measurement which appears in Hanafi texts, and to quote a Hanafi authority who conveniently establishes that the precise dimensions of the *jarib* depend upon local practice:

> (24) The *sheikhu'l-islam* Khvarharzade[18] has ascertained that the truth of the matter is that the *jarib* is whatever amount is customary and known in each [particular] region, and that no one of these amounts is singled out as binding. [This ruling] is to be preferred. [*Ch*, f. 31b]

This ruling effectively declares the *dönüm*, with all its local variations, to be the canonical measurement of land. However, when there was a need to provide an exact equation between a Hanafi and an Ottoman value, Ebu's-su'ud did so. An example is the rate of the poll-tax (*jizya*), a canonical tax unconnected with land, levied on adult non-Muslim males. The rate, according to the Hanafi texts, varies according to the wealth of the individual, a rich man possessing 10,000 or more *dirham*s paying forty *dirham*s in tax. A *dirham* in Hanafi texts is a silver coin, and the problem was therefore to establish how many Ottoman aqches there were to the *dirham*. Since this question was important in fixing the rate of the poll-tax, Ebu's-su'ud gave a very precise answer:

> (25) With the aqches circulating up to now, [ten-thousand *dirham*s] makes forty-two thousand aqches. With the new aqches, it makes forty-five thousand. [*Ch*, f. 31b]

He arrived at these figures by calculating the weight of silver in the aqche. A *dirham* was a term not only for the standard silver coin of the juristic tradition, but also of a weight which was in use in the Ottoman Empire. Before 1572, the Ottoman mints produced 420 aqches from a hundred *dirham*s of silver. After the debasement of 1572, they produced 450. The fatwa must therefore date from 1572, immediately after the debasement of the coinage.

Anomalies in Feudal Tenure

These fatwas on the validity of particular taxes and the value of specific measurements add nothing to Ebu's-su'ud's juristic theory of land and taxation, and only the ruling on the value of the *dirham* had any practical importance. Their main function was presumably to satisfy the questioners' aspirations to piety by producing a fictitious equation between Hanafi doctrine and Ottoman custom. However, other problems which arose out of the contradictions between Hanafi ideals and Ottoman reality were important for both theory and practice. These could arise either because the feudal practice on the lands in question did not conform to the ideal model which Ebu's-su'ud had first laid out in the Law-Book of Buda, or because the lands enjoyed a particular status in Hanafi tradition.

The provinces of central Anatolia fell into the first category. In this region, revenues from the land did not go exclusively to the fief-holder. Instead, one portion from each parcel of revenues went to a fief-holder, while the other portion belonged to the private estate (*malikane*) of an individual. The fief-holders held their share of the revenues at the discretion of the Sultan, on condition of performing military or other services. The estate revenues were the private property of their owners. This method of dividing the revenues from the lands pre-dated the Ottoman conquest of Anatolia, and clearly worked in practice, but Ebu's-su'ud was the first to construct a juristic theory to describe the system:

(26) Is it the usufruct of the land or a tithe on the produce that is meant by the estate (*malikane*) of a village?
Answer: It is neither. It is the real substance (*raqaba*) of the land. [The sum] received from the share of revenues allocated to a fief (*divani*) is the proportional tribute on the land of one in ten or one in eight. What is taken as *chift*-tax is the fixed tribute. The peasants who occupy the land are tenants. [The sum taken for] the estate is the rent on the land, which [the peasants] pay to the [interested] party. [*D*, 37]

The reality of the system was simply that the peasants paid taxes to both the fief-holder and the estate-owner. The ultimate ownership of the land itself was not an issue. Ebu's-su'ud, however, has to assign ownership, as this is a requirement of Hanafi theory. In his view, therefore, the real substance of the land is the property of the estate-owner. The land itself is tribute land and so, in Hanafi theory, owes fixed and proportional tribute to the sovereign. It is these taxes that make up the portion of the revenues due to the fief-holder, who is the sovereign's appointee. This neat formulation does not, however, account for the portion which the peasants pay to the estate owner. Ebu's-su'ud explains it as rent. The substance of the land belongs to the estate owner, but the peasants have the usufruct. The relationship is therefore one of landlord and tenant.

The practical effect of Ebu's-su'ud's theory of land tenure in central Anatolia was to maintain the status quo, but what is remarkable about it as a theory is how it differs from his account of feudal land in western

Anatolia, the Balkan peninsula and Hungary. These lands, he insists, were the property of the Treasury, and his definition of their legal status clearly aims to extend the Sultan's powers to dispose of them at will. In central Anatolia, however, he concedes that the land is the property of the estate owners. The effect of this concession is to surrender some of the Sultan's theoretical powers to a local interest group. Ebu's-su'ud probably had two motives in doing this. The first was simply the need to find a way of reconciling actual practice with Hanafi theory. The second was political. In the first three decades of the sixteenth century, central Anatolia had experienced several dangerous rebellions against Ottoman authority, and continuing unrest thereafter. Any apparent diminution of the rights of estate-owners could have the effect of alienating a powerful section of the local population and reigniting armed resistance to Ottoman rule.

Lands in Syria and Palestine were a problem for a different reason. Islamic tradition asserts that both regions fell to the Muslims during the reign of 'Umar, the second of the Rightly Guided Caliphs who succeeded the Prophet, and for this reason enjoyed a special religious status. Furthermore, the area included Jerusalem, one of the three most sacred sites of Islam. After the conquest of Syria and Palestine in 1516, the Ottoman Sultan acquired prestige as the ruler of a holy land, but also faced the problems of exactly which lands were holy, and precisely what this meant in practice. These were questions which Ebu's-su'ud had to answer:

(27) Are all the Arab realms Holy Land, or does it have specific boundaries, and what is the difference between the Holy Land and other lands?
Answer: Syria is certainly called the Holy Land. Jerusalem, Aleppo and its surroundings, and Damascus belong to it. Some say it is only Arbaha. Some say it is Damascus and Palestine. [*D*, 851]

When asked to define the specific qualities of the Holy Land, Ebu's-su'ud continued:

(28) ... Since the Holy Land is distinguished from other regions by the purity of its essences, it has become the alighting place for the stations of the Prophets (prayer and salutation be upon them). The merit of acts of worship which take place there is, for that reason, greater... [*D*, 852]

The next, and perhaps more pressing, question was whether these lands enjoyed a preferential tax status, as some versions of the Islamic conquest of Syria suggested they should. Ebu's-su'ud, with an eye to maintaining tax revenues, had to rule that they did not. In order to achieve this, he had to find an authoritative tradition of 'Umar's conquest which could establish Syria as tribute land:

(29) Is the land of Syria and Aleppo tribute land or tithe land?
Answer: It is tribute land. His Majesty 'Umar (may God be pleased with him) imposed [tribute]. It is true that he himself conquered Jerusalem and the other Syrian lands by composition, but later the land was, at his command, conquered by force at the hands of Abu 'Ubaida b. Jarrah, Khalid b. Walid and Sharahbil b. Hasana and Zeyd b. Sufyan (may God Most High be pleased with them), and tribute was imposed. [*Ch*, f. 31b]

About a century earlier, the Egyptian jurist Ibn Humam (d. 1457) had quoted a slightly more detailed version of the same tradition of the conquest of Syria.[19] Ibn Humam was writing during the period of the Mamluk Sultans of Cairo, whose domains included Syria and, like Ebu's-su'ud, his purpose in quoting the tradition was clearly to uphold the Sultan's right to tax Syria to its capacity, against those who claimed that it enjoyed special exemptions. In the formation of the tradition, it appears that the party which supported a lower rate of taxation for Syria had buttressed their claim with the story that 'Umar had acquired Syria by treaty. The opposing party had accepted this, but superimposed on it the story of a second conquest by force, since this was the normal legal condition for the imposition of tribute. Syria, therefore, was a Holy Land, but not one which enjoyed fiscal privileges.

Conclusion

It is above all for his work on defining the laws of land tenure and taxation that Ebu's-su'ud gained the reputation of having reconciled the *qanun* with the *shari'a*. What he did was essentially very simple. From a mass of often localised custom, he isolated the basic common elements in the system of feudal tenure and taxation. Having done this, he described the legal relationship between the taxpaying occupants of the land, the fief-holders and the Sultan in terms which he borrowed from the Hanafi tradition. The clarity of the resulting statements gives the impression that he was simply expounding the law as it had existed from time immemorial, concealing the fact that he was, in reality, creating a legal fiction. Feudal tenure as it existed in the Ottoman Empire was a system which divided the interest in the land between the Sultan, the fief-holders and the peasant occupiers, but where there were no real owners. The Hanafi jurists, on the other hand, treated land as a commodity, subject to the normal laws of property exchange. Ebu's-su'ud, like some of his Hanafi predecessors, overcame the discrepancy between Hanafi doctrine and feudal reality by declaring the Treasury to be owner of the land, and by describing peasant tenure in terms such as loan or lease, which he borrowed from the Hanafi laws of property. At the same time, he redefined Ottoman *chift*-tax and tithes in Hanafi terms as fixed and proportional tribute. The effect was not simply to harmonise the feudal law with the holy law, but also to reinforce the Sultan's control over the land, and to give him greater powers of discretion over rates of taxation.

Notes

1. G. Ostrogorski, *Pour l'Histoire de la Féodalité Byzantine*, Corpus Bruxellense Historiae Byzantinae, Subsidia 1, Brussels: Editions de l'Institut de Philologie et d'Histoires Orientales et Slaves (1954).
2. Irène Beldiceanu-Steinherr, 'Fiscalité et formes de la possession de la terre arable dans l'Anatolie pré-ottomane', *Journal of the Economic and Social History of the Orient*, 19 (1976), 233–322.
3. al-Marghinani, *al-Hidaya*, Cairo: Matba'a Mustafa al-Babi al-Halabi (1972), vol. 6, p. 37.
4. Ibn Humam, *Fath al-Qadir*, Cairo: Matba'a Mustafa al-Babi al-Halabi (1972), vol. 6, p. 33.
5. al-Marghinani, *al-Hidaya*, vol. 6, p. 33
6. Abu Yusuf, *Kitab al-kharaj*, Cairo: Matba'a al-Salafiyya (1976), p. 63.
7. Al-Khassaf, *Kitab ahkam al-awqaf*, Cairo: Matba'a Diwan Umum al-Awqaf al-Misriyya (1904), p. 35.
8. Ibn Bazzaz, *al-Fatawa al-Bazzaziyya*, in margins of *al-Fatawa al-Hindiyya*, Bulaq: Imperial Press (1912/13), vol. 4, pp. 92–3.
9. Qadikhan, *al-Fatawa al-Khaniyya*, in margins of *al-Fatawa al-Hindiyya*, Bulaq: Imperial Press (1912/13), vol. 3, pp. 591–2; Ibn Humam, *Fath*, vol. 6, p. 37, adopts a formula very similar to Qadikhan's. See Baber Johansen, *The Islamic Law of Tax and Rent*, London: Croom Helm (1988), p. 84ff.
10. Ahmad al-Rumi, *Risalat al-aradi*, Süleymaniye Library, Istanbul, MS Kasidecizade 682, f. 50b.
11. The Law-Book of Buda has been discussed, with varying degrees of comprehension, in Ö. L. Barkan, 'Caractère religieux et caractère séculier des institutions ottomanes', *Contributions à l'Histoire économique et sociale de l'Empire Ottoman*, Collection Turcica III, Louvain: Editions Peeters (1981), pp. 11–58; John R. Barnes, *An Introduction to Religious Foundations in the Ottoman Empire*, Leiden: E. J. Brill (1987), pp. 21–49; Halil İnalcık, 'Islamization of Ottoman laws on land and land tax', in Christa Fragner and Klaus Schwarz (eds), *Festgabe an Joseph Matuz*, Berlin: Klaus Schwarz Verlag (1992), pp. 101–18. The text is given in Ö. L. Barkan, *Kanunlar*, Istanbul:

Burhaneddin Matbaası (1943), p. 296.

12. Colin Imber, 'The status of orchards and fruit trees in Ottoman law', *Tarih Enstitüsü Dergisi*, 12 (1982), 763–74.
13. Ö.L.Barkan, *Kanunlar*, p. 267.
14. University Library, Istanbul, MS T2,088, f. 59b.
15. *MTM*, 53.
16. al-Quduri, *Matn*, Cairo: Matba'a Mustafa al-Babi al-Halabi (1957), p. 46.
17. This fatwa is missing in the printed version of the 'New *Qanun*' in *MTM*.
18. The reference is to Khvarharzade of Bukhara (d. 1090).
19. Ibn Humam, *Fath*, vol. 6, p. 32.

6

Trusts in Mortmain

Trusts and their Function

Much of the land and immoveable property in the Ottoman Empire was neither feudal nor allodial, but trust in mortmain, with its income assigned in perpetuity to a charitable cause that the founder had named in the trust deed, such as poor relief or the maintenance of a mosque.

The Hanafi jurists categorise trust in mortmain (*waqf*)[1] as alms (*sadaqa*), linking it through this definition to the institutions of maintenance (*nafaqa*) and alms-tax (*zakat*). The function of alms is to support the destitute, and through these three institutions the jurists created a theoretical scheme of poor relief for the Muslim community. The law obliges individuals to pay maintenance in fixed shares to indigent members of their family, and, if a pauper receives no maintenance, it entitles him to relief through the alms-tax. Furthermore, if a person owns less than the legal minimum above which he becomes liable to pay the alms-tax, the law makes him eligible for support from a trust. The poor, in juristic theory, are the ultimate beneficiaries of trusts. If a founder of a trust does not specify its purpose, then its income goes to the poor, and he must always name a charitable cause that will exist in perpetuity – typically the poor – as the beneficiary when the original object of his benevolence no longer exists.

Obviously, this elegant juristic scheme of poor relief could not fully work in practice, primarily because the alms-tax never existed as a reality. Ebu's-su'ud's definition, when pressed, of the Ottoman sheep-tax as alms-tax was a crude legal fiction.[2] Nevertheless, the scheme was not wholly imaginary. Families undoubtedly supported their needy members, although it is most unlikely that they observed the fixed shares of maintenance that the jurists envisaged. Furthermore, charitable trusts, most notably the soup-kitchens belonging to large mosques, really did support the poor, and the income from trusts really could be reassigned to the indigent when the original charitable purpose had become extinct. This Ebu's-su'ud makes clear in a fatwa:

(1) Travellers do not come to the lodge which the founder [of the trust]

built for them. Is it possible in law for the food designated for travellers
to be given to the local poor?
Answer: Yes, provided that there are poor people [there]. [*D*, 311]

However, both in theory and in reality, trusts did more than support
the destitute. The law permitted the foundation of trusts for any cause
that promoted Islam, the jurists specifying in particular the endowment
of mosques, fountains, inns, roads and bridges; the provision of
cemeteries; and the support of travellers, holy warriors and the poor.
These were the institutions that ensured the continuity of Muslim
worship: mosques for congregational prayer, fountains for the canonical
ablutions before prayer; inns, bridges, roads and the support of travellers
for the performance of the Pilgrimage; and cemeteries for Muslim burial.
To support warriors was essential for the continuity of the holy war
against the infidels, and to give alms to the poor is an obligation on the
faithful. Furthermore, it was trusts that supported Islamic education,
through the endowment of both primary schools and the higher colleges
attached to large mosques. At the same time, many individuals of modest
means set up trusts to provide, for example, oil for the lamps in their local
mosque or, most frequently of all, to pay for the repeated recitation of the
Quran, for their soul after death.

Islam, in short, was wholly dependent upon trusts in mortmain. They
provided the physical fabric of mosques and colleges, the stipends of
religious functionaries and teachers, as well as the lighting in mosques
and the continuous murmur of recitation which, for the faithful, signified
the presence of God. In supporting the colleges, trusts ensured the
continuity and dissemination of religious knowledge. It was the colleges,
in fact, that provided the material support for the juristic profession.
Trusts, however, were as important in affairs of the world as they were in
matters of religion. It was the colleges that trained the judges who served
in the law-courts. The provision of inns and bridges would, on most routes,
benefit merchants and other travellers more than pilgrims. Water supply,
whether a simple fountain or a major undertaking, like the supply to
Istanbul which successive Sultans had endowed, was essential to the
maintenance of life, and cemeteries were essential to the orderly disposal
of the dead. Without trusts, Islamic society could not have functioned.

One form of trust did not benefit Islam or the Muslim community.
This was the family trust where, typically, the founder stipulated that the
income go first to himself and thereafter to his descendants in perpetuity.
These foundations contravene the basic definition of a trust as 'alms',
since wealthy descendants are as eligible for their benefits as poor ones,
but this did not prevent the jurists from declaring them legal. Instead,
they circumvented the problem of illegality by insisting that, for the trust
to be valid, the income after the extinction of the founder's line must go

to the poor, and by invoking an opinion attributed to Abu Yusuf, which validates family trusts on the grounds that to permit them is to encourage the foundation of trusts that ultimately benefit the destitute.[3] It is quite clear, however, that the usual motive for establishing a family trust had nothing to do with the poor, but was to get round the rules of inheritance. In Hanafi law, a person can bequeath only one third of his estate. The remaining two thirds the law divides in fixed proportions between the heirs. If, however, a person converts all his property to trust in mortmain, then he retains control of it during his lifetime, ensures that it remains intact after his death, and is able to nominate whomever he wishes as beneficiaries. It was an inheritance device which could, for example, benefit females who, as canonical heirs, would receive only half the share of males, but who, as beneficiaries of a trust, would normally receive an equal share, unless the founder stipulated otherwise. The founder's freed slaves frequently also benefited in this way. Thus, while the visible function of trusts was in the public realm, they also operated in the private sphere of the family.

The Formation of Trusts

The Ownership of the Property to be Converted

Without the 'public' trusts, Islam and Islamic society could not have survived. However, since there had never been an Islamic 'church' and, before the nineteenth century, there was no Islamic 'state' identifiable as a corporate entity, the establishment of trusts was solely the responsibility of individuals, the size of a trust institution usually reflecting the founder's status in society. The mosque of the Süleymaniye, for example, with its associated hospital and colleges, still dominates the skyline of Istanbul above the Golden Horn, and reflects in architecture the concept of the Sultan as universal sovereign. It is, nonetheless, the foundation of an individual. In law, the status of the Süleymaniye, together with the properties and income which supported it, was no different from the status of a trust which, for example, a humble individual had set up to supply oil for the lamp in his local mosque.

Since every trust is the creation of an individual, the founder can use only his own property for the endowment. This rather obvious rule applies to the sovereign as much as to his subjects, as Ebu's-su'ud's predecessor in office, Kemalpashazade, rather pointedly makes clear:

(2) The Sultan of the Age converts a village to trust for [the benefit of] Zeyd and his descendants, giving them its canonical taxes as income. Is this licit for Zeyd and his descendants?

Answer: Yes, provided that the village which the Sultan has made trust is his [own] property. [*Ch*, f. 65a]

Equally obvious is the rule that a trust is not valid when a third party has a lawful claim to the property. This was not a problem that appears in juristic literature, but was the subject of an Ottoman Imperial decree, which the Sultan issued probably at Ebu's-su'ud's instigation. The problem was that debtors, by converting their property to trust, hoped to put it beyond the reach of their creditors:

(3) When the debtor Zeyd is in good health, he surreptitiously takes property from his creditors, and converts all his property to trust for his descendants. Is his trust valid?
Answer: It is neither valid nor irrevocable. Judges are forbidden to validate and register as trust the amount of a debtor's property that is tied up in the debt. [*H*, p. 42]

The Nature of the Property

The founder, therefore, must own the property that he wishes to convert to trust, and it must not be subject to a claim. The question then remains as to whether it belongs to a category of property that he may lawfully convert. The Hanafi tradition offers three different opinions on this matter. The jurists agree unanimously that it is lawful to convert real estate, and this was inevitably the major source of income for large foundations. It was, for example, the revenue from 217 villages, together with rents from commercial property in the capital, that made up the income of the Süleymaniye.[4] The rents from houses and shops in different quarters of Istanbul supported the primary school which Ebu's-su'ud himself had established in the suburb of Eyüp.[5] Where the jurists differ is over the conversion of moveable property. The tradition ascribed the most stringent and least practical view to Abu Hanifa, who maintains that the conversion of moveable property to trust is forbidden. Abu Yusuf, the tradition asserts, permits the conversion of moveable property that is an adjunct to the land. It is possible, for example, to convert land to trust, together with the slaves, animals and implements used in its cultivation. The jurists attribute the most lenient view to Shaibani, who, 'it is reported, permitted the conversion to trust of such moveables as it is customary [to convert]: hoes, shovels, adzes, saws, coffins and their coverings, cooking-pots, cauldrons and Qurans'.[6]

Of the three opinions, Shaibani's was clearly the most practical, permitting as it does the donation of tools for the maintenance of land and buildings, funerary equipage for mosques, cooking-vessels for the mosque kitchens which fed college students and the poor, and books for libraries. The purpose of the tradition seems to have been to enable individuals to make small donations to trusts.

In practice, the conversion of moveables became widespread and not confined to small donations. Moveables often, in fact, formed all or part of the capital endowment of a trust. It seems that, in particular, the conversion of animals or cash became so popular that these practices gained the grudging consent of the more liberal jurists. Qadikhan, for example, in a ruling which his successors frequently quote, permits the conversion to trust of a cow to supply milk to travellers at a hospice.[7]

Cash endowments presented more of a legal problem, since the most obvious source of income from such an endowment was interest on loans, and the law absolutely forbids usury. There was, however, a tradition which permits the conversion to trust not only of cash, but also of other fungibles. Qadikhan summarises the arguments: '[It is reported] from Zufar (may God have mercy on him) that a man converted to trust cash, food and things that can be measured or weighed. [Zufar] said: "It is permissible". He was asked: "How can this be?" He said: "The cash is given in a commenda contract [as capital to a commercial partner], and the profits of the partnership are given as alms to the cause for which the trust was established. What is measured or weighed is sold, and its price used as trading capital, or in a commenda contract ..."' Here, the use of the money for profitable commercial transactions preserves the capital sum, provides an income for the trust, and avoids the taking of interest. The probability, however, is that the commenda contract is a legal fiction, serving to justify the existence of trusts which, in reality, derived their income from lending money at interest. Cash trusts, in short, were legally suspect. In an indisputably valid trust, the endowment capital should be non-fungible and, since a trust is eternal, indestructible. Cash is neither of these things and, what is more, 'it opens the gateway to usury'. The fact that the jurists attribute the tradition to Zufar, and not to Abu Hanifa, Abu Yusuf or Shaibani, indicates that they remained uneasy about the cash trust.

Despite the scruples of the academic jurists, it was the permissive views of Shaibani and Zufar that Ebu's-su'ud adopted in the controversial question of whether or not it is permissible to convert moveables and cash to trust. In a treatise defending the institution of the cash trust, he takes as his starting point Shaibani's view that custom sanctions the conversion of certain moveables. He states further that the specific moveables which the Shaibani tradition lists – hoes, shovels and so forth – are simply examples of what was customary in Shaibani's age. The list was not prescriptive, and jurists in every age will sanction what is customary in their own time: 'they have even designated as permitted what Shaibani has designated as unlawful, as in the conversion of animals and clothes to trust'.[8] In Ebu's-su'ud's view, the only factor limiting what a person may or may not convert is contemporary custom. He had no hesitation, for example, in allowing the conversion of animals to trust. In the following fatwa, the thought that this might be illegal does not even arise:

(4) It is said that sheep and cattle in a fold were designated as trust, but that their numbers were not stated. Is [the trust] valid?
Answer: Their number must be stated. [The case] is not like the one of trees in an orchard, where it is sufficient to define the boundaries. [*Ch*, f. 64b]

Ebu's-su'ud's attitude here was entirely practical. Animals were an important source of income for some trusts, for example, the sheep and cattle belonging to dervish lodges in the countryside.[9] To declare that animals could not be made trust might satisfy some legal purists, but it would also ruin these and other institutions. Ebu's-su'ud's aim was to find a juristic formula that would allow the practice to continue.

He took the same view of cash trusts.[10] A register of charitable trusts in Istanbul, dated 1546,[11] indicates that the majority of them, and especially the smaller ones supporting such things as recitation in a local mosque, relied on cash endowments for their income. Indeed, the majority of trusts that Ebu's-su'ud himself had validated during his time as judge of Istanbul between 1533 and 1537 were of this type. Furthermore, it is perfectly clear from the register that their income came from lending cash at interest. The records do not attempt to disguise loans as commenda contracts or interest as commercial profits, and it was this flouting of the legal prohibition on interest payments that became a source of controversy.

At some time between 1546 and 1547, the Military Judge of Rumelia, Chivizade Mehmed, declared cash trusts to be unlawful, and persuaded the Sultan to abolish them by decree.[12] As Mufti, Ebu's-su'ud responded with a fatwa pronouncing them valid. In 1548, the Sultan issued a second decree, countermanding the first and restoring the trusts. It was not, however, the end of the argument, since the fundamentalist scholar, Mehmed of Birgi, in a series of treatises composed between the mid-century and his death in 1573, attacked Ebu's-su'ud's position. Juristically, the arguments of Chivizade and Mehmed of Birgi adhere closely to the mainstream Hanafi tradition and, in terms of the tradition, are clearly correct. Ebu's-su'ud's ultimate concern was not, however, with the juristic texts, but with what was practical and what was in the public interest, and it was clearly not in the public interest to abolish cash trusts. In their support of religious institutions, especially in poor neighbourhoods, they maintained the fabric of Muslim piety. Also, they were the only readily available source of credit in Istanbul and other Ottoman towns and cities. To abolish them, as the fundamentalists wished, would have damaged both religious and economic life.

Ebu's-su'ud did, however, have to confront the problem of interest payments. It was from loans at interest that the cash trusts derived their income, and no Hanafi authority had ever permitted usury. On this point, neither Shaibani nor Zufar were of any help. He called instead on the literature of 'stratagems' (*hiyal*), devices for circumventing certain legal obstacles.[13] In the collection of legal exemplars which he made for working judges, he included a model for a certificate confirming the validity of a cash trust. In it, he refers not to the payment of interest, but instead uses the euphemism that was in common usage, 'legal transaction' (*mu'amala shar'iyya*).[14] This, he makes clear to a questioner, was simply an old trick for circumventing the prohibition on usury:

(5) To be valid, how should a legal transaction be carried out?
Answer: The trustee legally sells some merchandise to 'Amr for 1,100 aqches. He delivers the merchandise to 'Amr who, after taking possession, sells it to Bekr for 1,000 aqches. After receiving [the merchandise], Bekr says: 'Give the money for it to Zeyd' and gives the merchandise to the trustee as a pledge for 1,000 aqches. This has been considered permissible. [*Ch*, 54b]

This clumsy device disguises a loan at interest as a double sale and an un-redeemed pledge, and requires two collaborators, apart from the borrower, Zeyd. It is unlikely, however, that trustees ever in reality resorted to this trick. The fact that a few founders of trusts required borrowers to deposit a pledge with the trustee, or to name a guarantor, suggests that they lent the money and received the interest directly. However, for the scrupulously pious, stratagems for avoiding the payment of interest were available.

Ebu's-su'ud in fact had a more urgent and, again, more practical concern than concealing interest, and this was to prevent extortion by controlling the percentage at which it was payable. The maximum permissible according to the Ottoman Law Books issued from the time of Bayezid II (1481–1512) was 15 per cent,[15] and it is clear that Ebu's-su'ud himself issued a fatwa confirming this rate, which the Sultan had subsequently enacted as an Imperial decree. The date of the decree is unknown, but there is a record of the Sultan sending the same instruction to the judges in the Peloponnesos in 1565:[16]

(6) Zeyd performs transactions at ten for twelve (20 per cent), thirteen (30 per cent) or even more. In our time, the Sultanic decree and the noble fatwas of His Excellency the Mufti of the Age are that ten should not be given for more than eleven and a half (15 per cent). If, after this admonition, [Zeyd] does not obey, but still persists, what should happen to him?

Answer: A severe chastisement and a long imprisonment are necessary. He should be released when his reform becomes apparent. [*Ch*, f. 54b]

Is it licit to perform a transaction of ten for twelve?
Answer: It is absolutely forbidden. The judge should chastise the offender. [*Ch*, f. 54b]

What Ebu's-su'ud did was to permit the loan of money at interest, under the euphemistic designation of 'transaction' or 'legal transaction', but to make the charging of interest at more than 15 per cent a criminal offence. For those borrowing from trusts, the standard rate was 10 per cent.[17]

By permitting the use of cash and moveables as endowments, Ottoman custom made it possible for persons of modest means to found trusts in mortmain. Without this permission, the possibility would have disappeared and existing trusts would have fallen into ruin. This was a point which the Imperial decree of 1548, lifting the ban on cash trusts, made in its preamble: 'the trustees and heirs of the funds of existing trusts are using the opportunity to embezzle the endowment cash, with the result that mosques, places of worship and other charitable purposes are falling into ruin; and it is commonly known that, because most charitable donors do not dispose of real estate, it has caused a diminution in charitable works ...'[18]

Ebu's-su'ud's successful defence of Ottoman custom against the main juristic tradition meant that, except in the couple of years before 1548, a person could convert to trust not only real estate but also moveables, and in particular, animals, cash and, following the opinion of Zufar, 'goods that can be weighed and measured'. A founder could, in fact, convert most property, provided it was his, and not the subject of a claim.

The Mode of Conversion

Before doing so, he had to identify the property. With real estate and non-fungibles, this was not a problem. In juristic theory, however, a cause for the invalidity of the conversion of cash or fungibles to trust is that they cannot be specifically identified. In defence of the cash trust, Ebu's-su'ud made an analogy with the general rule which permits a trustee to sell non-productive land belonging to the trust and to purchase good land in its place, even though the trustee had not identified the new land at the time of the foundation.[19] What happened in practice was that the founders of a cash trust identified not the individual coins, but the exact sum of the endowment, and it is this that the trustee had to keep intact. In the case of cash trusts which he registered as judge of Istanbul, Ebu's-su'ud, like all other judges, scrupulously recorded the capital sums. He was equally scrupulous when dealing with other types of trust:

(7) A gold cup and a silver belt have been converted to trust. Their weight has not been declared, but it is said that their description is known to the interested parties. Is this enough?
Answer: It is more prudent to give the detailed description. [This makes them] more secure against the possibility of substitution. [*Ch*, f. 64b]

The same caution and respect for the integrity of the trust makes him hesitant to accept collective memory as the decisive factor in maintaining the boundaries of land belonging to a trust or to an individual, even though this was the customary form of evidence in boundary disputes:

(8) Is it sufficient to say simply that the boundaries of a property are 'known'?
Answer: It is sufficient for the validity of a certificate [confirming title], provided they really are known, and provided it is not a source of trouble. [*Ch*, 64b]

Once the founder has identified the property, the next stage is to convert it to trust in mortmain. Hanafi law recognises two types of trust, which the tradition ascribes respectively to the opinions of Abu Hanifa, and of Abu Yusuf and Shaibani. In Abu Hanifa's view, the capital (*'ayn*) of the trust remains in the ownership of the founder, who donates the benefits as alms. He may at any time revoke the trust or sell the capital. When he dies, the capital passes in the normal way to his heirs. The trust becomes irrevocable only by the decree of a judge, or by bequest, in which case the capital is deducted from the third of the estate which the testator may dispose of freely. Qadikhan remarked of this kind of trust that 'the people have not followed the opinion of Abu Hanifa';[20] and, clearly, revocable trusts were never popular. In practice, most trusts conformed to the definition which the tradition ascribes to Abu Yusuf and Shaibani: 'The meaning of trust is the passing of the capital from the property [of the founder] to God Most High, and making it in perpetuity the property of God Most High, and making over the benefits to mankind'.[21] The capital of the trust thus ceased to be the property of the founder. Nonetheless, since the trustee could not use the income except in accordance with his stipulations, the founder retained control both during his own lifetime and posthumously: 'Even if [the founder's] ownership in reality lapses with [the creation of] the trust, in effect it remains his property, by virtue of the words of [the Prophet] (peace and blessings be upon him): "Alms are effective until the Day of resurrection"'.[22]

Since there were two types of trust, it was essential for the founder to make clear at the outset whether his trust was revocable or irrevocable.

For the vast majority of founders who wished to establish a trust in perpetuity, Qadikhan recommends a procedure which was to become standard practice in the Ottoman Empire. The founder should first deliver his trust to the trustee, and then bring an action against him, demanding its return, in accordance with the principles of Abu Hanifa. The judge would then rule that, in accordance with the opinions of Abu Yusuf and Shaibani, the trust was irrevocable, and enter this judgement in the trust-deed.[23] Ebu's-su'ud recommends exactly this procedure:

> (9) A person wishes to convert some of his property to trust. How should he do this to ensure that the trust is irrevocable?
>
> *Answer*: He should convert it to trust, assign its expenditures in perpetuity, and deliver it to the trustee. He should then go to the judge, and give the details of how he has assigned the expenditures and delivered [the trust] to the trustee. After the trustee has confirmed [this], he should demand the property back from the trustee, saying: 'It is not trust in the opinion of Abu Hanifa. I have retracted and will take [back] my properties.' The trustee should then say: 'It is binding according to the two Imams (i.e. Abu Yusuf and Shaibani)', and not return the property. The judge, for his part, should say: 'I have decreed that the trust is valid and irrevocable', so that it does not revert. [*D*, 299]

When a founder did not follow this procedure or, conversely, failed to state specifically that his trust was revocable, problems inevitably followed. Here, Ebu's-su'ud has to sort out a case where the founder died before he had made up his mind:

> (10) Zeyd converts a vineyard to trust in mortmain. The trust-deed records that the trust was adjudged valid according to the opinion of whichever [of the three Imams] the founder sees fit. After the vineyard has been used for a few years in accordance with the trust-deed, Zeyd dies. Does the vineyard become an irrevocable trust with the [judicial] decree that [the trust] is valid?
>
> *Answer*: In the opinion of the three Imams, the conversion of real estate to trust is valid. However, in the opinion of the Greatest Imam (i.e. Abu Hanifa), it is not irrevocable. To say that it was adjudged valid according to whichever [Imam] the founder sees fit, admits the possibility of its being attributed to the opinion of the Greatest Imam. Where there is doubt, no judicial decree is valid.
>
> If, however, it had been recorded that the trust had been adjudged valid in accordance with the opinion of the two Imams [Abu Yusuf and Shaibani], there would be agreement and the trust would be irrevocable. The decree of a judge is valid in a case where juristic

opinion is not unanimous (*mas'ala mujtahad 'alaihi*) and, in the opinion of the Two Imams, validity is inseparable from irrevocability.

In this case, the said founder converted the vineyard to trust, specified the expenditure and died when the trust was operating uninterruptedly in accordance [with his stipulations]. If this is proven by the evidence of just witnesses, [the trust] should be disposed of through the bequest, and considered part of the third [of the estate, of which a testator may freely dispose]. If the third [of the deceased's property] is sufficient [to encompass the entire vineyard], then all the vineyard remains [as trust]. If it is not, then the portion [of the vineyard] which the third [encompasses, remains as trust]. The trust is irrevocable, and no one may alter it. [*Ch*, ff. 62b–63a]

The founder here had not only failed to specify at the outset whether the trust was revocable or irrevocable, but had clearly also died intestate and not disposed of the property by will. Ebu's-su'ud's solution is to deem that the founder had established the trust according to the principles of Abu Hanifa. The next step is to prove that the trust had been continuously in existence since the time of its foundation. If proof is forthcoming, this is evidence that the founder had not revoked it and that it was still in existence at the time of his death. If this is the case, then Ebu's-su'ud deems it to be part, or all, of the bequest of one third of the deceased's estate. If it makes up more than one third of the estate, then only the portion that comprises the third remains trust property. By this device, according to Abu Hanifa's rules, the vineyard, or part of it, becomes trust in perpetuity. The solution respects both the integrity of the trust and the rights of the heirs, whose canonical shares of the inheritance remain untouched.

Cases such as these were presumably rare. Almost all trusts, it seems, were in perpetuity, and there was a standard procedure for ensuring that they could not revert. In irrevocable trusts, the founder's ownership of the property is extinguished. The problem is to establish at exactly what moment this happens, and it is at this point in the procedure that Hanafi opinion divides. The tradition makes both Abu Yusuf and Shaibani agree that the founder's title lapses, but they differ on when it does so.

Abu Yusuf maintains that this occurs at the moment when the founder declares verbally that the property is trust. The jurists make an analogy with manumission, where the master loses ownership of his slave at the instant when he declares him to be free.[24] Shaibani, by contrast, holds that the founder's ownership lapses only on delivery of the property. Normally, this means delivery to a trustee (*mutawalli*); but, in the case of a mosque, it occurs when a congregation (or, in the opinion of some, an individual) has prayed there; in the case of an inn, when the first traveller has stayed in it; in the case of a fountain, when the first person has drunk water from it; and in the case of a graveyard, after the first burial with the owner's permission.

In Ottoman practice, it was Shaibani's view that prevailed. In most cases, however, it was unimportant to establish precisely when the founder's ownership expired and the property became trust. What really mattered was registration in the records of the local court, and it would usually have been sufficient to say that the time of registration was the decisive moment in the creation of a trust. Without such a record, as Ebu's-su'ud makes clear, the trust does not exist, and the property belongs to the founder or his heirs. With such a record, they have no rights of ownership:

> (11) Zeyd makes a village trust for his descendants. If his descendants are poor, can they sell it?
> *Answer*: If it is registered, no. [*Ch*, f. 62b]

In a more difficult case, however, it might be necessary to return to pure Hanafi theory and the strict definition of 'delivery'. In answer to a question on the subject, Ebu's-su'ud in fact rules that it is possible to cancel a trust after registration, 'especially before delivery to the trustee',[25] and in the following he uses this rule in order to find an equitable solution:

> (12) The guardian Zeyd builds a mosque with an orphan's property and dies bankrupt. Is the sale of the mosque permissible?
> *Answer*: If prayer has not been performed in it, yes. [*Ch*, f. 63a]

Here the trust itself is legal, since the law gives a grudging consent to a guardian's borrowing from his ward, provided he can repay.[26] In this case, however, whatever his original prospects of discharging the debt, the guardian had died insolvent, and the only way of recovering the money is to declare the trust invalid and sell the mosque. After delivery, the mosque is in effect consecrated. It is the property of the Almighty and cannot be sold. The only solution to the problem is therefore to prove that delivery to the trust, which in the case of a mosque takes place on the first performance of prayer, has not taken place. In this case, the orphan can sell the mosque and take the money, but if delivery has occurred, there is no solution.

The Administration of Trusts

With the delivery of the property, the founder's ownership lapses. After delivery, the capital of the trust belongs to God, as does any physical structure, such as a mosque, which the trust supports. The income from the capital belongs in general to 'mankind', but in particular to the causes that the founder names. The control of the trust passes to the trustee. He assigns the revenues in accordance with the stipulation of the trust-deed, and is responsible for the management in general. It is the founder who appoints the trustee in the first instance, and many founders in fact appointed themselves to this position. He may also, by stipulating, for example, that the trusteeship remain within his own family, retain posthumous control over future appointments. A trustee on his death-bed may also appoint his own successor. It is usually the trustee who is responsible for appointing the servants of the trust – for example, the imam, muezzin or caretaker of a mosque – but, again, a founder may reserve such positions for his descendants. Financially, a trust has to be self-supporting, and it is for this reason that the jurists lay down detailed rules to ensure that both the capital and the income of the trust remain unimpaired. A trustee may not, for example, lease trust property for more than one year at a time, or three years in the case of land, in order to prevent the tenant claiming the property as his own. A female slave belonging to a trust may be given in marriage, but not a male slave, since this would make the trust liable to pay dower to his wife. A mosque lamp may not burn beyond the period of the night prayer, as this would cause unnecessary expenditure. There are many rules serving the same prudential purpose.

A trust, in short, is a self-governing entity and, in answering questions on trusts, Ebu's-su'ud's major concern was to uphold their integrity, and to ensure that they operated in accordance with the founder's wishes.

For some trusts, the first threat to their existence came from the founder's heirs. This, it seems, happened not when the founder, in the normal way, registered the property and delivered it to the trustee, but when he formed it through the bequest of one third of his property. Since the execution of a will is mandatory, the trust so formed becomes irrevocable. The problem is more difficult when the founder made the bequest during his death sickness, but here Ebu's-su'ud rules, if possible, in favour of the trust:

(13) During his death sickness, Zeyd's mind comes and goes. If he says: 'Let the third of my property be trust. Let them build a school', can his heirs challenge [the bequest] after his death?
Answer: No. Someone who had lost his mind would not speak so many words. [*D*, 815]

A constant danger to a trust already in existence was the erosion of the capital. The first safeguard against this is the rule that makes the trustee liable for capital loss:

(14) The trustee Hind gives her brother Zeyd some of the trust's property, taking from him a valuable pledge. Then, unbeknown to Hind, Zeyd by some means or other takes the pledge from her. He then becomes bankrupt and cannot repay the trust. Is Hind liable?
Answer: Yes. Not to keep secure a pledge [given as security] against trust property is a cause for compensation. [D, 319]

A second safeguard is a rule, on which Ebu's-su'ud insists, that if income is insufficient to meet expenditure, then the trustee should cease paying stipendiaries and beneficiaries, and instead use existing income to augment the capital:

(15) Zeyd builds a school, making the condition that three aqches [per day] should go to the teacher, and that seven Thirtieth [portions of the Quran] should be recited for seven aqches. He converts twenty-thousand aqches to trust, stipulating that it should be converted to real property, but after the conversion, the income does not cover expenses. In law, should [the income] be used for restoring the capital, or should it be disbursed?
Answer: If it is impossible to cover expenditure out of the capital, then the capital should be restored. [D, 329]

The same principle applied if buildings fell into disrepair: the trustee diverted income from stipendiaries and beneficiaries to reconstruction. Furthermore, it was a principle which Ebu's-su'ud regarded as inviolable, overriding even the wishes of the founder:

(16) There is a clause in a trust-deed: 'When the capital of the said trust is restored, the salaries of the trustee, the clerk and the revenue-collector should not be taken for the repair'. Are the aforenamed excluded [from the prohibition on paying stipends]?
Answer: No. The said condition is illegal. It is a superfluity. [D, 327]

An obvious corollary of the two rules is that, if a trustee does pay stipendiaries or beneficiaries during the period of restoration, he becomes liable to compensate the trust:

(17) The capital [of a trust] is being restored [in accordance] with the command of the Sultan and the opinion of the judge. If the trustee pays stipends, is he liable to pay compensation?
Answer: Yes. Restoring the capital has priority over all other expenditure. [D, 324]

Thus the cost of restoring the capital or making repairs fell on the stipendiaries and beneficiaries of the trust or, if he were responsible for the loss of capital, on the trustee.

Ebu's-su'ud's rules were uncompromisingly harsh, but were probably inevitable in the economic circumstances of the age. There were, it appears, no secure means of investing capital against future needs. Trusts simply disbursed their income directly to beneficiaries. When, for example, a trust relied for its income on agricultural land, it paid its stipendiaries once a year, after the harvest, and a stipendiary received payment only for the portion of the year when the crops were in the ground:

(18) Zeyd becomes a professor at a college whose revenue is annual after the harvest. When he is in office, the college is bestowed on 'Amr before sowing. Can Zeyd claim anything from the revenue from the grain for the said year?
Answer: No. [*Ch*, f. 65b]

Ebu's-su'ud was equally exacting in his demands on the tenants of a trust. Like earlier, Hanafi jurists, he forbade long-term tenancies as a safeguard against the loss of the property:

(19) If Zeyd has been in occupation of trust land for many years, can the trustee take it from him for no legal reason, and give it to another person?
Answer: It is unlawful to occupy trust land for a long time. [*D*, 318]

He also adhered to the Hanafi tradition in forbidding leases at less than the 'fair rent', meaning the current average rent for an equivalent property, but it is clear that he regarded the 'fair rent' as the minimum. Higher rates were permissible:

(20) A plot with a rent of two hundred and forty aqches a year is trust for [the founder's] children and children's children. It has fruit trees [on it] and is productive. Its rent is paid annually. Is it permissible in law for Zeyd to increase it excessively, to one thousand aqches, which is more than the fair rent?
Answer: Yes. [*D*, 304]

These rules governing tenancies and fixing a minimum, but not a maximum rent, aimed to ensure that both the capital and the income of the trust remained intact. A corresponding set of rules served to limit expenditure, many of them laying down the conditions which employees and other beneficiaries of the trust had to fulfil before receiving a stipend. These too belonged to the mainstream Hanafi tradition, as Ebu's-su'ud demonstrates when, in answering the question of whether a student who is not resident in a college is entitled to a stipend, he simply quotes an earlier Hanafi authority:

> (21) The student Zeyd does not live in the room of the college which he attends, but comes every day to attend classes. Is he entitled to receive a stipend?
> *Answer*: 'No one is permitted to receive [a stipend from] the income of a college trust, unless he lives in [the college] more than he lives in his own house; unless most of his effects are there; and unless he is occupied in study. A person who attends classes [in the college], but lives in his [own] home is not entitled to receive [a stipend from] the income [of the college].' *Khizanat al-akmal*,[27] at the end of the chapter on trust. [*Ch*, f. 65a]

Many similar fatwas deal with the stipends payable to imams, professors and other employees of trusts, all embodying the principle that payment is due strictly for duties discharged. Ebu's-su'ud's first concern, as always is with the financial integrity of the trust.

His second concern is to enforce the wishes of the trust's founder as he expressed them in the trust-deed. Nevertheless, he is prepared to permit an alteration in the founder's terms when it is clearly in the financial interest of the trust to do so:

> (22) The benefactor Hind has several cash trusts, and had [the following] entered in her trust-deed: 'So long as she lives, she may not change or alter [the terms of the trust]'. However, because the trustee does not respect the founder's condition[s], lending the money to bankrupts and to places where it is impossible to collect it, and because some of the debtors are elsewhere, the renewal of the contract each year is not possible. Since it is certain that the trust is suffering great injustice and damage, it would be more profitable to the trust if [the capital] were converted to real estate. Can [the founder] therefore make the following condition: 'The cash should be collected, and real estate bought [immediately] with part of the sum, and [more] with the remainder when it is convenient [to do so] (?)', and convert all the cash to real estate?
> *Answer*: She can. [*D*, 300]

Here, Ebu's-su'ud permits an important alteration in the founder's original terms, because his overriding concern is always to preserve the capital and income of the trust. When these are not at stake, he insists that the terms should be observed:

(23) Zeyd makes it a condition that certain of the learned class recite the Mighty Quran over his grave on Mondays and Thursdays. The learned who now perform the recitation do it at home, because the animals of the quarter wander over the graves, [leaving] their droppings. Is the stipend which they receive licit?
Answer: No. [*D*, 307]

Inevitably, however, problems arose in interpreting the founder's conditions. This was particularly the case in trusts where the trusteeship or the benefits went to the founder's own family, and the problem after the first generation was to determine who was eligible. In the following, it is a trusteeship that is in question:

(24) The founder's two children jointly hold a trusteeship vested in [his] descendants, one generation succeeding the other. They both die, leaving Hind, the daughter of the founder's son, and Zeyd, his daughter's son. Are they entitled to hold the trusteeship jointly?
Answer: Yes, and [the expression] 'one generation succeeding the other' is evidence not only of the order of descent, but also that the trusteeship is vested in the children's children and below. [*D*, 320]

There are two possible problems here. The first is whether a grandchild through a daughter is strictly a descendant of the founder since, in law, descent is through the male line. In the law of trusts, however, the jurists usually admit descent through the female line,[28] and so the problem does not arise. The real question hinges on the phrase 'one generation succeeding the other' (*batn^{an} ba'd batn^{in}*). In Arabic, the term *batn* implies the members of a single generation, so that when a founder uses this phrase it implies that the trusteeship or the benefits of a trust go only to a single generation of descendants at any one time. The next generation succeeds to the trusteeship or benefits only when the last member of the previous generation is dead. In this case, therefore, the founder's granddaughter and grandson are entitled to the succession, since none of the previous generation is alive. Ebu's-su'ud's answer is also pre-empting two possible misunderstandings in the future, which arise out of the use of this phrase. The first is a possible confusion with another phrase used in trust-deeds, 'generation after generation' (*nasl^{an} ba'd nasl^{in}*), which refers not to a single generation, but to all living descendants. These phrases, it seems from Ebu's-su'ud's fatwas, were a constant source of confusion in the administration of Ottoman trusts. The second point which he raises in his answer is that this mode of descent is in perpetuity. He does so, it seems, because in the Hanafi law of trusts, the status of the third generation of descendants is insecure. One view, for example, is that, if the founder does not specifically mention the third generation, nominating as trustees or beneficiaries only his 'children's children' and omitting his 'children's children's children', then the third generation does not benefit.[29] Ebu's-su'ud seems to be forestalling the possibility of such a claim. His own personal preference was clearly for the orderly succession of one generation at a time, in perpetuity, as he emphasises in a fatwa which, remarkably, openly rebuts two earlier and respected Hanafi authorities:

> (25) 'A man makes a trust for his children and does not mention the mode of succession. All generations are included in it, because of the generality of the noun "children". But it goes to the first generation so long as it endures, and when it dies out, to the second. After the third, the nearest and furthest [descendants] have a share. That is to say, the order of descent is not a condition after the third generation.' Should practice be based on this opinion?
> *Answer*: No. Radiyy al-Din Sarakhsi mistakenly wrote this in his *Muhit*. The author of *Durar wa Ghurar* also put faith in [this opinion].[30] [*Ch*, f. 63b]

Ebu's-su'ud's main concern was, it seems, for orderly descent.

The Role of the Sultan

Although the Hanafi jurists make trusts as far as possible autonomous institutions, they nonetheless assign the judge, and through the judge the sovereign, a role in their establishment and government. If, for example, a joint owner of a piece of land wishes to convert his share of the property to trust, he must first seek a judicial decree, since one opinion within the Hanafi tradition forbids the division of land in this way, 'and in disputed cases the decree of a judge is decisive'.[31] For a similar reason, a judicial decree is necessary in order to make a trust irrevocable. In appointing trustees, the judge also has residual powers. 'If the trustee dies when the founder is still alive, then the decision in the appointment belongs to the founder. After the founder's death, the decision belongs to his executor, not to the judge; but if he has no executor, then the decision belongs to the judge.'[32] If the trustee wishes to acquire a debt on behalf of the trust, or to rent out land for a period longer than the trust-deed stipulates, he must seek the judge's permission. In these, and other cases, the Hanafi jurists give judges the power to intervene in the affairs of trusts. Their aim seems, however, to be to restrict these powers to the minimum necessary for the good administration and continuity of the trust.

These were also Ebu's-su'ud's concerns. However, in Ottoman practice there were more restrictions on the autonomy of trusts than the juristic tradition envisaged. Registration in the records of a court was, in practice, a condition for the validity of a trust, and, once registered, the inclusion of trust property in both the detailed cadastral surveys of the Empire, and in separate registers of trusts, brought them under bureaucratic surveillance, and so under the control of the Sultan and his agents.

The first restriction was on the formation of trusts. A person could convert only his own property. He could not convert land or revenues in the royal demesne:

> (26) A tithe on the produce of a plot of land goes to a cavalryman. Is it valid in law to convert it trust?
> *Answer*: Unless it is [the founder's] property, no. [*Ch*, f. 63a]

Since the revenues of this piece of land already went to a cavalryman, the inevitable assumption must be that it is royal demesne assigned as a military fief, and therefore inalienable.

Since royal demesne comprised all agricultural land apart from the relatively few allods and lands already registered as belonging to existing trusts, this prohibition played a vital part in maintaining the Sultan's control over the alienation of land to trusts. There were only two ways to overcome this restriction. The first was to petition the Sultan to grant the land as an allod, and then to convert it to trust. This, it seems, was how the large non-royal trusts came into being. The second was to take advantage of the rule in Ottoman land law, which makes the ground itself, and the trees and vines growing on it, subject to separate ownership. Ebu's-su'ud permitted the use of this device but, by assimilating it to the Hanafi rules on the conversion to trust of a portion of jointly-owned property, he ensured that the practice remained under the Sultan's control:

> (27) Zeyd plants a vineyard on royal demesne and converts it to trust. Is this valid in law?
> *Answer*: With a judicial decree, yes.
> [Proof-text]: 'According to Muhammad [Shaibani], it is not permissible to convert jointly-owned property to trust. But if the judge decrees it to be permissible, then it is permitted by the unanimous [opinion of the jurists].' *Jami' al-Fusulain*.[33] [*Ch*, ff. 63a–b]

The ruling treats the land and vines as jointly owned property (*musha'*). If the owner of a portion of the property – here the vines – wishes to convert his share to trust, he may do so with the permission of the judge, but not without. Since judges receive their authority by virtue of their appointment by the Sultan, this keeps the alienation to trust of vines and trees ultimately under royal authority.

By restricting the creation of new trusts, these rules clearly aim to prevent the alienation of feudal lands, whose revenues the Sultan needed for distribution as military fiefs. They did not affect trusts that were already in existence. Ebu's-su'ud, however, clearly wished to bring the internal affairs of trusts under royal authority, petitioning the Sultan to issue decrees limiting trustees' rights to dispose freely of trust lands and to make appointments. An opinion, which Hanafi tradition ascribes to Abu Yusuf, permits trustees to exchange real estate belonging to a trust, or to sell it when it becomes unproductive and to buy new property with the sum raised. This procedure is legal, provided only that it has the sanction of the trust's founder. After 1544, however, it also required the sanction of the Sultan:

(28) There are legal warrants for the sale and exchange of property belonging to trusts. Has an Imperial decree nonetheless been issued, preventing sale and exchange?
Answer: It was issued in 951/1544. It was decreed that this transaction should take place [only] with royal permission. [*H*, p. 42]

The decree, it seems, had two aims. Supervision of sale and exchange would prevent embezzlement and loss to the trust, as a proof-text which the compiler has added seems to suggest. More importantly perhaps, it would prevent trusts acquiring, without the Sultan's consent, lands belonging to the royal demesne. It was thus another measure to prevent the alienation of revenues available for assignment as fiefs.

Ebu's-su'ud also sought to control salaried appointments to trusts. This might, in some cases, mean simply that he wished to ensure that a candidate entitled to a post by the terms of the trust deed, was properly qualified:

(29) The founder, Zeyd, stipulated that the professorship of the college which he has built goes to his sons and his sons' sons. Zeyd's son is a candidate [for the office]. If he has been a candidate for two years, is entitled to the college, and is seeking [the position], is it permissible to give the college to an outsider?
Answer: So long as it becomes evident in a gathering of men competent to decide, that his learning entitles him [to the position], it should not be given to an outsider. [*D*, 303]

Appointment to a teaching post was thus dependent on a favourable assessment of the candidate's ability by established members of the religious-juristic profession.

The control of appointments was, however, more far-reaching. In the year of Ebu's-su'ud's accession as Military Judge of Rumelia, the Sultan, evidently on Ebu's-su'ud's petition, issued a decree requiring all trustees to act only in collaboration with judges. The same decree also nullified the stipulation in some trust-deeds that no governor or judge should infringe the autonomy of the trust. The effect was to give the Sultan ultimate control:

(30) The founder, Zeyd, reserves to whichever of his descendants is trustee, the power to dismiss, appoint and carry out other business of the trust, adding: 'Let no judge or governor interfere in my trust. If they interfere, may God's curse be upon them.' Can some judges and governors disregard the founder's stipulation and interfere?

Answer: In about 944/1537, the stipulations in trust-deeds written in this way were [more closely] defined, and a decree issued as follows: 'Trustees having the rank of district governor should, in accordance with the Noble *shari'a*, personally submit to the Porte (i.e. the Sultan) dismissals and appointments as they occur. Those occupying a lower rank should, together with the judges of the district and again in accordance with the Noble *shari'a*, submit [to the Sultan dismissals and appointments] as they see fit. In matters which accord with reason and the law, judges should not oppose trustees, nor trustees judges.

If the founders mean: 'Let governors and judges be cursed when they interfere, no matter how corrupt the trustee', then they are themselves cursed. If they mean: 'Let the *shari'a* be cursed', they are again cursed themselves. Stipulations which contravene the Noble *shari'a* are all superfluous and void.

[Proof-texts]: 'The conditions of the founder are observed like [authoritative] texts, unless they contravene the *shari'a*.' al-Kafi.[34]

'If the founder stipulates that the trusteeship belongs to himself, and stipulates that neither the judge nor the sovereign power may dismiss him, if he is not to be relied on in the trusteeship, then the condition is invalid, and the judge may dismiss him and appoint someone else.' Qadikhan. [*H*, p. 44]

This extension of royal surveillance over trusts may have served partly, as Ebu's-su'ud implies, to check corruption. Its prime purpose must, however, have been to bring the trusts, which in Hanafi theory are autonomous or nearly autonomous institutions, firmly under the control of the Sultan. By the time that Ebu's-su'ud relinquished the post of Military Judge in 1545, the Sultan had acquired the power not only to control the conversion to trust of land and trees, but also to supervise the appointment of trustees and stipendiaries, and the acquisition and disposal of trust property.

In 1569, the degree of royal control became spectacularly apparent when, with the authorisation of a fatwa of Ebu's-su'ud, Selim II abrogated the trusts belonging to the wealthy monasteries of the Orthodox Church.[35] These trusts offended against two legal principles. First, they consisted largely of rural land which, by Ebu's-su'ud's definition, belonged to the royal demesne. Second, in Hanafi law, it is forbidden to create trusts directly for the benefit of churches or monasteries. It is nonetheless clear that, in reality, such trusts were commonplace. Not only did wealthy ecclesiastical institutions continue to exist, but Ebu's-su'ud had to issue a special instruction to his fatwa clerks 'not to say "trust for a church", because trust for a church is invalid'. They had instead to write 'for the poor of the church'.[36] If there were no trusts for the benefit of churches and monasteries, this instruction would not have been necessary. Ebu's-su'ud was, it seems, enforcing the rule for the first time. By ruling that monastic lands were royal demesne and the trust of monasteries invalid, Ebu's-su'ud effectively left the monks with no legal property except the monastic buildings themselves. His aim was not, however, to destroy the monasteries, but to bring the legal status of their possessions into conformity with Ottoman feudal law and with the Hanafi law of trusts. In so doing, he also raised an immediate cash sum for the Sultan, and gave him the legal power to raise revenues from monastic property in future.

The first step in this procedure was to confiscate the properties. The second step was to resell to the monks the houses, flocks, vines and other properties which, by Ottoman law, could be subject to individual ownership. The land itself became royal demesne. To raise the money for the repurchase, the monks levied a tax on the Orthodox faithful. After the monks had, as individuals, bought back the property, they individually converted it to trust, not however 'for the church' or 'for the monastery', but 'for travellers and the poor', since this form of words conforms to the Hanafi rules. The land itself passed into the ownership of the Treasury, as royal demesne. The monks retained the right of occupation, but on condition of paying the entry fine and other taxes due on the soil:

(31) Some Christian subjects become monks in a monastery. The registrar of the province takes from them the flocks, vineyards, orchards and mills, which are in their ownership, and sells them back to them. If they convert the said property to trust for the poor and travellers, can any outsider later interfere in the said trust?
Answer: If what they have converted to trust are things like animals, vineyards, mills or shops, and so long as they did not make them trust for the monastery, but trust for the poor and travellers, no one may intervene. Fields and arable lands can never be [converted to] trust, but they may receive them from the fisc on payment of an entry fine, and no one may intervene, provided there is an entry in the [cadastral] register as follows: 'The monks should have possession [of the land]

and, after they have paid all their dues like other subjects, no one may intervene. When the monks die, the ones who take their place should have possession', and provided [the fields] are not [recorded] as trust. [*D*, 453]

The creation of trusts was the simplest way for the monks to keep the repurchased property within the community. Another method, which Ebu's-su'ud also permitted, was by bequest, but the rules, as he laid them out, were far more cumbersome:

(32) Is it permissible for the monks in a monastery to bequeath the vineyards, houses and lands which they bought from the fisc, to the monks who will live in the monastery after them?
Answer: Provided that there are no heirs, and provided that they bequeath all their property, apart from lands, to the monks living in the monastery; and provided that the monks [in question] are limited to a well-defined group, whether they are rich or poor, their bequests are valid. No one from the fisc may intervene.
   If, however, they are innumerable and make up a large group, it is invalid to make a bequest to all of them. It is necessary, in order that no one may intervene, to make the bequest to the poor among them.
   If they have heirs, these are able to refuse any [bequest] beyond the third [which the testator may freely dispose of]. They cannot interfere in the third. In this way, no one may intervene. If their heirs accept [this arrangement], it is in its entirety a valid bequest, and no one may interfere. Nevertheless, a Sultanic decree is necessary in order to prevent anyone intervening in their lands. [*D*, 452]

The problem with a bequest is that Ebu's-su'ud is insisting that the monks follow the Hanafi rules. In practice, almost every monk would have heirs, since inheritance is not confined to direct descendants, and each heir has a canonical right to a fixed share of the estate. For the property to pass to the other monks in the monastery, the heirs would have to forego their portion of the property.
   Ebu's-su'ud's rulings on monastic trusts had several important consequences. The confiscation and resale of the properties produced an immediate cash sum for the Sultan, a useful windfall in the year in which he was planning the invasion of Cyprus. The designation of monastic lands as royal demesne also allowed him to collect taxes from it in future. However, the new régime, which gave the monks ownership of vines, buildings and properties other than the land itself, allowed the monasteries to survive, and to keep the assets within the monastic communities, whether by way of trusts or by bequests. To achieve this, all Ebu's-su'ud had to do was to apply Ottoman feudal law, as he himself had

formulated it, and the Hanafi law of trusts. It was a juristic sleight of hand that served, above all, the interests of the Sultan.

Conclusion

It was perhaps the Sultan who gained most from Ebu's-su'ud's rulings on trusts, since they gave him the ultimate control over both their creation and their internal government. An Ottoman tradition, however, remembered Ebu's-su'ud as the jurist who, in defending the conversion of cash and moveables against the attacks of zealots, had 'preserved the trusts of the Muslims',[37] and it is his permissive view on cash trusts that was to enter the Hanafi tradition. In this respect, his greatest service was to the continuity of the Muslim community in general.

Notes

1. J. Krcsmárik, 'Das Wakfrecht vom Standpunkte des Sarî'atrechtes nach der hanafitischen Schule', *Zeitschrift der Deutschen Morgenländischen Gesellschaft*, 45 (1891), 511–76.
2. See above, Chapter 5, no. (21).
3. Qadikhan, *al-Fatawa al-khaniyya*, in margins of *al-Fatawa al-Hindiyya*, Bulaq: Imperial Press (1912/13), vol. 3, p. 272.
4. K. E. Kürkçüoğlu, *Süleymaniye Vakfiyesi*, Ankara: Vakıflar Umum Müdürlüğü Neşriyatı (1962).
5. Ö. L. Barkan and E. H. Ayverdi, *Istanbul vakıfları tahrir defteri: 953 (1546) târîhli*, Istanbul: Baha Matbaası (1970), section 2,494.
6. al-Marghinani, *al-Hidaya*, Cairo: Matba'a Mustafa al-Babi al-Halabi (1972), vol. 6, pp. 216–17.
7. Qadikhan, *al-Fatawa*, vol. 3, p. 311.
8. Ebu's-su'ud, *Risala sharifa ma'mula fi sihha waqf al-nuqud*, Library of the Topkapı Palace, Istanbul, MS A1,541, f. 376b.
9. Ö. L. Barkan, 'Kolonizatör Türk dervişleri', *Vakıflar Dergisi*, 3 (1942), p. 310, section 19.
10. J. E. Mandaville, 'Usurious piety: the cash waqf controversy in the Ottoman Empire', *International Journal of Middle Eastern Studies*, 10 (1979), 289–308.
11. Ö. L. Barkan and E. H. Ayverdi, *Istanbul vakıfları tahrir defteri*.
12. Text of decree in *K*, ff. 70a–70b.
13. *Encyclopaedia of Islam*, 2nd ed., Leiden: E. J. Brill, vol. 3 (1971), art. 'Hiyal' (J. Schacht).
14. Ebu's-su'ud, *Bida'at al-qadi*, Süleymaniye Library, Istanbul, MS Laleli 3,711, chapter 1.
15. For example, Ahmed Akgündüz, *Osmanlı Kanunnameleri*, Istanbul: Fey Vakfı Yayınları, vol. 3 (1991), p. 93, section 42.
16. Süleymaniye Library, Istanbul, MS Laleli 706, f. 265b.

17. On usury in the Ottoman empire, see Neşet Çagatay, '*Riba* and interest concept, and banking in the Ottoman Empire', *Studia Islamica*, 32 (1970), 53–68; R. C. Jennings, 'Loans and credit in early 17th century judicial records: the *Sharia* Court of Anatolian Kayseri', *Journal of the Economic and Social History of the Orient*, 16 (1973), pp. 168–216; Bistra Cvetkova, 'Le crédit dans les Balkans, XVIe–XVIIIe siècles', *Contributions à l'histoire économique et sociale de l'Empire ottoman*, Collection Turcica III, Louvain: Éditions Peeters (1981), pp. 299–308.

18. Mahmud b. Süleyman el-Kefevi, *Kata'ib*, f. 70a.

19. Ebu's-su'ud, *Risala sharifa*, ff. 377a–b.

20. Qadikhan, *al-Fatawa*, vol. 3, p. 286.

21. Ibn Bazzaz, *al-Fatawa al-bazzaziyya*, in margins of *al-Fatawa al-hindiyya*, Bulaq: Imperial Press (1912/13), vol. 6, p. 248.

22. Ibid., p. 251.

23. Qadikhan, *al-Fatawa*, vol. 6, p. 288.

24. al-Marghinani, *al-Hidaya*, vol. 6, p. 208.

25. *Ch*, f. 62b.

26. 'If [the guardian] does this (i.e. borrows his ward's money) and he is capable of discharging the debt, there is no harm in it' (Qadikhan, *al-Fatawa*, vol. 3, p. 561).

27. The reference is to *Khizanat al-fatawa al-akmal fi'l-furu'* of 'Ali b. Muhammad al-Hanafi (d. 1128).

28. Qadikhan, *al-Fatawa*, vol. 3, p. 324. Founders who wish to exclude female descendants and male descendants through the female line should state this specifically in the trust-deed.

29. Ibn Bazzaz, *al-Fatawa*, vol. 6, pp. 373–4.

30. The references are to *Kitab al-Muhit* by Radiyy al-Din Sarakhsi (d. 1149) and to *Durar al-hukkam fi sharh ghurar al-ahkam* by Molla Khusrev (d. 1480).

31. Qadikhan, *al-Fatawa*, vol. 3, p. 302.

32. Ibn Bazzaz, *al-Fatawa*, vol. 6, p. 251.

33. The reference is to the *Jami' al-Fusulain* by Badr al-Din of Simavne (d. 1416).

34. The reference is to *al-Kafi fi'l-wafi*, a commentary on *al-Wafi fi'l-furu'* of Nasafi (d. 1310).

35. Aleksandar Fotić, 'The official explanation for the confiscation and sale of monasteries (churches) and their estates at the time of Selim II', *Turcica*, 26 (1994), 33–54.

36. Süleymaniye Library, Istanbul, MS Esad Efendi 1,017, f. 96b.

37. 'Ata'i, *Hada'iq al-haqa'iq fi takmilat al-shaqa'iq*, Istanbul: Imperial Press (1851/2), p. 186

7

Marriage and its Dissolution

Marriage in Islamic law is, in several important respects, the opposite of the canon-law marriage of Catholic Europe. In the canon law, marriage is monogamous and indissoluble except by death, with the wife's property and certain legal capacities passing to her husband. Islamic law, by contrast, permits polygamy, allows the dissolution of marriage, keeps the wife's property separate from her husband's, and requires the husband to make a payment to her as an essential element in the marriage contract.

In the pre-modern Islamic world, as much as in the pre-modern European world, the typical family would undoubtedly form around the persons of the wife and husband, with the husband in law and in custom occupying the position of head of household. An Islamic wife would, in general, enjoy greater legal rights to dispose of her affairs and her property, but suffer greater social restrictions. However, whereas the canon lawyers saw such a family unit as the ideal, the Islamic jurists clearly did not, since the logic of Islamic law leads towards the formation not of a nuclear family, but of a patriarchal household.

The obvious first step in the formation of such a household is the rule that a man may marry up to four women at the same time. The law also permits him to have sexual intercourse with his female slaves, and affiliates to him the offspring of such unions, provided he recognises them as his. If he does not, then the law fixes descent in the mother, and they inherit her servile status. Since, in legitimate unions, descent is in the male line, there is no distinction in legal status between a man's child by his wife and, provided that he has acknowledged it, his offspring by his slave.

The laws of divorce serve to emphasise a wife's subordinate position within a household. A man has an unrestricted right to repudiate his wife, whereas a woman's right to obtain a separation from her husband is extremely limited. Furthermore, after a divorce or separation, guardianship of the children remains with the husband. The woman has a right to the custody of her children up to the age of about 7 in the case of boys, and later in the case of girls. When the period of custody is over, the child reverts to its father and, since descent is from the father, the ex-wife severs her last link with her ex-husband's household. The factors which mitigate the subordination of the wife are the right to keep her own property and her right to a dower from her husband. In practice, the latter usually came to her in two portions, the lesser portion paid on marriage, and the greater on divorce or the death of the husband. Effectively, therefore, it acted as an insurance policy against widowhood or divorce.

It was probably, in fact, the jurists' insistence on the wife's unconditional right to receive a dower from her husband and to keep her own property intact that ensured that the otherwise highly inequitable laws of marriage actually worked in practice. Certainly, marriage, divorce, maintenance and custody form an area of the law where Ebu's-su'ud follows Hanafi tradition closely, making only a few modifications.

The Contract of Marriage

The Registration of Marriage

Marriage comes into existence as the outcome of a contract,[1] whose validity is dependent on the fulfilment of certain juristically-determined conditions. In Hanafi theory, the contract is an entirely private agreement, requiring no judicial intervention or registration. In the Ottoman Empire, however, it was customary, at least in cities, to register marriages with the judge. A fatwa of Ebu's-su'ud makes it clear that, by his time in office, an Imperial decree had made registration compulsory:

(1) Now that a Sultanic decree has been issued [commanding] that no marriage be concluded without the cognisance of a judge, is a marriage [concluded] without such a cognisance valid?
Answer: No, lest it give rise to dispute and litigation. [*D*, 36]

The purpose of registration, as Ebu's-su'ud's answer implies, was to provide evidence of marriage in case of dispute, and presumably also to prevent irregular or illicit unions. If, however, all the elements of the contract were intact, the judge had no right to reject the marriage:

(2) In the presence of witnesses, Zeyd marries his minor daughter to 'Amr's minor son, and 'Amr accepts. If it is without the cognisance of a judge, is the said marriage valid?
Answer: The position [of the two fathers] as guardians is flawless. Yes, the judge cannot but accept. [*D*, 38]

Here, the validity of the marriage is not in doubt. A father, as guardian, has an absolute right to contract his minor child in marriage. The contract was witnessed and, at this stage of a child marriage, dower is not payable. The implication of Ebu's-su'ud's somewhat elliptical answer is that the children's guardians must register the marriage with the judge but, since there is no defect in the contract, the judge cannot refuse the registration.

The effect of registration is to remove the marriage contract from the purely private to the public sphere, but without in any way affecting the essence of the contract itself.

The Verbal Formula

The formula for the conclusion of a marriage is not fixed, but must nevertheless consist of two parts, an offer from the bride's party and an acceptance from the bridegroom's. Neither the bride nor the groom need be present. Their guardians or agents may contract the marriage in their absence although, if the bride is an adult, it does not become effective until she has given her consent. To be valid, the offer must use either a term denoting marriage, such as 'I have married myself/my daughter to you', or else, significantly, a term which denotes the transfer of owner-ship, such as 'I have given' or 'I have sold myself/my daughter to you'. The implication of this formula is that the contract effects a conveyance of property from the bride to the groom.

Ottoman marriage contracts seem to have adhered to these conven-tions, using such phrases as 'I have come to X as his legitimate spouse', to denote marriage, or 'I have given' to denote a transfer of property, with the groom replying: 'I have received and accepted'. The question of whether or not a particular phrase was valid in concluding a marriage never arises in Ebu's-su'ud's fatwas, suggesting that in his day the issue was never a problem.

Witnesses

The Hanafi jurists stipulate that there must be two male witnesses to a contract of marriage, or else two women and one man.

This rule is so straightforward that Ebu's-su'ud rarely received queries on the subject. He did, nevertheless, modify Hanafi doctrine in two respects. The first is the question of marriage by hearsay. In Hanafi doctrine, an agent contracting a marriage on behalf of a woman may, provided that he mentions the woman's name and the name of her father and grandfather, go to a random group of witnesses and inform them of the espousal by word of mouth. If the witnesses know the woman, and the bridegroom wishes to marry her, he need only mention her name.[2] Ebu's-su'ud makes it quite clear that this procedure is no longer permissible:

(3) In marriage, is witnessing by hearsay acceptable?
Answer: Not in our time. [*D*, 35]

The second modification which Ebu's-su'ud made to Hanafi doctrine concerns the question of whether there is a legal requirement for the witnesses to see the bride's face. The issue is important, since Muslim brides are usually veiled and women's faces are normally hidden from all men, except for those in the immediate family. The Hanafi solution was not to require the bride to unveil, provided that she spoke the words giving herself in marriage.[3] Ebu's-su'ud, however, clearly required the witnesses to see her face:

(4) In order to witness [the marriage], is it a requirement in law for all who are present to see [the bride] Hind's face?
Answer: No. It is enough for two people to see it. [*Ch*, f. 36b]

The reason for these modifications of the Hanafi rules was clearly to prevent deception.

The Permission of the Guardian

A third element in a valid contract of marriage is normally the permission of the woman's guardian.

Hanafi law appoints him from her male agnatic relatives, encapsulating their role in a Saying of the Prophet: 'Marriage belongs to the agnates', and further refining the notion by listing the male agnates in a hierarchical order according to their proximity of kinship to their ward: father, paternal grandfather, full brother, half-brother on the father's side and so on.[4] Non-agnatic kin can act as guardians only in the absence of agnates, but even here their right is controversial.[5] In the absence of agnates or, in the opinion of some, agnates and other permitted relatives, the judge acts as guardian on behalf of the sovereign.[6] However, the jurists envisage that, in most cases, the bride will pass from the authority of one of her agnatic kin, usually her father, to the authority of her husband.

They also very strongly imply that the guardian's consent is a condition for the validity of the contract. Qadikhan, for example, introduces his section on guardians with the Saying of the Prophet: 'There is no marriage without a guardian'. However, having enunciated this principle, he at once qualifies it with the statement: 'This is a condition for the validity of marriage in the case of minors, slaves and lunatics'.[7] In other words, the Hanafi prohibition on a woman's marrying without her guardian's permission is not absolute. There is a view within the Hanafi tradition that an adult woman with full legal capacity may give herself in marriage.

In 1544, however, when Ebu's-su'ud was Military Judge of Rumelia, and probably on his petition, the Sultan issues a decree forbidding women to marry without the permission of their guardian. The effect of the decree was not only to restrict women in their choice of marriage partner, but also to restrict the discretion of the judges in their interpretation of the law. They could no longer, after 1544, accept marriages when the guardian had not given his consent; and, with the decree making registration of marriage compulsory, they effectively became responsible for enforcing the prohibition. This exercise of Sultanic power in an area that was within the sphere of the Holy Law clearly worried some judges. The questioner in the following fatwa opened his argument with a quotation from an authoritative text:

(5) 'One of the conditions for [a valid] marriage is [authorisation by] the guardian. This is a condition for the validity of the contract in the case of minors, the insane and slaves, but there are differing opinions concerning an adult woman who marries herself. Abu Sulayman relates from Muhammad [Shaibani] that her marriage is void. Abu Hafs relates [also] from Muhammad [Shaibani] that her marriage is valid if she does not have a guardian. If she has a guardian, her marriage is dependent on his permission. If he gives his permission, it is permitted, but if he refuses, it is void, regardless of whether or not the husband is her equal.' Qadikhan.

Is the decree of a judge, who rules in accordance with these cases, valid? *Answer*: In the year 951/1544, judges were commanded not to accept marriages without the authorisation of the bride's guardian.

The questioner here has been excessively cautious in his choice of text, since neither of the opinions which he quotes gives an adult woman an unrestricted right to conclude her own marriage. The quotation from Abu Hafs gives her this right only if she has no guardian. This was probably in fact the answer that the questioner was seeking. He was in all probability a judge faced with the problem of whether to accept a marriage where the woman had no guardian, and was seeking a way round the decree. Ebu's-su'ud's answer makes it clear that the decree applies in all cases.

A supplementary question guardedly raises the question of authority, suggesting that the right of judges to use their discretion in selecting from the range of Hanafi opinion overrides the will of the Sultan:

In which case: The judge of the time decrees: 'Traditions and opinions on this subject are not unanimous. I shall act in accordance with the alternative opinion. It is permissible to adjudge the marriage to be valid.' Is his decree permissible in law?

Answer: Since it is forbidden, it is most certainly not permissible. The authority of judges derives from the licence and authorisation of the Lord of the Caliphate. They are commanded to act according to the soundest opinion, and forbidden from [acting according to] controversial opinions, especially since the corruption of the age is as clear as daylight. There are altogether thirty-two [such controversial] cases.

This apart, the originals of the Noble decrees prohibiting, forbidding and restraining in this matter are preserved in the courts of the Three Cities [of Istanbul, Bursa and Edirne] and copies of them have been made.

The corruption of [this practice] is clearer than daylight. Once embarked on this course, how many households will be ruined! [H, pp. 28–9]

The answer makes it clear that the reason for the original prohibition was a conviction that to allow women to act free of male restraint would lead to the collapse of households, and that this was one of thirty-two cases where the Sultan had forbidden judges to act in accordance with controversial opinions within the Hanafi tradition. These, however, were merely asides. The reason that judges must accept the prohibition, and give judgement accordingly, is that their authority derives from the Sultan, whom they cannot therefore disobey. Furthermore, by giving the Sultan the title 'Lord of the Caliphate', he is invoking the right which the theological tradition accords to the Caliph, to use his independent reasoning in the interpretation of the *shari'a*. As Caliph, therefore, the Sultan possesses the power to limit the discretion of his judges in making choices between divergent juristic opinions.

In his fatwas, Ebu's-su'ud makes it clear that there can be no exceptions to the ban on marriage without the consent of the woman's guardian:

(6) Without the authorisation of a judge, Hind, in the presence of a few people, says: 'I have given my daughter, the minor Zeyneb, to my brother 'Amr's son, the minor Bekr'. 'Amr says: 'I have received and accepted Zeyneb on behalf of Bekr'. Is this a marriage?

Answer: It has been commanded that it should be with the judge's authorisation. [*D*, 37]

As a female, a mother cannot act as guardian and, in the absence of male agnates, the judge must assume the role. In this case, therefore, the judge's 'authorisation' as guardian, and not, as in other cases, simply his 'cognisance' is essential to the validity of the marriage. It is clear too that Ebu's-su'ud did not regard the consent of the male guardian as a mere external formality in the formation of the contract. His authority to contract the marriage was absolute, overriding the wishes of female members of his family:

> (7) Hind is a minor. Can her father Zeyd give her in marriage to 'Amr without the consent of her mother, Khadija, and her grandmother, 'A'isha?
> *Answer*: Yes. [*Ch*, f. 35a]

A guardian also has a right to dissolve a marriage which his ward has concluded during his absence:

> (8) When their father is absent, the twelve-year-old Hind's adult sister gives her in marriage to Zeyd. If the father returns after they are married, can he separate Hind from Zeyd, saying: 'The marriage did not have my permission'?
> *Answer*: Yes. [*Ch*, ff. 42b–43a]

The enactment of the decree forbidding women to marry without the authorisation of their male guardian had two further consequences. The first was to upset the hierarchy of generations. This becomes clear in the following:

> (9) Hind, who has a married son, marries a fresh-faced youth. Her son, Zeyd, is overcome with shame and, on the wedding night, throws a few stones at his mother's house. Are the executive authorities able to interfere?
> *Answer*: No, never. Nor is her marriage valid without Zeyd's consent. [*D*, 44]

The questioner here is simply trying to secure an acquittal for the son, by emphasising that he threw only 'a few' stones, and pointing to his shame as an excuse for his behaviour. Ebu's-su'ud, however, while also exempting the son from punishment, seizes upon the illegality of the marriage. The implication of the question is that the son is the mother's nearest guardian and, this being the case, the marriage is not valid without his consent. In questions of guardianship in marriage, males have an absolute authority over females, even when the latter belong to a senior generation.

The second consequence of the decree is to render a woman's marrying without her guardian's permission a criminal offence:

> (10) In the presence of Muslim [witnesses], Hind says: 'I have married 'Amr as his legitimate wife'. 'Amr, in accepting, says: 'I have received and accepted [her]'. In addition, the marriage fee is paid to the judge.

If the aforenamed couple are united with only this much [of the formalities of the marriage contract], are they liable for anything in law?
Answer: So long as Hind does not have the permission of her nearest
guardian, a chastisement and separation are necessary. [*Ch*, f. 36b]

In strict Hanafi law, the omission of an element in the contract
invalidates the marriage and necessitates separation. It does not, however,
incur a penal sanction. Here, Ebu's-su'ud is insisting on both separation
and punishment, separation because the marriage is invalid, and
chastisement because the couple are in breach of a Sultanic decree.

The Consent of the Bride

A valid marriage also requires the consent of the bride. The jurists do not
see this as an element in the contract itself, but rather as something which
is necessary in order to bring it into effect. The contract remains in
suspense until the bride has agreed. The consent of the bridegroom is not
necessary, presumably since an adult male has an unrestricted right to
contract his own marriage and, even if a guardian has contracted a
marriage on his behalf and against his will, he has an unrestricted right of
divorce.

A guardian cannot, therefore, coerce his female ward into marriage
but, in the case of a virgin bride, the notion of consent is negative rather
than positive. A virgin need not express her consent to the marriage
verbally. In keeping with traditional views of maidenly bashfulness, the
law considers her behaviour a sufficient indication. If, on receiving the
news of the betrothal, she is silent, or else laughs or cries, this is consent.
Refinements of this principle involve the further categorisation of silence
and weeping. Laughing in all circumstances signifies consent. If her
guardian gags her, her consequent silence is not consent, provided, on
removal of the gag, she immediately says: 'I do not agree'. If she weeps
tears, but without making a sound, this is consent. If she weeps, but raises
her voice or screams at the same time, it is not.[8] In the case of a bride who
has been previously married, the law assumes that she will not be too
bashful to express her wishes, and her verbal consent is obligatory.

It seems most unlikely that guardians would have scrupulously
observed these rules, since this part of the marriage contract was entirely
private. The law did not require the bride to declare her consent before
witnesses, and, even when the registration of marriages became
compulsory, judges did not make a record of the bride's consent, since it
did not form part of the contract itself. Consent, it seems, was a question
left entirely to the consciences of guardians, and therefore rarely appears
as an issue in Ebu's-su'ud's fatwas. In the following, Ebu's-su'ud balances

a woman's right to reject a marriage against a guardian's right to refuse his permission:

> (11) Zeyd's fiancée, Hind, does not consent to separation from Zeyd and marriage to another man. If her father nevertheless marries her to Bekr, and Zeyd later demands her, is Hind still able to refuse Bekr and [instead] marry Zeyd?
> *Answer*: Bekr cannot take her if she did not consent to the marriage [which] her father [had arranged]. So long as the father did not give his consent, Hind cannot marry Zeyd. Agreement is necessary.

Here, neither marriage is valid, the one because the woman has not consented, and the other because the guardian has not given his permission. With this problem solved, the answer to the supplementary question, which was clearly the enquirer's major concern, is simple:

> In which case, assuming that [Hind] does in the end marry Bekr, can Zeyd take back his property which has passed to Hind and her relatives?
> *Answer*: Yes. [D, 42]

He could in fact take back his property on the cancellation of the engagement, even if his ex-fiancée did not marry the other man in the case.

Equality

Another condition for the validity of marriage is the equality (*kafa'a*) of the spouses. A Saying of the Prophet: 'Women ... should not be given in marriage except to equals',[9] establishes the general principle, with the Hanafi tradition defining equality essentially in terms of religion and lineage (*nasab*), meaning descent on the father's side.

It is, as the Saying of the Prophet implies, only women who may not marry social inferiors, 'because a noble woman will refuse to share a bed with a vile man, and [the law] must be observed with regard to her. The case is different on his side, because it is the husband who seeks a bed-companion, and the meanness of the bed does not disgust him.'[10] This prohibition had two important legal consequences. The first is the rule that, if a woman contracts herself in marriage to a man who is her inferior, her guardians can separate them, 'in order to rid themselves of the shame' arising from such a marriage.[11] Since descent in Islamic law is through the male line, the offspring of such a marriage would acquire their father's low status, and so shame the mother and her kinsmen. There was no such problem if a man of high status married a low-born woman. The second consequence of the prohibition is that a Muslim woman cannot marry a non-Muslim man, as he is her inferior with regards to religion. A Muslim man, on the other hand, can marry a non-Muslim woman.

Elements in assessing equality other than descent and religion, such as profession, piety and intelligence, were matters of juristic discussion, as was wealth, and even the husband's ability to pay his wife's dower and maintenance,[12] although in practice this must usually have been the most important factor in assessing whether a prospective husband was the bride's equal.

Since a husband had to pay his wife dower and maintenance commensurate with the status of her family, marriages where the man was not the woman's equal must have been extremely rare. It is for this reason perhaps that Ebu's-su'ud received so few questions on equality. When he did so, the problem was one of balancing the claims of Muslim piety against the claims of wealth. This is very clear in the following example, although the question here is not whether inequality invalidates a marriage, but whether wealth or learning carries a greater weight:

(12) Zeyd is a man of learning. He is betrothed to the Muslim Hind, the daughter of 'Amr, and sends some of the advance dower. Before they are married, can 'Amr, with her consent, give Hind not to Zeyd, but to the wealthy Bekr?
Answer: It is unworthy of a Muslim that they should prefer anyone to a man of learning.

In fact, there is no legal reason why the girl's father cannot cancel the engagement. The advance dower is returnable, and does not create an obligation to contract the marriage. This Ebu's-su'ud's answer implies, while taking a strong moral line in the opposite direction. A supplementary question follows:

In which case, what in law should happen to 'Amr when he prefers the said Bekr on the grounds that Zeyd is poor?
Answer: Zeyd's learning is better than 'Amr's worldly goods. He should prefer learning. [*Ch*, f. 36a]

The answer makes it clear that, in Ebu's-su'ud's view, Muslim learning bestows a higher social status than wealth, and that it would therefore be wrong, although not illegal, for the father to cancel the engagement.

The same question of whether wealth or piety carries a higher status appears in the following:

(13) Bekr is the son of 'Amr, who holds a military fief [worth] 15,000 aqches [per year]. With the permission of the judge, he marries Hind,

the daughter of the muezzin, Zeyd. When Hind's brother, the absent Bishr, returns, can he, in law, separate them on the grounds that there is no equality?

Answer: If Hind is an adult and gave her consent to the marriage, Bishr cannot separate them, and refuse to give [her in marriage]. However, Bishr's consent is necessary. [*Ch*, f. 36a]

The brother here presumably considered his sister, as the daughter of a fairly humble mosque official, to have too lowly a social status to marry the holder of a valuable military fief. In law, however, a woman of humble birth may marry a man of superior status. The question of equality does not therefore arise, unless the reason for the brother's objecting to the marriage was that he considered his sister to be socially superior to her husband on account of their father's religious vocation. In either case, Ebu's-su'ud sees no objection to the marriage on the grounds of equality. What he does do, however, is to remind the questioner that the marriage, although it has the permission of the judge who acted as her guardian in her brother's absence, will now need the consent of her brother as her nearest agnatic relative.

Dower

The dower (*mahr*) is a sum which the husband must pay to the wife.[13] It is as indispensable to the contract as it is central to the Hanafi theory of marriage. It is already clear from the words of the contract that the jurists conceived of marriage as, in part at least, a property transaction, since the woman, her guardian or agent may make the offer of marriage with words denoting a transfer of property to the man. The dower, however, passes not from the woman to the man, but from the man to the woman, suggesting that what is happening is an exchange of property between the parties. The question of what the husband acquires in exchange for the dower is one which the jurists answer unequivocally: 'the dower is an exchange for the vulva, and must be paid'.[14] By the payment of the dower, the husband acquires, quite literally, the ownership (*milk*) of the wife's vulva, and it is this ownership that renders sexual intercourse licit.

It is the payment of the dower, therefore, that, in Hanafi theory, distinguishes marriage from fornication, the legal definition of fornication being sexual intercourse where there is no ownership (*milk*) or quasi-ownership (*shubhat al-milk*).[15] Sexual intercourse is permissible, therefore, only in marriage, where the dower represents an 'exchange for the vulva', or between a master and his female slave, whom he has acquired through purchase. When sexual intercourse takes place outside marriage or the bond of slavery, if the couple do not receive the fixed penalty (*hadd*) for fornication, the man must pay the woman her 'fair dower' (*mahr al-mithl*).

The jurists underline the notion of the dower as representing, in effect, the price of the vulva in an analogy which they make in order to explain the rule that the minimum sum payable as dower is ten *dirhams*. In cases of theft, ten *dirhams* is the minimum value of the goods which a thief must steal in order to incur the fixed penalty of amputation of a hand. Ten *dirhams* is therefore the minimum value of a human limb, and therefore the minimum sum payable as dower: 'The estimation of [the price] by which a limb is rendered licit is authorised in law by [the degree] of dignity [attached] to it. This is ten *dirhams* in [the case of] the fixed penalty for theft, and [the price] for rendering licit the vulva is estimated by [analogy with] this.'[16]

The Hanafi theory that dower represents an exchange for the vulva is important in practice, in that it provides a basis for the solution of common legal problems, such as whether a wife is entitled to a dower in an unconsummated marriage. In reality, however, the dower came to acquire an entirely different function, and this was to provide some security for women in pre-modern Islamic societies, where mortality was high and divorce frequent. It became the custom, seemingly throughout the Islamic world, to divide the dower into two portions, the advance dower payable on marriage, and the more substantial deferred dower payable to the wife on widowhood or divorce, or to her heirs if she predeceased the husband. The jurists accepted the practice of dividing the dower as having the sanction of custom, without, however, attempting to construct an explanatory theory.

Bride-price, Earnest-money and Nuptial Gifts

The dower is an essential element in an Islamic contract of marriage, and is unequivocally the property of the wife. In popular practice, however, it was only one of several exchanges of property which might occur on betrothal or marriage. A bridegroom might, for example, pay the bride's guardian a bride-price, or the couple might exchange gifts before or after the wedding. The problem with such payments or exchanges was to determine the ownership of the property in cases of dispute, usually following the dissolution of the engagement or marriage.

In solving these problems, the Hanafi jurists would, where it is possible to do so, assimilate the payment to dower or, more often, to a contract such as hire or gift, which is extraneous to the contract of marriage. The late fifteenth-century Ottoman jurist, Hamidi, for example, assimilates the bride-price to hire. In a section on the payment which is 'made over to the woman's guardian, and called *aghirliq* or *qaftanliq*', he quotes from a commentary on the *Hidaya*: 'A man gives something to one of the woman's relatives. If it is by way of a fee for the hire of his efforts [in procuring the marriage], it cannot be reclaimed after annulment, and there is no indemnity. If it is by way of a bribe, what is still in existence may be reclaimed, but there is no indemnity for what has been destroyed.'[17]

Ibn Bazzaz illustrates the range of options available in assigning ownership where there is a dispute over extra-canonical payments made on marriage. He cites the case of a man who offers his daughter in marriage with a large marriage-portion (*jihaz*), receives earnest-money (*dest-peyman*) from the suitor, but does not then give the marriage-portion. The first option is to consider the earnest-money as giving the suitor an unconditional right to the marriage-portion: 'If the father did not provide her with a marriage-portion, [the bridegroom] may reclaim from him the excess of the marriage-portion over the earnest-money payable for a girl of her status (*dest-peyman mithliha*). The value of a marriage-portion [compared with] earnest-money is that, for every *dinar* of earnest-money, there are three or four *dinar*s of the marriage portion.' If the father refuses to pay this sum, the bridegroom can demand the return of the earnest-money. This option seems to be an attempt to regularise what were clearly established elements in marriage. It is clear, however, that neither the earnest-money nor the marriage-portion were part of the contract of marriage itself.

Ibn Bazzaz continues by citing two further options. The first of these denies the bridegroom any rights against the bride's father: 'The truth is that he has no recourse against the woman's father because, in marriage, property is not a goal'. The father, therefore, is under no obligation to pay the marriage-portion, since it is not an element in the contract of marriage, and he keeps the earnest-money, which is in the nature of a gift. The second option also refuses the return of the earnest-money, 'because it is an advance dower ... and is therefore in exchange for the person (*nafs*) of the woman ... So how can the husband seek a marriage-portion ... given that in the person of his wife, he has already received the exchange [for the earnest-money]?' This view assimilates the earnest-money to the advance dower, and so incorporates it fully into the contract of marriage. His wife is already the return for the dower, and so he cannot demand a marriage-portion in addition.

This is one of Ibn Bazzaz's two favoured solutions to the problem: 'When earnest-money is included in the contract [of marriage], it is an advance dower', and in this case, the bridegroom cannot demand a marriage-portion. If, however, it is not included in the contract, it is assimilated to an onerous donation (*hiba bi-shart al-'iwad*): 'If it is not included in the contract and not made subject to a contract, then it becomes an onerous donation'.[18] By defining it as an onerous donation, Ibn Bazzaz obliges the father of the bride, if he wishes to keep the earnest-money, to give a countervalue, in this case the marriage-portion. Otherwise the law will treat the earnest-money as a gift, which the donor may reclaim.

Ebu's-su'ud is far more restrictive than Ibn Bazzaz. He is reluctant to admit to the validity of any nuptial payment that he cannot assimilate to the advance dower:

> (14) Zeyd is betrothed to 'Amr's daughter, Hind. He sends some cash and garments as *kalin*. In return, 'Amr sends some clothes equivalent to them in value, consisting of shirts, trousers and other items. After a while, when [the couple] have separated, can Zeyd take back the cash and clothes which he gave as earnest-money, under the name *kalin*?
> *Answer*: *Kalin* is the advance dower. It is not a gift for which an equivalent should be sent. It must be given. [*D*, 31]

Ebu's-su'ud is here redefining and regularising a popular custom. *Kalin*, the earnest-money which the husband pays on betrothal, he redefines as advance dower, making it part of the marriage contract itself. Since, on marriage, he receives the return for this payment in the form of his wife or, more precisely, her vulva, he cannot demand it back. He also rebukes the questioner for misunderstanding the nature of *kalin*. A fiancé should not give it in the expectation of receiving a countervalue. Whether or not the payment of a countervalue was customary, by declaring it unnecessary and by redefining *kalin* as advance dower, Ebu's-su'ud was bringing popular usage within the scope of the *shari'a*.

He does the same in the following:

> (15) Zeyd does not marry his daughter Hind to 'Amr, until he has received from 'Amr three hundred aqches as *aghirliq*. After the marriage, can 'Amr take back the three hundred aqches from Zeyd?
> *Answer*: Yes. If it is certain that, had 'Amr not given [the three hundred aqches to Zeyd], Zeyd would not have given his daughter in marriage, then it is not *aghirliq*. It is a bribe. [*D*, 30]

Like Hamidi, and earlier Hanafi jurists,[19] in cases where the guardian makes payment of the bride-price a condition for giving a woman in marriage, Ebu's-su'ud assimilates the bride-price to a bribe (*rishwa*). Since, in law, a bribe cannot be subject to ownership, the money still belongs to the bridegroom and not to the bride's guardian.

A third form of property transfer on marriage, after *kalin* and *aghirliq*, was *ergenlik*, whereby a bride makes a gift to her new husband, and herself receives a gift in return:

> (16) At the time of [their] marriage, Hind gives Zeyd a vineyard as *ergenlik*. In return, Zeyd gives her a kaftan. When they separate after a

year, can Hind take the vineyard from Zeyd?
Answer: Yes. It is a bribe. She gives its countervalue back to Zeyd.
[*D*, 32]

Ergenlik means literally 'bachelorhood', suggesting that the payment was perhaps a symbolic compensation to the husband for robbing him of his youthful freedom. If this is the case, then offering payment to a man to induce him to marry would be a bribe, and not therefore subject to ownership by the husband. The same principle emerges in the following:

(17) Hind gives *ergenlik* to her husband, Zeyd. After Hind's death, are her heirs able to take it from Zeyd?
Answer: Yes, it is a bribe. [*D*, 34]

Since it is a bribe, the wife remains the legal owner of the *ergenlik*, even though it may be in the possession of her husband, and it therefore forms part of her estate after her death.

These answers suggest that, in Ebu's-su'ud's view, none of the property transfers which occurred at the time of the marriage, apart from the dower, effected a transfer of ownership. Even when the wife receives a countervalue for the *ergenlik* which she pays her husband, he does not, as he could well have done, treat it as an onerous donation, which would have transferred the ownership of both the gift and its countervalue. Instead, he treats it as a bribe. His aim in undermining the legal validity of these customary payments, which presumably many regarded as essential elements in the contract, must have been to bring the practice of marriage strictly into accordance with Hanafi doctrine.

The Value of the Dower

In Hanafi law, the value of the dower is negotiable between the parties. The minimum permissible dower is ten *dirham*s, which translated conveniently into Ottoman currency as ten aqches. If the contract does not specify the amount, the bride is entitled to a fair dower (*mahr al-mithl*), which reflects her social status. The question then is to determine what is a fair dower:

(18) Is Hind's fair dower known by her mother's dower, or by what?
Answer: It is known by comparison with women on her father's side.
Another answer: It is known by comparison with her sisters. *D*, 58]

Since descent is in the male line, it is the social status of her father's family (which includes her sisters) that determines her value. This is the standard Hanafi rule. The exception seems to be the dower of a freed slave, who legally has no lineage. In her case, it is the status of her former master or of her husband that is relevant:

> (19) Hind is the freed slave of the lord who was previously Pasha of Algiers, and wife of Hasan Pasha, son of Khair al-Din Pasha. She brings a suit claiming: 'My marriage was for a thousand gold ducats'. When the heirs [of Hasan Pasha] say [in response to her claim]: 'Your marriage was for ten *dirhams* [of silver]', she cites a certificate. However, the certificate is in Algiers and, because a long period has elapsed, she cannot produce evidence in Istanbul. If she can produce evidence in Algiers, can she receive in cash the dower of a thousand gold ducats?
>
> *Answer*: If this is suitable as her fair dower, yes. Otherwise she cannot receive it until the evidence of the witnesses has been transferred. However, in view of Hasan Agha's fame, [the probability of marriage for] ten *dirhams* is remote.
>
> *In which case*: In law, what sort of person should be used in comparison [in assessing] Hind's fair dower?
>
> *Answer*: The comparison is with Hasan Agha's fame, and should be determined and agreed by experts. [*D*, 66]

Hasan Pasha, three times governor of Algiers, and son of the renowned Khair al-Din Barbarossa, died in Istanbul in 1572. When his widow claimed her deferred dower of 1,000 gold ducats, Hasan Pasha's heirs objected, declaring that her dower had been ten *dirhams*, the minimum possible in law, presumably on the grounds that she was a former slave. The widow could produce evidence only in Algiers, and not in Istanbul where the case was being heard. Ebu's-su'ud, in effect, rules in her favour, dismissing the idea that she could have been married for ten *dirhams* only, and suggesting that the dower be estimated in relation to the status of her husband. This is a reversal of the normal rule, where it is the woman's status that determines the dower, but necessary in the case of a slave, who has no family with whom it is possible to make comparisons.

When the contracting parties have agreed upon the dower, the next problem is the form in which it should be paid. If they fix the value in whatever currency is in circulation, then there is no problem, but if they fix it in goods, then it is essential to specify goods that have a precise value. It is not, for example, sufficient to specify simply 'a slave' since, without further definition, it is impossible to estimate the price. It was this rule which allowed Ebu's-su'ud to rescue the heirs of a husband who had married for an impossibly expensive dower:

(20) Zeyd marries Hind for a hundred loads of musk and a hundred loads of saffron, with each load being thirty *batman*s; a hundred male and a hundred female slaves; and a hundred camels. Because [this] is impossible to pay, can Zeyd's heirs, when he dies, give Hind nothing more than her fair dower?

Answer: Yes. The value of the goods is unknown. [*D*, 69]

Here, the heirs are hoping not to pay on the grounds that they cannot afford to. Ebu's-su'ud exempts them, but not for this reason. In agreeing to the dower, the husband had not defined the goods closely enough to assign them a market value. For this reason, the named dower is invalid, and the woman is entitled only to her fair dower.

In short, therefore, the value of the dower is negotiable between the parties. It cannot, however, be less than ten *dirham*s and, if the contract does not name a sum, then the woman receives a fair dower. The dower, however, is an exchange for the vulva, raising the question of what happens in a case of non-consummation. The general rule is that if, in a valid privacy (*khalwa sahiha*) where there is no impediment to sexual intercourse, it is the impotence of the husband that prevents consummation, the woman receives her dower in full. The husband has, in effect, taken possession of the vulva, and the failure to consummate arises from a defect on his part. If, however, it is a defect in the wife that renders intercourse impossible, she receives only half her dower. The same is true if the husband divorces her before the valid retirement:

(21) Zeyd divorces his wife Hind before consummation. Can Hind take her entire dower?

Answer: She takes half of what has been named as advance and deferred dower. [*Ch*, f. 42b]

In this case, he has not taken delivery of the exchange.

Although the theory that it is paid in exchange for the vulva is central to the Hanafi understanding of dower, the law did allow the parties to take other considerations into account when negotiating its value. Typically, a woman may demand a more valuable dower if her husband is to take her from the town or village where she is living, or the man may pay more on condition that his bride is a virgin. In these cases, however, the extra payment for the fulfilment of the condition must be in addition to the value of the fair dower. The fair dower thus represents the exchange for the vulva. The additional sum represents what the husband pays for the fulfilment of the condition. Ebu's-su'ud makes this principle clear:

(22) 'Amr's daughter, the adult Hind, is in Istanbul. Zeyd then marries her on condition that [she] go to Egypt [with him]. At the time of the

contract, two hundred gold ducats were fixed as dower, and Hind agrees [to the dower]. After marriage, can she not go [to Egypt]?
Answer: Yes. But if the two hundred gold coins are in excess of her fair dower, and if [the excess] was paid on condition of [her] going to Egypt, she loses the surplus over her fair dower. [*D*, 51]

The same rule applies in the following:

(23) Zeyd marries Hind, thinking she is a virgin. She turns out not be, and he divorces her. Does she receive her full dower?
Answer: If virginity was not stipulated in the contract, yes. If it was stipulated, and the named dower was made greater than the fair dower in order [to accommodate the condition of her] virginity, she does not receive the surplus over her fair dower. [*Ch*, f. 40a]

Finally, when the parties have negotiated the amount of the dower, it is binding on the husband to pay. Any disavowal on his part nullifies the contract:

(24) When Zeyd marries Hind, he says to her agent 'Amr: 'I do not consent to [a dower of] more than three thousand aqches'. 'Amr nevertheless marries her for six thousand. When Zeyd hears this, he says: 'I would not have agreed', but still cohabits with Hind. Is Zeyd liable for the six thousand?
Answer: If he does not accept that [the dower] was six thousand, but [still] cohabits with Hind, he has committed fornication. Not accepting the dower entails not accepting the marriage. [*D*, 55]

The Time of Payment

The next question after the value of the dower is the time of its payment. The Hanafi tradition does not lay down any rules as to the precise moment when the wife should take possession. The problem is rather to establish the moment when the payment becomes binding on the husband.

The marriage contract itself creates an obligation to pay dower. In Hanafi theory, however, dower is a consideration for the vulva, creating an obligation on the part of the wife to deliver herself to her husband. The question then is whether the dower is payable on completion of the contract, or after a valid privacy, when there was no impediment to intercourse. The jurists, it seems, solved the problem by making half the dower payable on completion of the contract, and the full dower payable after a valid privacy. It is, it seems, for this reason that a husband is liable for half the dower if he divorces his wife before the valid privacy, or if he cannot consummate the marriage on account of a physical defect in his wife. He becomes liable for the full dower on consummation, 'because the delivery of the exchange is realised by intercourse',[20] or after a valid retirement where it is a defect in himself that prevents consummation.

These rules make it clear when, in law, the dower becomes an obligation on the husband. In practice, however, the suitor usually paid the advance dower before the marriage. The question then was whether the bride acquired ownership at this stage. Ebu's-su'ud makes it clear that she did not:

(25) Zeyd is betrothed to Hind, and sends a cash sum and gold and silver rings, as advance dower. If Zeyd renounces the marriage, or dies before it, is the advance dower returnable?
Answer: Yes. [D, 54]

In other words, the bride can take possession of the dower before the marriage, but does not acquire ownership before the completion of the contract. The sum is therefore returnable on cancellation of the marriage. This accords exactly with Hanafi doctrine. If, however, the bridegroom did not pay the dower in advance of the marriage, the question is whether it becomes payable on completion of the contract or after a valid privacy. Hanafi logic would suggest the latter, as the valid privacy is when the husband takes delivery of the exchange. Ebu's-su'ud, however, did not accept this solution:

(26) When Zeyd gives his daughter to 'Amr, they agree upon five thousand aqches as an advance dower. Zeyd gives his daughter in marriage, and delivers her to 'Amr before she receives the money. Can 'Amr not give the five thousand aqches?
Answer: No, and the girl can prevent [herself] being taken to him. [D, 56]

The effect of this ruling is to make the payment of the advance dower obligatory upon completion of the contract. Without payment, the bride has no obligation to deliver herself to her husband. The jurists are not so specific in designating the time of payment. Ebu's-su'ud's aim in making the rule is obviously to prevent disputes, by removing an uncertainty in the law.

The husband must therefore pay the advance dower on completion of the contract. Most contracts, however, divided the dower, raising the question of when the second portion fell due. This, Ebu's-su'ud's answer makes clear, was determined either by negotiation or by custom:

(27) Can Hind, in law, demand and receive her deferred dower when

her husband is alive?
Answer: In the custom of this land, if the term is not fixed, she does not receive it before death or divorce. [*D*, 63]

This, it seems, was the practice in most of the Islamic world.

The Matrimonial Régime

Maintenance of the Wife

In addition to dower, the law requires a husband to pay his wife maintenance (*nafaqa*)[21] for so long as the marriage is in existence. In one opinion, attributed to Shaibani, the obligation comes into effect with the contract of marriage. In another opinion, attributed to Abu Yusuf, it comes into effect with the delivery of the bride to her husband's house. It is due until the death of the wife or, in the case of divorce or the death of the husband, until the expiry of the waiting period during which she may not legally remarry (*'idda*). The payment itself is in the form of food, clothing and lodging, with the status of the wife determining its value. The clothing, however, should not comprise items, such as shoes, which the wife needs to go out of doors. If the standing of the wife is sufficiently high, then the law also obliges the husband to pay the maintenance of her servant. The couple may themselves fix the amount of maintenance due by mutual agreement, or they may rely on the ruling of a judge. In a case where the husband is absent, the intervention of the judge is essential in fixing maintenance. In theory, maintenance should not be paid in cash,[22] although in Ottoman practice it often was.

Maintenance, like dower, is not a gratuitous payment. The jurists understand it as being due in exchange, or compensation for the husband's right to confine his wife to his house (*ihtibas*). It is for this reason that payment does not include outdoor clothes or shoes. In exchange for maintenance, the husband may prevent access to his wife and prevent her from going out without his permission. If she does so, she is disobedient (*nashiza*) and forfeits her right to maintenance. It seems to be a general understanding within the tradition that the wife's confinement is for the sexual gratification of her husband, hence the juristic discussions of whether a wife who is too ill or old to endure intercourse is also entitled to maintenance. Dower is the payment which gives the husband ownership of his wife's vulva. Maintenance is the payment that ensures his exclusive use. Qadikhan demonstrates this principle in a case involving the marriage of a female child: 'A man gives his minor daughter in marriage. He may demand dower from the husband, but he may not demand maintenance when she is unable [to endure] men, because maintenance is recompense for confinement on the husband's account, and a minor girl who is in this position is not confined on her husband's account. As for the dower, it is an exchange for the vulva. He has ownership of her vulva and dower may be demanded from him.'[23]

Of the numerous practical problems which arise out of the theory of maintenance, the first is the question of when it falls due. Ebu's-su'ud seems, in essence, to follow the view of Shaibani, that it becomes payable on completion of the marriage contract. However, his answer in the following fatwa suggests that he is seeking a compromise with the view of Abu Yusuf, which makes payment follow the delivery of the wife to the husband's home:

(28) While Zeyd's wife, the virgin Hind, is still in her mother's house, she has [the rate] fixed [of] maintenance due from Zeyd. Can she afterwards take from Zeyd the maintenance which was estimated at a fair rate?
Answer: Yes, provided her staying in the house and not joining Zeyd was a result of Zeyd's neglect, and was not from her side, and provided the judge ordered her to incur a debt [repayable by Zeyd to make up the amount of her maintenance]. [D, 138]

In other words, she receives maintenance for the period before moving to her husband's house, but only on certain conditions. If it was she who refused to join her husband, she receives no maintenance and, furthermore, it requires the intervention of a judge to fix the maintenance and to order her to take it in the form a debt repayable by her husband.

Once the wife is in the husband's house, Ebu's-su'ud applies the standard Hanafi rules on the degree of liberty to which she is entitled. She may not leave the house without her husband's permission, even to visit her parents:

(29) Zeyd beats Hind because she has gone out without his permission to her father's house. What is necessary?
Answer: Not much is necessary. [D, 148]

She may, however, visit relatives within the prohibited degrees of marriage, if the husband permits, and, within the limits which the following fatwa clearly lays out, still receive maintenance:

(30) By saying to her husband Zeyd: 'I'll be back soon', Hind gets permission to go and see her siblings. She does not come back for a long time, but lives [instead] with her siblings. Can she take from Zeyd the maintenance for this period?

Answer: If he said 'Come!' and she did not do so, no maintenance is due. Otherwise, if she stayed away for more than thirty days, the maintenance lapses. [*D*, 150]

The rule here could not be clearer. The wife may, at her husband's discretion, leave the house to visit relatives and still receive maintenance for up to thirty days. On the payment of maintenance, the husband also acquired the right to restrict visitors coming to see his wife. His discretion is not, however, absolute. He may prevent her parents, relatives and children from a former marriage from entering the house to see her, but not from standing outside the door and talking. He must, however, allow her parents a weekly, and other relatives a yearly, visit:

(31) Can Zeyd stop his wife Hind's parents from visiting her every Friday?
Answer: No. [*D*, 159]

This is the amount of freedom which the law allows a wife, and which Ebu's-su'ud in no way modifies. Independence beyond this limit is the cause of loss of maintenance.

A husband can unilaterally suspend the payment of maintenance if his wife is absent without his authorisation. A wife, however, has no matrimonial authority and, if she wishes to enforce the payment of maintenance during her husband's absence, she must apply to a judge, who may empower her to take it in the form of a debt repayable by her husband. Ebu's-su'ud's answer to the following makes it very clear that it is only with the judge's authority that she can do this:

(32) Zeyd's wife, Hind, has the amount of her maintenance fixed. However, she does not demand the maintenance for five or seven years, but lives on her own resources. Can she then take the maintenance from Zeyd?
Answer: If the judge fixed [the maintenance] on [the condition] that she spend from her own [resources], and reclaim it from Zeyd, and if she did [in fact] spend it in order to reclaim it from Zeyd, yes. [*Ch*, f. 40b]

Here, the wife's rights against her presumably absent husband depend on what the judge determined. In the next case, she has an absolute right to reclaim unpaid maintenance, because she had fixed the precise sum due by mutual agreement with her husband, and this has the same binding force as a judicial decree:

(33) Zeyd fixes twenty aqches per day as maintenance on his wife, Hind. He makes a five-year journey away from the region, and sends

her one thousand or two thousand aqches every one or two years. If Zeyd is a person of sufficient means to [pay] the said maintenance, can Hind, in law, take the arrears of the maintenance that was fixed? *Answer*: So long as they are alive, and the marriage still in existence, yes she can. If Zeyd dies or divorces her, or the judge orders her to take [the sum] due as a loan, she can [reclaim the arrears of maintenance from her husband's estate]. [*D*, 151]

The rules on the payment or non-payment of maintenance during the absence of the husband or wife raise serious problems when the husband either deserts his wife or drives her from the home. Here, the logic of the Hanafi rules leads to inequitable solutions, presenting Ebu's-su'ud with the problem of how to apply the law without creating flagrant injustices.

If a husband drives his wife from the home, she is bound to lose her maintenance, because she is technically 'disobedient' and, in forcing her out, the husband has renounced his right to keep her in confinement, for which maintenance is payable. A wife, therefore, who flees domestic violence forfeits her maintenance. In these circumstances, Ebu's-su'ud does his best to help the wife within the limits that the law allows:

(34) Zeyd beats his wife, Hind, and drives her from his house. The said Hind goes to her mother's. Can she have maintenance fixed on Zeyd? *Answer*: No, not unless Zeyd comes to get her. However, if Hind wishes to go to Zeyd's house, and Zeyd does not consent [to this], the judge can fix maintenance. [*D*, 149]

Here the woman loses her maintenance, because she is absent without her husband's explicit permission. In order to reclaim the maintenance, the wife must show that she is willing to return to the marital home. If her husband refuses his consent, it is possible to interpret this as his permitting her to be absent. In this case, the judge can fix maintenance as, technically, she is no longer disobedient. What Ebu's-su'ud seems to be doing is to create a legal fiction in order to entitle to maintenance a woman who is a victim of domestic violence.

In cases of desertion, however, Hanafi law offers no solution to the wife's difficulty. It is pointless for her to ask the judge to allow her to borrow against the husband's assets, since there is no hope that he will repay the debt. Nor can she ask the judge to dissolve the marriage, as this would contravene a Hanafi legal maxim: 'Inability to pay maintenance does not entail the right to obtain a separation'.[24]

In practice, however, there was a solution to the problem, and this was for the deserted wife to obtain a separation not from a Hanafi but from a Shafi'i judge. This was possible, since Shafi'i doctrine, unlike Hanafi, permitted a wife to obtain a judicial separation in a case of desertion. This was the Ottoman practice; and, in fact, Ebu's-su'ud's own handbook for judges includes a model of a document certifying that a woman had received permission from a Hanafi judge to obtain a separation in a Shafi'i court, and that the Hanafi judge had put that court's decree into effect.[25] He also validates the practice in a fatwa:

(35) Hind's husband disappears, and she is unable to obtain maintenance. Is it permissible for her to act as a Shafi'i and marry another man?
Answer: It is permissible, so long as there is a need for maintenance. [*Ch*, f. 39b]

At some point, probably after 1552,[26] a Sultanic decree rendered this solution impossible. This is clear from a supplementary answer which Ebu's-su'ud has added to a fatwa of Kemalpashazade (d. 1534):

(36) Hind's husband is absent, and she is unable to obtain maintenance. She acts as a Shafi'i, and a Shafi'i judge separates [her from her husband] and she marries another. If Zeyd then returns, can he take his wife back?
Answer: No. [Kemalpashazade]
Another answer: There has been a Sultanic prohibition, forbidding the practice of acting as a Shafi'i in the lands of Rumelia and Anatolia (*diyar-i Rum*). [Ebu's-su'ud] [*H*, p. 30–1]

The decree to which Ebu's-su'ud refers affected two important areas of the law. In the first place, it made it impossible for deserted wives to obtain a judicial separation. In the second place, it made it impossible to obtain absolution from an oath, since this was possible only under Shafi'i law.[27] This too had important consequences for spouses, since oaths were among the commonest causes of the dissolution of marriage.

Insofar as it regulates an area of the law which falls within the scope of the *shari'a*, the decree forbidding Hanafis to act as Shafi'is resembles the decrees which the Sultan issued following petitions from Ebu's-su'ud. However, since the effect of this particular decree is to create legal problems, rather than to solve them, and since, before its promulgation, Ebu's-su'ud had clearly approved of the practice of using a Shafi'i judge to dissolve the marriage of a deserted wife, it is very unlikely that it was issued on his initiative.

The Affiliation of Children

Descent (*nasab*) in Islamic law is in the male line. This is true of blood-relationships, and also of foster-relationships, which are important since, like consanguinity, they create a bar to marriage. The descent of a foster-child is through the man by whom the foster-mother acquired her milk, so that in law a boy and girl suckled by separate foster-mothers, both of whom had acquired their milk by the same man, are foster-brother and sister, and may not marry.[28] The only free person whose descent is through the mother is the offspring of an illicit union. The rule is that a child must be conceived within wedlock. The marriage of the parents after conception does not cancel illegitimacy:

(37) Is the child born of fornication which Zeyd and his wife committed before marriage, heir to both Zeyd and Hind?
Answer: It is heir to Hind, but not to Zeyd. [*D*, 28]

However, the general tendency of the law is, whenever possible, to affiliate a child to a man. In marriage, if a woman gives birth to a fully-formed child only six months after the wedding, the child is affiliated to the husband; so too is a child born to a woman within two years of a divorce. The law in these cases establishes descent by giving the legal fiction of the minimum and maximum terms of pregnancy precedence over biological reality.

If a man wishes to disclaim the paternity of a child born at any time after the first six months of wedlock, he must resort to the process of mutual anathema (*li'an*). This requires him to swear by God four times in the presence of a judge, that he is truthful in accusing his wife of fornication, and then formally to invoke God's curse if he is not telling the truth. Following him, the wife must swear four times that her husband is lying, and then invoke the curse of God on herself if he is telling the truth. The procedure takes this specific form in order to deflect the fixed punishments for false accusation of fornication and for fornication, from the husband and wife respectively.[29] After these formalities, the judge separates the couple and affiliates the child to its mother.

However, unless he resorts to mutual anathema, the law will always affiliate the child to the husband, even when it patently is not his:

(38) Zeyd is absent for three years. Then he comes home and finds his wife, Hind, to be pregnant. What is the decree of the Noble *shari'a*, when she says: 'I am pregnant by you'?
Answer: If he confirms [what she says], fine. Otherwise they should pronounce mutual anathema. [*D*, 784]

If a husband does use mutual anathema to deny paternity, there is nonetheless another route to affiliation with a male, which appears in a supplemen-tary answer to one of Ebu's-su'ud's fatwas:

(39) The child of Zeyd's wife, Hind, is by fornication with another [man]. If Zeyd dies when it has been established that [the child] is by another man, does the child inherit from Zeyd?
Answer: [Fornication] is not established unless [Zeyd and Hind] have pronounced mutual anathema, and the child has been assigned to its mother. If they have done so, then the child cannot inherit. [*D*, 29]

This is the same rule as in the previous fatwa, but it also has a supplementary answer:

Answer: Quasi-marriage is sufficient for affiliation. [*Ch*, f. 37b]

In other words, if the act of fornication can be said to resemble marriage, then it is possible to establish paternity in the biological father, from whom the child could then inherit. The notion of quasi-marriage is another fiction to prevent illegitimacy, and analogous to the notion of quasi-ownership to prevent the punishment for fornication.

The important role of legal fictions in the laws of affiliation makes possible what is, in effect, adoption. If a man claims that a slave is his son or daughter, his claim is effective, provided only that the slave is such that he or she 'could have been born to someone like him'. This 'adoption' gives the former slave the same status as a biological child. If, for example, a man 'adopts' a male and a female slave who are married, they become brother and sister, and their marriage is invalid.[30] Ebu's-su'ud validates this practice, but with a modification:

(40) Zeyd's slave, 'Amr, is of unknown descent. When Zeyd is in good health, he calls 'Amr 'my son', and dies after making this avowal. It would have been possible for Zeyd to have had a son like 'Amr. If Zeyd has a son, Bekr, can 'Amr also inherit?
Answer: If it is established by proof (*bayyina*) that 'Amr's descent by birth is unknown, yes. Otherwise, no. [*D*, 25]

The important point here is that the owner's declaration by itself is insufficient to bring about affiliation. It becomes effective only if he can bring proof that the slave's descent is unknown.

The rules governing the status of the offspring of female slaves are different from those governing the offspring of free women. The descent of the child of a female slave is fixed in the mother, and not in the father, and it inherits her servile status. If the father is free but the mother a slave, the offspring too is a slave. There is, however, a very important exception to this rule. If a master has a child by his female slave and acknowledges the child as his, then the child is free and the mother acquires a privileged status as 'mother of a child' (*umm walad*). Her master loses the right to sell her, and on his death she becomes free. The master need not acknowledge his child by his slave, but the law puts strong moral pressure on him to do so.[31] Once he has recognised such a child, it enjoys the same legal status as his offspring by a wife.

These rules are clear, and were evidently well known enough not to cause problems, as they do not form a subject of Ebu's-su'ud's fatwas. The questions which came before Ebu's-su'ud arose essentially from the separation of the husband's and wife's property, and the temptations which a wife's female slave offered to her husband. To start with, there were disputes over actual ownership:

(41) Hind gives her husband a female slave as a gift. When Zeyd has produced children by the slave, Hind denies the gift. If [Zeyd] cannot bring proof, are his children affiliated to Zeyd?
Answer: Not without proving the gift. [*D*, 545]

Here, the husband is caught by a technicality. A court would give preference to the wife's word, unless he could provide counter-evidence, because, in property disputes, the word of the person who transferred the ownership – here the wife – has priority. The descent of the children is meanwhile fixed in the mother, and they inherit her status as slaves. The husband, as frequently happened, found himself the father of slaves in his own household.

Ebu's-su'ud was undoubtedly happy with this outcome, since he usually refuses to affiliate a man's offspring by his wife's female slave, even though the law provides him with the means to do so. Qadikhan summarises the rule: 'If the man [who has produced a child by his wife's or other person's slave] says: "The owner of the slave made her licit to me", there is no affiliation unless the owner confirms that he [or she] made [the slave] licit to him, and that the child is by him. If he [or she] confirms him in both these things, [the child] is affiliated [to him]; but otherwise, it is not.'[32] In short, if a wife permits a husband to have intercourse with her slave and both recognise the child, it is affiliated to the husband. Nevertheless, this is a rule which Ebu's-su'ud is prepared to disregard:

(42) Hind gives her husband, Zeyd, permission to have intercourse with her female slave, Zeyneb. Zeyd has intercourse with Zeyneb and a child is born. Hind then dies, and the judge (?) says: 'Prove that she gave you permission to have intercourse with Zeyneb'. Assuming that

Zeyd is unable to bring proof, can it be confirmed by oath?
Answer: Even if he proves it, the child's affiliation is not established. [Ownership of] the child that was born is divided among the heirs, like the rest of Hind's estate. [*D*, 547]

Here, Ebu's-su'ud's insistence that proof of the wife's permission would not serve to affiliate the child seems to contravene the rule as Qadikhan formulated it, and to contravene the spirit of the law, which presumes in favour of affiliation to a male.

The same is true of the following:

(43) Zeyd has intercourse with the female slave Zeyneb, owned by his wife, Hind. The said Zeyd has children by Zeyneb. When the said Hind dies, are her heirs able to sell Zeyd's children by Zeyneb?
Answer: If Hind dies while she is Zeyd's wife, a share in Zeyneb and her children passes by inheritance to Zeyd. Although affiliation to Zeyd is not established, they become free. The other heirs attach the children to Zeyd's share [of the inheritance], and take their own shares from [the remainder of] the estate. [*D*, 549]

In this case, unless the wife gave the husband permission to have intercourse with the slave, and he acknowledged the children as his, the law does not affiliate the husband's children to him during the wife's lifetime. As slaves, they and their mother pass by descent to the heirs on their owner's death. As an heir, therefore, the husband acquires part-ownership of his own children and of their mother. According to Qadikhan, ownership of the mother should result not only in the children's freedom, but also in their affiliation: 'If he acquires ownership of the slave for a single day, then the child is affiliated to him'.[33] Ebu's-su'ud, however, chose to ignore this rule, which he could have invoked in order to establish the children's descent. Instead, he attributes the children solely to the husband's share of the estate, and the mother solely to the joint estate of the other heirs. By thus depriving the husband of a share in the ownership of the slave, Ebu's-su'ud is preventing the affiliation to him of his children. In thus circumventing Qadikhan's rule, Ebu's-su'ud is showing a systematic unwillingness to affiliate the off-spring of slave women when the father is not their master. This was an attempt, perhaps, to regulate succession within the household.

Guardianship, Custody and the Maintenance of Children

When husband and wife are separated through death or divorce, the law makes a clear distinction between the guardianship (*walaya*) and the custody (*hidana*) of the children. It assigns guardianship to male paternal kin in a hierarchy of authority, beginning with the father and paternal grandfather. Custody, however, it assigns to female maternal kin, giving priority to the mother and maternal grandmother, and then to the other female kin, again in a descending order of authority. It was important to fix the hierarchy of female maternal kin, since if a divorcée or widow remarries, she automatically loses the custody of her children, making it essential to assign another female custodian.

Guardianship of a male child lasts until puberty, of a female child usually until marriage. Custody, on the other hand, is shorter. A boy comes out of female custody and reverts to his father or other guardian, in the dominant tradition, when he can 'eat, drink and dress on his own', and a girl until she menstruates or, in a tradition attributed to Shaibani, 'when she reaches the point of lust'.[34]

It was the Shaibani tradition that guided Ebu's-su'ud in his ruling on the limit of the period of custody for girls:

(44) In law, how long is the period of custody for female children?
Answer: Even when they are no longer in need of custody, it is better [that the male guardians do] not take them for a while, unless they are sexually mature (*mushtahat*). [D, 6]

He clearly shared the view which is implicit in the tradition, that female sexuality is unmanageable without male tutelage:

(45) The child Hind's maternal grandmother, Zeyneb, has the right of custody. When Hind reaches ten years, in law, can her father Zeyd remove her from Zeyneb?
Answer: If she is sexually mature, and Zeyneb is unable to control her, yes. [D, 8]

This is a point on which he insists, allowing women the custody of sexually mature girls only when there is no male alternative:

(46) Hind is married to a stranger. Can Hind's mother take from her her fifteen-year-old daughter?
Answer: If there is no male agnate within the prohibited degrees of marriage, yes she can. But if there is, he takes her. [Ch, f. 40b]

Conversely, he recognises that males have no right of custody before the ages at which the law considers children to be independent:

(47) The infant Zeyd has a married brother, 'Amr, and a paternal uncle, Bekr. In law, which of them has the right of custody?

Answer: A male has no [right of] custody. The right to educate [the child] belongs to the brother. [*D*, 7]

Furthermore, when the child does leave custody, Ebu's-su'ud insists that it comes under the tutelage of the guardian who is nearest in the legal rather than the geographical sense, however inconvenient this may be:

> (48) Zeyd divorces his wife, Hind, and [goes to] live in another region. His son by Hind, the minor 'Amr, reaches the age of nine and Hind's right of custody drops. Can his brother, Bekr, without Zeyd's knowledge, take 'Amr from Hind, saying: 'He's my brother's son'.
> *Answer*: No. [*D*, 13]

The child must, in this case, revert to its father.

While the child is in the custody of its mother or one of her female relatives, its male guardian remains responsible for the payment of maintenance. In the case of divorce, the rule is straightforward. The father pays the entire maintenance, which the mother, in case of non-payment, may claim against him as a debt. Ebu's-su'ud makes this standard rule very clear in the following pair of fatwas:

> (49) Zeyd's divorced wife, Hind, comes to the judge and gets him to fix maintenance for her small child by Zeyd. Zeyd does not accept. Can he take the child from Hind when it is still in need of custody?
> *Answer*: No. [*D*, 4]

The next question follows on:

> (50) After a while, Hind seeks the cash which she has had fixed. Zeyd makes excuses and does not pay. Can she have the said Zeyd imprisoned?
> *Answer*: Yes. [Non-payment would] lead to the destruction of the infant. It is not like a grown child. [*D*, 5]

The reason why the ex-wife can have her ex-husband incarcerated is that he is her debtor, and non-payment of debt is one of the cases for which the law formally prescribes imprisonment.

The rule, therefore, for the payment of children's maintenance after divorce is simple. It is the responsibility of the father. This leaves the problem of who pays maintenance if the father dies. The rule here is less straightforward. If the child is still a minor, the wife retains custody, but guardianship passes to the nearest agnate, perhaps a paternal grandfather or paternal uncle, who then assumes responsibility for the maintenance. However, if the mother of the child was still married to the father at the time of his death, she inherits from her husband and, by virtue of the inheritance, becomes responsible for a share of the maintenance. As a general rule, a woman's fixed share in an inheritance is half a man's, so her share of the maintenance is half the guardian's. This explains the ruling in the next fatwa:

> (51) When Zeyd dies, his wife, Hind, has [maintenance] fixed on her minor daughter, Zeyneb. She brings up Zeyneb with maintenance from her own resources. Eight years later, can Hind take the cash, which she has spent on maintenance, from Zeyd's father, 'Amr?
> *Answer*: Not all of it is owed by him. If Zeyneb has no property, one third is assigned to Hind, and two thirds to 'Amr. [*Ch*, f. 40b]

The ruling here accords precisely with a case which Qadikhan cites, where a father dies leaving his child, the child's mother and a paternal grandfather: 'The [child's] maintenance is owed by the two of them, in thirds: a third by the mother and two thirds by the grandfather'.[35] Here, as in all questions of guardianship, custody and the maintenance of children, Ebu's-su'ud applies the Hanafi rules without any modification.

The Dissolution of Marriage

Hanafi marriage was a fragile institution. A husband has an unrestricted right to repudiate his wife, and to make vows which, if he breaks them, result in divorce. Furthermore, it is possible to establish a foster-relationship or affinity between the spouses even after marriage, and this too breaks the matrimonial bond. Apostasy by either of the spouses has the same effect.

Annulment through Foster-relationship, Affinity and Apostasy

Foster-relationship, like affinity, is a bar to marriage and so, as a rule, foster-relative would not marry in the first place. In the following, Ebu's-su'ud makes the prohibition plain:

> (52) Before they are weaned, Hind suckles her infant daughter, Zeyneb, together with Khadija's infant daughter, Fatma. Is it possible for Zeyneb's elder brother, Zeyd, then to marry Fatma?
> *Answer*: No. [*Ch*, f. 39b]

Problems did, however, arise either when the spouses only learned of the foster-relationship after marriage, or through the practices of polygamy and child marriage, where sometimes a mature wife would suckle an infant whom the husband had married. In this case, the husband becomes his infant wife's foster-father, since it is through him that his elder wife acquired her milk, and the marriage automatically becomes invalid. Furthermore, simultaneous marriage with a mother and daughter is illegal, so he also loses his elder wife.

Knowledge of the prohibitions of fosterage must have been widespread, giving rise to one of the evergreen problems of Ottoman fatwa collections:

> (53) Zeyd sucks his wife Hind's breast, but no milk comes out. Is Hind forbidden to Zeyd?
> *Answer*: No, not even if milk does come out. So long as he did not suck it before the age of two and a half years, prohibition is not established. [*Ch*, f. 38b]

The questioner fears that the husband's sucking his wife's breast makes him her foster-son. (If this were the case, it would also make him his own foster-father, since it is through him that his wife acquired her milk.) In the answer, however, Ebu's-su'ud puts him out of danger. Foster-relationship is created only if the sucking infant is under two and a half years old, and hence the rule that, even if a husband sucks his wife's milk, the marriage remains intact.

Affinity too creates a bar to matrimony and, like fosterage, can come into effect after the marriage has taken place. This is a possibility because of a rule of law that any form of sexual contact creates affinity. If, for example, a man touches a woman, or even looks at her with lust, marriage to any of her female relatives is prohibited. It was a rule which led the jurists to create an elaborate taxonomy of lust, in order to establish precisely which acts were sufficiently lascivious to create affinity. It was also a rule that threatened marriages, since if a married person had any kind of sexual contact with one of their spouse's relatives, the marriage instantly dissolved. In an age of overcrowded accommodation and poor lighting, this rule was an ever-present threat to marriage, but Ebu's-su'ud was not prepared to mitigate its harsh effects:

> (54) Zeyd mistakenly thinks that his mother-in-law, Khadija, is his wife, Hind. He begins to have intercourse with her but, before penetration, he realises his mistake and stops. Does this harm Hind's marriage to him?
> *Answer*: Yes. It is permanently unlawful. [*Ch*, f. 35b]

There was, however, an even more potent threat to marriage than affinity, and this was apostasy (*ridda*) since, if a Muslim becomes an apostate and abandons the Faith, his marriage dissolves at once. This may at first seem to be an entirely academic problem since, in an age of faith, almost no-one voluntarily renounced Islam. However, in the Hanafi tradition, in order to become an apostate, a person had to do no more than to pronounce one of the many 'profane words' (*alfaz al-kufr*) which the jurists considered to be blasphemous. Concern with the profane words was so strong in the sixteenth century that the Egyptian Ibn Nujaim (d. 1563) even made 'the utterance of profane words on the tongue' his primary definition of apostasy,[36] stressing that the words themselves, and not the inward belief or intention of the speaker, are what is legally relevant. The fatwas of Ebu's-su'ud's predecessor Kemalpashazade indicate the same concern with profanities in the Turkish-speaking world. These show that an even slightly irreverent remark about God or an angel, about the *shari'a* or its practitioners, or even about a legal document, or any invective against a Muslim's faith, were profane words, which caused the speaker to become an apostate and dissolved his or her marriage. When the law deemed even the slightest profanity to be the cause of apostasy, the marriages of the pious who were aware of these rules could break up under even the minor stresses of everyday life.[37]

Ebu's-su'ud shared the prevailing juristic view of profanity, and his fatwas show that his usual solution to the problem of marriages which dissolved as a result of profanities was the traditional one of prescribing a 'renewal of marriage' (*tajdid al-nikah*). This appears to have been a brief and simplified ceremony before an imam, lacking many of the elements of a regular contract of marriage. This form of renewal had the effect of allowing the law of apostasy to run its course, constantly reminding people of the dire effects of blasphemy, but without in the end causing too great an inconvenience.

For women, however, the law created an opportunity. A wife has no matrimonial authority, and cannot therefore repudiate her husband. Apostasy provided one of the few ways out of an unwanted marriage and it was, furthermore, one which Ebu's-su'ud was prepared, in limited circumstances, to condone:

(55) Zeyd beats his wife, Hind, who is guilty of no offence. When 'Amr says: 'It's against the *shari'a*. Why are you beating her?', Zeyd replies: 'I don't recognise the *shari'a*'. What should be done?
Answer: He becomes an infidel. Hind is irrevocably divorced (*ba'in*). She receives her dower and marries whichever Muslim she wishes. [*D*, 90]

The husband's offence here is not his beating his wife, but blasphemy against the *shari'a*. This is what makes him an apostate and dissolves the marriage. Ebu's-su'ud is, however, prepared to pronounce the dissolution final, rather to insist on a renewal, thus allowing a maltreated wife to escape a violent husband. In other cases, too, where the blasphemy emanates from the husband and the wife does not consent to a renewal, Ebu's-su'ud allows the apostasy to end the marriage. The wife's consent, it seems, is crucial.

These rules did not escape the attention of some women who hoped, by themselves blaspheming, to put an end to their marriages. This, however, was something which the law did not permit, since to allow would, in effect, give women the ability to repudiate their husbands. In dealing with such a case, Ebu's-su'ud follows Hanafi precedent:[38]

(56) Zeyd's wife, Hind, blasphemes on purpose. Zeyd thinks that a divorce (*talaq*) has occurred, takes some of his things and leaves. Has an irrevocable divorce occurred?
Answer: Repudiation does not occur through blasphemy. The couple become separated through annulment (*faskh*) of the marriage. However, after bringing the wife back to Islam by an eloquent chastisement, Zeyd should forcibly renew the marriage and take [her back].

In a supplementary answer, he defines the process of 'forcibly renewing the marriage', showing that in this case a simple renewal before an imam is not enough:

In which case, what degree of force towards Hind is licit?
Answer: [Bringing her back to Islam] is by great force and long imprisonment. After she has come to Islam, she becomes Zeyd's wife through the judge's marrying her to Zeyd in the presence of two witnesses. Then he takes her home by force. [*D*, 98]

Here, where the woman deliberately blasphemed in order to dissolve the marriage, Ebu's-su'ud insists on what would be a regular contract of marriage, except that it is effective without the woman's consent, and she receives no dower. He adopts the same solution in other similar cases and, in so doing, blocked an escape route which beckoned to women in unhappy marriages.

Divorce

Hanafi law gives a husband unfettered powers to repudiate his wife. By contrast, a woman's powers to obtain a separation from her husband are extremely limited. Divorce, however, is a 'claim of God' (*haqq Allah*) and not a 'claim of man' (*haqq al-'ibad*) and so, in legal theory, it is not the will of the husband that brings it into effect, but the will of God. What this means in practice is that whenever a husband pronounces a valid formula for repudiation, such as 'You are divorced' or 'Be divorced!', a divorce follows automatically, regardless of whether he intended it or not, and regardless of whether or not there are witnesses present:

(57) Zeyd says: 'Let my lawful wife be forbidden to me!' but does not intend it. Does the divorce take place?
Answer: Yes. [D, 70]

Since intention in divorce is irrelevant, it follows that a correct divorce formula is valid even if the husband pronounces it in jest or anger:

(58) In anger, Zeyd says 'Be divorced! Be divorced!' three times to his wife, Hind. What kind of divorce has befallen the said Hind?
Answer: A triple divorce is binding.[39] [D, 73]

Furthermore, in Hanafi law, divorce is valid, even if the husband pronounces the words under duress. Although this rule is perfectly in keeping with the logic of the law, it is manifestly unjust. Nevertheless, to ignore it would be to ignore a claim of God, and Ebu's-su'ud insists on its application. The most that he is prepared to do is to find a way of compensating the husband for one of the obligations which divorce entails:

(59) The district governor, Zeyd, tortures 'Amr, and makes him divorce his wife. Can divorce occur through compulsion?
Answer: Yes. Compulsion does not cause invalidity in matters such as divorce. Its only effect that is apparent here is that if Hind has had intercourse [with 'Amr], the person who used compulsion compensates 'Amr for half the dower for which he is liable. [D, 80]

The half dower presumably refers to the deferred dower, for which a husband becomes liable on divorce. In this case, since he pronounced the divorce formula under compulsion, it is the person who compelled him who is liable.

There are only two cases where the divorce formula is ineffective. The first is where the husband pronounces it when he is in a state of insensibility:

(60) Zeyd quarrels with his wife, Hind, in a dream, and says to Hind: 'Be divorced, three times!' Is she divorced?
Answer: He must be careful not to say it when he is awake. [D, 86]

(61) Zeyd eats hemp and drinks beer. When he is senseless, he divorces his wife three times. Is his repudiation credited?
Answer: If he could not distinguish the earth from the sky, no. [D, 87]

To be unable to distinguish between earth and sky is a standard juristic test for drunkenness. The second case is when the husband audibly accompanies the formula with the Arabic expression 'God willing':

(62) The illiterate Zeyd says: 'May my wife be divorced three times, God willing!' If he does not understand the sense of saying 'God willing', does the divorce occur?
Answer: No. It is not necessary to understand its sense. [*D*, 75]

Once again, it is the formula itself, and not the speaker's intention, that is legally effective. The words 'God willing' invalidate the divorce, because nobody can know God's will.

In repudiating his wife, a man may declare the divorce to be either revocable (*raj'i*) or irrevocable (*ba'in*). An irrevocable divorce is effective the moment he pronounces the formula. The divorced wife may not, however, remarry until she has completed a waiting period (*'idda*) of three menstrual cycles from the time of the divorce; or four months and ten days from the death of her husband; or, if she is pregnant, until the delivery of the child. Marriage within the waiting period is invalid. Ebu's-su'ud goes further, and makes it a criminal offence:

(63) Hind marries Zeyd, thinking that her waiting period is complete, when it is not. Is this permissible?
Answer: A severe chastisement is necessary. Thinking [the waiting period to be complete] is not an excuse. [*D*, 106]

If, however, the husband pronounces a revocable divorce, the repudiation does not become effective until the completion of the waiting period. During this time, the marriage is still in existence:

(64) Zeyd divorces his wife, Hind, and then dies during her waiting period. Does Hind inherit from Zeyd?
Answer: If it is a revocable divorce, yes. [*D*, 112]

If she were no longer his wife, she would not be entitled to inherit. However, after the end of the waiting period, the divorce is no longer revocable:

(65) Zeyd repudiates his wife, Hind, with a revocable divorce. When Hind has completed her waiting period, she wishes to marry 'Amr. Can Zeyd stop her?
Answer: No. After the waiting period, the divorce is irrevocable. [*D*, 82]

After one or two divorces, the couple may remarry immediately if they wish to do so; and, given the ease and involuntary nature of divorce, this must have happened frequently. If, however, a husband has repudiated his wife three times or, alternatively, if he has pronounced the divorce formula three times on a single occasion, the couple may not remarry until the ex-wife has contracted, consummated and been divorced from an intermediate marriage (*tahlil*). A function of the intermediate marriage was undoubtedly to deter husbands from carelessly pronouncing triple divorces since, if a man wished to remarry the same woman, he would have to endure the shame of knowing that she had had intercourse with another man. Furthermore, it was within the power of the intermediate husband not to repudiate the wife. However, a deterrent will work only if enforced, and evasion of the intermediate marriage was clearly an idea that horrified Ebu's-su'ud:

(66) By mistake, Zeyd repudiates his wife, Hind, with a triple divorce. They still want and desire one another, and keep one another company. If he wishes to marry her [again] without an intermediate marriage, is this permissible in law?
Answer: We take refuge in God Most High. Is this possible? [*D*, 128]

It is, however, clear that many couples tried to avoid the intermediate marriage, or else devised stratagems to prevent its being consummated. Ebu's-su'ud would tolerate neither of these things, and in one case even makes it plain that a particular device to avoid the intermediate marriage merited death:

(67) When Zeyd repudiates his wife Hind with a triple divorce, he does not elect for an intermediate marriage. The deputy judge, 'Amr, says to Zeyd: 'Become an infidel. Then become a Muslim again.' When Zeyd – we take refuge in God – has become an infidel and then a Muslim again, 'Amr marries Hind to Zeyd. Is the marriage which he has contracted valid?
Answer: The deputy judge is an infidel before Zeyd is. It is possible licitly to execute both of them. [*D*, 132]

What the deputy judge has done is to recommend that the man renounce Islam to become an apostate, and thereby cancel his obligations as a Muslim. When he reconverts to Islam, he would therefore carry no pre-existing obligations, and he could remarry his former wife without an intermediate marriage. Since apostasy carries the death penalty, Ebu's-su'ud's reaction is perhaps understandable. Other cases which came before Ebu's-su'ud concerned strategies which couples used to prevent consummation of the intermediate marriage, none of which he would tolerate, apart from one, which had the sanction of the juristic tradition:

(68) Zeyd repudiates his wife, Hind, with a triple divorce. If they arrange an intermediate marriage with an old man who is incapable of intercourse, or with a twelve-year-old lad, is it licit [for Hind] to marry Zeyd afterwards?
Answer: A seminal emission is not necessary. Yes, so long as it is established that there was penetration. Otherwise, no. [*D*, 133]

The rules which Ebu's-su'ud prescribes for intermediate marriage are standard. The only way in which he slightly modifies the Hanafi tradition is to bring enforcement clearly into the sphere of royal authority. In the first place, he makes failure to observe the requirement of the intermediate marriage a criminal offence:

(69) Zeyd repudiates his wife Hind with a triple divorce. Then, without there being an intermediate marriage, he has [himself re-]married to her, and has intercourse with her. What should happen?
Answer: A severe chastisement and a long imprisonment are necessary. [*D*, 129]

The marriage would also be invalid. There is in fact a tradition from Abu Hanifa prescribing 'chastisement' for this offence,[40] but Ebu's-su'ud went further in involving the authorities. Enforcement of intermediate marriage clearly depended to some degree on the vigilance of the community, and it is clearly with a view to maintaining public involvement that, in a supplementary answer to a question, Ebu's-su'ud hints that the executive authorities should also punish anyone who fails to notify them if a couple has evaded an intermediate marriage:

(70) What should happen in law to those people who knew that Zeyd had married Hind without an intermediate marriage, but remained silent?
Answer: It is necessary to inform the authorities. [*D*, 131]

Presumably the authorities would then take action against the people who had failed to notify them of the illegal marriage. Together with the compulsory registration of marriages, these rules bring matrimony firmly under the surveillance of the government.

Annulment by the Wife

While a husband's powers to end a marriage are unrestricted, a woman's
are extremely limited. If, on marriage, she finds that a husband has a
hideously deforming disease, she may ask a judge for a separation. She
may do the same if he is impotent. However, she may exercise this right
only if his impotence is evident on the first night of the marriage, and not
if it appears subsequently. The judge, however, must grant the husband a
year's delay, and can separate the couple only if the husband fails to
consummate within this period.

In these cases, it is the authority of the judge that effects the separation. Only on two occasions can a wife pronounce a divorce on her own
authority. The first of these is the 'option of puberty' (*khiyar al-bulugh*).
When there has been a child marriage, the wife has a restricted right to
pronounce divorce on the attainment of puberty. She can do this only if it
was someone other than her father or paternal grandfather who gave her
in marriage, and only on the very first appearance of the menstrual blood.
If she delays even for the time it take to bring witnesses, she loses this
option.[41] The second occasion is when the husband delegates his own
power of divorce to his wife. Again, however, the wife's option lapses if
she does not exercise it immediately. If she goes away to think about it,
she loses the option. Furthermore, she has to use the correct formula,
using the word 'self' as the object of the verb:

(71) Zeyd says to his wife: 'May your wish be in your hand'. If the wife
at that moment says: 'I myself have divorced', or if she says: 'Be
divorced from me with an irrevocable divorce!' is she divorced?
Answer: No. [*Ch*. f. 41a]

Here, the first formula is wrong because the word 'myself' is the subject of
'divorced' and not the object. The second formula is wrong because the
wife does not use the word 'myself' and, more importantly, because a wife
cannot divorce her husband. She has to use his authority to divorce herself.

Although a wife can exercise this power only at a specific instant, the
husband is able to designate a moment when she will be able to exercise it
in the future. The right was clearly valuable when a husband
disappeared, leaving his wife without maintenance. It was, however,
extremely restricted, and Ebu's-su'ud ensured that it remained so:

(72) When Hind says to her husband Zeyd: 'If you don't come back
from [your] visit within a year, is my wish in [my] hand?' Zeyd replies:
'Yes'. Assuming that the said Zeyd does not return within a year, can
Hind divorce herself with three divorces?
Answer: Yes, provided she does not delay, once the year is up. [*D*, 77]

(73) When Zeyd goes to another place, he says to his wife Hind: 'If I am not back within six months, your wish is in your hand', and sets out. If he does not return within four years, is Hind divorced from him by repudiating herself?
Answer: No. She can only do so when the six months are up. [*D*, 78]

Here, Ebu's-su'ud is insisting on applying the letter of the law. A woman has the authority to divorce herself only at the time that her husband has designated. As with the option of puberty, this power is confined to a single moment.

The other method of divorce open to a woman is not limited in time, but involves a financial penalty. This is a *khul*, whereby a wife asks her husband for a divorce, and her husband repudiates her for a consideration. This transaction, in legal theory, is 'an exchange of property for the person. The husband possesses one of the objects of exchange, and [the wife] possesses the other, this being her person, as a realisation of equivalence.'[42] The amount which the wife must pay is negotiable, but the usual understanding is that she should renounce all, or some, of her dower and the maintenance, in other words, the financial obligations on the husband which arise out of the married state. To demand more than the value of these payments is permissible in law, but immoral by the standard of piety. This is the view of the jurists, which Ebu's-su'ud shares:

(74) Is it permissible for Zeyd to take more as an exchange for the *khul* than what he has given to Hind?
Answer: It is not proper. One should not do this. [*D*, 104]

If, however, the consideration for the *khul* is the dower or maintenance, which would otherwise be an obligation on the husband, Ebu's-su'ud makes absolutely no concessions to the wife. She has an absolute liability to pay:

(75) Hind concludes a *khul* with her husband, Zeyd, on condition that she pay the seven years' maintenance of their infant son from her own resources. The judge confirms the *khul* and issues a certificate. If the infant then dies, can the said Zeyd reclaim the infant's seven-year maintenance from Hind?
Answer: Yes. [*D*, 103]

A boy remains in the custody of the ex-wife usually until the age of 7. The maintenance during this period is, however, an obligation on the ex-husband, which here the ex-wife undertook to pay as the price of divorce. The death of the child does not release her from the obligation. What she owes, in fact, is not the maintenance itself but its value, which remains as a debt due to the husband even after the death of the child.

Suspended Divorces

In Hanafi law, the ordinary formula for divorce is, in effect, an oath.[43] The jurists define an oath (*yamin*) as a 'power' (*quwwa*),[44] and the divorce formula has in itself the power to dissolve a marriage, even against the wishes of the speaker. This aspect of the formula is even more obvious in the 'suspended divorce' (*al-talaq bi'l-ta'liq*).

This is a vow on divorce. The law recognises three types of vow. The first is a vow by God, where the speaker says, for example: 'By God, I will not do X!' He must then either refrain from doing X, or else make an act of atonement (*kaffara*), usually by freeing slaves or feeding the poor. The second and third type are vows on manumission and vows on divorce. This is where a person says, for example: 'If I do X, my slave is freed', or 'If I do X, my wife is divorced'. If he then does X, the manumission or divorce follows automatically. In both these vows, the intention of the speaker is legally irrelevant. Both men and women may make vows on manumission but, since she has no matrimonial authority, a woman may not make a vow on divorce.

Since vows on divorce are so easy to make, and yet have such serious consequences, they form an important topic both in the classical works of jurisprudence and in collections of Ottoman fatwas. Some jurists are more ready than others to suggest to husbands ways of escaping from the consequences of vows on divorce, but Ebu's-su'ud is not, as a rule, eager to help, usually preferring to adopt a very literal interpretation of the words of the oath:

> (76) Zeyd says to his wife, Hind: 'If I get into bed with you, be divorced from me three times!' If Zeyd then does it [*sic*] with Hind on a carpet or mattress, without getting into bed, is she divorced from him three times?
> *Answer*: No, but they must never again get into bed. [*D*, 126]

Such is the strength of a vow on divorce that it is valid even if the man has vowed to perform an illegal act:

> (77) Zeyd says: 'If I don't divide 'Amr into four quarters and kill him, may my wife be divorced three times!' In law, assuming that he cannot kill 'Amr, is his wife divorced?
> *Answer*: If this is his custom, the divorce occurs at the final breath of whoever dies first out of Zeyd, 'Amr or Hind. [*D*, 117]

Here, the last breath of any one of the protagonists is the last moment when the husband can execute the vow. If the husband or the wife die first, the point might seem merely academic, but it is not. If the husband dies without fulfilling his vow, his wife is irrevocably divorced at the moment before he expires, and in consequence cannot inherit from him, as she ceases to be an heir. Similarly, if the wife dies first, she is divorced at her last breath, and the husband cannot inherit from her.

The consequences of vows on divorce were so serious that the jurists devised ways of circumventing them, which Ebu's-su'ud, if asked directly, was prepared to recommend. One of these methods, when a man had vowed never to marry, was to use an unauthorised agent to conclude the contract. This was possible if the man did not personally authorise the agent, but instead appointed him through an intermediary. Some men, however, vowed never to get married, even through an unauthorised agent. Here, because the questioner asks him directly, Ebu's-su'ud recommends a way round this vow:

(78) Zeyd says: 'If I do such-and-such a thing, may every woman I marry be divorced, and if I marry a woman through an unauthorised agent, may she still be divorced!' [If he does what he has vowed not to do,] is it possible for Zeyd to take a woman in marriage?
Answer: Both parties should be married through an unauthorised agent. If Zeyd accepts [the marriage] before the woman accepts, and then the woman accepts, no divorce occurs. [*D*, 122]

The solution is possible because neither of the parties formally initiates the marriage, and the man's acceptance does not bring the contract into existence, since he makes it before the woman has formally consented to her agent's offer. It is the woman's agreement, and not the man's, that seals the contract. Since the man neither initiates nor concludes the marriage, divorce does not occur.

The method of circumventing the vow which Ebu's-su'ud suggests is cumbersome, but this is the point. In making an oath, the swearer has made a unilateral contract with God and, if an oath is to retain its force as a divine power, evasion should not be made easy.

Suspended divorces were the commonest form of vow on divorce, but there were also two other formulae, each of them constituting a vow of sexual abstention.[45]

The first is *zihar*. This is a form of words where a man compares his wife to his mother, or to any woman who is forbidden to him in marriage. The effect of the vow is to forbid sexual contact between the partners until the husband has performed the specific penance of freeing a slave, fasting for sixty successive days, or feeding sixty paupers. If he does not perform the penance, the marriage dissolves. *Zihar* was hardly a common form of divorce, but it was nevertheless a lurking menace because, for example, a Turk might affectionately call his wife 'my girl' which, in Turkish, could also mean 'my daughter'. The jurists, however, had ruled that in cases where the expression is one that, by custom, simply expresses endearment, then it is not *zihar*, unless this is what the husband had intended by the words. Phrases, therefore, which could constitute *zihar* do not normally do so, unless this is what the husband intended. This is the usual basis of Ebu's-su'ud's rulings on the subject, except where a man uses such a formula when the marriage contract is in formation:

(79) Zeyd betroths his daughter, Hind, to 'Amr. In answer to [Zeyd's] saying: 'Take her!', 'Amr says: 'If from today I take Hind [in marriage], may she be my daughter, my mother and my sister!' Is Hind's marriage to 'Amr still valid?
Answer: It is necessary for the marriage to be contracted twice as a precaution. It is permissible that this be done in one session. [*D*, 116]

The man's answer here is an integral part of the marriage contract, as it constitutes an acceptance of the father's offer of his daughter in marriage. The man obviously spoke the words affectionately, but Ebu's-su'ud's answer underlines the seriousness of the oath. He insists on a double contract of marriage, because the man's words might, in the eyes of God, have the effect of *zihar*, dissolving the first contract and necessitating the second.

He is equally punctilious on the question of *ila*, the second vow of sexual abstention. This is where a husband vows not to have intercourse with his wife (or female slave). If he breaks the vow, he must perform an act of penance. If he fulfils it, a divorce occurs automatically after four months. If he pronounces *ila* without a time limit, then remarriage to the same woman is impossible. There is, however, an opinion within the Hanafi tradition that, if the husband also pronounces a triple divorce, this cancels the effect of the *ila*, allowing the couple to remarry after the ex-wife has undergone an intermediate marriage. If, however, he repudiates her with less than a triple divorce, the *ila* is irrevocable:

(80) Zeyd says: 'If, from this moment, I have intercourse with my wife, Hind, may she be divorced from me three times!' Then, without having intercourse [with her], he divorces her with an irrevocable divorce. If he marries her again after the waiting period, is the marriage valid?
Answer: It is *ila*. There is no way out of this. [*D*, 114]

Here, the form of the suspended divorce amounts to a vow of abstention from intercourse, and is therefore *ila*, and the single divorce that the husband pronounces is not sufficient to cancel its effect. Ebu's-su'ud's answer, however, suggests that he would not be willing in any circumstances to offer a stratagem to escape the consequences of the vow.

Conclusion

The rules of divorce rest essentially on a notion of the magic power of words, which the jurists have harnessed to a theological end. The function of the rules on divorce and suspended divorce, where a single misplaced word can dissolve a marriage, seems to have been to emphasise to believers the inexorability of the divine will, and to make them aware of the divine presence in the most intimate aspects of everyday life. It is perhaps for this reason that Ebu's-su'ud was usually unwilling to exercise juristic ingenuity in absolving couples from the consequences of these words. By allowing the law to run its full course, he was emphasising the power both of the Almighty and of his chosen representatives on earth, in the form of the Sultan and the Ottoman legal establishment, to whom God had entrusted the application of His will in the form of the *shari'a*.

In other areas of the law of marriage, Ebu's-su'ud is equally authoritarian, but in a rational rather than a magical sense. He brings the contract of marriage under government surveillance by making registration compulsory, and apparently also by requiring the community to inform on any couple who have remarried after a triple divorce without the wife's first undergoing an intermediate marriage, and by making such a remarriage a criminal offence. With these regulations, marriage ceased to be a purely private contract, but came under the authority of the Sultan. Within individual households, he increased the power of women's male guardians by making their permission an absolute condition for the validity of a marriage, their authority in the household in a sense reflecting the authority of the Sultan in the Empire.

Others of Ebu's-su'ud's rulings served simply to regularise the practice of marriage. By forbidding witnessing by hearsay, and by requiring the two witnesses to see the bride's face, he clearly aimed to outlaw clandestine marriages, and his tendency to classify nuptial gifts as bribes suggests that he wished to outlaw them altogether and to confine the exchange of property strictly to the dower. In this he was clearly unsuccessful, since nuptial gifts continued to cause legal problems in the following centuries.

Notes

1. Aliah Schleifer, 'The legal aspects of marriage according to hanafi *fiqh*', *Islamic Quarterly* 39/4 (1958), 193–219; Judith Tucker, '*Muftis* and matrimony: Islamic law and gender in Ottoman Syria and Palestine', *Islamic Law and Society*, 1/3 (1994), 265–300.
2. Qadikhan, ed. and trans. Moulvi Mahomed Yusoof Khan Bahadur and Moulvi Wilayat Hussain, *Fatawa-i-Kazee Khan relating to the Mahomedan Law of Marriage, Dower, Divorce, Legitimacy and Guardianship according to the Sources*, Lahore: Law Publishing Company (1977), section 22.
3. Qadikhan, *Fatawa*, section 22.
4. Ibid., sections 229, 233.
5. Ibid., sections 239, 243.
6. Ibid., section 244.
7. Ibid., sections 227, 228.
8. Ibid., section 96.
9. al-Marghinani, *al-Hidaya*, Cairo: Matba'a Mustafa al-Babi al-Halabi (1972), vol. 3, p. 291.
10. Ibid., p. 293.
11. Ibid., p. 294. In the Ottoman Empire, this rule became irrelevant after the decree of 1544, forbidding women in any circumstances to marry without the consent of a male guardian.
12. Qadikhan, *al-Fatawa*, section 194.
13. Mona Siddiqui, '*Mahr*: legal obligation or rightful demand?', *Journal of Islamic Studies*, 6/1 (1995), 14–24.
14. al-Marghinani, *al-Hidaya*, vol. 3, p. 300.
15. Such as when, for example, a man has intercourse with his son's female slave. The only importance of the notion of quasi-ownership is as a device to avert the fixed penalty for the offence.
16. Ibn Humam, *Fath al-qadir*, Cairo: Matba'a Mustafa al-Babi al-Halabi (1972), vol. 3, p. 320.
17. Hamidi, *Jami' al-Fatawa*, Library of the Topkapı Palace, MS R665, f. 46a.
18. Ibn Bazzaz, *al-Fatawa al-Bazzaziyya*, in margins of *al-Fatawa al-Hindiyya*, Bulaq: Imperial Press (1912/13), vol. 4, pp. 150–1.
19. Qadikhan, *Fatawa*, section 459.
20. al-Marghinani, *al-Hidaya*, vol. 3, p. 322.
21. Ya'akov Meron, *L'obligation alimentaire entre époux en droit musulman hanéfite*, Bibliothèque de Droit Privé, vol. 14, Paris: R. Pichon & R. Durand Auzias (1971).
22. Qadikhan, *Fatawa*, section 685.
23. Ibid., section 443.
24. Ibid., section 742.
25. Ebu's-su'ud, *Bida'at al-qadi*, Süleymaniye Library, Istanbul, MS Laleli 3,711, chapter 3.
26. An apparently semi-official collection of legal exemplars, copied in 1552, has specimen documents concerning the dissolution of a Hanafi marriage by a Shafi'i judge. British Library, MS or. 7,268, ff. 9a–b.
27. *D*, 659. On the procedure for dissolving an oath by application to a Shafi'i judge, see Qadikhan, *Fatawa*, vol. 2, section 1,614.

28. Qadikhan, *Fatawa*, section 637.
29. Joseph Schacht, *An Introduction to Islamic Law*, Oxford: Clarendon Press (1964), p. 179.
30. Qadikhan, *Fatawa*, section 350.
31. Ibid., sections 362–3.
32. Qadikhan, *al-Fatawa al-Khaniyya*, in margins of *al-Fatawa al-Hindiyya*, Bulaq: Imperial Press (1912/13), vol. 1, p. 569.
33. Ibid.
34. Qadikhan, *Fatawa*, section 551.
35. Ibid., section 859.
36. Ibn Nujaim, *al-Bahr al-ra'iq*, Cairo: al-Matba'a al-'ilmiyya (1893), vol. 5, p. 119.
37. Colin Imber, '"Involuntary" annulment of marriage and its solutions in Ottoman law', *Turcica*, 25 (1993), 39–73.
38. Qadikhan, *Fatawa*, vol. 2, section 1,895.
39. The problem here is that the husband has pronounced a double divorce three times. He has therefore divorced his wife six times. As Ebu's-su'ud's answer shows, this is legally a triple divorce.
40. *D*, 131.
41. Qadikhan, *Fatawa*, section 597.
42. al-Marghinani, *al-Hidaya*, vol. 4, p. 219.
43. On oaths, see Norman Calder, '*Hinth, birr, tabarrur, tahannuth*: an enquiry into the Arabic vocabulary of vows', *Bulletin of the School of Oriental and African Studies*, 51 (1988), 214–39.
44. al-Marghinani, *al-Hidaya*, vol. 5, p. 66.
45. G. R. Hawting, 'An ascetic vow and an unseemly oath? *Ila* and *zihar* in Muslim law', *Bulletin of the School of Oriental and African Studies*, 56 (1994), 113–25.

8
Crimes and Torts: Offences against Property

Crimes and Torts

There is nothing in the Hanafi tradition that corresponds precisely to the concept of penal law.[1] Instead, the jurists group what other legal systems might classify as criminal offences under four headings. In the first category are the offences which incur a fixed penalty (*hadd*, pl. *hudud*). In the second are delicts (*jinayat*), comprising homicide, injury to the person, and some cases of damage to property. In the third is usurpation (*ghasb*), a term which covers misappropriation and damage to property. In the fourth are offences which incur discretionary punishment (*taz'ir*).

Offences in the first category are fornication (*zina*), false accusation of fornication (*qadhf*), wine-drinking (*shurb al-khamr*), theft (*sariqa*) and highway robbery (*qat' al-tariq*). For fornication, the penalty is stoning to death for a free married Muslim, 100 lashes for others, and fifty lashes for slaves. Wrongful accusation and wine-drinking both incur eighty lashes for a free person and forty for a slave. The penalty for theft is amputation of a hand, and for highway robbery, death by the sword where there is homicide alone, amputation of a hand and foot where there is looting alone, and crucifixion where there is both. These penalties are 'claims of God' (*haqq Allah*), meaning in practice that they are not pardonable and not commutable, and that it is the duty of the sovereign to put them into effect.

These penalties correspond with the notion of criminal law to the extent that their execution is a duty of the public authority, but here the resemblance ends. The function of a criminal law is to punish and deter. If it is to do this, it must be applicable in practice, and this is not the case with the fixed penalties. The Hanafi jurists quote a Saying of the Prophet: 'Avert the fixed penalties as much as you are able' and, in order to put this precept into practice, lay down over-strict rules of procedure which render conviction for these offences very difficult or, in the case of fornication and theft, virtually impossible. A successful prosecution for fornication, for example, requires the evidence of four male eyewitnesses to the act, whose probity the judge has investigated, and who must be able to say: 'We saw him having intercourse with her like a stylus in a collyrium jar'.[2] If the evidence of the witnesses fails, they become liable to the fixed penalty of eighty lashes for false accusation of fornication. Even in the case of wine-drinking, where the standard of evidence is not so stringent, there is a requirement to prove that the defendant drank voluntarily, and an anecdote about Abu Hanifa, which appears as the answer in a fatwa, probably of Ebu's-su'ud, indicates that the evidence must be absolutely definitive. Circumstantial evidence is not acceptable:

(1) [What happens] if a wine jar is found in Zeyd's possession?
Answer: 'It is related of Abu Hanifa (may God have mercy on him) that he went on a Pilgrimage and, when he entered Medina, he saw the people gathering around a man. They said: "We found him with a wine-skin, and we wish to inflict the fixed punishment on him". Abu Hanifa replied: "He's got an instrument of fornication with him, too. So stone him." And they left the man and scattered.' [*Ch*, f. 96a]

False accusation and highway robbery are easier to prove, but the function of the penalty for false accusation is simply to prevent anyone from bringing forward a prosecution for fornication. It is, in the end, only highway robbery that corresponds to the notion of a criminal offence.

The unreality of the fixed penalties had an important effect on practice, by removing the punishment of fornication and theft from the domain of the *shari'a* and into the realms respectively of private and royal justice.

The second and third categories of offence, delicts and usurpation, belong under the heading of tort rather than of crime. They are technically 'claims of men' (*haqq al-'ibad*), meaning that it is the injured party or, in the case of homicide, his heirs who bring the claim. The penalties which they incur are not, strictly speaking, punishments, but rather a form of compensation which restores the status quo between the perpetrator of the act and his victim, who also has the option of pardoning the offender or of composing with him for an agreed sum. In cases of killing and injury, the law does distinguish between intentional and unintentional acts, and regulates the penalties accordingly. However, in cases of misappropriation and damage to property, the offender's intention is irrelevant to the legal outcome of the act.

The offences which incur discretionary punishment form the fourth category, covering misdemeanours such as sodomy, bestiality, magic or taking opium,[3] which do not fit under any other heading. It is here perhaps that the jurists come closest to the notion of a criminal law. It is the judge or the sovereign (*imam*) who has the duty of inflicting the penalties, whose purpose is not to compensate but specifically to deter and to punish.[4] It is the judge too, or the sovereign, who has the duty of assessing the severity of the penalty, the jurists confining themselves to recommending the different levels of punishment which will deter people in different classes of society. A mere warning will deter the nobility and the learned, whereas nothing but a severe beating will deter the rabble.[5] The jurists also transfer the concept of discretionary punishment to the household, where they accord husbands the right to beat their wives 'as a discipline and a corrective'.[6] The husband within the household occupies the same position as the sovereign within society at large. The jurists understand the term 'discretionary punishment' (*ta'zir*) to mean strokes of the lash, with the addition, if the judge or sovereign sees fit, of imprisonment. It does not, it appears, extend to include the death penalty. Nonetheless, they do condone extra-judicial execution, classifying it as administrative punishment (*siyasa*), a term which has the general sense of repressive action by the government for the maintenance of public order.

In the theoretical scheme of the law, the offences which occur discretionary or administrative punishment form a residual category, covering only those cases which defy classification as offences which incur fixed penalties, delicts or usurpation. In practice, the opposite was true.[7] Since, in many areas of what in other legal systems would constitute criminal law, Islamic law is either impractical or inadequate, it is inevitable that Islamic authorities would, to a large extent, ignore juristic prescription and deal with criminal offences at their discretion. Furthermore, the area of discretionary punishments is not one that the Hanafi jurists had greatly systematised, their most sustained effort in this direction being to classify personal insults in order to establish which, because they affront or shame Muslims, incur a penalty. This was a matter of great concern, as is clear from the numerous queries which Ebu's-su'ud received on the subject, for example:

(2) [What should happen to] the non-Muslim Zeyd, who insults the Muslim 'Amr and his wife with – we take refuge in God – the f. word? *Answer*: He is liable for a severe chastisement and a long imprisonment. [*Ch*, f. 90b]

Nonetheless, it does not amount to a general systematisation of the law. The result was that, in matters of crime, Islamic authorities came to enjoy virtually unlimited powers to act as they pleased, without feeling the need to be bound by juristic rules. This was particularly true in the area of offences against property, where Islamic law is at its most impractical. It was a development which was to find a faint reflection in 'post-classical' Hanafi jurisprudence.

This too was the situation in the Ottoman Empire. The pursuit of criminals was largely a matter for the district governors and fief-holders, who executed the punishments and received fines as part of their income. Criminal procedure was not, however, completely arbitrary. The first general Ottoman Law-Book of c. 1490 opens with a criminal code, consisting largely of a tariff of fines, lashes and other penalties for specified offences. Between c. 1490 and c. 1540, the code went through a number of recensions, accreting clauses which add to or modify the original tariff and lay down some rules of procedure. In some of its details and in some of the concepts which it employs, the code does reflect Hanafi law; but, by and large, it is very different. The criminal code, in theory at least, bound the provincial authorities. It did not, however, bind the Sultan, whose absolute discretion in criminal matters is apparent in the institution of penal servitude in the galleys. During the sixteenth century, whenever a large fleet put to sea, the Imperial Council, acting in the Sultan's name, would issue decrees to provincial authorities commanding that anyone 'guilty of a grave offence, but not meriting capital punishment (*siyasa*)' should be condemned to the galleys.[8] These orders, sentencing men either collectively or individually, overrode the provisions of the criminal code and instead derive their authority directly from the will of the Sultan.

Offences against Property: Hanafi Theory

Theft

Hanafi jurists classify most property offences under two headings, theft (*sariqa*) and usurpation (*ghasb*). The first of these is a claim of God, incurring the fixed penalty specified in the Quranic verse: 'As for the male thief (*sariq*) and the female thief (*sariqa*), cut off their hands'.[9] The jurists have amplified the Quranic ruling, prescribing amputation of the right hand for the first offence and of the left foot for the second. Usurpation, by contrast, is a claim of man, and does not incur a criminal sanction.

Marghinani defines theft 'in its lexical sense' as 'taking something from another person by secrecy and stealth', adding that in legal usage there are further qualifications.[10] Since the Quran lays down a severe penalty, a strict legal description of the offence is clearly essential. This the jurists provide, structuring their definition around the penalty itself, and focusing their discussion on the criteria necessary for putting it into effect.

To incur amputation, the thief must be a sane adult, who has stolen from custody goods worth ten *dirham*s or more, which he does not own, and in which he has no share or quasi-ownership (*shubhat al-milk*). This is the basic definition, which jurists further refine. For example, the theft of 'things of trifling value, which are found ownerless in the realms of Islam, such as wood, hay, reeds, fish, birds, game, arsenic or lime', does not incur amputation,[11] nor does the theft of things that rot quickly, such as milk, meat or fresh fruit. The strict definition of removal from custody places further restrictions on the use of the penalty. There are two types of custody. One is a place such as a house or a room, which is custody by definition, and custody by a guardian, such as when a person is sitting with his goods, or sleeping with them under his head. A bath-house, or any room which the public has the right to enter, is not custody. However, theft from custody does not necessarily incur amputation, since the next question is how the thief removed the goods. If he pierced the wall of a house and inserted only his hand, he does not suffer amputation, since the breach of custody is incomplete. Even if he did enter the house, and passed the goods to an accomplice on the outside, neither suffers the penalty, nor does the thief who threw goods from inside the house out onto the road. There is no penalty for a slave who steals from his master or mistress, 'since access is customary', nor for a guest who steals from his host, since 'his act is perfidy and not theft'.[12]

The notions of partnership and quasi-ownership place further restrictions. A creditor, for example, does not suffer for stealing money from his debtor. There is no amputation for stealing from the Treasury, because it is the property of the public, of which the thief is a member, nor for theft from a spouse or close relative, since the law attributes quasi-ownership to the thief. It is this notion of quasi-ownership that is ultimately the most crucial in averting the punishment, since it underlies a specific rule which makes amputation impossible unless, in effect, the thief asks for it voluntarily: 'If the thief claims that the object stolen is his property, then amputation drops, even if he does not bring proof'. The doubt (*shubha*) which the thief's avowal raises creates quasi-ownership and causes the penalty to drop.

Even without this very restrictive definition of theft, the normal rules of procedure would render conviction virtually impossible. The usual standard of proof in Hanafi law is two male eyewitnesses, or one man and two women, which would be very difficult to achieve for an offence which the jurists define as taking 'by stealth'. Juristic discussions of theft do not, in short, belong to the realm of practical law.

This lack of reality creates a paradox which the jurists never resolve. The reason which they give for the severity of the penalty is that it is a deterrent (*zajr*). Marghinani, for example, explains the rule that the amputated limb must be cauterised, as follows: 'If it is not cauterised, it leads to the loss [of the thief's life], and the fixed punishment is a deterrent and not a destroyer [of life]'.[13] Ebu's-su'ud, in his commentary on the Quranic verse in question, explains the inclusive phrase 'the male thief and the female thief' as serving to provide 'the maximum of deterrence'.[14] However, while explaining that the purpose of the penalty is to deter, the jurists also make it perfectly plain that the purpose of the rules of procedure is to prevent the punishment from ever actually happening in practice. In explaining, for example, why the Hanafis adopt the theft of ten *dirhams* as the legal minimum for amputation, as against the three *dirhams* of the Shafi'is and Malikis, Marghinani states: 'In our opinion, adopting the [larger] sum is better, as a stratagem to avert the fixed penalty'.[15] Again, in rebutting the argument attributed to Shafi'i, that to let amputation drop if the thief claims ownership of the property leads to 'the closure of the door of punishment', Marghinani asserts: 'In our opinion, doubt averts the punishment, and doubt comes into being with the claim, because of the possibility [that he is speaking the truth]'.[16] Amputation, in fact, is not a real penalty and cannot, therefore, in reality act as a deterrent.

The Hanafi jurists seem to have had two motives for removing theft from the sphere of practical law. The explicit motive was to act in accordance with the Prophetic principle of avoiding the fixed penalties. An implicit motive was perhaps to define theft so restrictively as to move all unlawful seizure of property into a legal category which, with its stress on the maintenance of equivalence between individuals, corresponds more precisely with the intellectual structure of Hanafi law. This category is usurpation (*ghasb*).

Usurpation

Marghinani defines usurpation 'in its lexical sense' as 'taking something from another by force, in order to make use of it', and 'in law' as 'taking property which has a market value and esteem, without the owner's permission, in such a way as to extinguish his possession [of it]'.[17] He next makes a distinction between usurpation when it is intentional and when it is unintentional: 'If [usurpation] is undertaken knowingly, then its legal effect is [to create] a sin (*ithm*) and a debt. But if it is undertaken unwittingly, then [its effect is also to create] liability, because it is a claim of man, and one does not take the motive into account.'[18] In other words, if the usurpation is deliberate, the law deems the usurper to be a sinner, who must answer to God for his wrongdoing, but the sin has no legal consequences. In law, there is no distinction between deliberate and unintentional usurpation. Both incur the same degree of liability.

The basic rule in a case of usurpation is that the usurper must return what he has taken to its owner. If the goods are fungible, and have been destroyed in his possession, then he must return the precise equivalent. If he is unable to do so, he must, in opinions attributed respectively to Abu Hanifa, Abu Yusuf and Shaibani, restore to the owner the precise value of the goods on the day of the court action, on the day of the usurpation, or on the day when similar goods were no longer procurable. In the view of Marghinani, the return of the goods is preferable to the return of the value: 'the return of the value is secondary as a means [of achieving a solution to the problem], because it is defective. Perfection lies in the return of the object and the quality of ownership.' Others, however, claim that 'the fundamental obligation is the value, and the return of the object [merely] a means of achieving this'.[19] If the object has lost value when in the possession of the usurper, then the usurper, when he returns it, is also liable to compensate the owner for loss.

In Marghinani's definition, the concept of usurpation applies only to moveable property: 'Usurpation in its real sense is realised only with regard [to moveable property] and nothing else, because the extinction of possession is by removal'. He attributes this view to Abu Hanifa and Abu Yusuf, who reasoned that 'usurpation is the establishment of possession through the extinction of the owner's possession, by an action against the object, and this cannot be imagined in the case of immoveable property. The owner's possession is extinguished only by expelling him from it, and this is an action against him, and not against the property.' The consequence of this rule is that illegal occupation is neither a crime nor a sin, and also that the illegal occupier is not liable for damage which occurs through natural causes. If, however, he is himself the cause of destruction or damage to the property, then he is liable: 'because it is destruction, and compensation for the property is incurred. An example is when he removes soil [from the property], because it is an action against the property itself [and not against the owner].'[20]

Usurpation can, in certain cases, result in the legal transfer of ownership from the original proprietor to the usurper. This happens, in the first place, if the usurper irreparably damages the object. In this case, he is liable to compensate the proprietor for the full value of the undamaged object, while he becomes owner of the remains. In the second place, 'when the usurped object is changed through the actions of the usurper, so that it loses its designation and its benefit is increased, the proprietor loses ownership of it. The usurper becomes owner, and compensates [the original proprietor], ... such as when someone usurps a sheep and slaughters ... and cooks it, or wheat and grinds it, or iron and makes it into a sword.'[21] A third case where transfer of ownership can occur is when the property increases in value through the actions of the usurper. An example of this which the jurists often give is when a person misappropriates a white cloth and increases its value by dyeing it red. In this case, the original owner of the cloth may either demand the value of the undyed cloth from the usurper and transfer ownership to him; or he may demand the return of the cloth, and compensate the usurper by paying him the value of the dye.

It is clear from these rules that the overriding concern of the jurists in cases of misappropriation and damage to property was to restore the *status quo ante* between the individuals concerned, by ensuring that the compensation given is precisely equivalent in value to the loss suffered.

The law is thus essentially a theoretical exercise in working out solutions to problems of misappropriation in accordance with the principle of 'equivalence' which underlies much Hanafi law, and for which, in cases of damage to life and property, the jurists find a justification in the Quranic verse: 'If someone transgresses against you, transgress against him in the same manner as he has transgressed against you'.[22] Their solutions are invariably elegant, but less often practical. In particular, by excluding intent as an element in calculating the legal consequences of the act, they ensure that the laws of usurpation are in practice inadequate for dealing with cases of theft and malicious damage.

Theft and Usurpation: The Influence of Practice

This lack of practicality was perhaps unimportant for academic jurists, who saw their function as the guardians of tradition, and whose concern was with the intellectual and religious structure of the law, rather than with its application. However, it is clear that, in dealing with property offences, and especially with theft, practice was very different from theory, and that eventually some jurists began to superimpose justifications for what actually happened on their expositions of the traditional rules.

An example is Ibn Bazzaz (d. 1414) who in the main body of his chapter on theft (*sariqa*), presents a traditional definition of the offence itself and a restatement of the rules governing the infliction of the fixed penalty. However, he opens his chapter with a quotation: 'If a defendant denies the theft, most of the sheikhs have said "[The governor] chastises him if he finds him in suspicious circumstances, in that he saw him associating with thieves, or sitting with wine-drinkers [even] though he was not drinking"'. This ruling has three effects. First, it abrogates the normal rules of procedure, which would require the victim of the theft to produce witnesses if the suspect denied the charge. Instead, it allows conviction on suspicion alone. Second, it removes theft from the category of offences which incur a fixed penalty, and redefines it as an offence which incurs discretionary punishment. Finally, the ruling seems to imply that it is the public authority and not the victim of the theft who brings the thief to trial and produces evidence.

Ibn Bazzaz reinforces these ideas with an anecdote which he appends to the ruling:

'Isam b. Yusuf came into the governor['s apartment] and a thief was brought before him, who denied [the charge]. ['Isam] was asked [about the proper procedure], and he said: '[The defendant who has] denied [the charge] must [take] an oath, and the plaintiff must [produce] evidence.' The governor said: 'Bring whips and scourges!' and had not given ten lashes before [the thief] confessed and brought the stolen goods. 'Isam said: 'Praise be to God! I have never seen an injustice more closely resemble justice than this.'[23]

While meticulously describing it as an injustice (*zulm*), that is, as contrary to the *shari'a*, the anecdote clearly aims to legitimise the governor's action. In so doing, it also legitimises the practice of bringing cases of theft before the administrative authorities, the abolition of the canonical rules of procedure, and the use of torture to extract a confession. What Ibn Bazzaz is in fact doing is to justify what was obviously the practice in his own time. Ibn Humam (d. 1457) was later to do the same thing, when he reluctantly concedes the permissibility of the lash as a punishment for theft:

> [It is reported] from Abu Yusuf that it is permissible to apply the lash (*ta'zir*) in cases of [illegally] taking property (*akhdh al-mal*). But in the opinion of Abu Hanifa, Shaibani and the other Imams, it is not permissible. In the *Khulasa* there is the following: 'I have heard from a reliable authority that flogging for taking property is permissible, if the judge or governor sees fit'. The sum of this is that a man who does not attend congregational prayers [and is therefore of bad character] may be flogged for taking property, by electing to act in accordance with the sheikhs who hold this view, such as Abu Yusuf.[24]

This ruling, like Ibn Bazzaz's, effectively puts theft into the category of offences which incur discretionary punishment. Ibn Humam achieves this by defining theft simply as 'taking property' (*akhdh al-mal*), and avoiding the technical term *sariqa*.

Over two centuries earlier, Qadikhan (d. 1196) had already hinted that the canonical laws of theft had no practical relevance. In his *Fatwas*, he does not make theft the subject of a single chapter, but instead, in the chapter on oaths, he groups together 'Problems concerning theft (*sariqa*), taking (*akhdh*) and usurpation (*ghasb*)' into a single short section, making no clear distinction between the categories.[25] He does devote a complete chapter to usurpation, but what is most striking about it is that most of the cases which he cites concern not the misappropriation of property, but liability for damage. This development is quite consistent with the logical structure of the law, since the principle which underlies the specific rules is compensation for loss, and damage to property is as much a cause of loss as misappropriation. Furthermore, since in practice most cases of misappropriation, that is, of theft in a non-restrictive sense, had become a matter for the administrative authorities, it is natural that some jurists should shift the burden of the discussion to questions of compensation for damage which occurs without the physical removal of the property. Nonetheless, in dealing with questions of damage, Qadikhan follows Hanafi principles to the letter.

The chapter opens with the following case: 'A man has a cloth which he is carrying. [Another] man takes hold of it. The owner of the cloth pulls it away and it is torn. Shaibani said: "The man who took hold is liable for half its value. But if the person who pulled the cloth was the man who took hold of it and was not its owner, then he is liable for the full value."'[26] This case is, in several respects, typical of the ones which follow. First, it makes no distinction between accidental and malicious damage. The concern of the law is solely with who caused the damage, and not with his motives. In this case, the man who took hold of the cloth and its owner are jointly responsible for the tear, and so the proprietor receives compensation for only half the loss. The fact that the owner was simply trying to regain his own property is irrelevant. He receives full compensation only if the man who seized his cloth was solely responsible for the tear. Second, where there is a chain of causation, it is the direct rather than the indirect cause that is relevant in assessing who is liable. In this case, the indirect cause of the damage is the man's seizing the cloth. The direct cause is his holding it and the owner pulling, making them jointly responsible for the tear. The man who seized the cloth is fully liable only if the owner did not also pull. This distinction between the direct and the indirect cause is important, and becomes clearer in the numerous other cases which Qadikhan cites. For example, a person is liable for fire damage only if he was the direct cause of the conflagration, for example by dropping cinders. If he lights a fire, and subsequently a wind blows up and carries sparks to a neighbouring building, he is not liable,[27] because the immediate cause of the damage is the wind's blowing and not his lighting the fire. If a man sends his dog to kill a sheep, he is liable. But if the dog pauses before attacking the sheep, the law deems the dog to be the direct cause of the loss, and not its owner, who therefore escapes liability.[28] In none of these cases is intention relevant, whether in dropping the cinders, lighting the fire, or sending the dog against the sheep.

Underlying all the cases which Qadikhan cites is the Hanafi view that the function of the law of usurpation is to restore the *status quo ante* between individuals by fixing compensation which is precisely equivalent in value to the loss. It is this equivalence between the parties rather than actual possession or ownership that the law seeks to maintain. This is most apparent perhaps in cases of commixture, as in the example of the man who dyes cloth belonging to another person. An example which Qadikhan quotes is of a man who usurps a beam and incorporates it into his own house. He becomes owner of the beam, but must pay compensation for its value. If the value of the house and the beam are equal, either person may compensate the other, but if they cannot agree, the house is sold and the price divided equally between the two parties. Similarly, if a chicken swallows a pearl, if the value of the pearl is greater than the value of the chicken, the owner of the pearl becomes owner of the chicken, paying compensation for its value, and vice versa. The principle in both cases is that 'the owner of the more valuable of the two properties may take possession of the other [and give compensation for its value]. But if the value of the two [properties] is equal, they are both sold and the price divided between the parties.'[29] Questions of malicious intent, such as wrongfully taking the beam, or of negligence, such as dropping pearls in someone else's chicken-coop, do not enter into the solution.

To the extent, therefore, that he treats usurpation as having the sense primarily of damage or commixture, Qadikhan is showing the influence of legal practice. In its sense of the illegal removal of property, usurpation would come under the jurisdiction of the administrative authorities. This does not, however, mean that all the solutions which he offers to problems of damage and commixture are strictly practical. The lack of a distinction in Hanafi law between malicious and unintentional removal, damage or commixture, and the exemption from all liability of the person who was the indirect cause of a loss, means that some solutions seem to contravene a natural sense of justice, and it is undoubtedly for this reason that some cases of damage and commixture came to be the concern of administrative justice.

Offences against Property: Ottoman Practice

The Ottoman Criminal Code

In its treatment of property offences, Ottoman secular law, *qanun*, exemplifies the fact already implicit in the formal juristic texts, that the rulings of the jurists had little or no influence on practice. It was practice that influenced the jurists, rather than the other way round.

The basis of Ottoman criminal law was the tariff of fines and strokes which survives in the manuscript of the so-called '*Qanun* of Sultan Mehmed', dating probably from the early 1490s. For cases of theft this prescribes, according to what is stolen, either a fixed fine, a fine varying according to the means of the offender, a flogging, or flogging together with a fine of one or two aqches for each stroke. The actual number of strokes is at the discretion of the judge. The two factors which determine the level of the fine are the object stolen, and the offender's means. The theft of a horse, for example, incurs a fine of 100, fifty, or thirty to forty aqches, according to whether the offender is rich, in average circumstances, or poor. Although it underwent some modification and formal rearrangement, this original tariff remains as the basis of subsequent recensions of the code. The later versions, made between 1500 and about 1540, also saw the addition of a large number of additional clauses, including an enumeration of offences which incur hanging. These are stealing a prisoner [of war?], luring away another person's male or female slave, abducting a boy, breaking into a shop or house, and 'patently committing theft several times'.[30] An entirely separate clause also prescribes the death penalty for arson.

It is clear that the development of the Ottoman criminal code in its various recensions owed very little to Hanafi jurisprudence. In the sections dealing with theft, the compilers make a gesture towards the *shari'a* by prefixing the prescribed penalty with the condition: 'If the offender's hand is not to be amputated', but it is unlikely that this was ever more than a form of words. To denote strokes of the lash, they borrow from the jurists the term *ta'zir*. The use of this word, together with the prescription of the lash, might serve to put the penalties technically into the juristic category of discretionary punishment. However, in addition to flogging, the code also prescribes fines, which are alien to the Hanafi tradition. The jurists admit fines to the category of discretionary punishment only on the condition that the money be returned to the miscreant when he has shown repentance for his act.[31] By contrast, fines were an essential part of Ottoman feudal society, since they went to the governors and fief-holders who were responsible for the maintenance of law and order, and for whom the profits of justice were a source of income. In short, any resemblance between the criminal code and the *shari'a* in the area of property offences is entirely superficial.

Most of the penalties which the code prescribes, particularly in the clauses added to the original tariff, seem to have come about as an ad hoc response to crimes which were especially prevalent in the early sixteenth century. Only in one area do the codifiers develop, albeit very hesitatingly, a general legal principle. This is the recognition of criminal intent as an element in fixing the penalty. This appears in the statute dealing with arson, which ends with the phrase: 'If [the miscreant] commits the offence intentionally, he shall be hanged'.[32] In the juristic tradition, setting fire to property is not a criminal act but 'usurpation', incurring only liability for damage, regardless of whether or not it was deliberate. A similar way of thinking appears in a clause on crop damage by animals. This states that, if a man does not fence off his corn, and another man's animals trample on it, 'no sin (*günah*) shall attach itself to the owner of the animals', unless he drives them into the corn deliberately.[33] The implication is that, if he does so, he will have to pay compensation. In its externals, this clause simply follows the Hanafi rules for usurpation. The Hanafi jurists would also award compensation only if the owner drove his animals into the corn. However, their reasoning is different from the codifiers'. They would look only at the immediate cause of the damage. If the owner did not drive the animals into the crops, he is not the direct cause, and for this reason is not liable. The codifiers, however, look not at the cause, but at the intent. The owner of the cattle is 'sinful' only if he intentionally drives the animals into the corn, and only if he is 'sinful' must he pay compensation. It is thus the owner's intent, and not the fact that he is the immediate cause of the damage, that makes him liable. This line of reasoning distinguishes the codifiers from the Hanafi jurists, but it is one that is very weakly developed. In essence, the statutes on property offences which appear in the Ottoman criminal code are no more than an ad hoc accretion of clauses around the core of the original tariff of strokes and fines.

Ebu's-su'ud's rulings

Theft

The last redactor of the general Ottoman Law-Book, of which the Criminal Code forms the opening section, was most probably the Chancellor, Jelalzade Mustafa, who undertook the work in about 1540, when Ebu's-su'ud was Military Judge of Rumelia. As the senior judicial member of the Imperial Council, Ebu's-su'ud must have followed the work of redaction closely. There is, however, no evidence that he had any direct role in making the new recension of the Law-Book; and, since relatively few of his fatwas deal with the criminal offences covered by the Criminal Code, it seems that in penal affairs its application fell largely to the secular authorities, who were responsible for law enforcement and for executing punishments. It is nonetheless clear that, while he never refers directly to the Criminal Code, Ebu's-su'ud was willing to defend its application in practice, however much its statutes might differ from the ideals of the *shari'a*.

In the realm of property offences, the main concern of the code is with theft and damage. These are precisely the areas where the Hanafi prescriptions are most unreal. Theft (*sariqa*) as a criminal offence the jurists removed from the realm of practical law, and although, in theory, the laws of usurpation (*ghasb*) could apply to theft, they too are unrealistic, since they do not take into account the usurper's intent, or impose a penalty. Nevertheless, usurpation in its primary sense of taking property without the owner's permission is the closest that Hanafi law came to a working definition of the offence, and it was one that Ebu's-su'ud was able to develop by tacitly introducing a notion which the jurists had rejected. For Ebu's-su'ud, usurpation, when it is intentional, incurs a penalty:

(3) Zeyd removes a stone from a castle wall and uses it for the floor of his house. In law, is he liable for its price?
Answer: It is pulled up and replaced [in the castle wall]. Zeyd is flogged. [*D*, 727]

In the Hanafi view, removing the stone is usurpation, and the questioner is assuming that, since the usurper has incorporated it into his own house, he becomes the owner of the stone, but is liable to compensate its original owner for its value. Ebu's-su'ud, however, punctiliously prescribed the preferred Hanafi solution of returning, when it is possible to do so, the usurped object. However, in contrast to the strict Hanafi prescriptions, he also imposes a penalty, evidently because the offender intentionally removed the stone, without permission and knowing that it was not his. By doing this, he brings usurpation, which the jurists in effect define as a tort, into the sphere of the criminal law.

For practical purposes, therefore, Ebu's-su'ud redefines theft as intentionally taking property without the owner's permission and, by prescribing flogging as the penalty, brings it into the category of offences which incur a discretionary punishment. This concurs with the implied definition of theft in the Criminal Code.

He also makes it clear that, in cases of theft, the normal standards of proof, confession by the defendant or the evidence of two male eyewitnesses, do not apply. He does this by quoting an anecdote about how 'Ali, the fourth Caliph of Islam, conducted an enquiry into an abduction, after the established procedure in court had failed to identify the culprit:

(4) How are thieves[34] to be 'carefully examined'?
Answer: His Excellency 'Ali (may God ennoble his face) appointed Imam Shuraih as judge. It so happened that, at that time, several people took a Muslim's son to another district. The boy disappeared and, when the people came back, the missing boy's father brought them before Judge Shuraih. [When he brought] a claim [against them on account of the loss of his son], they denied it, saying: 'No harm came to him from us'. Judge Shuraih thought deeply and was perplexed.

When the man told his tale to His Excellency 'Ali, [the latter] summoned Judge Shuraih and questioned him. When Shuraih said: 'Nothing came to light by the *shari'a*', ['Ali] summoned all the people who had taken the man's son, separated them from one another, and questioned them separately. For each of their stopping places, he asked: 'What was the boy wearing in that place? What did you eat? And where did he disappear?' In short, he made each of them give a detailed account, and when their words contradicted each other, each of their statements was written down separately. Then he brought them all together, and when the contradictions became apparent, they were no longer able to deny [their guilt] and confessed to what had happened.

This kind of ingenuity is a requirement of the case. [*D*, 725]

The story clearly serves two purposes. First, it justifies the removal of criminal cases from the *shari'a* courts, which the figure of Shuraih represents, to the administrative authorities, represented here by 'Ali. Second, it serves to justify non-canonical methods of criminal investigation and thief-taking, such as occur in the Ottoman Criminal Code in cases, for example, of thefts from caravanserais.[35]

Theft, therefore, as Ebu's-su'ud defines it, is the unauthorised and deliberate taking of property. The investigation and punishment of theft is a matter for the administrative authorities, who may use whatever method of investigation and standard of evidence is appropriate to the case. Other fatwas emphasise these points. In reply to a question as to whether a ruler may inflict extra-judicial punishment (*siyasa*), Ebu's-su'ud cites two proof-texts which refer to the sovereign's right to deal specifically with cases of theft. The first of these, from the jurist al-Zaila'i (d. 1342), closely resembles the quotation with which Ibn Bazzaz opens his chapter on theft:

(5) '[An example of] administrative punishment is what is related from the jurist Abu Bakr al-Aghmash. When a person accused of theft denies [the charge], the ruler (*imam*) may act according to what, on balance, he considers best. If he strongly suspects that [the accused] is the thief and has the stolen goods with him, and he punishes him, [then] this is licit. It is the same if the ruler saw him sitting with dissolute people in a wine party, or associating with thieves, and his suspicions were overwhelming. [The jurists] have also permitted killing (*qatl al-nafs*), as in a case where a man comes up to a person with a drawn sword, and he strongly suspects that [the man] is going to kill him.' [*Ch*, f. 88b]

Like Ibn Bazzaz before him, Ebu's-su'ud follows this quotation with the story of 'Isam b. Yusuf and the governor, which seems to justify the use of torture in cases of theft in order to extract a confession. The effect of the two quotations is to give the authorities unlimited procedural and punitive powers.

It seems from the Criminal Code that the normal punishment for theft was the lash. However, it also imposes money fines, and these too Ebu's-su'ud seems willing to justify:

(6) If the judge or governor sees fit to impose a money fine (*ta'zir bi'l-mal*), is this permissible in law?

Answer: 'I have heard from a reliable person that a money fine is permissible if the judge or governor sees fit. A case in point is when a man does not attend Friday prayer. It is permissible to punish him with a fine.' *Khulasa*.[36]

In which case, in what manner is the fine imposed?

Answer: 'A fine is permissible if [the judge or governor] sees benefit (*maslaha*) in it. Our Lord the Seal of *Mujtahids* Rukn al-Din al-Vanjani al-Khurazmi said: "This means that we take his property and place it in deposit. If he repents, it is returned to him, as is the custom with horses and weapons belonging to rebels." The Imam Zuhr al-Din al-Timirtashi al-Khurazmi upholds him in this. It is said that a case in point is that, when a man does not attend Friday prayer, it is permissible to fine him.' Ibn Bazzaz. [*Ch*, f. 89a]

The proof-texts here do not go the whole way in justifying money fines, but they are probably the nearest that the Hanafi tradition comes to treating fines as a legitimate form of punishment. In its post-1490 recensions, however, in certain cases of theft the Criminal Code also prescribes hanging. Ebu's-su'ud finds a text to justify this as well:

(7) Can a thief be executed by administrative decree?

Answer: 'In the *Munya*,[37] the ruler may execute a thief by administrative decree (*siyasat*[an]), because he foments corruption on the earth.' *Durar wa Ghurar*.[38] [*Ch*, f. 87b]

'Fomenting corruption on the earth' is a catch-all phrase deriving from the Quran,[39] which jurists and governments frequently invoke in order to justify punitive actions outside the scope of the *shari'a*.

The effect of Ebu's-su'ud's rulings on theft is to remove the offence altogether from the scope of the Holy Law, to justify what happened in practice, and in particular to justify the provisions of the Criminal Code. The general public, however, was clearly more familiar with the canonical punishment of amputation, without being aware of the stringent conditions for its implementation. As a result, Ebu's-su'ud sometimes found himself warning his questioners not to try to put this particular ordinance of the *shari'a* into practice:

(8) Zeyd takes 'Amr's donkey without his knowledge and sells it. Is he a thief (*sariq*)?

Answer: His hand is not cut off. [*D*, 729]

Damage

Malicious damage, like theft, fell within the scope of the Ottoman Criminal Code. Hanafi law, on the other hand, treats malicious damage simply as usurpation, incurring restitution of the loss but no penalty. Ebu's-su'ud follows the Criminal Code and makes it a penal offence. This is already clear from the case of the man who removes the stone from the castle wall. This is as much a case of damage to the castle as it is of theft of the stone, and Ebu's-su'ud's remedy, return of the stone plus the lash, shows him observing the Hanafi rule that the miscreant must restore the damage, but requiring in addition a penalty. The same principle is at work in a clause in the Criminal Code which stipulates that 'if a person kills another's hen, dog or other animal' he must pay compensation and also receive strokes of the lash.[40] In other cases of damage, Ebu's-su'ud ignores the Hanafi principle of compensation altogether. Arson, for example, which the Hanafi jurists categorise as usurpation, Ebu's-su'ud treats straightforwardly as a crime. In this he is following the Criminal Code:

(9) Zeyd sets fire to a meadow and burns it. What should happen to him?
Answer: He should receive the lash (ta'zir). [*Ch*, f. 85b]

In short, where damage is intentional, Ebu's-su'ud abandons the Hanafi tradition and treats it as a crime. It may or may not incur compensation, but it will always incur a penalty.

It is only in some cases of damage or loss through negligence or by accident that Ebu's-su'ud gives the appearance of following strictly the Hanafi rules of usurpation. The following two cases are examples:

(10) Zeyd mounts 'Amr's horse as a courier and loses it. Is compensation necessary?
Answer: Yes.
In which case: What if Zeyd has a Sultanic decree [authorising him] to take horses for courier service?
Answer: Compensation is required in any case. He was not commanded to lose [the horse]. Even if he were commanded, it is the person who loses it who is liable. [*Ch*, f. 76b]

Here, a courier in the service of the Sultan has requisitioned a horse and subsequently lost it. It is he, rather than the Sultan, who is liable to pay compensation, since he is the direct cause of the loss, and it is always the direct cause that is relevant in attributing liability. A similar line of reasoning appears in the following:

(11) Concerning a woman who took her husband's horse to tie up in the stable and let it loose, and it disappeared. Does she pay compensation?
Answer: If she let it loose because it could not be controlled, no. [*Ch*, f. 85b]

The woman is liable only if she herself set the horse free. If it broke free because she could not control it, then the horse itself is the cause of the loss, and the woman owes nothing.

In both of these cases, however, Ebu's-su'ud probably had concerns other than pure Hanafi doctrine. In the first, by making the courier liable for the loss, he is protecting the Sultan. As the question clearly implies, he could equally well have invoked the rules of compulsion (*ikrah*), whereby a person is not liable for the consequences of his action if he carried it out under duress. The standard definition of compulsion is a threat to life, and a royal command constitutes compulsion, since the ruler has powers of life and death over his subjects. By this rule, it would have been possible to make the Sultan liable for the loss of the horse, and it is evidently to forestall this possibility that Ebu's-su'ud states somewhat sarcastically that the Sultan's decree did not contain an order to lose the horse. Furthermore, royal couriers were notorious for abusing their privileges[41] and, by making them personally liable for loss, Ebu's-su'ud may have been seeking to check their misdemeanours.

In the second case, where the woman frees the horse, it seems more than likely that what concerns Ebu's-su'ud is not to establish the direct cause of the loss, which is the relevant question in Hanafi law, but to establish the woman's intention in letting the horse go. If she did not free it deliberately, then she is not liable. If she freed it on purpose, she is. Certainly, in the following, it seems to be the intention rather than the cause that is the point at issue:

(12) The people of a village take it in turns to guard their animals. During Zeyd's watch, 'Amr's donkey goes missing. Assuming that Zeyd has not transgressed, is compensation necessary?
Answer: No. [*D*, 728]

In Hanafi law, anyone who is the direct cause of a loss is a 'transgressor' whether the loss is intentional or not. Here, however, the answer seems to depend on whether the loss occurred through the intention or negligence of the watchman. Where there is no intent or negligence, the watchman is not liable.

In cases of damage to, or loss of, other people's property, Ebu's-su'ud seems therefore to have modified the Hanafi law of usurpation in two ways. In the first place, he treats intent and negligence as factors which determine the legal consequences of the act. Loss or damage to another person's property incurs compensation only if it was wilful or the result of negligence. Second, he insists that malicious damage incurs a penalty and not merely compensation.

Illegal Occupation

The Hanafi jurists also classify as usurpation damage which comes about as a result of the illegal occupation and use of other people's land, an offence which is unknown to the Ottoman Criminal Code. In these cases, Ebu's-su'ud follows the Hanafi rules without any important modifications. He nonetheless manipulates them in order to circumvent their often inequitable solutions.

In dealing with these cases, the Hanafi jurists observe three important principles. First, the illegal occupation of land is not, in itself, an offence. It incurs neither a penalty nor the payment of compensation. Second, the ownership of the land is separate from the ownership of buildings, trees or plants on the land; and, third, the illegal occupier is liable for any damage which he might cause. By the normal principles of usurpation, however, the third of these rules also works in reverse. If the illegal occupier increases the value of the land, for example, by planting trees, then the owner, on regaining possession, must either make him remove the trees or else compensate him for their value. Qadikhan illustrates this rule with the example of a man who grows wheat on usurped land. In this case, the owner of the land has two options. Either he may wait until the wheat has grown, and then order the usurper to remove the crop, or he can pay the value of the crop. The fact that the usurper sowed his wheat on land that does not belong to him does not affect his ownership of the wheat. If it comes into the possession of the owner of the land, then the owner of the land must compensate him for its value.[42]

Ebu's-su'ud clearly regarded these rules as inequitable, and finds a way round them when he can. When he cannot, the wording of the answers suggests that he is not at all satisfied with the solution:

(13) Grass capable of being mown and sold grows on Zeyd's property. Without Zeyd's permission, certain people mow it and feed it to their cattle. Is this permissible in law?
Answer: If the grass grew on its own, it is not forbidden. If Zeyd cultivated it, it is not licit. God is wiser and more knowing. [*Ch*, f. 77a]

The problem here is damage, and underlying the answer are the principles that what grows on the land does not follow ownership of the soil and that what grows without cultivation is not subject to ownership.

Uncultivated meadow is therefore available for common use, even if the soil itself is not common property. Only when the owner or occupier of the land has cultivated the crop himself does it belong to him and, therefore, only if he has cultivated it himself can he claim compensation for its loss. This is logical enough in terms of Hanafi doctrine, but an inconvenience to owners or occupiers of pastureland. In the case above, where the loss has already occurred, Ebu's-su'ud can offer no solution, except perhaps for the owner of the land to claim that he had cultivated the grass. In a case where no loss has yet occurred, the solution is to invoke judicial authority:

(14) One year Zeyd does not sow the field which he occupies, and grass grows. The people of the village wish to turn their animals onto the grass. Can Zeyd prevent them, and keep the grass for himself?
Answer: Yes. He can stop them with a judge's decree. [*Ch*, f. 86a]

After the occupier has obtained the decree, he acquires sole right to the use of the meadow. The decree, however, does not make him owner of the grass. It simply forbids access to the other villagers. The solution nevertheless allows the occupier exclusive use of the meadow without contravening Hanafi principles.

The greatest source of inequity in the Hanafi law of usurpation is, however, the rule which makes an owner or occupier liable to compensate the usurper for increasing the value of the property. Ebu's-su'ud was clearly not ready to accept the injustices which this rule can cause:

(15) Zeyd's land is fallow and, without his permission, 'Amr sows seed in it and there is a crop. Can the said Zeyd give the value of the seed and the cost [of labour] and keep it for himself?
Answer: No. But if he sows seed on it and ploughs again, what grows belongs to Zeyd. He gives 'Amr whatever is the price of seed wrongfully (*ghasb^{an}*) sown in a place belonging to someone else (*il yeri*). [*Ch*, f. 78b]

The questioner here is proposing one of Qadikhan's two solutions to the same problem, and Ebu's-su'ud is rejecting it in favour of his own. What the legal owner must do is to scatter his own seed and, by running the plough over the land, mix the two batches of seed together. By Hanafi rules, if someone mixes his property with another person's, so that they cannot be separated, he becomes owner of the entire property, and compensates the other party for his loss. Here, by mixing his seed with the usurper's, the legal owner or occupier of the land becomes owner of all the seed. He must, it is true, compensate the usurper for the loss, but the phrase which Ebu's-su'ud uses, 'the price of seed which has been wrongfully sown in a place belonging to someone else', is a very strong hint that the amount of compensation due to the usurper is negligible or non-existent. This was a solution that observes the letter of the Hanafi rules of usurpation, while entirely undermining the principle.

It is also typical of Ebu's-su'ud's treatment of property offences. Where the law is totally impractical, as it is in the case of theft, he ransacks the Hanafi tradition to find justifications for removing it altogether from the jurisdiction of the *shari'a*. In cases of damage or loss, he tacitly modifies Hanafi principles by introducing the notion of intent as a relevant factor in prescribing penalties or compensation. In cases of illegal occupation, he manipulates Hanafi rules to arrive at as just a remedy as is possible, even if it is not the solution that the Hanafi jurists had intended.

Loss of Amenity

The cases so far have dealt with theft and the loss of property belonging to another person, and with damage to property and land. The relative scarcity of fatwas on these subjects indicates that property offences in general fell outside the scope of the *shari'a* and within the jurisdiction of the secular authorities. However, another area of the law of property did come under the jurisdiction of the *shari'a*, and this was the loss of amenity. It was also an area where Hanafi principles were of limited use.

The first problem was the tendency of the Hanafi jurists to give owners unfettered freedom within the boundaries of their own property. They are, to start with, exempt from liability for accidents which occur there. If, for example, a wall on the property collapses onto a visitor or the visitor's possessions, the owner is not liable. He is liable only if, in certain circumstances, a leaning exterior wall collapses onto a passer-by on the street. Similarly, if a gutter falls and injures a person or damages property, the owner is liable only if it was the portion of the gutter overhanging the street that fell. In both cases, liability arises from the fact that the object that caused the damage or injury was occupying the air of the street, and not the owner's property. More importantly, some jurists exempt an owner entirely if an action which he undertakes exclusively on his own property causes damage to his neighbour. If a man pours water in his own house, and it floods the house next door, he is not liable, 'because pouring water in his own property is absolutely licit to him'. The only restraint, in this view, is a moral one: 'Between himself and God Most High, he should refrain from this, if another man is harmed by it'. This is the strict rule, although 'there are some sheikhs who hold the opinion that, if he pours water in his own house, and he knows that it will go onto another person's land, he is liable [in law]'.[43] This is a very grudging admission of liability.

The second problem was the tendency of the Hanafi jurists to consider only damage to the physical fabric of the neighbouring property, and not intangible damage, such as loss of light or air.

The logic of Hanafi reasoning is therefore to place no restrictions on what a person may do on his own property, and to disregard any loss of amenity which his activities may cause to his neighbours. These were principles which Ebu's-su'ud did not accept. Instead, by admitting people's right to stop harmful activities or to prevent harmful developments on adjacent property, he accepted that loss of amenity could be the basis of a legal claim. The problem then was to set the limits on this right, and he did this by applying a set of simple general rules.

The first rule was that the cause of the loss of amenity must be new. The tortuous argument in the following case arises because Ebu's-su'ud is actually breaking this rule, but cannot be seen to be doing so:

(16) Zeyd has a privy near a mosque. Since Muslims who come to the mosque are upset by its smell, can they say to Zeyd: 'Remove it from here and build it somewhere else'?
Answer: If he is a Muslim, it is incumbent [on him] to remove it, [even] before [anyone] tells [him to]. So much the less then is it possible for him, after being told, to make excuses, saying it has been there for a long time. Since the harm from that abomination increases day by day, it has the legal effect of being a new [source of] harm. [*Ch*, f. 83a]

Here, the legal as opposed to the pious argument for removing the privy is that, however old-established the privy itself may be, the smell coming from it is renewed daily, and is therefore new, giving the neighbours, in this case the mosque-goers, a rightful claim to have it removed.

The second rule restricting a neighbour's right to prevent harmful development is that the damage must be actual and not potential:

(17) On ground which he owns, Zeyd builds a mill which operates all year, right up against and overlooking the house which 'Amr owns. In law, can 'Amr prevent him building, saying: 'I'm afraid that one day it will be knocked down by the wind, and knock down my house as well'?
Answer: No, so long as Zeyd owns the ground.

(18) Zeyd builds a pastry-shop near to shops belonging to several other people. The owners say nothing. Can they then have it removed, saying: 'It might damage us'?
Answer: No. [*Ch*, f. 84a]

The second answer also suggests a third rule, that neighbours should exercise the right to object before the development happens.

The fourth rule is that, before neighbours can prevent a development, they must show that it will cause great harm:

(19) The light entering Zeyd's house is confined to its windows and glass. His neighbour 'Amr builds a wall on his own land and blocks the light coming through the windows and glass. Can he get 'Amr to demolish his wall?
Answer: If it causes great harm, it is necessary to remove it. [*Ch*, f. 82b]

The question then is to define what is meant by great harm. It is a notion that did not apply, among other things, to the loss of an unrestricted supply of fresh air, even if it could apply to loss of light:

(20) Zeyd wishes to build a canopy on [the flat roof of] the house which he owns. Can the neighbours stop him, simply because he blocks the air?
Answer: No. [*Ch*, f. 82b]

Great harm is a subject which Ebu's-su'ud deals with at length in a detailed answer to a question, where he also provides a test for whether loss of light constituted great harm:

(21) Zeyd wishes to add a storey to the single-storey house which he owns, and which adjoins the [two-]storey house owned by 'Amr. 'Amr prevents him, saying: 'It will block my light and air, and shut in my windows and glass. I will not let [you] build [it].' Zeyd brings a builder and experts and shows them [his house]. The builder says: 'It is his property from earth to sky. He can do what he likes [with it].' When Zeyd wishes to add to his one-storey house, can 'Amr stop him?
Answer: According to the Great Imam [Abu Hanifa], a person can do as he pleases on his own property. Whether or not he harms his neighbours, he cannot be stopped. According to the two Imams [Abu Yusuf and Shaibani], if a person causes harm, he can be stopped. The later sheikhs, in order to respect both opinions, have elected, if he simply causes harm, to act according to the opinion of the Great Imam, but if he causes serious harm, to act according to the opinion of the two Imams. As it happens, this is the most appropriate and suitable [course of action].
　　If Zeyd extends his house upwards by adding an upper storey, and this causes harm to 'Amr, if it is impossible to prevent the harm in any other way, Zeyd should be prevented from adding the upper floor. If it is possible to prevent the harm by any other means, he should build [the upper floor] and prevent [the harm] by other means. If he does not cause serious harm, he should certainly not be prevented.
　　To block his air or view is not a harm recognised in law, nor is it to

block the sun. [However,] to block out the light of the windows and glass so excessively as to prevent the reading and writing of the Quran is serious damage. If it does not prevent these things, it is not serious damage. [*Ch*, ff. 84b–85a]

The test here for whether the loss of light constitutes great harm is as practical as it is pious. If it is too dark to read and write the Quran, it will certainly also be too dark to carry out household tasks.

Taken together, these fatwas provide very clear guidelines as to whether a neighbour can claim loss of amenity in order to prevent a development. If the claim is to be successful, the development must cause great harm, which need not necessarily be to the physical fabric of the neighbouring property. The harm must, however, be actual and not simply potential, and it is not possible to bring a claim if the source of the nuisance is long-standing, or against a new development once it is completed. On the related question of disputes concerning easements on land belonging to another person, Ebu's-su'ud seems to have an equally clear set of principles, although his fatwas on this subject are rare:

(22) Zeyd brings water to the front of a caravanserai, and sites a cistern for the people to make use of, on ground which 'Amr owns. Can 'Amr block the cistern, and stop the people from benefiting?
Answer: No, not if he agreed to letting the water pass and there is no reason to block it. If there is no damage from the water's flowing past, but there is from the cistern's being cleared out, that is a reason to block it. [*Ch*, f. 84a]

From this example, it appears that the first rule is that the owner or occupant of the land must agree to the easement. Once he has done so, he cannot withdraw his consent, unless it causes damage to his land that was not part of the original agreement. As in cases of loss of amenity, these rules are clear and straightforward, allowing Ebu's-su'ud to arrive at equitable solutions that would not have been possible if he had shared the general Hanafi prejudice in favour of the absolute rights of property owners.

Notes

1. Joseph Schacht, *An Introduction to Islamic Law*, Oxford: Clarendon Press (1964), p. 187.
2. al-Quduri, *Matn*, Cairo: Matba'a Mustafa al-Babi al-Halabi (1957), p. 94.
3. Qadikhan, *al-Fatawa*, in margins of *al-Fatawa al-Hindiyya*, Bulaq: Imperial Press (1912/13) vol. 3, p. 481.

4. al-Marghinani, *al-Hidaya*, Cairo: Matba'a Mustafa al-Babi al-Halabi (1972), vol. 5, p. 346.

5. Ibn Humam, *Fath al-qadir*, Cairo: Matba'a Mustafa al-Babi al-Halabi (1972), vol. 5, p. 345.

6. Ibid.

7. Baber Johansen, 'Eigentum, Familie und Obrigkeit im hanafitischen Strafrecht', *Die Welt des Islams*, 19 (1979), 1–73.

8. Colin Imber, 'The navy of Süleyman the Magnificent', *Archivum Ottomanicum*, 6 (1980), 265–9; Uriel Heyd, *Studies in Old Ottoman Criminal Law*, Oxford: Clarendon Press (1973), pp. 304–7.

9. Quran, 5:38.

10. al-Marghinani, *al-Hidaya*, vol. 5, p. 354.

11. Ibid., p. 363.

12. Ibid., p. 387.

13. Ibid., p. 393.

14. Ebu's-su'ud, *Irshad al-'aql al-salim ila mazaya al-kitab al-karim*, in margins of Fakhr al-Din Razi, *Mafatih al-ghaib*, Istanbul: Imperial Press (1872/3), vol. 3, p. 571.

15. al-Marghinani, *al-Hidaya*, vol. 5, p. 356.

16. Ibid., p. 408.

17. Ibid., vol. 9, p. 315.

18. Ibid., p. 318.

19. Ibid., p. 321.

20. Ibid., p. 325.

21. Ibid., p. 332.

22. Quran, 2:190.

23. Ibn Bazzaz, *al-Fatawa al-bazzaziyya*, in margins of *al-Fatawa al-Hindiyya*, Bulaq: Imperial Press (1912/13), vol. 6, p. 430.

24. Ibn Humam, *Fath*, vol. 5, p. 345.

25. Qadikhan, *al-Fatawa*, vol. 2, p. 42ff.

26. Ibid., vol. 3, p. 234.

27. Ibid., p. 251.

28. Ibid., p. 248.

29. Ibid., p. 242.

30. Ottoman Criminal Code, section 74, in Uriel Heyd, ed. V. L. Ménage, *Studies in Old Ottoman Criminal Law*, Oxford: Clarendon Press (1973).

31. See below, no. (6).

32. Ottoman Criminal Code, section 92.

33. Ibid., section 110.

34. The term here is *surraq*, meaning 'people who commit *sariqa*'.

35. Ottoman Criminal Code, sections 83–5.

36. The reference is presumably to *Khulasat al-fatawa* by al-Bukhari (d. 1147).

37. The reference is to *Munyat al-Mufti* by al-Sijistani (d. 1240)

38. The reference is to *Durar al-hukkam fi sharh ghurar al-ahkam* by Molla

Khusrev (d. 1480).

39. Quran, 5:37.
40. Ottoman Criminal Code, section 112.
41. Ed. and trans. R. Tschudi, *Das Asafname des Vezîrs Lutfî Pascha*, Türkische Bibliothek 12, Berlin: Mayer & Müller (1910), Turkish text, pp. 10–11, German text, pp. 11–12.
42. Qadikhan, *al-Fatawa*, vol. 3, p. 246.
43. Ibid., p. 461.

9
Crimes and Torts:
Offences against the Person

Offences against the Person: Hanafi Doctrine

In Hanafi law, there is no absolutely clear boundary between offences against the person and offences against property. The jurists discuss most property offences under the heading of usurpation (*ghasb*), which has the primary sense of unlawful removal of or damage to property, but can also refer to the abduction of human beings. They discuss killing and wounding under the heading of delicts (*jinayat*), but this category can also comprise abduction, or damage to property by animals, or collapsing buildings. Qadikhan, in fact, repeats several of his cases under both headings.

The reason for the overlap is simply that the same essential principle applies in both kinds of offence. In cases of killing and wounding, the law aims not so much to punish the offender as to maintain the precise equivalence between individuals. Where there is loss or damage to property, the offender must restore to the owner the precise value of the loss. Where there is killing or wounding, the assailant must suffer damage which is precisely equivalent to the damage which he has inflicted on his victim. In one place, Qadikhan makes the analogy between liability for wounding and liability for damage to property particularly clear. He cites a case where A bites B's arm, and B pulls it away. As a result, A loses a tooth and B loses flesh in his arm. Immediately after this, he repeats the case which opens his chapter on usurpation, where A grabs hold of B's cloth, which B pulls away from him, causing it to tear. In both cases cash compensation is due, and in both cases the problem is to decide who is liable and for what amount.[1]

To claim compensation, the victim must bring a private suit against his assailant. In cases of homicide, it is the next-of-kin who initiate the action, as they are heirs to the claim of the deceased. If the plaintiff proves his claim, the law will seek to maintain equivalence between the parties by imposing talion (*qisas*), blood-money (*diya*) or fair compensation (*hukumat al-'adl*). The parties may also in some cases compose for an agreed sum. If they do not do this, the problem is to determine which of the penalties is applicable.

This depends first on whether the assailant took the victim's life or 'what is less than life' (*ma dun al-nafs*) and, second, on whether the act was intentional, quasi-intentional or accidental. In determining intent, the law does not examine the mental state or motives of the killer, but only external appearances. The definition of a deliberate killing or wounding is one where the assailant uses an offensive weapon (*ala jariha*) such as a sword, the weapon itself being proof of intent. Quasi-intent is where the assailant uses an instrument, such as a stone or cudgel, which is not usually used for killing. Other cases of killing and wounding are accidental. All discussions of whether or not the act was deliberate revolve around the nature of the weapon used. Where there is no weapon, there is, strictly speaking, no offence. The law does not, for example, classify strangling as a delict, because the killer does not use a weapon: the authorities should execute him by administrative decree (*siyasat^(an)*) if he has offended more than once.[2]

The simplest rules are those for intentional killing. It is a sin (*ithm*) and incurs talion. The next-of-kin (*wali al-dam*) must either forgive the killer or claim his life. He can claim blood-money only if the killer consents. Lack of equivalence between the killer and his victim does not, in most cases, affect the law of talion. Hence, a free man may be executed for killing a slave, or a man for killing a woman because, the jurists argue, they are equal in the degree of protection that the law affords them; and because what is at issue is the destruction of life, and all people's lives, unlike their limbs, are equal in value.[3] There are only a few cases where the next-of-kin cannot demand talion for intentional killing. There is, for example, no talion if a father or grandfather kills his child or grandchild. He becomes liable instead to pay blood-money. Finally, the law of talion does not demand equivalence in the manner of death. However the murderer killed his victim, execution is always with the sword.

The rules for cases of intentional wounding are less straightforward. In principle, either the parties may compose for an agreed sum, or the injured party may demand talion. This is not, however, as simple as in the case of homicide, because in matters short of life, the law demands exact equivalence between the parties. Hence, talion is impossible between a man and a woman, since the law gives a woman half the value of a man; nor is it possible between a free person and a slave. Talion is, however, permissible between a Muslim and a non-Muslim. A second restriction in the application of the law is the rule that the injury inflicted as 'vengeance' must be the exact equivalent of the original injury. There is, for example, talion for knocking out a tooth or cutting off a hand. Difference in size between the affected limbs does not matter, since it is the utility or beauty of the limb that the law takes into account, and not its size. On the other hand, there is no talion for a bone other than a tooth, 'because regard for equivalence in bones other than teeth is impossible, because of the probability of excess or deficiency. This is not the case with a tooth, because it is filed with a file. If it is pulled out at the root, the [assailant's] tooth is also pulled out, so that the two are equivalent.[4] Similarly, there is no talion for amputating part of the penis or tongue, because these are distensible organs, and to inflict precisely the equivalent injury is impossible. Underlying these rules is the concept of a limb as property. Anyone who causes the loss of a limb must suffer a loss of precisely equivalent value: 'Limbs are treated as property (*amwal*) and equivalence is lacking where there is a difference in value. [This] is known by the valuation of the law.'[5] Talion is operative only where the limbs are equal in value, and where it is possible to inflict an equal injury.

The notion of limbs as having a precise value is more obvious still in the rules for the payment of blood-money, a sum which is not negotiable, but fixed by law. Blood-money is payable in two categories of killing. The first is where the killing is quasi-intentional. This is a sin, and the killer must perform a penance (*kaffara*), either by freeing a slave or by fasting for two successive months. It also incurs blood-money. In the case of quasi-intentional homicide, liability is for the 'heavier' blood-money (*diya mughallaza*), which the jurists fix at 100 camels of four specified types, in four groups of twenty-five. To qualify as 'heavier' blood-money, payment must be in the form of camels, an archaic rule which remained embedded in the juristic tradition. The second category is where the killing is accidental. This is not a sin, but nonetheless requires a penance from the killer and payment of 'normal' blood-money (*diya muhaqqaqa*). This consists again of 100 camels of less valuable breeds, but may be commuted for 1,000 gold *dinars* or 10,000 silver *dirhams*. Tradition asserts that Abu Yusuf and Shaibani also permitted payment in cows, sheep or garments, a rule which Abu Hanifa resisted because 'the amount can be estimated only with reference to something of known value, and these things are unknown in value. For this reason, they cannot be used in estimating compensation. Valuation by camels is known through widespread traditions, which we lack with regard to other things.'[6] The point is that the sum due as compensation is fixed and, in juristic theory, it is camels that provide the standard for valuation.[7]

The heavier blood-money represents the full value of a human life, but is relevant only in cases of quasi-intentional killing. In other cases, normal blood-money is the standard measure of assessment. It is payable not only in cases of accidental death, but also for a number of legally-specified injuries. It is due, for example, if an assailant strikes a person and causes him to lose his sight, hearing, taste or smell, or if he hits someone in the back, causing impotence or deformity. It is due also for the loss of both organs, where these occur in pairs. In such cases as these, it is due for the loss of the utility of the organ. In others, as with the permanent loss of a beard, it is payable for loss of beauty.

For many other types of injury, the law prescribes a fixed proportion of the normal blood-money. The loss of one of a pair of organs, for example an eye, or a female breast, incurs half blood-money. The loss of a finger incurs one tenth, and the loss of a single joint of a finger one thirtieth, unless it is the thumb, in which case the figure is one twentieth. Head wounds form the subject of a special section in legal texts, which divide them into ten or more categories, ranging from a superficial scratch to a blow which penetrates the skull, and lay down a tariff of blood-money payable for each type. For some injuries, the assailant does not pay a fixed proportion of blood-money but a 'fair compensation' (*hukumat al-'adl*). The amount is not, however, entirely at the judge's discretion. There are various ways of estimating its value, but the one which Qadikhan[8] and other jurists favour, is for the judge to estimate the value of the wounded person had he been a slave, and then to estimate the loss in value which the wound in question would cause. The value of the loss is the value of the compensation.

The law also treats abortion and miscarriage under the heading of blood-money. The general rule is that the loss of the foetus incurs payment to the heirs of the dead infant of the minimum blood-money (*ghurra*) of 500 *dirhams*, or of a slave or horse of the same value. If the foetus is a slave, the blood-money is one twentieth of its value if it is male, and one tenth of its value if it is female. This is payable, however, only if the abortion was deliberate: 'The condition for liability for the minimum blood-money is that [the mother] should have drunk an abortifacient, intending to abort the child'.[9] If there was no intention, there is no blood-money. If the cause of the miscarriage was a blow to the woman, then the assailant is liable to pay the minimum blood-money if the foetus is born dead, and the full blood-money if it is born alive and dies subsequently.

The rules for the payment of blood-money place an exact value on human life and limbs. The purpose in fixing the sums so precisely is clearly to ensure that equivalence is maintained between the individuals. As in the laws of talion, the assailant must suffer exactly the same loss as his victim.

The next question is who pays the blood-money. In cases of intentional killing or wounding, where talion is not inflicted, it is the offender himself who pays the sum due, over a period of three years. In cases of quasi-intentional homicide, it is not the killer himself but his communal group (*'aqila*) who pay. In cases of quasi-intentional wounding, it is the assailant himself. In cases of accidental killing or wounding, it is the communal group that pays, unless the sum due is less than one twentieth of the full blood-money. The communal group, like the individual, pays the blood-money over a period of three years, reckoned from the moment of the judgement. If, however, instead of the plaintiff's demanding talion or blood-money, the parties compose for an agreed sum, this is payable immediately, as the liability arises out of a contract.[10]

Clear though these rules may be, there remains the problem of identifying the communal group. The jurists make it clear that the function of the group is to render mutual aid to its members, and for this reason they exclude women, minors, the insane and slaves, whom the law does not deem capable of bringing assistance (*nusra*). Equally, an infidel cannot belong to the same communal group as a Muslim, and vice versa.[11] A communal group, therefore, consists of males of the same religion. However, when they come to defining the term more closely, the jurists devote most of their efforts to preserving an archaic tradition of the communal group as consisting of the registered members of a garrison in a city, or as members of a tribe. They make only glancing references to possible senses of the term in their own time: 'If today it is through trades that they mutually assist one another, then their communal group consists of tradesmen. If it is through confederacy, then it is their confederates.'[12] Or: 'If a person kills accidentally, and blood-money becomes due, the people of the killer's quarter or village are his communal group'.[13] Juristic asides such as these suggest that, in reality, the communal group was not strictly defined. It consisted of a group with shared economic interests, a kinship group, or a group resident in the same district. The important element is that its members must be capable of rendering mutual aid. The communal group is jointly responsible for discharging certain delictual liabilities incurred by any of its members, and serves to alleviate the burden of paying blood-money. The author of the delict pays only his share as a member of the group.

The same concept of mutual aid appears in other areas of the law of delicts. It is, in the first place, often the presence or absence of assistance that determines culpability in cases of killing in self-defence. The basic rule is that a person is not culpable if he kills an assailant who has drawn an offensive weapon: 'When an attacker draws a sword against Muslims, they may kill him'. By attacking a Muslim, the assailant is technically a rebel (*baghi*), and his blood is no longer protected.[14] However, when the aggressor's weapon is not technically offensive, the right to kill in self-defence depends on whether or not assistance will be forthcoming: 'A person draws a weapon against a man by night or day: or he draws a cudgel against him by night in a town, or by day on a road away from town. The person who is threatened kills intentionally. He is not liable for anything.'[15] He may not by day kill an assailant who is armed with a non-offensive weapon, because the townsmen will come to his help. This is not the case at night or outside the town: 'At night, help will not reach him, and he is constrained to defend himself by killing'.[16] Rather similar rules apply to a householder's right to kill a thief whom he finds breaking into his house.

The idea of mutual aid is also a factor in determining liability for homicide in cases where the killer is unknown. In these cases, it is the inhabitants of the village or quarter, or the owner of the property where the body was found, who pay the blood-money. Liability arises because, in allowing a murder to take place, they have failed in their duty of protection. If, on the other hand, the body is found in a place which is not near to any habitation, the blood is unavenged: 'and the sense of "near" ... is defined by [the ability to] hear a voice, because when it is [too distant to hear] help cannot reach [the victim], and negligence (*taqsir*) cannot be attributed to anyone'.[17] If the body is found in a public place – a main street, a congregational mosque, a public bridge, or a market-place without an owner – it is the public treasury that is liable to pay the blood-money, since these places, like the treasury, are the shared property of the public.

Before blood-money becomes payable, it is necessary first to establish that the corpse is intact. If less than half a body is found, no action is taken. Second, the body must be that of a 'slain man' (*qatil*). The marks of a slain man are indications of beating or wounding, or blood coming from the eyes, ears, or any organ from which it does not normally issue.

If there is such a corpse and the killer is unknown, the inhabitants of the village or quarter where it came to light must submit to compurgation (*qasama*). Qadikhan describes the process:

A slain man is found in a quarter. The people of the quarter are liable for compurgation, and their communal groups for blood-money. It is for the next-of-kin of the slain to choose fifty men from among the old and pious; [or] if he wishes, he may choose the young men for compurgation. The choice in the matter belongs to the next-of-kin of the slain and not to the ruler (*imam*), because the claim is his.[18]

When the next-of-kin has chosen the fifty compurgators, each of them must swear: 'By God, we did not kill him and do not know the killer'. The extreme formalism of the law requires that there must be exactly fifty oaths. If there are fewer than fifty compurgators, some of them must repeat the oath. If there is only one, he must repeat the oath fifty times. The law excludes lunatics and minors from the process, because their word is not reliable, and women and slaves, because they are not 'people who bring aid'.

The compurgation releases the inhabitants of the village, quarter or household from liability for talion, but not from blood-money: 'Blood-money is payable because of a killing which, to all appearances, came about through them, since the slain man was found among them ... And it is incumbent because of their negligence [in the matter of] offering protection, as in [a case of] accidental killing.'[19] The burden of paying the blood-money is shared among the communal group or groups of all the male inhabitants.

When the corpse is found in an open space within a community, then it is the community that is liable. If, however, it is found on property belonging to an individual, it is the individual who is liable, and not the community. The question then arises of whether liability rests solely with the owner of the property, as in the doctrine attributed to Abu Hanifa and Shaibani, or whether with the tenants and other inhabitants, as in the doctrine attributed to Abu Yusuf. This was to become an issue in Ebu's-su'ud's time.

So far, cases of homicide have been intentional, quasi-intentional or accidental. As a fourth category, the law also recognises indirect killing (*qatl bi-sabab*) and injury. In these cases, the general rule for establishing liability is the same as in incidents of damage to property where there is a proximate and an ultimate cause: it is the direct and not the indirect cause that is relevant. For example, if a person digs a well in a public road, and somebody falls in and is killed or injured, then the person who dug the well is liable. But if a third person places a stone by the well, and somebody trips over it and falls in, then liability rests with the person who planted the stone, and not with the person who dug the well. If a person tells an assassin to kill somebody, then it is the assassin and not the person who instructed him who is liable. The assassin is exempt only if he acted under compulsion.

The most usual application of the rules for indirect killing and injury is, however, to cases of harm arising from animals, obstacles on the ground, or collapsing buildings. In establishing who is liable in these cases, the law takes into account not only the direct and indirect causes, but also the ownership of the ground where the death or injury occurred. In general, a person is not liable for an indirect death or injury which happens on his property. If a person falls into a well or is struck by falling masonry within the boundaries of an individual's estate, he or his next-of-kin receive no compensation. A person is, however, liable for damage which occurs outside his own property. If he lives in a cul-de-sac, there are limitations on this liability. A cul-de-sac is the shared property of its inhabitants, and so anyone who lives there may place firewood, tether his animal or sprinkle water in the road in front of his house, because 'these things are necessities of living, [and it is] as in a shared house'.[20] If however, he wishes to erect a privy which occupies space in the street, or put in an overhanging gutter, then he must first get the permission of the other inhabitants of the street, whether or not they are put to inconvenience. Only then will he be exempt from liability for any harm which they may cause.

Such permission is not necessary in a public road, because it is impossible to seek the permission of all members of the public. In a public road, however, passers-by have more rights, and the householder greater potential liabilities. If a person makes a privy or drain in a public road, or builds a shop there, passers-by have a right to remove the obstacle, as they would on their own property. Furthermore, if he places any obstruction in the public road which causes death or injury, he or his communal group become liable: 'If a person digs a well or places a rock in the public road, and a person is destroyed as a result, his communal group must pay blood-money. If an animal is destroyed, he pays compensation from his own property.'[21] The same rule applies if an overhanging gutter or similar projection falls on a passer-by. The householder is the direct cause of the accident, because he has responsibility for the gutter, and liable because the section which fell and caused the injury was 'occupying the air of the [public] road'.[22] He remains liable if somebody suffers injury through tripping over the gutter lying in the road. It is as though the gutter's owner had tripped the injured person. If, however, a third person removes the gutter and places it elsewhere, causing somebody an injury, then he, and not the owner of the gutter, is the direct cause of the injury, and therefore liable.

In the public road itself, everybody has a right of free passage, but one that is 'restricted by the condition of safety' (*muqayyad bi-shart al-salama*). Passers-by are liable for any harm which they or, more often, their animals cause. A rider, or rather his communal group, is liable if his animal bites or kicks someone, or if it causes damage or injury by kicking up large stones. If, however, the animal is moving, the rider is not liable for minor injuries from its hooves or tail, from its kicking up dust or pebbles, or from its dung, urine, sweat or saliva. The law does, however, make a distinction between an animal which is moving or which has stopped of its own accord, and an animal which the rider has brought to a halt: 'If [the animal] was moving, then stopped [of its own accord] and urinated or dropped dung, the rider is not liable. But if the rider stopped it for some reason other than urinating or dropping dung, then the rider is liable for any [harm] which results from this.'[23] By stopping the animal, the rider somehow becomes the proximate cause of the damage or injury. If a person goads an animal, causing it immediately to kick, bite or bolt, then the person who goaded it is liable since he, and not the rider, is the direct cause. If a tethered animal causes damage or injury, then the owner is liable, but if he did not tie it up, the law treats it as a stray. The owner is not liable, because the animal has moved from the spot where he left it, and so the animal itself and not the owner is the direct cause of the harm. Other detailed rules, following the same general principles, deal with damage and injury by animals being led or driven, either singly or in caravans.

Offences against the Person: Ottoman Practice

The Ottoman Criminal Code

In its section on homicide and wounding, as in its section on property offences, the Ottoman Criminal Code of c. 1540 is an amalgam. It preserves intact the statutes from the Code of c. 1490, adding to them additional matter from the originally independent criminal code of c. 1500, as well as some entirely new clauses. There is no systematisation of the material. The code presents, for some offences, a tariff of money fines, for others strokes of the lash or strokes plus a fine, and for some the exposure of the offender to public scorn. Other clauses lay down, unsystematically, rules of procedure, or else regulate the tariffs.

The clauses which prescribe money fines, for tearing out the hair or beard, for blows to the head which draw blood, and which lay bare the bone, for striking with a knife or arrow, and for homicide, represent the most archaic layer in the text. They derive from the Code of c. 1490, with the fines remaining unchanged in later recensions. Clauses added in the early sixteenth century prescribe the lash for unlawful beating or for tearing out someone's beard, despite the earlier clause prescribing only a fine for the latter offence. It lays down the same punishment for fighting between men and for fighting between women who are not 'veiled ladies' (*mukhaddarat*), and lashes plus a fixed fine for drawing a sword against someone in the road. It establishes exposure to shame for shooting an arrow at someone in the road: 'he shall be led with an arrow through his ear'.[24] For cutting purses or knifing someone, 'he shall be led with a knife through his arm'. If he does either of these two things habitually, 'then his hand shall be cut off'.[25]

None of these provisions has any affinity with Hanafi law. Nevertheless, there are a few sections of the Code which clearly do reflect the Hanafi tradition, most obviously in the case of homicide. The Code of c. 1490 and all later recensions impose a fine for homicide only if talion is not inflicted, and a clause in the Criminal Code of c. 1500 reinforces the view that talion was the normal penalty: 'A person who kills somebody should be killed in place of the person whom he killed'.[26] This clause appears reworded in the Code of c. 1540. Another affinity which the Code of c. 1490 and all subsequent recensions have with Hanafi law is in their classification of blows to the head into those which draw blood, and those which lay bare the bone. This is a much simplified version of the Hanafi scheme. The clause which appears in the Code of c. 1540, laying down a procedure for cases of homicide where the killer is unknown, also derives in part from the juristic tradition: 'If a person is found killed within a [town-]quarter or somewhere between villages, [the people in the vicinity] shall certainly be examined and compelled to find the killer or defray the blood-money. But if no sign of killing is found [on the dead body, the people] shall not be hurt, merely because a corpse has been found [in the vicinity].' This clause reproduces the Hanafi rules, except that, for compurgation, it substitutes the duty of finding the killer.

Other clauses in the Code present rules which probably derive from a popular rather than a learned understanding of the Holy Law, most notably the rule that stipulates that an infidel or slave should pay half the fine of a free Muslim for the same offence. This reflects, in a very general sense, the inferior status which the jurists accorded to non-Muslims and to slaves, although the particular rule has no justification in the Hanafi tradition. Rather similar is the clause which distinguishes between women who are 'veiled' and those who are not. If two 'veiled ladies' fight, it is their husbands and not they who pay the fine. The distinction seems to arise from a popular interpretation of the Holy Law which makes the payment of maintenance to a wife conditional on her remaining confined to the house, and which, in general, subjects unmarried women to the tutelage of a male guardian. A woman who remains secluded is therefore, in the popular view, more obedient and pious than one who does not, a distinction in religious merit which coincides with a difference in social status, since only women in relatively wealthy households could afford not to work outside the home. The compilers of the Criminal Code have turned this difference in piety and social status into a legal distinction. It was, furthermore, one which Ebu's-su'ud himself accepted, when he ruled that, if a woman who is not a 'veiled lady' brings a case to court, the defendant may refuse to accept the case, if the plaintiff appoints an agent and does not appear in person.[27] Thus the notion of a 'veiled lady' became a quasi-legal concept which arose out of the general precepts, although not the specific doctrines of Islamic law, and from the beliefs and practices of Muslim society. Nevertheless, the jurists knew of no such concept; and, for this reason, when he came to define the term, Ebu's-su'ud dissociated it from all notions of specifically Islamic piety, and linked it instead to secular standards of behaviour and economic status: 'What is taken into account in [defining] who is a veiled lady is not respect for the ordinances of the Noble *shari'a*. For this reason, there are veiled ladies among infidel women. If she does not appear before strangers, and does not manage her affairs, she is a veiled lady.'[28] It is unlikely, however, that the compilers of the Code or the Ottoman public at large were so careful in their definition of the term. Most probably, they thought of it as a concept of Islamic law.

In some respects, therefore, the Ottoman Criminal Code, in all its recensions between c. 1490 and c. 1540, does show the influence of Hanafi law and, in the clauses on differential fines and 'veiled ladies', of what Muslims at large probably believed Hanafi law to be. Nonetheless, most of its provisions have no counterpart in the law of the jurists. For the

Hanafis, killing and wounding give rise to a private claim. It is up to the victim or his next-of-kin to produce the culprit in court and there to demand talion or blood-money or to compose for a cash sum. In a case of homicide where the killer is unknown, it is up to the victim's next-of-kin to select the compurgators from the inhabitants of the district where the body was found. Talion and blood-money are imposed not on behalf of the ruler or the community but on behalf of the victim or his heirs and, in legal theory, serve not so much as punishment as to maintain equivalence between the parties. In the Criminal Code, on the other hand, injury to the person gives rise to a public claim. It is the public authorities who sentence offenders to the lash, fines or exposure to scorn, and who are the recipients of fines. The Code also indiscriminately mixes punishments for inflicting injuries with punishments for affray, suggesting that its underlying concern is with the maintenance of public order, a concept which is entirely absent from the Hanafi law of delicts. In cases, then, of wounding and affray, it was the Criminal Code that was applicable. In cases of homicide, however, Hanafi law remained paramount. The Criminal Code involves the public authorities in investigating killings, and dispenses with compurgation, but the claim for talion or blood-money remains with the deceased's next-of-kin. The authorities collect a fine for the offence only if no such claim is made. In essence, therefore, wounding and affray fell under the jurisdiction of the Criminal Code, and homicide under the jurisdiction of the *shari'a*.

Ebu's-su'ud's rulings

Wounding and injury

It is presumably for this reason that almost all of Ebu's-su'ud's fatwas on offences against the person concern homicide. Very few deal with woundings or other injuries, evidently because most of these cases were the responsibility of secular justice and the administrative authorities. When he did receive such questions, Ebu's-su'ud usually treated them strictly in accordance with Hanafi law, effectively as civil offences, incurring fixed compensation which the assailant paid to his victim. The solutions which he offered are as mechanistic as the Hanafi jurists evidently intended them to be:

(1) The child Zeyd removes one of the child 'Amr's eyes. 'Amr then removes one of Zeyd's teeth. For what are the said children liable?
Answer: Zeyd gives 'Amr 5,000 *dirham*s of silver, and receives from 'Amr 500 *dirham*s. [*D*, 751]

Full blood-money is 10,000 *dirhams*. Loss of an eye incurs half blood-money, and loss of a tooth one twentieth, and hence the answer. The solution to the following is equally straightforward:

> (2) Zeyd fights 'Amr in play. They both fall and 'Amr's arm is broken. In law, is Zeyd liable for anything?
> *Answer*: If [the arm] is permanently crippled, he is liable for half blood-money. [*Ch*, f. 110b]

Arms, like eyes, occur in pairs, so the loss of one, like the loss of an eye, incurs half blood-money.

Homicide

Since homicide came largely under the authority of the *shari'a*, Ebu's-su'ud's fatwas on this subject are numerous. As in cases of wounding and injury, he applies Hanafi law and makes no reference to the fines which the Ottoman Criminal Code imposes in certain cases. Nonetheless, because he has to deal with such a variety of instances, his application of the Hanafi rules is far from mechanistic, making large concessions to common sense, custom, equity and administrative practice.

The most obvious departure from the prescriptions of the jurists is the abolition of the communal group (*'aqila*) who, in the legal textbooks, are responsible for paying the blood-money in cases of quasi-intentional killing and of accidental killing and wounding. However, by the sixteenth century, the communal group had no existence outside works of jurisprudence, and Ebu's-su'ud comes very close to saying this:

> (3) When a killer cannot pay, is his communal group (*'aqila*) liable for blood-money?
> *Answer*: There are no *'aqila* in these lands. [*Ch*, f. 114b]

Ottoman practice also differed from Hanafi theory in another respect. For the jurists, homicide gives rise to a purely private claim by the next-of-kin against the killer. When the killer is unknown, the community where the corpse came to light must pay blood-money after a process of compurgation. In Ottoman practice, it was the executive authorities that pursued the killer or, if the killer was unknown, ordered an investigation. In such cases, the Criminal Code lays on the community the obligation to find the culprit. Although, in cases of homicide, the Hanafi jurists do not oblige the government authorities to intervene or investigate, it is clear that Ebu's-su'ud approves of their involvement. In the following case, he clearly hopes that a criminal inquiry will help circumvent an absurdity in Hanafi law:

(4) There is a sheepfold near a village. A man's head is found there. Can the executive authorities say to Zeyd, an inhabitant of the village: 'Find the killer, or pay the blood-money!'
Answer: It is necessary to investigate with care. But if nothing is proved against [the villagers], no blood-money or compurgation is necessary. [*Ch*, f. 106b]

The absurdity is that a head constitutes less than half a body and so, in this case, there is no 'slain man', and therefore no blood-money. This explains the last part of Ebu's-su'ud's answer. However, since he makes it a principle to award blood-money whenever it is possible to do so, he demands a thorough investigation to bring the killer to light. Otherwise no blood-money will be paid. It seems clear, however, that he does not approve of the authorities' action in making a single member of the village responsible for finding the killer or paying the blood-money. Responsibility must be communal.

The involvement of the executive authorities in investigating killings and in pursuing killers and bringing them to court does not, however, alter the fact that homicide is, in modern terms, a civil offence. It is the next-of-kin, and not the government, who bring the claim, and who retain the right to demand either talion or blood-money, or to forgive the killer.

Exemptions from Liability

If the victim's next-of-kin exempt the killer, he escapes all liability for talion or blood-money, although in these circumstances the executive authorities might collect a fine under the provisions of the Ottoman Criminal Code. The right to absolve a killer is never in doubt. The only question which worried one of Ebu's-su'ud's questioners was whether forgiveness was more meritorious that prosecution:

(5) 'Amr kills Zeyd. Is it better that Zeyd's heirs kill him, or bring a claim against him?
Answer: If 'Amr is a pious and devout person, and the said wounding[29] occurred by accident, then forgiveness is better. If he is a wicked person, it is better to bring a claim. [*D*, 741]

The answer here presents a purely moral principle. There were no legal restraints on the heirs to determine their course of action. The following case, however, introduces a legal complexity:

(6) Zeyd is shooting a gun in some place and hits 'Amr, who dies on the

third day. If he hit him accidentally, must the said Zeyd pay blood-money?

Answer: Yes.

In which case, 'Amr dies within three days but, while he is still able to move every limb, he says: 'I have forgiven [Zeyd]. Do not seek [compensation for] my blood.' Can Zeyd, simply because 'Amr said this, not pay blood-money to his heirs?

Answer: If the killing was deliberate, he can refuse unconditionally. If it was accidental, his absolution is valid from the third [part of his estate, which he can bequeath by testament.] If the third of his property suffices [to cover the full] amount of his blood-money, yes, [Zeyd can refuse to pay.] Otherwise, he must pay the shortfall. [*Ch*, f. 107a]

The problem here is that it was not the heirs who forgave the killer, but the killer's victim before he died. The question, then, is whether the victim's words of forgiveness are legally valid and, if so, whether they would deprive the heirs of the right to claim blood-money. Ebu's-su'ud's starting point is to declare the victim's absolution effective, but this alone does not solve the problem, except in the case of intentional killing, which would incur talion and not blood-money. In a case of accidental killing, however, absolution by the victim would deprive the heirs of blood-money, which effectively forms part of the inheritance from the dead man. In Hanafi law, a person may bequeath by testament a third of his property, and Ebu's-su'ud solves the problem by treating the blood-money as a bequest. As such, it comes from the third portion of the deceased's property. However, if the heirs do not receive the full amount of his blood-money through the third, the killer must make up the deficiency.

A second case where the killer is exempt is when he kills in self defence:

(7) The executive authorities seize Zeyd, saying: "Amr died from your blow.' Zeyd replies: "Amr attacked me. I accidentally struck him with a knife.' Is Zeyd liable for anything of talion or blood-money?

Answer: If it is proved that he could escape in no other way, he is liable for neither talion or blood-money. [*D*, 742]

The questioner here, presumably a judge, had good reason to be puzzled by this case. Strictly speaking, the answer is clear. A knife is an offensive weapon. The killing is therefore deliberate, and so the killer is liable for talion. The killer, however, described the act as unintentional and, although a strict interpretation of Hanafi law would not admit this, it does raise the possibility that the penalty should be blood-money. The answer offers a solution to the dilemma. In Hanafi law, if a person kills, even deliberately, in self-defence, he escapes liability. The jurists, however, restrict this general rule to cases where the assailant draws an offensive weapon, or where the assault occurs at night or in a deserted place, where no help is at hand. These conditions for justifying homicide are obviously too restrictive, and so Ebu's-su'ud replaces them with the more flexible formula: 'If he could escape in no other way'. What he does not do is to say what would be the solution if self-defence is not proven.

A related category of homicide, which Ebu's-su'ud enthusiastically exempts from liability, is killing in order to prevent a sexual assault:

(8) Zeyd enters Hind's house and tries to have intercourse forcibly. Since Hind can repel him by no other means, she strikes and wounds him with an axe. If Zeyd dies of the wound, is Hind liable for anything? *Answer*: She has performed an act of Holy War. [*D*, 781]

By wounding and ultimately killing her assailant, the woman has prevented an act of fornication,[30] which is an offence against God, and hence Ebu's-su'ud's enthusiasm for her action. It is also a ruling which concurs with the opinion of some 'post-classical' jurists, with Ibn Bazzaz, for example, stating bluntly: 'If a man coerces a woman, she may kill him'.[31] Ebu's-su'ud is equally forceful in applying the same principle to cases of homosexual assault:

(9) When Zeyd wishes to sodomise the beardless 'Amr, ['Amr] has no other way to escape, and so kills Zeyd with a knife. He explains the case in the presence of the judge, and the people of the village bring testimony, saying: "Amr is truthful'. Is [their testimony] heard? *Answer*: There is no need for testimony. So long as Zeyd is a wicked person, 'Amr cannot be touched. Their testimony [merely] reinforces [this]. [*Ch*, ff. 108b–109a]

There were also cases of domestic injury or homicide where the killer escapes liability. The first of these is where a slave-owner injures or kills his slave. The slave is the absolute property of the owner, who may therefore do with him as he wishes. Killing or injuring one's slave is a sin, but does not incur a legal liability for talion or blood-money. Nonetheless, when the slave is guiltless, Ebu's-su'ud invokes a ruling of Qadikhan which imposes flogging for a master who kills his slave:

(10) If Zeyd puts out his slave 'Amr's eyes ...? *Answer*: A great torture in the next world. In this world, a severe chastisement is necessary. [Proof-text] 'If a man kills his slave ... he is chastised, but there is no liability for talion or blood money.' Qadikhan. [*Ch*, ff. 107b–108a]

However, where he deems the slave to have provoked the killing, he exempts the master altogether:

> (11) When Zeyd's slave is drunk and insensible, he enters the private harem. Zeyd is disturbed and kills [the slave] with a sword. For what is Zeyd liable?
> *Answer*: Apart from his sin, there is no punishment in this world. [*Ch*, f. 108a]

The two answers together effectively produce a new rule. Ebu's-su'ud, following Qadikhan, reclassifies the offence of killing or injuring a slave as one that incurs discretionary punishment (*ta'zir*). Next, by imposing punishment in the first case but not in the second, he produces the rule that, if a master deliberately kills or injures his slave, he is liable for a penalty, but that if the slave provoked the assault he is morally but not legally liable.

The second instance of the law's exempting a domestic killer is a rule which gives – especially males – the right to kill a female in the same family and her lover, if he catches them *in flagrante*. This was a rule which the jurists expressed with increasing confidence as the centuries progressed. Qadikhan, in the twelfth century, is somewhat cautious in his formulation, permitting a person to kill a man whom he finds fornicating with his own or anyone else's wife, but only if he has told them to refrain, and they have ignored his warnings.[32] Ibn Bazzaz, in the early fifteenth century, is slightly less cautious, allowing a husband to kill his wife's lover and also his wife, 'if she is submitting [to the lover]'.[33] Ibn Nujaim in the sixteenth century is the boldest: 'The principle in this matter is that it is licit for a person to kill a Muslim whom he sees committing fornication. He holds back only lest he should kill him without it being certain that he is, in fact, committing fornication.'[34] The same essential principle emerges in a clause in some recensions of the Ottoman Criminal Code, giving a husband the right to kill his wife and her lover, if he catches them 'while they are committing fornication'. However, it also lays on the husband the obligation of immediately bringing a group of people to the house to bear witness to what has happened. In this case, 'the claims of the dead person's heirs should not be heard'.[35]

It is perhaps this clause in the code that Ebu's-su'ud is invoking in his answer to the following question:

> (12) Zeyd kills his wife, Hind, and [her lover] 'Amr at the moment of fornication. Are Hind's and 'Amr's heirs able to inflict talion on Zeyd, or to take blood-money from him?
> *Answer*: No. [The matter] should on no account be investigated. It is forbidden. [*D*, 777]

In other cases, however, Ebu's-su'ud extends the exemption beyond the limits of the code, to the brothers of the offending woman and to her female ascendants:

(13) One night, on Zeyd's property, 'Amr and Zeyd's sister Hind commit fornication. Zeyd kills 'Amr and Zeyd's mother kills Hind. Can the executive authorities interfere [in this case]?
Answer: No, never. [*D*, 778]

He does not, it seems, go as far as Ibn Nujaim in exempting from liability any Muslim who kills a fornicator. The exemption, it appears, applies only to members of the guilty woman's family. In another respect, however, Ebu's-su'ud is more permissive than Ibn Nujaim, since he allows a man to kill an illicit couple when he sees them merely in each other's company, with no evidence of fornication:

(14) Zeyd sees his sister, Hind, in a house with 'Amr, who is outside the prohibited degrees of marriage (*namahrem*). He kills Hind and wounds 'Amr, who dies on the following day. Zeyd acknowledges that he killed Hind and 'Amr, and goes to another place. Now his paternal uncles are not guarantors for Zeyd, but 'Amr's brother, Bekr, brings a claim (*qawl*) and, in contravention of the law, forcibly and wrongfully takes two hundred gold coins from the aforenamed persons. When he returns, can Zeyd lawfully recover the entire sum from the person to whom they paid it?
Answer: Yes. [*D*, 779]

Here, Ebu's-su'ud may be basing his answer on a technicality. The highly tendentious question implies that the money which the dead man's brother took from the killer's uncles was not blood-money or a sum formally agreed in court by composition between the parties. It is perhaps technically for this reason that Ebu's-su'ud allows the killer to take back the money, but the reality seems to be that he is approving the killing.

The essence of Ebu's-su'ud's rulings seems, therefore, to be that the men and senior women in a family may kill a female family member and a man who is not a close relative, if they find the two associating in any way. This is a rule which accords more or less with the various statements on the subject by 'post-classical' jurists. It is not a classical Hanafi doctrine, but it is nevertheless one that emerges logically from the laws of fornication. The Hanafi tradition treats fornication as a heinous crime but, at the same time, renders prosecution impossible. A consequence of this is to remove the punishment of fornication from the public to the private sphere, making it the responsibility of the female offender's family. However, the real source of post-classical Hanafi doctrine that allows the private punishment of fornicators seems to be the customary law of the Islamic world, the jurists having assimilated the popular 'code of honour' to formal legal practice. This 'code', in essence, measures a family's honour by the yardstick of the behaviour of its younger women, and permits members of the family, usually men, to kill those who transgress the norms of modest female behaviour.

Since these honour killings were so established in popular custom and, furthermore, had found a justification in juristic texts and in the Ottoman Criminal Code, Ebu's-suʻud clearly had no choice but to accept that, in these cases, the killer was exempted from liability. It seems, too, from the tone of his fatwas that it was a rule that he thoroughly approved.

A person, therefore, who kills in self-defence, kills his slave or, in certain instances, kills a fornicator is exempt from talion or blood-money. In these cases, the identity of the killer is known. When the killer is unknown, the community or the owner of the property where the corpse was found, is liable. If, however, the corpse has no signs of wounding, there is no liability. This rule applies in the following case:

(15) Zeyd drinks arak away from home. When he is returning, he dies near ʻAmr's house. There is no mark of wounding, but he has vomited. Is ʻAmr liable for blood-money?
Answer: No.
In which case, if someone says in evidence: 'Zeyd drank arak in such-and-such a place, and [then] set off [for home]', is his evidence accepted?
Answer: There is no need for evidence. There is no blood-money for this kind of dog. He killed himself. [*D*, 759]

Ebu's-suʻud's exemption of the household where the dead man had been drinking, or of the community where his body was found, may spring largely from his dislike of Muslims who drink alcohol. Nonetheless, he does no more than apply the Hanafi rule. There is no sign of wounding, and therefore no blood-money.

The Assignment of Liability

In homicide cases where there is no exemption from talion or blood-money, the first problem is to assign or apportion liability. This may be a problem where there is more than one killer, or in cases of indirect killing.

In the following two cases, Ebu's-suʻud straightforwardly applies the Hanafi rules:

(16) Zeyd, 'Amr and Bekr unlawfully kill Bishr with offensive weapons. Should all of them be killed on the demand of the heirs?
Answer: Yes, even if there were a hundred of them. [*D*, 746]

This unequivocal answer applies two rules. First, the law deems the killing to be intentional, because the killers used offensive weapons. The penalty therefore is talion. Second, in Quduri's formulation: 'If a group of people kill a person intentionally, talion is inflicted on all the group'.[36] All of them, therefore, must suffer the penalty. The second case is one of quasi-intentional or accidental killing:

(17) If several infidels beat an[other] infidel to death, what is their liability?
Answer: They are liable for blood-money. [*D*, 758]

Here there is no mention of an offensive weapon, and the law therefore deems the killing to be accidental or quasi-intentional according to the instruments used. In either case, the penalty is blood-money, for which the offenders are jointly liable.

A third case is somewhat different:

(18) Zeyd attacks 'Amr's house with a few accomplices. A small son of 'Amr's is trampled underfoot by the aforesaid people. If he dies ...?
Answer: After a severe chastisement, all must undergo a long imprisonment. The person who trod on and killed [the boy] must pay blood-money. [*Ch*, ff. 107a–b]

In answering, Ebu's-su'ud assumes that only one of the invaders could have been responsible for the boy's death, and so assigns to him liability for blood-money. However, in order not to exempt the others who were accessory to the killing, Ebu's-su'ud, as he frequently does, invokes the power to impose discretionary punishment.

Blood-money is payable for death or injury resulting from an accident as much as it is for death or injury resulting from an assault. For this reason, the problem of apportioning blood-money also arises in cases of accidents where more than one person is the cause:

(19) Zeyd hires four workmen. When they are building a house, it falls down, killing one of them. Who is liable for the blood-money?
Answer: If it fell through the action of all of them, the share of the one who is killed is not paid. The rest of the blood-money falls to the remainder. [*Ch*, f. 111b]

The answer is self-explanatory, and applies also in the following case:

(20) Zeyd is an officer of the novice Janissaries. He wishes to circumcise a lad and, as his novices and servants are cleaning and sweeping out [the] houses [in preparation for the ceremony], one of the beams of a house is struck and falls on top of them. If one of the novices dies, what is necessary in law?

Answer: However many people struck the beam are liable for blood-money. If one of the people who struck [the beam] is also the person who died, he is liable for a portion of the blood-money, and [so this portion] drops. The rest is taken from the other people who struck [the beam].

Zeyd is not liable for blood-money, provided he is not one of the people who struck [the beam]. [*Ch*, f. 113b]

This last rule, exempting the person who is not the immediate cause of the accident, is perhaps reasonable in cases where the death is unintended. However, in strict Hanafi law, where a person kills deliberately at the command of another, the person who gave the order escapes all legal liability. This solution is clearly unsatisfactory, and Ebu's-su'ud predictably remedies the injustice by imposing a discretionary punishment on the person who issued the command. In effect, he recommends life imprisonment:

(21) Zeyd says to 'Amr: 'I'll kill you!' He sends his servants and has 'Amr killed with offensive weapons. What are Zeyd and his servants liable for in law?

Answer: Talion is inflicted on the servants. Zeyd is imprisoned for many years. [*D*, 745]

This case is simple enough. Ebu's-su'ud is, however, more circumspect in answering a similar question where there might be extenuating circumstances to lessen the gravity of the offence:

(22) Zeyd tells [one of] his men [Bekr] to kill 'Amr, who is approaching his house at night. The aforesaid [Bekr] strikes 'Amr, who dies of the blow. Is either Zeyd or Bekr liable for talion or blood-money?

Answer: A person who kills with an offensive weapon is liable for talion. If he said 'Kill!', Zeyd is liable for three years' imprisonment. If it was possible to fend him off in another way, killing 'Amr is not licit. [*Ch*, f. 113a]

The answer here is the same as in the previous example, except that the final sentence implies that the householder and his servant are exempt, if there was no other way of keeping out the intruder.

Cases such as the last two, where the killer acted under compulsion, belong conceptually to the general category of indirect killing. In all such cases, the question is whether to assign liability to the direct or the indirect cause; and, in Hanafi law, the answer is always the same. If a person is not the direct cause of the killing, he is exempt. In some cases, this produces a solution which Ebu's-su'ud accepts without reserve:

> (23) Although Zeyd is [guilty of] no previous crime, the people of the village hand him over to the executive authorities and have him hanged. If it then becomes clear that he was blameless, are the villagers liable for blood-money?
> *Answer*: The person who hanged him is liable. [*Ch*, f. 112b]

This is the unmodified Hanafi solution to the problem. The villagers are the distant cause of the death, the executive authorities the indirect, and the hangman the direct cause. The hangman is therefore liable. It would in theory have been possible to fix liability on the executive authorities since, as representatives of the Sultan, they were in a position to coerce the hangman. However, as an upholder of government authority, this was a course which Ebu's-su'ud would not take, and the hangman must therefore bear the entire responsibility. In the next case, however, he slightly modifies this position:

> (24) Zeyd's goods are stolen. He delivers the suspect, 'Amr, to the executive authorities, and gets them to torture him. 'Amr dies during the torture. Zeyd did not personally torture 'Amr, but he was [nonetheless] the cause. In law, can 'Amr's heirs take blood-money from Zeyd?
> *Answer*: They can have him severely chastised and imprisoned for a long time. They receive blood-money from the torturer. [*D*, 666]

On the question of blood-money, Ebu's-su'ud again follows Hanafi doctrine in making the person liable who is the direct cause of the death, and he again exempts the executive authorities. In fixing liability on the torturer, he is also following an opinion of Ibn Bazzaz: '[A torturer] kills a person in the sovereign's prison before anything is proven against him. The killer is liable for talion.'[37] This time, however, Ebu's-su'ud admits to the possibility of the person who is the indirect cause receiving discretionary punishment. This was probably in response to the promptings of the dead man's heirs, who clearly wanted him to receive a penalty.

Cases such as these, where a person acting voluntarily or under coercion kills on behalf of another, are the most straightforward cases of indirect killing. The same principles also apply in cases of accidental death or injury which do not involve a third party. Here too, a person is liable only if he is the immediate cause of the accident. The jurists sometimes illustrate this principle with a bizarre and, for this reason, memorable example. If a person digs a well in the public road, and a man falls in and dies from the fall, then the person who dug the well is liable. If, however, the man who falls into the well dies of hunger because he cannot climb out, and not because of the fall, the person who dug the well is not liable, because he is the indirect and not the direct cause of the death.

This hypothetical case illustrates an important principle in assigning liability, and also highlights the fact that its strict application can produce results which contravene natural justice. It is for this reason that Ebu's-su'ud is prepared to disregard the strict logic of the law if it seems to him to produce the wrong solution:

> (25) In a wrestling match, Zeyd goes out voluntarily to wrestle, and defeats one or two people. Then some people goad and strip 'Amr, and he wrestles with Zeyd. Zeyd, by his own manoeuvre, comes beneath 'Amr. His neck is fractured, and he dies fifteen days later. Is 'Amr liable for anything?
> *Answer*: He is liable for blood-money. It is irrelevant that [Zeyd] was wrestling voluntarily and died as a result of his own action. [*D*, 756]

Here, the questioner is prompting Ebu's-su'ud to exempt the wrestler on the grounds that he is not the direct cause of the death. He does this by first stating that the wrestler's opponent was fighting voluntarily, while the wrestler himself was 'goaded'. The aim here is obviously to establish that the people who goaded him, and not the wrestler himself, were the direct cause of the accident. The argument fails because, unless they used irresistible force, the law deems their goading to be an indirect and not a direct cause. The questioner's second argument is more persuasive. By making the opponent 'die of his own manoeuvre', he is making him the direct cause of his own death. The fact that this happened while wrestling makes his adversary the indirect cause. As the indirect cause, the adversary should not be liable. Despite its making sense in law, Ebu's-su'ud dismisses this argument out of hand. His priority is to award blood-money, and to do so he will ignore legal subtleties.

The same is true in the following case:

> (26) In a time of plague, Zeyd brings the minor 'Amr to Istanbul without permission. If 'Amr dies of the plague, can his heirs take the blood-money from Zeyd?
> *Answer*: Yes. [*D*, 754]

In strict logic, it was the plague that killed the boy, and not the man who took him to Istanbul. The man, by taking him to Istanbul, is only the indirect cause of the death, and so should not be liable. However, to argue like this would exempt the man from the consequences of his irresponsibility and deprive the heirs of blood-money, and Ebu's-su'ud understandably pursues a different line of reasoning. The element in the question which allowed him to arrive at the answer which he gave is the fact that the man took the boy without the authorisation of, presumably, the boy's guardian. He is therefore solely responsible for the boy's infection by the plague. From this point, it might be possible to argue by analogy with the rule that applies to schoolteachers who beat their pupils. They escape liability for any injury they might cause only if the beating has the consent of the boy's father.[38]

In these two cases, Ebu's-su'ud ignores the strict rules assigning liability in cases of indirect killing. Where, however, they seem to provide a reasonable solution, he will apply them meticulously:

(27) Zeyd and 'Amr collide while hunting. They are both knocked from their horses. Three days later, Zeyd dies from the blow of 'Amr's horse. Is 'Amr liable for anything?
Answer: If they collided while they were both galloping, 'Amr is liable for half blood-money. [*Ch*, f. 111a]

The answer here rests on the rule that if a moving animal causes damage, then the person who is riding it, or who goaded it, is the direct cause of the damage and therefore liable. If the animal was moving of its own accord, no-one is liable. Here both men were riding, and so the solution to the problem depends on establishing which of them was moving at the time of the accident. If one of them was stationary, he was the indirect cause of the accident, and so not liable. If they were both moving, they were jointly the direct cause and, for this reason, both are liable. The solution follows logically from these principles.

In most cases, therefore, of indirect killing, it seems that Ebu's-su'ud tried to avoid the more bizarre solutions which could result from a mechanistic application of the Hanafi rules. His main concerns seem to have been to ensure that blood-money was paid, and that anyone who was an accessory to, that is, the indirect cause of, a killing should also receive a penalty. Nevertheless, in some areas, the rigidity of Hanafi logic prevented his achieving these aims.

The most obvious example is in cases of poisoning. In legal terms, poison is not an offensive weapon, and so poisoning someone incurs blood-money and not talion. In most cases, however, the poisoner avoids any liability. The reason for this is that, since he usually adds the toxin to his victim's food or drink, which the victim then consumes voluntarily, poisoning is technically an indirect killing. By taking the poison, the victim is the direct cause of his own death. The poisoner is the indirect cause, and so escapes liability. He becomes liable to pay blood-money only if he literally forces the poison down the victim's throat. However, most jurists, starting, it would seem, from Kasani, obviously considered the total exemption of a poisoner from any liability to be absurd, and circumvented the problem by ruling that he should receive discretionary punishment, not for administering the poison but for deceiving the victim into consuming it.[39] This was a convenient legal fiction, which Ebu's-su'ud adopts in the following case:

(28) Zeyd's wife Hind cooperates with 'Amr in killing the said Zeyd, by getting him to drink poison. If they confess voluntarily, for what are they liable?
Answer: If they made him drink it with their own hands, they are liable for blood-money. If Zeyd drank it himself, they are liable for a severe chastisement and a long imprisonment. [*D*, 755]

The use of discretionary punishment provides a reasonable solution in most cases of poisoning. There is, however, a further problem if someone poisons at the behest of another. In Hanafi logic, this produces a chain of causation. The victim, by drinking the poison, is the direct cause of his own death. The poisoner, by giving it to him, is the indirect cause. The person for whom the poisoner is acting is the remote cause. The poisoner receives a discretionary punishment for deception, but the person who is the remote cause is exempt from any liability. Ebu's-su'ud disagrees with this solution, but cannot quite bring himself to say so:

(29) Zeyd is sick. Bekr says to 'Amr, the doctor who is treating him: 'If you give Zeyd a poisoned drink and kill him, I'll give you so-and-so many aqches'. If he does this, in law, what is the liability of Bekr and 'Amr?
Answer: If 'Amr himself put the drink into Zeyd's mouth, he is liable for blood-money. If he put it into [Zeyd's] hand, and [Zeyd] drank it himself, there is no blood-money. After a severe chastisement, a long imprisonment is necessary. In truth, a punishment is necessary for Bekr as well. [*Ch*, f. 112b]

The rules for indirect killing thus made it impossible to award blood-money in most cases of poisoning. They have equally strange consequences in the case of a boy who dies as a result of a mishap during his circumcision. The boy's father or guardian has authorised the circumciser to cut the boy's foreskin, and so he, and not the circumciser, is responsible for any wounding or damage to the glans, or for death resulting from cuts in this area. For wounds in any area other than the glans, or for death resulting from these wounds, the circumciser is liable.

In the first case, the father or guardian is the direct cause of the wounds, in the second case, the circumciser. By the nature of the operation, wounds would tend to occur in both areas, causing a legal problem, whose bizarre solution Kemalpashazade states with no explanation:

(30) While Zeyd is circumcising a lad, he cuts off his penis, together with the glans. What is Zeyd liable for in law?
Answer: If the lad dies, half the blood-money. If he recovers, the full blood-money. [*Ch*, f. 112b]

In answering the same question, Ebu's-su'ud feels constrained to give an explanation:

(31) When the circumciser, Zeyd, circumcises 'Amr, he goes too far and cuts further than the glans. If 'Amr is wounded and dies of the wound ...?
Answer: If the glans heals, and he dies of the wound which he cut in excess, he is liable for the full blood-money. If it does not heal, and the death can be attributed to the wound in its entirety, half the blood-money drops, because cutting the skin was permitted, but he remains liable for half the blood-money for the place which he cut in excess. In fact, if the glans was cut off and [the lad] recovers, [the circumciser] must pay full blood-money. If [the lad] dies, [the circumciser] is liable for half blood-money [for the wound]. The *Khulasa* classified this as a strange case. [*Ch*, ff. 112b–113a]

Unattributed Homicide

In cases of homicide where the killer is unknown, it is the location of the corpse that determines who is liable. If it is found on an individual's property, then the individual is liable for blood-money. If it is found in the open in a village or town quarter, then the community is liable. If it is found away from habitation, then the treasury is liable.

These rules arise in the first place from the notion that householders and communities are responsible for the security of life and limb within their boundaries. It is for this reason that Ebu's-su'ud will, if somewhat grudgingly, exempt them from liability if they brought assistance, but nonetheless failed to prevent the killing:

(32) In a village at night, brigands attack Zeyd's house and kill two men with weapons of war. The people of the village heard Zeyd's shouts and screams and brought him aid and assistance. Are the people of the village liable for blood-money?

Answer: No. They suffer punishment in the next world if they were able to repel [the attack and failed to do so.] [*Ch*, f. 106a]

The second and more important function of the rules is to ensure the payment of blood-money in most cases of homicide. This is a principle which overrides the notion of blood-money as a penalty for failure to prevent the killing. Ebu's-su'ud, as a result, sometimes imposes blood-money even when the individual or community was in no position to save the victim:

(33) At the proper season, the people of a village all go to the summer pasture. For a period of three or four months there is no one living in the said village. When it is empty, a man is found killed. If the killer is not known, who is liable for blood-money?
Answer: If [the corpse] was found on someone's property, the owner. If it was found in the village, the inhabitants. [*Ch*, f. 112a–b]

The same rule applies if a member of the community is absent at the time of the homicide. He is liable with the rest of the community:

(34) A slain man is found in a village, and the people of the village are liable for blood-money. Is a share taken from one of the villagers, Zeyd, who is on a journey?
Answer: If he has houses [*sic*] in the village, yes. [*Ch*, ff. 105b–106a]

Blood-money is therefore payable in almost all instances of unattributed homicide. The first problem in such cases is to establish whether an individual is liable, or the community. Before an individual can be liable, the corpse must be found on his property (*milk*). The second question is therefore to determine what is meant by property. In Ottoman feudal law, a person cannot own the soil, but he can own moveables, and trees and buildings which are above the soil, so that by this definition a house, for example, or a vineyard are his property. In homicide cases, however, Ebu's-su'ud restricts his definition of property to dwellings, possibly to prevent injustices, since it is generally easier to guard a house than a property which is away from home. However, he justifies this restriction on technical grounds. The owner of a vineyard owns the vines, but not the soil beneath them, and so is not liable for homicides on the land:

(35) Zeyd plants a vineyard on land that is royal demesne (*miri*). If the said vineyard is Zeyd's property (*milk*), why is Zeyd not liable for the blood-money of 'Amr, who is found killed and wounded on the said vineyard?
Answer: The existence of blood-money relates to the ground. The

fact that the trees on it are property does not make blood-money necessary. If it happens that the property which is on ground that is not owned is a dwelling, be it a house or a tent, [the owner] is liable provided he is resident there, because he has not brought assistance. [*Ch*, f. 106a]

He applies the same rule when a corpse is found on a threshing floor:

(36) With 'Amr's permission, Zeyd establishes a threshing floor on his land. The said Zeyd is found killed on the threshing floor. If the killer is not known, are the people of the village or 'Amr liable for blood-money?
Answer: A threshing floor cannot be a true property (*milk sahih*). It is not like a house. The people of the village are jointly liable. [*Ch*, f. 106a]

It is only, therefore, if the corpse is discovered in a dwelling that the owner is liable. This rule is straightforward enough if the owner actually lives there, but causes a problem if he is absent, and the occupant is a tenant or a guest. The question in this case is whether the owner is liable, or the occupant. This was a problem which Ebu's-su'ud encountered continuously during his first five years as Mufti but was unable to answer satisfactorily, since the Hanafi tradition offers two opposing solutions. The opinion attributed to Abu Hanifa and Shaibani makes the owner liable, even if he is not in residence at the time of the killing. The opinion attributed to Abu Yusuf makes the owner liable only if he is in residence. If he is not, it is the occupant who pays the blood-money. It was the second solution that appealed to Ebu's-su'ud, leading him in 1550 to petition the Sultan to issue a decree, making it mandatory for judges to give rulings in accordance with the opinion of Abu Yusuf. In the text of the petition, he makes his reasons clear:

(37) There have been many enquiries [like the following]: 'There has been a killing in the wineshops which the infidels occupy by lease, and the killer is not known'. Or: 'The district governor's officers came to a village with chained prisoners, and forcibly billeted them in a house, ejecting the owner. At night, some of the prisoners are found hanged or killed. If it is not known who did it, who is liable for blood-money and compurgation?'
According to the Great Imam [Abu Hanifa], in cases like these, if the place in question is [private] property, [liability for] blood-money falls on the owner. If it belongs to a trust, then it falls to the trust. In the opinion of Abu Yusuf, blood-money falls on the occupier. So if a corpse is found in a place where a guest is staying and the killer is

unknown, if the guest is the sole occupant of the house, and the owner is not in residence, then the owner is liable for neither blood-money nor compurgation.

[The following] submission is therefore made to the Sublime Threshold. In cases such as these, where the owner of the property is uninvolved and in another place, to act in accordance with the opinion of the Great Imam and to make him liable for blood-money leads to deficiencies and carelessness in the occupants' vigilance. To act in accordance with Abu Yusuf's opinion, and to make the occupants responsible for blood-money, is to make them take greater care in protecting and guarding [the premises], and is considered more suitable for the prevention of wrongdoing.

A note added to the text of the petition records the date of the decree enacting its recommendations as law:

A decree was issued on this matter, commanding [judges] to act in accordance with the opinion of Abu Yusuf, in Rabi' al-awwal 957/ February–March 1550. [*H*, p. 58–9; *D*, 767]

In all such cases which occurred after the date of the decree, Ebu's-su'ud rules that the occupant pays the blood-money, and not the absent owner. For example:

(38) A slain man is found in a rented mill ...
Answer: The lessee pays the blood money. Judges have been commanded to act according to this opinion. [*Ch*, f. 104b]

The problem which remained was that, if a sole occupant was killed and the killer was unknown, there was no-one to pay the blood-money. This was a problem which Ebu's-su'ud left unresolved:

(39) Zeyd lets his house, which he owns, to the cavalryman 'Amr. The said 'Amr is found wounded in the house. If his killer is unknown, must Zeyd pay blood-money?
Answer: If [the house] was independently in 'Amr's possession, and Zeyd in no way interfered, no.
In which case, the house was in 'Amr's possession. Zeyd in no way interfered, and the judge imposes blood-money on Zeyd. In law, is the judgement effective?
Answer: If the judge gave judgement on this side of Rabi' al-akhir [*sic*] 957/ March–April 1550, it is not effective. Judges have been forbidden from imposing blood-money in cases like this. Their judgements are void. [*Ch*, f. 104b]

Taken together, the effect of these rulings is to undermine the principle of Hanafi law that it is the owner who pays blood-money if a corpse is found in his property and the killer is unknown. Ebu's-su'ud first narrows the definition of 'property' to mean a dwelling. Then he makes the occupant of the dwelling liable, and not the owner. He thus, in practice, severs the link between blood-money and property. An inevitable effect of this is to transfer onto the community or the treasury the responsibility for any unattributed killing that occurs outside a house or a tent. The question then is whether the community is liable, or the treasury. This is a problem to which Ebu's-su'ud gives a very clear answer:

(40) Zeyd is found killed in a street in a [town] quarter, a street in a market, or a street outside a town. His killer is not known. In which of these cases is blood-money necessary, and on whom does it fall?
Answer: In places within earshot, [that is] in streets or markets [which belong] to a village or [town] quarter, the people of the nearest [village or town quarter] are liable for blood-money and compurgation. In roads far from villages or [town] quarters, there is no compurgation, and blood-money falls on the treasury. Lands in the royal demesne (*aradi'l-mamlaka*) are also like this. When there is a populated place within earshot, blood-money and compurgation are obligatory. Where there is no population, blood-money falls on the treasury. It does not fall on the peasants who have the use of the land. [*Ch*, ff. 107a–b]

In short, if the corpse is found anywhere outside a house, but within earshot of a community, the community is liable, regardless of who owns the land. This reformulation of Hanafi law serves to exempt not only individual landowners from liability but also, in one case, the treasury. The normal Hanafi rule is that if a corpse is found in a town on a public road, it is the treasury that defrays the blood-money. The road is the shared property of the public and so too, in Hanafi theory, is the treasury. So the treasury is liable on behalf of the public.[40] Ebu's-su'ud, in these cases, reinterprets Hanafi tradition, and makes the community liable:

(41) Zeyd is found at night, killed on the main street. The judge decrees that the people of the quarter do not pay blood-money. In law, should the said [judicial] decree be altered and cancelled?
Answer: Yes. The unconditional expressions found in the text[s refer to] public roads, far from [town] quarters. When they are near to [town] quarters, [blood-money] falls on the people of the quarters, not the treasury. [*Ch*, f. 106b]

The treasury, therefore, in Ebu's-su'ud's formulation of the law, is liable in two cases of unattributed homicide. The first is when the corpse is found on roads and cultivated lands around, but out of earshot of, a settlement. The second is when the corpse is found on property belonging to a trust, but again only if this is out of earshot of anyone who could have brought assistance to the dead man:

(42) At night, when the tenants are [away] at home, a slain man is found in shops which belong to the trust of a mosque. What does the Noble *shari'a* decree?
Answer: So long as the shops belong to the trust of a mosque, and are definitely not the property of an individual, and so long as there is no [town] quarter that is within earshot, then blood-money falls to the treasury. [*D*, 761]

In two cases, no blood-money is due. The first, which applies after the decree of 1550, is when a sole occupant is found dead in a house. Before 1550, if the occupant was a tenant or guest, the owner would have been liable. The second, as Ebu's-su'ud explained to a questioner, is when a corpse is found on waste ground far from any habitation. This is the view of some[41] but not all jurists[42] in the Hanafi tradition:

(43) When a fatwa was sought concerning a homicide, the Noble Answer gave the following ruling: 'When the killing is in a remote spot, no blood-money is necessary'. What is 'a remote spot'?
Answer: No one is liable for blood-money if the place of the homicide is out of earshot of a village, and if it is not a public road, royal demesne, or the villagers' pastureland. If, on the other hand, it is a public road, royal demesne or the villagers' pastureland, and so long as it is out of earshot [of any village], the blood-money falls on the treasury. [*D*, 763]

If, however, the corpse is found near a community, there is no ambiguity. The community is liable. The only problem that can arise is when there are two communities within earshot, and it is necessary to assign liability to one of them. This Ebu's-su'ud solves simply, if mechanistically, by making the nearest one liable:

(44) A voice can carry to several villages from the place where Zeyd is found killed, but one of the said villages is nearer than all the others. Are all liable for blood-money?
Answer: It falls on the nearest village. [*Ch*, f. 105a]

This was the traditional answer to the problem, but it is one which Ebu's-su'ud underlines when he rewrites the response to a question put previously to Kemalpashazade. He seems to have felt that Kemalpashazade had not made the point absolutely clear:

(45) Zeyd is found killed near a small town. The killer is not known. If a voice could reach the whole town [from the spot where the corpse was found], does blood-money fall on the whole town, or on the people of the quarter which is on that side?
Answer: It falls on the people of that quarter. (Kemalpashazade)
Answer: It falls on the people of [the quarter which is] nearest. (Ebu's-su'ud) [*Ch*, f. 105b]

Conclusion

It is clear that, in cases of offences against the person, homicide was the area where Hanafi law applied most consistently in practice. It is clear too that, in the interests of practicality, Ebu's-su'ud greatly simplified the Hanafi rules. In cases of accidental killing, he did not pretend that the killer's communal group was liable to pay blood-money, obviously because communal groups, as they appear in the pages of the jurists, did not exist in the real world. He left it to the killer to raise the money in whatever way he could. In cases where the strict application of Hanafi principles exempts either a killer or an accessory to a killing, such as a master who kills his slave or a man who employs an assassin, he uses discretionary penalties to make sure that guilt is punished. In these cases, he is in effect treating what the Hanafi tradition would classify as a sin with no consequence in law, as a crime which incurs a punishment. In cases of unattributed homicide, he departs from the Hanafi tradition, in that he no longer links ownership with liability. When a corpse is found in a dwelling, it is the residents and not the owner who bear the responsibility to pay blood-money. When the corpse is found outside, it is almost always the community at large that is liable, and not the owner of the ground. Furthermore, although homicide gives rise to a private claim, it is clear that Ebu's-su'ud approved of the secular practice of investigation and prosecution by the authorities. However, it was obviously not his intention to make radical changes in the law. He keeps intact, for example, the strange rules for dealing with cases of poisoning. His aim instead was obviously to modify Hanafi law only to the extent that was necessary in order to render it practical, and to prevent its sometimes peculiar logic from causing flagrant injustices.

Notes

1. Qadikhan, *al-Fatawa al-khaniyya*, in margins of *al-Fatawa al-hindiyya*, Bulaq: Imperial Press (1912/13), vol. 3, p. 437.
2. Qadikhan, *al-Fatawa*, vol. 3, p. 440.

3. al-Marghinani, *al-Hidaya*, Cairo: Matbaʻa Mustafa al-Babi al-Halabi (1972), vol. 10, pp. 220, 236. Baber Johansen, 'Der *ʻisma*-Begriff im hanafitischen Recht', *Actes du VIIIe Congrès International des Arabisants et Islamisants*, Aix-en-Provence: Edisud (1978), pp. 97–101.
4. al-Marghinani, *al-Hidaya*, vol. 10, p. 234.
5. Ibid., p. 236.
6. Ibid., p. 275.
7. On the law of homicide in general, see J. N. D. Anderson, 'Homicide in Islamic law', *Bulletin of the School of Oriental and African Studies*, 13 (1951), 811–28.
8. Qadikhan, *al-Fatawa*, vol. 3, p. 434.
9. Ibid., p. 446.
10. al-Marghinani, *al-Hidaya*, vol. 10, p. 240.
11. Qadikhan, *al-Fatawa*, vol. 3, pp. 449–50.
12. al-Marghinani, *al-Hidaya*, vol. 10, p. 395.
13. Qadikhan, *al-Fatawa*, vol. 3, p. 448.
14. al-Marghinani, *al-Hidaya*, vol. 10, p. 232.
15. Ibid.
16. Ibid.
17. Ibid., p. 387.
18. Qadikhan, *al-Fatawa*, vol. 3, p. 451.
19. al-Marghinani, *al-Hidaya*, vol. 10, p. 377.
20. Ibid., p. 310.
21. Ibid., p. 312.
22. Ibid., p. 307.
23. Qadikhan, *al-Fatawa*, vol. 3, p. 455.
24. Ottoman Criminal Code, section 48, in Uriel Heyd, ed. V. L. Ménage, *Studies in Old Ottoman Criminal Law*, Oxford: Clarendon Press (1973).
25. Ottoman Criminal Code, section 49
26. M. ʻArif (ed.), 'Qanunname-yi al-i ʻosman', *Tarih-i osmani encümeni mecmuası*, suppl. (1911), p. 7. The Code does not distinguish between accidental and deliberate killing.
27. Friedrich Selle, *Prozessrecht des 16. Jahrhunderts im Osmanischen Reich*, Wiesbaden: Otto Harrassowitz (1962), p. 50.
28. *D*, 156.
29. 'Killing' would be a more appropriate word. The reference instead to wounding suggests that this might be a 'floating answer', which originally belonged to a different, although similar question.
30. By modern legal definition, she has prevented an act of rape. However, Islamic law does not recognise rape *per se* as an offence. It is treated as fornication and, in theory, the woman is as culpable as her attacker. However, assuming that the rapist and his victim do not suffer the fixed penalty for fornication – which in practice is impossible to inflict – the law gives the victim two claims. She may claim blood-money for any physical injury that she has suffered, and she may claim a 'fair dower' (*mahr al-mithl*) for the man's possession of her vulva. In the case of the fair dower, the man must pay the same as he would if he were her husband.
31. Ibn Bazzaz, *al-Fatawa al-bazzaziyya*, in margins of *al-Fatawa al-Hindiyya*, Bulaq: Imperial Press (1912/13), vol. 6, p. 432.

32. Qadikhan, *al-Fatawa*, vol. 3, p. 441.
33. Ibn Bazzaz, *al-Fatawa*, vol. 4, p. 32.
34. Ibn Nujaim, *al-Bahr al-Ra'iq*, Cairo: al-Matba'a al-'ilmiyya (1893), vol. 5, p. 42.
35. Ottoman Criminal Code, section 13.
36. al-Quduri, *al-Matn*, Cairo: Matba'a Mustafa al-Babi al-Halabi (1957), p. 90.
37. Ibn Bazzaz, *al-Fatawa*, vol. 6, p. 433. In making the torturer liable for talion, Ibn Bazzaz is assuming that the killing was intentional. In making him liable for blood-money, Ebu's-su'ud is assuming that the death was accidental or quasi-intentional.
38. Qadikhan, *al-Fatawa*, vol. 3, p. 445.
39. al-Kasani, *Bada'i' al-sana'i' fi tartib al-shara'i'*, Beirut: Dar al-Kitab al-'Arabi (1982), vol. 7, p. 235. However, some jurists, including Ibn Nujaim, applied the exemption rigidly.
40. al-Marghinani, *al-Hidaya*, vol. 10, p. 386.
41. Ibid., p. 387.
42. Qadikhan, *al-Fatawa*, vol. 3, p. 452.

Conclusion

In asserting that Ebu's-su'ud reconciled the *qanun* with the *shari'a*, Ottoman tradition is emphasising his piety and religious merit rather than his secular legal skills. By bringing the laws of mankind into harmony with divine law, he was executing the Will of God on earth. Since he was a man who shared the religious and superstitious outlook of his humbler contemporaries, this too is undoubtedly what Ebu's-su'ud himself believed. Despite his distinctly practical mind, he was a man who, in common with his age, was strongly aware of the immanence of the divine, and of God's intimate presence in the life of every individual. It is clear, for example, that he believed in the magical effects of vows made in God's name, and in the efficacy of the saints, and that God speaks directly to man through dreams. The importance which he attached to vows is especially evident in fatwas dealing with the dissolution of marriage through oaths and profane words. His devotion to saints is evident in, for example, a letter to his dissolute son, Shemsü'd-din Ahmed, whom he berates for abandoning the observances of the Companion of the Prophet, Abu Ayyub, supposedly interred in the Istanbul suburb of Eyüp, where Ebu's-su'ud founded a school and is himself buried.[1] Several anecdotes refer to his belief in premonitory dreams,[2] and in his Commentary on the Quran he illustrates the truth of the verse: 'Do not say that those who are killed in the Path of God are dead. No, they are living,'[3] by recording a dream which he had in the year 1532/3, where he encountered in the flesh the Prophet's martyred Companions.[4] Given his religious and superstitious outlook, there can be no doubt that he hoped, through his legal activity, to bring down divine favour on himself, the Sultan and the Sultan's Muslim subjects, by putting into effect the ordinances of God. In this respect, he is a figure typical of a pre-Enlightenment age.

Ebu's-su'ud's harmonisation of secular practice with the *shari'a* worked in three areas in particular. First, there was his description of the principles of feudal land tenure and taxation, using concepts which he borrowed from the Hanafi laws of property. Since land and taxation were *par excellence* the areas where secular authority was paramount, it is especially for this work of re-definition that Ebu's-su'ud acquired the reputation of having brought the *qanun* into conformity with the *shari'a*.

This delineation of secular law in Hanafi terms did not enter the academic Hanafi tradition, but was to become a canonical element in Ottoman law, especially with the promulgation of the 'New *Qanun*' after 1673. This was a systematic compilation of texts on land law, which adopted Ebu's-su'ud's Law-Book of Buda of 1541 as the basic statement of the principles of tenure. The 'New Qanun' remained in force until 1858. Apart from land tenure and taxation, the *qanun* also embraced criminal law, especially in the areas of property offences, wounding and affray. In this sphere, however, Ebu's-su'ud did little to accommodate the *qanun* to the *shari'a*, beyond finding Hanafi texts which could serve to justify current practice.

Second, by investing the Ottoman Sultan with the title of Caliph, Ebu's-su'ud accorded to him powers over the interpretation of the *shari'a*, and in so doing brought royal decrees within the scope of the Holy Law. This equation of royal and divine justice also acquired a canonical status in the late seventeenth century with the compilation, perhaps by the editors of the 'New *Qanun*', of the 'Petitions' (*Ma'ruzat*). This is a collection of Ebu's-su'ud's fatwas which illustrate the principle of systematising the application of the *shari'a* through royal decrees, together with some of his petitions to the Sultan requesting legislation.

Third, there was his justification, in Hanafi terms, of trusts which lent cash at interest. Despite the violent opposition of religious zealots, his ruling on the legitimacy of these trusts entered the juristic mainstream, so that Ibn 'Abidin in the early nineteenth century was still quoting Ebu's-su'ud as an authority.

These were the areas where, in the assertion of Ottoman tradition, Ebu's-su'ud brought secular law and practice into harmony with the *shari'a* and, in so doing, put into effect God's will on earth. Viewed, however, from this side of the Enlightenment, his achievements seem rather different. He was, above all, a practical jurist working in the service of a dynasty, and his 'harmonisation' of the two types of law served distinctly secular purposes. Ebu's-su'ud's basic text on the law of land tenure and taxation is the 'Law-Book of Buda', which he composed in response to the urgent need for a concise statement on the principles of Ottoman feudal tenure before its introduction into the newly annexed province of Hungary. The statement does more, however, than simply outline the existing law. The most important effect of his redefining tenure and taxation in Hanafi terms was to increase the Sultan's control over the occupants of the land and his powers of discretion over rates of taxation.

His redesignation of the Sultan as Caliph had a more generalised effect. The theological tradition from which, in part, the notion of the Caliphate derives, grants the Caliph discretion in the interpretation and application of the *shari'a*, blurring the clear distinction which the jurists make between royal and juristic authority. To describe the Sultan as Caliph had the ideological function of justifying his secular rule in Islamic terms, and had the actual result of enhancing his powers over the substance of the law. This enhanced authority is visible, for example, in the increased government surveillance over the administration of trusts and over contracts of marriage, as well as in the rationalising decrees which followed Ebu's-su'ud's petitions, limiting judges' discretion in certain areas of the law. Seen therefore from a secular viewpoint, Ebu's-su'ud's pious work of harmonisation served to legitimise and uphold the existing Ottoman order and, above all, to enhance the authority of the Sultan.

His defence of cash trusts against the attacks of zealots certainly served a pious end, in that it helped to preserve many religious institutions whose upkeep depended on the income from such trusts. However, it also served the entirely worldly purpose of keeping intact what seem to have been the only source of non-extortionate credit in Ottoman towns and cities.

In his approach to the details of the law, Ebu's-su'ud's concern was with the practical task of finding more or less equitable solutions to everyday problems, within the constraints of a highly conservative legal tradition. When Hanafi law was unworkable, as it was, for example, in dealing with theft, he made it clear, while supporting his view with canonical authority, that the case fell wholly within the sphere of the secular law. When Hanafi law goes part of the way towards providing a solution, he adopts it with modifications, as, for example, when he demands a penalty in addition to restitution or compensation, in cases of malicious damage to property. When Hanafi law is practical and, in his view, equitable, Ebu's-su'ud follows it to the letter.

What the Islamic juristic tradition did not allow him to do was openly to espouse completely new legal principles. Even when defending cash trusts or redefining feudal tenure, he achieved his ends by manipulating pre-existing concepts. Occasionally, it is true, he did introduce new ideas or abandon old ones. For example, in prescribing a penalty for malicious damage, he is in fact introducing a notion, foreign to strict Hanafi law, that intention is a relevant factor in determining the legal consequences of an act. In dealing with cases of unattributed homicide, he severs the link which Hanafi jurists make between ownership of the property where the corpse is found and the payment of the blood-money. Nevertheless, he did not and, within the constraints of juristic conventions, could not openly admit that he was using a new legal concept or discarding an old one. Still less could he, or his successors, develop non-traditional concepts to produce a change in the intellectual structure of the law. Ebu's-su'ud's fatwas were available to future generations as a source of authority in solving individual problems, but not as a basis for speculative reasoning.

From a strictly modern and strictly secular perspective, Ebu's-su'ud appears as a creative jurist whose originality, in a tradition which forbade innovation, led nowhere. This, however, is a view which would have been incomprehensible to Ebu's-su'ud himself. For him, the *shari'a* was the closest that human investigation could come to discovering the will of God. The function of the jurist was to pass the tradition intact to the next generation, and to solve the problems of everyday life by applying its rules as nearly as was practically possible. The skill of the jurist lay in manipulating the rules and concepts available to him in the legal tradition, and applying them to the exigencies of his own day.[5] This is precisely what Ebu's-su'ud did.

Notes

1. Peçevi, ed. M. Uraz, *Peçevi Tarihi*, Istanbul: Yeni Şark Maarif Kütüphanesi (1968), p. 42.
2. 'Ata'i, *Hada'iq al-haqa'iq fi takmilat al-shaqa'iq*, Istanbul: Imperial Press (1851/2), p. 184.
3. Quran, 2:154.
4. Ebu's-su'ud, *Irshad al-'aql al-salim ila mazaya al-kitab al-karim*, printed in margins of Fakhr al-Din Razi, *Mafatih al-ghaib*, Istanbul: Imperial Press (1872/3), vol. 2, p. 52.
5. I would thus disagree with Wael B. Hallaq's conclusion that 'the juridical genre of the *fatwa* was chiefly responsible for the growth and change of legal doctrine in the schools, and that our current perception of Islamic law as a jurists' law must now be further defined as a *muftis'* law: 'From *fatwas* to *furu'*: growth and change in Islamic substantive law', *Islamic Law and Society*, 1/1 (1994), 29–65.

English Equivalents of Legal and Technical Terms

advance dower: *mahr mu'ajjal*.
allod: *milk* (when used of land).
alms-tax: *zakat*.

blood-money: *diya*.

caliph: *khalifa*.
caliphate: *khilafa*.
candidate: *mulazim*.
cavalryman: *su eri, sipahi*.
certificate: *hujja*.
claim of God: *haqq Allah*.
college: *madrasa*.
compurgation: *qasama*.
contract: *'aqd*.
cottager: *bennak*.
custody: (of property) *hirz, ihraz*; (of children) *hidana*.

deferred dower: *mahr mu'ejjel*.
discretionary punishment: *ta'zir*.
disobedient: (of wife) *nashiza*.
district: *sanjaq*.
district-governor: *sanjaq beyi*.
divorce: *talaq*.
dower: *mahr*.
dowry: *jihaz*.

enemy: *harbi*.
estate: *malikane*.

fair compensation: *hukumat al-'adl*.
fair dower: *mahr al-mithl*.
fief: *timar*.
fifth: *khums*.
fixed tribute: *kharaj muwazzaf*.
forbidden: *haram*.
fornication: *zina*.

governor-general: *beylerbeyi*.
Grand Vizier: *sadr-i a'zam*.
gross deception: *ghabn fahish*.
guardianship: *walaya*.

highway robbery: *qat' al-tariq*.
holy war: *jihad, ghaza*.

imamate: *imama*.
imperial Council: *divan-i hümayun*.
intermediate marriage: *tahlil*.
irrevocable: (of marriage) *ba'in*.

janissaries: *yenicheri*.
judge: *qadi*.
jurisprudence: *fiqh*.

law-book: *qanunname*.
letters patent: *berat*.
licit: *halal*.

maintenance: *nafaqa*.
Military Judge: *qadi 'asker*.
mutual anathema: *li'an*.

next-of-kin: *wali al-dam*.

onerous donation: *hiba bi-shart al-'iwad*.

penance: *kaffara*.
poll-tax: *jizya*.
poor cottager: *jaba bennak*.
profane words: *alfaz al-kufr*.
professor: *mudarris*.
proof: *bayyina*.
proportional tribute: *kharaj muqasama*.
protected resident: *musta'min*.

realm of Islam: *dar al-Islam*.
realm of war: *dar al-harb*.
repudiation: (of wife) *talaq*.
revocable: (of marriage) *raj'i*.
royal demesne: *ard al-mamlaka, aradi'l-mamlaka, miri* (when used of land).

subject: *ra'iyyet*, pl. *re'aya*.

talion: *qisas*.

third: *thulth*.
tithe: *'ushr*.
tributary infidel: *kharaj*.
tribute: *kharaj*.
trust, trust in mortmain: *waqf*.
trustee: *mutawalli*.

valid privacy: *khalwa sahiha*.
veiled lady: *mukhaddara*.

waiting period: *'idda*.

Glossary

aghirliq: a payment made on marriage by the bridegroom to the bride's father or guardian.

alfaz al-kufr: profane words, which have the legal effect of causing the apostasy of the speaker.

aqche: an Ottoman silver coin, the standard unit of account in the Ottoman Empire.

'aqd: a contract; a fixed form bilateral transaction, which changes the legal status quo, usually by transferring property. A valid contract requires an offer and an acceptance, and the fulfilment of certain juristically predetermined conditions.

'aqila: the group of persons jointly liable with the offender for payment of *diya* in cases of accidental killing or injury.

ard al-mamlaka: land, in juristic theory, assigned to the ownership of the sovereign.

'askeri: a member of the Ottoman military class, exempted from taxation, and with a right to collect revenue or receive a salary in exchange for a specified, usually military, service to the Sultan.

ba'in: an irrevocable divorce; irrevocably divorced.

batman: a non-standard Ottoman measure of weight, of between two and twelve kilogrammes.

bayyina: proof, normally by the testimony of two male eyewitnesses, or of one man and two women.

bennak: a peasant holding less than half a *chift* of land.

berat: letters patent; a Sultanic decree, addressed to the world at large and issued to an individual, bestowing on him a post, privilege or exemption.

beylerbeyi: a governor-general of a province.

bid'a: an innovation, especially one that is contrary to the *shari'a*.

chift: a yoke; a unit of land for fiscal purposes, nominally the area of land that a yoke of oxen could plough.

dar al-harb: enemy territory, not under a Muslim sovereignty.

dar al-Islam: territory under a Muslim sovereignty.

dhimmi: a non-Muslim permanently residing under a Muslim sovereignty, and enjoying protection of life and property in return for payment of the poll-tax.

dinar: a denarius; a gold coin worth ten silver *dirham*s, a fictitious unit of currency in juristic texts.

dirham: (1) a drachma; a silver coin, a fictitious unit of currency in juristic texts. (2) an Ottoman measure of weight, of about three to four grammes.

divan-i hümayun: the Ottoman Imperial Council, meeting in the Sultan's Palace, under the auspices of the Grand Vizier, and issuing decrees in the Sultan's name.

diya: blood-money; a fixed sum compensation payable in cases of accidental killing and injury, and in some cases of deliberate injury.

dönüm: a measure of land, based on a day's ploughing, c. 940 square metres.

ergenlik: a gift paid by a bride to the bridegroom, sometimes in exchange for another gift.

fatwa: a responsum issued by a qualified jurist.

fiqh: Islamic jurisprudence.

ghaza: holy war; a raid, razzia.

hadd (pl. **hudud**): a fixed penalty of the *shari'a*. The fixed penalties are for fornication, false accusation of fornication, theft, highway robbery and wine-drinking.

halal: licit.

haqq Allah: a claim of God, an absolute claim which precludes a negotiated settlement.

haram: forbidden in law.

harbi: an enemy dwelling in the *dar al-harb*.

harem: the women's apartments of a house, whose access is forbidden to men, except to the husband or close relatives.

hauz: land rented from the sovereign.

hiba bi-shart al-'iwad: a gift given in exchange for a countervalue. The legal effect of the countervalue is to make the gift non-reclaimable by the donor.

hidana: the custody of children by the mother.

hirz: the custody of property.

hukumat al-'adl: a sum payable in compensation for an injury for which there is no fixed sum of *diya*.

'idda: the waiting period following divorce or widowhood, during which a woman may not remarry.

ihraz: the removal of property from the *dar al-harb* into the custody and protection of a Muslim sovereignty.

ijtihad: the exercise of independent reasoning in using the legal sources to reach a judgement.

ila: an oath, by the husband, of abstention from sexual intercourse.

imam: (1) in a general sense, a leader. (2) in common usage, the prayer-leader in a mosque. (3) in theological usage, the Caliph, the supreme head *de jure* of the Muslim community. (4) in Hanafi usage, a *de facto* Muslim sovereign or army commander. (5) in Hanafi usage, an authoritative jurist of the School.

ithm: a sin, not necessarily incurring a legal penalty.

jaba bennak: a landless peasant.
jihad: holy war.
jihaz: a dowry, which the bride brings to the marriage.
jizya: the poll-tax payable by non-Muslims enjoying the protection of a Muslim sovereignty.

kaffara: a penance; an expiatory act, consisting usually of fasting or the manumission of slaves.
kalin: earnest money, paid on betrothal by a man to his fiancée or her guardian.
khalifa: literally 'successor'. The Caliph, the supreme head of the Islamic community.
khalwa sahiha: privacy between husband and wife, where there is no impediment to intercourse.
kharaj: land tax.
kharaj muqasama: a proportional levy in kind, of up to half the produce on a piece of land.
kharaj muwazzaf: an annual fixed tax on land.
khilafa: the Caliphate, the office and functions of the Caliph.
khul': a divorce by the husband, for a consideration, at the request of the wife.
khums: a fifth; the fifth portion of the spoils of war, due to the sovereign.

li'an: an invocation of God's curse by the husband on his wife, and by the wife on her husband, when the husband accuses the wife of fornication, and she denies it. The effect of *li'an* is to dissolve the marriage.

madhhab: a School of Islamic law. The *madhhab*s within Sunni Islam are the Hanafi, Shafi'i, Maliki and Hanbali.
madrasa: a higher college, attached to a mosque.
mahr: the sum payable on marriage by the husband to the wife.
mahr al-mithl: fair *mahr*; the sum, reflecting the status of the bride's father's family, payable by the husband to the wife, when no sum of *mahr* has been stipulated in the marriage contract.
mahr mu'ajjal: the portion of the *mahr* paid at the time of the marriage.
mahr mu'ejjel: the portion of the *mahr* payable on divorce, or on the death of the husband.
malikane: in Ottoman Anatolia, the portion of revenue from a fief which belongs to a private owner, and is not assigned to the fief-holder.
milk: (1) ownership.(2) property. (3) in Ottoman usage, an allod; land or immovable property in the ownership of an individual, and not assigned as a fief.
miri: (1) belonging to, or at the disposal of the Sultan. (2) the fisc.
mithqal: a measure of weight; about four or five grammes.
müd: a modius; a measure of capacity, varying from region to region.
mudarris: a teacher at a *madrasa*.
mufti: a jurisconsult, qualified to issue fatwas.
mujtahid: one who exercises *ijtihad*.
mukhaddara: a veiled lady, an upper-class woman, who does not go out of the house unveiled and unaccompanied.

mutawalli: an administrator of a *waqf*, a trustee.

nafaqa: maintenance, payable in marriage by the husband to the wife, and by economically active men to dependent members of their family.

nashiza: (of a wife) disobedient, behaving in such a way as to forfeit the payment of *nafaqa* by the husband, especially by leaving the house without his permission.

penjik: (1) an Ottoman tax on war booty. (2) an Ottoman transit-tax on prisoners-of-war.

qadi: a judge in an Islamic court.

qadi'asker: a chief judge in the Ottoman empire, with authority especially over the *'askeri* class, and with a seat on the *Divan-i hümayun*. There were two *qadi'asker*s, one for Anatolia and one for Rumelia.

qanun: a secular law or laws.

qanunname: a code of secular laws.

qasama: a process of compurgation in cases of homicide where the killer is unknown. It has the effect of releasing the community, group or individual from *qisas*, but not from *diya*.

qisas: talion inflicted in cases of deliberate homicide and some kinds of injury. The culprit suffers death, or an injury precisely equivalent to the one he has inflicted.

ra'iyyet (pl. **re'aya**): in Ottoman usage, a tax-paying, peasant subject of the Sultan.

raj'i: (of divorce) revocable.

sadr-i a'zam: the Grand Vizier, the Ottoman Sultan's chief minister, presiding over the *divan-i hümayun*.

salarliq: a tax of one-fortieth on crops.

sanjaq: literally, 'flag, standard'. In Ottoman usage, a subdivision of a province.

sanjaq beyi: the governor of a *sanjaq*.

shar': in Islamic texts, the common designation of the *shari'a*, the Holy Law of Islam.

shari'a: the common modern designation of the *shar'*, the Holy Law of Islam.

sheikhu'l-islam: literally 'the head-man of Islam', a designation sometimes applied to jurists of great repute. After Ebu's-su'ud's period of office, the term attached itself to the Mufti of Istanbul, the head of the Ottoman legal and religious hierarchy.

Shi'a: one of the two major sects of Islam. The Shi'a deny the legitimacy of the first three Caliphs to succeed the Prophet, maintaining that the Prophet designated his son-in-law, the fourth Caliph, 'Ali, as his rightful successor, and that thereafter the legitimate succession to the Prophet is in the line of 'Ali.

Shi'i: pertaining to, a member of, the Shi'a.

sipahi: a knight, a cavalryman holding a fief on condition of military service.

siyasa: (1) in pre-modern usage, extra-judicial coercion or punishment, exercised for the maintenance of good order. (2) in modern usage, politics.

su eri: literally 'army-man'. An archaic term for *sipahi*.

Sunni: a member of one of the two major sects of Islam. The Sunnis, unlike the Shi'a, uphold the legitimacy of the first three Caliphs to succeed the Prophet, Abu Bakr, 'Umar and 'Uthman.

tahlil: the intermediate marriage which a woman must undergo after a triple divorce, if she wishes to remarry her former husband.

talaq: divorce, repudiation of the wife by the husband.

tanfil: the distribution of spoil before battle; in effect, permission given to the troops to take and keep booty.

tapu: an entitlement to a piece of land.

tapu tax: an entry fine levied on a new occupant of a plot, giving him title to the land.

ta'zir: punishment inflicted at the discretion of the judge or administrative authority; a flogging, chastisement.

thulth: a third; the third portion of an estate, which may be bequeathed by testament, the remaining two thirds descending in fixed portions to the heirs.

timar: a military fief; a parcel of revenues, usually from a defined area of land, which a *sipahi* holds in return for military service.

'ushr: (1) in general, a tithe. (2) in Hanafi jurisprudence, the tithe payable on lands distributed to the Muslim conquerors by the Muslim sovereign at the time of conquest.

walaya: (1) sovereignty, authority. (2) guardianship.

wali: a guardian.

wali al-dam: literally, 'guardian of the blood'. A next-of-kin who has the right to claim *qisas* or *diya*.

waqf: a trust in mortmain; a charitable foundation, whose revenues are assigned in perpetuity to the purpose stipulated by the founder.

zihar: an oath where a husband compares his wife to a female relative within the prohibited degrees of marriage. The oath has the effect of dissolving the marriage.

zina: unlawful sexual intercourse.

Index